EARTHCURRENTS

EarthCurrents

The Struggle for the World's Soul

Howard A. Snyder

Abingdon Press
Nashville

EARTHCURRENTS

Copyright © 1995 by Howard A. Snyder

This book is printed on recycled, acid-free paper.

Snyder, Howard A.
　　EarthCurrents : the struggle for the world's soul / Howard A. Snyder.
　　　　p.　cm.
　　Includes bibliographical references and index.
　　ISBN 0-687-11449-7 (alk. paper)
　　　　1. Environmental policy.　2. Gaia hypothesis.　3. Ecofeminism.
　　I. Title.　II. Title : Earth currents.
　　GE170.S66　1994
　　363.7—dc20　　　　　　　　　　　　　　　　　　　　　94-40468
　　　　　　　　　　　　　　　　　　　　　　　　　　　　　CIP

Scripture quotations are from the New Revised Standard Version Bible, Copyright 1989 by the Division of Christian Education of the National Council of the Churches of Christ in the USA. Used by permission.

Those noted NIV are from the Holy Bible, New International Version®. Copyright © 1973, 1978, 1984 International Bible Society. Used by permission of Zondervan Publishing House. All rights reserved.

The excerpt on pp. 103-4 is reprinted by permission of the publishers from *Mind Children: The Future of Robot and Human Intelligence* by Hans Moravec, Cambridge, Mass.: Harvard University Press. Copyright © 1988 by Hans Moravec.

The table on p. 217 is reprinted by permission of Sage Publications, Ltd. from I. Hassan, "Schematic Differences Between Modernism and Postmodernism," *Theory, Culture and Society* 2, 3 (1985): 123-24.

94　95　96　97　98　99　00　01　02　03　—　10　9　8　7　6　5　4　3　2　1

MANUFACTURED IN THE UNITED STATES OF AMERICA

To
Dick
Jim
and Nancy
and in memory of Grace,
who still lives

CONTENTS

ACKNOWLEDGMENTS   9

PREFACE   10

INTRODUCTION   **Earth and Spirit**   11

PART ONE
KEY GLOBAL TRENDS: WHERE IS THE WORLD GOING?   21

CHAPTER ONE   **Looking to 2030**   23

CHAPTER TWO   **Online:** *The New Shape of Global Culture*   37

CHAPTER THREE   **Global Web:** *The Emerging World Economy*   46

CHAPTER FOUR   **Gender Power:** *The Feminist Revolution*   64

CHAPTER FIVE   **Fragile Greenhouse:** *The Environment at Risk*   75

CHAPTER SIX   **Vital Strings:** *DNA and Superstrings*   88

CHAPTER SEVEN   **Electric Minds:** *Artificial Intelligence and Virtual Reality*   102

CHAPTER EIGHT   **Western Decline:** *America's Final Hour?*   116

CHAPTER NINE   **New World Order:** *Global Culture or Clash of Civilizations?*   132

PART TWO
EMERGING GLOBAL WORLDVIEWS: WHAT ARE FOLKS BELIEVING?   151

CHAPTER TEN   **Global Economics:** *A Pragmatic Worldview*   152

CHAPTER ELEVEN   **Quantum Mystery:** *A New Scientific Worldview?*   164

CHAPTER TWELVE Life on a Living Planet: *The Gaia Worldview*   177

CHAPTER THIRTEEN Divine Design: *God in the Shadows?*   186

CHAPTER FOURTEEN The Force of Fate: *Determinism Revisited*   201

CHAPTER FIFTEEN Postmodernism: *The Death of Worldviews?*   213

PART THREE
PERSONAL MEANING IN THE GLOBAL CITY: AT HOME IN
    THE COSMOS?   231

CHAPTER SIXTEEN The Future and the Ecology of Meaning   232

CHAPTER SEVENTEEN Order, Surprise, and Beauty:
                The Coherence of Meaning   247

CHAPTER EIGHTEEN Story, History, and Truth   261

CHAPTER NINETEEN Worldviews and Worldstory   277

CHAPTER TWENTY End of Story/Beginning of Story   291

NOTES   307

ACKNOWLEDGMENTS

A number of people have contributed to the preparation of this book at various stages—stimulating my thinking, contributing ideas and information, or reviewing parts of the manuscript as it was being developed. I particularly want to thank Steven Djuric, David McKenna, Leonard Sweet, Larry Welborn, and John Stackhouse.

Many others have influenced my thinking on matters discussed in this book, and I owe them a debt of gratitude—especially Mary Olson, Rob and Julie Banks, Milo and Helen Kaufmann, Matt Zahniser, James Sire, Bill O'Brien, Norman Thomas, Lloyd Arnett, Mark Snyder, Jeff Scott, Calvin Reber, Peter Kuzmic, Kodo Nakahara, Melvin Kowsnowski, Wai-Kan Yu, Joe Culumber, Gordon Moyes, Alan Walker, and J. Rutfield Crank.

None of these friends, of course, is to blame for the contents of this book, and most would probably take issue with me at one point or another.

Thanks also to Vinson Samuel and Kathy Wetz for helping to track down some quotations.

PREFACE

*E**arthCurrents* is at once a survey of trends, a reflection on world-views, and a proposal for future hope and belief.

Travel to thirteen countries on six continents in 1993 gave me unusual opportunities to see today's global changes up close. I returned to Ohio convinced of what I had earlier read: We are living through a global revolution—not only politically and economically, but in every area of life and culture.

This book was written to answer my own questions as much as to inform other people. Flooded by news reports on topics ranging from street violence to genetics to international crises, I pondered: What is the connection? How can one get behind the headlines to understand what is really going on? What do today's changes mean for the future of Planet Earth, and for being human?

I have tried to deal with these difficult questions seriously, but not somberly. Occasionally some things may even be said pun-in-cheek. This is a serious book, but it's okay to have fun with it.

One suggestion for time-conscious or impatient readers: If you find the discussion too detailed or technical in some of the early chapters, read the highlighted sidebars and skip to the end of the chapter. In the last few pages of each chapter, I show the significance of each trend for the larger global struggle for the world's soul.

Howard Snyder

Earth and Spirit

> Today, everyone agrees that humankind stands at a watershed in its history.
>
> **—Mikhail Gorbachev**
>
> The first day or so we all pointed to our countries. The third or fourth day we were pointing to our continents. By the fifth day we were aware of only one Earth.
>
> **—Sultan Bin Salman al-Saud,**
> **Discovery 5 Astronaut**

Life is enormously complex yet surprisingly simple. One day we are confounded by its details. The next day we are intrigued by the patterns. In a thousand big and little ways, we try to figure it out. Today we do this as never before on a global stage, increasingly conscious of the thousands of currents that shape our lives.

This book is about trends and worldviews, and what they mean for the future of the human family. It describes a global struggle for the world's soul. It asks where the Earth is going, and how we will get there.

EarthCurrents is an exercise in cultural analysis, viewed globally. It focuses particularly on the years 1990-2030. The thesis is that eight global trends are shaping what and how the world's peoples believe, and thus are touching all our lives.

I stress the word *global*. We use it more and more, because the Earth is increasingly interconnected. We haven't paid enough attention, however, to what key global trends say about the meaning and quality of our lives. These trends are not like movie plots, distant from our daily living. They are shaping what we think is real, what we believe is true, and what we would die for.

EarthCurrents is also, necessarily, a book about how the universe holds together. The universe "out there," our larger home, but also our personal universe—the things that give meaning and purpose to life. I will argue that meaning has something to do with *coherence,* the interconnection of things. That's an important point, since so much of life presents us with fragmentation, brokenness, disintegration.

Many people—poets, scientists, ecologists, mountain-top-sitters—believe that everything in the cosmos is connected. Others disagree, pointing to disorder and chaos. Yet the universe does show pattern and order—*coherence*—as well as chaos. What holds things together? What is the glue?

In *The Hitchhiker's Guide to the Galaxy,* Douglas Adams tells of people busily trying to figure out the riddle of the universe. After stupendous work over many years, a massive computer spits out the answer: Forty-two.

Forty-two is the answer. The next job, of course, is to figure out the question.

Life is a lot like that. It is one thing to have data and information. It's quite another to know what to do with it, what it all means. And that is really the question of how everything holds together.

So this is a book about meaning, and not mere information. It shows how key global trends in science, technology, religion, economics, politics, and popular culture raise questions and give insights into the nature of the universe and the experience of human life.

Fads are not trends, though trend-watching can be a fad. Still, trends *are* important. Carefully noted and interpreted, they register deeper cultural shifts. This book is not a bandwagon-load of trends but an analysis of change in culture. A surface ripple on a river may simply show a pebble has dropped or a fish has jumped. But it also might signal a deeper cause—a submerged rock or underground spring. So analysis and interpretation are needed.

The trends studied here are *EarthCurrents*—global forces that will shape our lives over the next two generations. They open new avenues of understanding, possibly offering more fulfilling lives and relationships and a better future for all Earth's children. But they also spell dangers.

A Hinge of History?

This is a pregnant time to inventory key trends. Observers in many fields agree: The world is experiencing historic change, a period of fundamental transition. A hinge of history, some say. People differ wildly as to what this means and where we are going, which way the hinge will swing. But almost every cultural analyst sees this as an epochal time of change. In fact, a growing consensus states that the world is entering a period unlike anything experienced before in human history.

Globe-trotting futurist Alvin Toffler in *Powershift* speaks of "a mighty convergence of change," a "new civilization now spreading across the planet," and he calls the period from roughly 1950 to 2025 "the hinge of history."[1] David Harvey writes in *The Condition of Postmodernity*, "There has been a sea-change in cultural as well as in political-economic practices since around 1972."[2] Sam Keen, author of the best-selling *Fire in the Belly*, says, "All the metaphors of Western culture are beginning to change." Keen believes this is an epochal moment in history when we must be custodians rather than conquerors of the planet.[3] The Club of Rome says today's global changes represent "a major revolution on a worldwide scale" and titled its 1991 report *The First Global Revolution.*[4]

Haven't people always felt this way? Probably, to a degree. But today's global currents feed a widening consensus. "It seems that today, everyone agrees that humankind stands at a watershed in its history" says Mikhail Gorbachev, now head of the International Green Cross.[5]

This is a time of broad *moral and cultural* shift, not just technological change. Philosopher Cornel West calls it the Postmodern Moment. The science, philosophy, and much of the culture that have dominated the West for three centuries are changing.

Paradoxically, postmodern culture points simultaneously in opposite directions: toward both *fragmentation* and *integration*. The world is falling apart and coming together at the same time. Fragmentation: collapsing empires, growing pluralism and relativism, decaying family life, escalating violence, the shattering of old ideologies and scientific theories. And yet integration: increasing global connections, growing environmental consciousness, fresh forms of community, expanding communications networks, new proposals in science for a Theory of Everything (TOE). Such paradoxes signal an old order dying and a new, uncertain age aborning.

This sense of change and the coming of a radically new epoch cuts across all fields of knowledge. In working on this book I surveyed in particular three broad areas: science/technology, political science/economics, and philosophy/religion. Similar themes pop up in all these fields. I often found whole paragraphs describing change that could be lifted from a book or essay in one discipline and dropped into a discussion in another discipline—and it would make perfect sense! The feeling of ferment is everywhere.

For example, Alvin Toffler writes in *Powershift:* "Connectivity rather than disconnectedness, integration rather than disintegration, real-time simultaneity rather than sequential stages—these are the assumptions that underlie the new . . . paradigm."[6] Toffler is writing here about economics, but similar talk of connectedness, integration, and simultaneity pervades today's discussions of science, religion, and even politics. Emerging "new paradigms," or models, in widely different areas are remarkably similar at root.

Still, much is unclear. Language about new paradigms is often fuzzy, highly symbolic, and even contradictory. Many see only disintegration, not new patterns of connection. Yet something is afoot, something of deep significance. So we must look deeper.

A few things already are becoming clear. For example:

- The emerging new age of science, involving especially quantum physics, genetic research, astronomy, and space exploration, and the ongoing quest for a Theory of Everything will shape worldviews globally. The way we see and understand the physical world is shifting, and that means changing worldviews in other ways, too.
- Globalization—growing worldwide linkages and awareness—also will shape worldviews. The global marketplace of goods, services, and ideas sets up a global tension between relativism and holism; between recognizing many different views and options, on the one hand, and searching for an over-arching vision that shows how everything holds together and gives meaning to life, on the other. Globalization means interaction, different worldviews rubbing against each other. This process will bring worldview questions into sharper focus and will itself provide raw material for new thinking.

Eight Global Trends

In *EarthCurrents,* we will give special attention to eight global trends:

- the coming of online, instant-access culture
- the rise of a global economy
- the rapidly expanding influence of, and new roles for, women
- increasing environmental vulnerability and awareness: the Green Revolution
- scientific breakthroughs in understanding matter itself
- the rise of computer culture
- a startling decline in Western society
- a basic power shift in global politics

These changes share three things: Long-range influence, cultural rootedness, and an underlying spiritual base. This is what makes Earth-Currents.

First, EarthCurrents are often generations in the making, and *have long-term impact*. They gain momentum slowly and shape society for decades or even centuries. This separates them from fads and short-term shifts. EarthCurrents build over time and have long-range influence that outlasts the tides of more immediate change.

Take the 1991 Gulf War. When the war broke out, many thought it signaled a major power shift, or perhaps a new role for the United States. But the war came and went. Though it has some long-term effects, underlying trends that faced the world before the war are still with us. The war illustrated some basic trends, especially in communications, technology, and international relations, but it didn't change them. EarthCurrents don't die suddenly. You can't bomb them away.

Second, EarthCurrents become *progressively institutionalized*. At first this may happen counterculturally. Gradually they spread into the mainstream, and become more than simply the sum of individual opinion. They turn into social forces, currents broader than any person's or nation's control. Often this happens first through television, print, film and video, songs, and even clothing and hair styles.

An example of this was the so-called Consciousness Revolution of the late 1960s and early 1970s. Though centered primarily in the United States and Europe, this was a global shift, touching nearly every part of the world. Values and ideas that first appeared counterculturally passed into the mainstream in a few years.

I especially noticed this because I lived outside the United States from 1968 to 1975. When my family and I went to Brazil in 1968, the Hippies were wearing beads, beards, long hair, and bright colors. When we returned seven years later, the Hippies had vanished. But businessmen were sporting colored shirts and bright ties, and many had beards!

The example appears superficial, but it is not. These surface changes signal something deeper. Some of today's emerging cultural values, including greater emphasis on community and human relationships and concern for the environment, first got a countercultural foothold through the late-1960s movement.

Third and perhaps most important, EarthCurrents have *a fundamental spiritual basis*. They are not simply opinion, not just fleeting currents expressed in popular culture or counterculture. *Something deeper is at work*. Something of the nature of metaphor and worldview—the lenses through which we look. Something at the level of fundamental paradigms and values. EarthCurrents have a power that prods the spirit, not just the mind.

Thus the symbolic side of trends and movements is important. Participants in new movements often know this in their bones. We feel it if we remember the power of the Goddess of Democracy statue in Tiananmen Square in 1989, or the dismantling of the Berlin Wall, or the smashing of Lenin's statues in the (former) Soviet Union in 1991.

The round, blue-and-white photo image of Earth from the moon, widely used since the early 1970s, has become the icon of a new vision—literally, a new worldview. This one image has captured the imagination and moved the spirits of a new generation of Earthlings. We feel here the spiritual nature of the whole-Earth trend. We are beginning to see Earth as one whole, not as fragmented parts or different countries. It is no longer the earth, but Earth. And this touches the spirit. We begin to understand the words of Apollo astronaut Alfred Worden: "Now I know why I'm here—not for a closer look at the moon, but to look back at our home: Earth."

Trends and Worldviews

Trends reshape worldviews, and worldviews, more than we think, set our menu of choices, the options from which we make the decisions that shape our lives. Some of today's trends are startling. Together they spell a different world for ourselves and our children. They are reshaping the way we understand the world and life itself—in other words, our worldviews,[7] or, perhaps, our world sense or world feeling.[8] People are thinking things never thought before; they are forming new hybrid views. For example, some scientists and philosophers say the whole universe is one stupendous living organism (an ancient idea, but new in its modern form). Others say the cosmos is a hologram, every microscopic part mysteriously embodying the whole. Is there anything to such ideas? Is this science or mysticism? With the emergence of quantum physics, can the two be separated?

Trends let us peer into the future. While the future is not predictable, neither is it unconnected to past and present. Among all the imponderables and unpredictables, some things are certain. Deep, long-range currents won't end suddenly. Generations will continue to succeed each other, and each new generation will differ by degrees from its predecessor. A key question is how today's global trends will affect generational change, especially the transmission of values, morality, and life-orientation. Watching the ongoing waves of generations gives insight into the flow of time and history.

What Color Is Your Worldview?

Every person has a worldview, known or unknown. Or if not a worldview, then a world *sense*—that is, an attitude toward life, a certain perception of reality.

James Sire writes in *The Universe Next Door,* "Few people have anything approaching an articulate philosophy—at least as epitomized by the great philosophers. . . . But everyone has a worldview. Whenever any of us thinks about anything—from a casual thought (Where did I leave my watch?) to a profound question (Who am I?)—we are operating within such a framework. In fact, it is only the assumption of a worldview—however basic or simple—that allows us to think at all."[9]

A worldview is really a kind of Theory of Everything (TOE). It is a comprehensive vision that plausibly explains all that is to the satisfaction of those who hold it. The term "Theory of Everything" is generally used today in the scientific sense of a theoretical union of the four physical forces (gravity, electromagnetism, and the strong and weak nuclear forces), though the claims for such a theory often reach beyond physics into metaphysics. A *real* Theory of Everything, one worthy of its name, should be able to include everything that exists. A worldview and a Theory of Everything are, in this sense, synonymous.

Do we choose worldviews? Not initially. In most cultures for most of time, people probably never thought about worldviews. They knew only one way to see and experience the world, and that wasn't thought of as a worldview. It was simply reality, "the way things are." Or perhaps there were two alternatives: "Our way," the way things *really* are, and what outsiders, "those other people," think—known to be error, unreality, foolishness.

Occasionally history brings worldview conflict, times when concepts of the universe clash or compete. Now is such a time. This struggle is *global* as never before.

Do ordinary people really care about worldviews? Probably most do not. They simply live

> Key global trends are giving birth to a new set of worldviews that present us with conflicting ideas about the meaning of life.

and act or *feel* and *experience*. "Worldview" sounds abstract and intellectual—in other words, irrelevant. The problem with this attitude, however, is that it opens people to manipulation. If we are interested in truth—or even if we aren't sure "truth" exists, but are interested in our own well-being—then worldviews become important.

Some of these worldviews are not really new. Probably none is totally novel. But they come in new guises and disguises. We will investigate these and ask: What is really believable?

Many Dimensions

In dealing with these issues, it will help us to think *multidimensionally* as well as globally. An underlying theme in this book is dimensions and dimensionality. We think of space (three dimensions) and time, or spacetime. We speak of the "inner" and "outer" dimensions of our lives and of "outer space." Are there other dimensions?

Scientists, especially mathematicians, have long been fascinated with such questions. How many dimensions does the universe have? How does one set of dimensions help us understand others? Mathematician and computer-graphics expert Thomas Banchoff comments, "For over a century, mathematicians and others have speculated about the nature of higher dimensions, and in our day the concept of dimension has begun to play a larger and larger role in our conception of a whole range of activities."[10] The word *dimension* itself has many dimensions, from scientific to poetic. So we will think multidimensionally as we look at global trends and worldviews.

The Inner World

Some of life's dimensions are within us. Life is not only about the world "out there" but also about the world "in here," inside the brain, mind, and spirit. Much of life is wrapped up in our thoughts, feelings, and imagination. This also is part of reality—the most intimate reality to each of us. It is the world of hopes and dreams, fears and anxieties. These form the filter through which we interpret life and navigate the "outer" world of things, people, time, and space.

We must examine interior things—consciousness and feeling. We must look at the meaning of those last thoughts we have before falling asleep at night and those first glimmers and hopes that awaken our minds in the morning. We grow as we pay attention to such things. We learn by drawing on both sides of the brain, letting intuition, feeling,

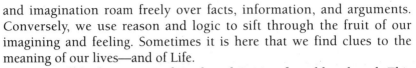

and imagination roam freely over facts, information, and arguments. Conversely, we use reason and logic to sift through the fruit of our imagining and feeling. Sometimes it is here that we find clues to the meaning of our lives—and of Life.

So we will look at issues of Earth and Spirit, of world and soul. This is the world we live in, and even more it is *the world that is emerging*. We live on Earth with space, time, and matter; yet somehow we live in a world where time and space curve together and where people often sense, even if only dimly, other dimensions beyond what can be measured by clocks and rulers. We live, apparently, in a multidimensional world.

The Shape of Our Quest

These complex issues and dimensions can be reduced to some fundamental questions:

- What key trends will shape our lives over the next thirty years?
- What are the main dangers we face?
- What are the signs of hope?
- Where will truth and meaning come from? Is there meaning?
- What are the options for hope and faith?
- What about God? Is God within, "out there," between us, or gone forever?
- Is a coherent life and worldview possible today?

We explore these questions throughout the book. We look first at global trends that will shape the next two generations (chaps. 2–9). We then explore key worldview options (chaps. 10–15). The last section explores more deeply questions of meaning and experience, and it suggests that a coherent, livable worldview is possible.

To set the stage, let's first look ahead two generations—to the year 2030.

PART ONE
KEY GLOBAL TRENDS

Where
Is
the
World
Going?

CHAPTER ONE

Looking to 2030

> The world has come to an end—at least the world
> we knew. The lay of the land has fundamentally
> changed, never to return to its original form.
> This earthquake has made us strangers in our
> own land.
>
> **LEONARD SWEET**[1]

Futurists keep reminding us that the year 2000 launches a new
millennium. John Naisbitt and Patricia Aburdene write in *Megatrends 2000:*

As we approach the year 2000, the millennium is reemerging as a
metaphor for the future. . . . The modern millennium ignites our vision for
a better world—alongside our nightmares of the world's end. . . . Beneath
the specter of nuclear weapons is a growing sense of hope that if we can
just "make it to the year 2000," we will have proved ourselves capable of
solving our problems and living harmoniously on this fragile planet. . . .

The most exciting breakthroughs of the 21st century will occur not
because of technology but because of an expanding concept of what it
means to be human.

Today we are emerging from a 20th-century version of the Dark
Ages—the combined impact of industrialization, totalitarianism, and
intrusion of technology into our lives. With most of the century behind
us and the millennium ahead, we are entering a renaissance in the arts
and spirituality. The magnet year 2000 is pulling forth bold experiments
in market socialism, a spiritual revival, and a burst of economic growth
around the Pacific Rim.[2]

This is Naisbitt's rosy assessment. According to *Megatrends 2000*, we
are about to enter a literal millennium—a golden age of global prosper-

ity. Minor glitches and problems may annoy us, but these will all be overcome in due time.

Others are less sanguine. It seems the world is filled with optimists and pessimists when it comes to the future. Optimists say: Humanity is finally coming to understand the world and solve its problems. Science and technology have wiped out many diseases and brought prosperity and growing world stability. History is the story of human progress. The mushrooming growth of knowledge and information spell hope that the next hundred years will be a time of unchecked prosperity and well-being for the whole planet.

Pessimists say: Life itself is threatened as modern "progress" is ruining the web of our relationships Irreparable harm is being done to the fragile fabric that sustains life. Rare species are rapidly vanishing. Diseases we thought were conquered are reappearing. Population is bulging beyond the capacity of many nations to feed themselves. Some countries grow rich while others sink into poverty. Prosperous nations show signs of social decay with mounting crime and the breakdown of family structures. "The future is an uncharted sea full of potholes," says Gerhard Casper in a postmodern mix of metaphors.[3]

We must be more precise and more comprehensive, which is only possible when we take a global view. Beneath the claims of optimists and pessimists lies a growing globalization which will reshape the world over the next two generations.

The Glue of Globalization

In the 1970s and 1980s people commonly divided the Earth into three "worlds": First, Second, and Third. The First World was the industrialized democratic nations, centered mostly in the Northern Hemisphere. The Second World was the Soviet Union, China, and other nations dominated by Communism. The Third World consisted of the poorer, economically less-developed nations, located mainly in the Southern Hemisphere.

These distinctions are now obsolete. Global economic links, the collapse of Communism, and the new information age make these divisions meaningless, or at least misleading. We are moving from three worlds to one: just Earth. This trend is the base force leading to a new global society by 2030. In science, entertainment, business, or politics, globalization is the shaping force.

Globalization is both the reality and the *consciousness* that the context of life has stretched from one's own city or nation to include the whole Earth. *For the first time in history, children are coming to adulthood*

with a global consciousness. The chief reasons for this are global communications, new environmental consciousness, and the impact of space exploration. Suddenly Earth is a small, beautiful, vulnerable planet, blue and white and green, a friendly presence in a cold cosmos. To see Earth from the moon—and, simultaneously, to begin to understand its ecology—is to transform human consciousness. Here is a consciousness revolution more basic than that of the 1960s.

Globalization is thus a change in both *perspective* and *reality.* A quick overview of the range of human experience drives the point home:

- *The environment.* New awareness of the global reach of environmental risks is prompting more cooperation in studying and reducing environmental hazards.
- *Technology.* Worldwide computerization, international cooperation in space exploration, and computer modeling of global weather patterns are all part of globalization.
- *Politics.* The rising tide of democracy (or democratic minorities), decline of ideology, and resurgence of ethnic identity all appear to be global trends. All these now occur on a live global stage.
- *Economics.* Business and commercial linkages, freer trade, and new technologies are fueling an emerging global economy. National identities and regional ideologies are melting in the hot bath of economic dynamism.
- *Popular culture.* The rise of a global pop entertainment culture and the "global teenager," broader roles for women, and the shift from hierarchies to networking are all part of the globalization phenomenon—as are relativism and the loss of moral certainty.
- *Science.* An increasingly international scientific enterprise is bringing breakthroughs in physics, genetics, and the earth sciences generally. Science has gone global.
- *Religion.* All the world's major religions are now global enterprises. Unprecedented worldwide missionary efforts and the emergence of new "hybrid" religions show that globalization is also a religious phenomenon.

> For the first time in history, children are coming to adulthood with a global consciousness.

- *Population.* Concern over world population growth is sparking expanded international cooperation. We face the squeeze of billions of people but only one Earth. Worldwide urbanization and migration of peoples and the colossal global refugee flood are also part of the picture.

The key point: *All of these trends are global.* They interact in a sort of global social dance, spurring global convergence—or conflict. We examine these trends in more detail in coming chapters.

As always, the future holds both hope and risks. It is not closed or determined. Partly it involves choices: personal choices and the broader will of groups, cultures, and humanity itself as they shape the flow of history.

Globalization is a long-term current that won't halt in the year 2000. If anything, it will speed up in coming decades. For this reason, we must look beyond 2000. A jump ahead to the year 2030 may be more useful. This is still only a generation or two, something we can imagine. Millennial models are not helpful here. A little generational thinking is a useful way of grasping the next third of a century.

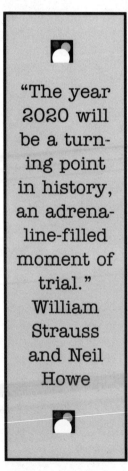

> "The year 2020 will be a turning point in history, an adrenaline-filled moment of trial."
>
> William Strauss and Neil Howe

Generational Thinking

When I ponder the flow of time and history, I think of my own family. Both my parents were born in October 1900. If my youngest son, born in 1972, marries by the year 2000 and in turn has a son or daughter in 2010, that grandchild of mine could still be alive in the year 2100. Four generations spanning two hundred years!

William Strauss and Neil Howe use this kind of generational thinking in their book *Generations: The History of America's Future 1584 to 2069.* Strauss and Howe view history in terms of generational cycles. "Again and again," they write, "this lifecycle approach to history revealed a similar and recurring pattern, one that coincided with many of the well-known rhythms pulsing through American history." This approach, they argue, solves a number of riddles: "why, for example, great public emergencies in America seem to arrive every eighty or ninety years—and why great spiritual upheavals arrive roughly halfway between" these cycles. Among other things, they predict a huge crisis about the year 2020, "a major turning point in American history and an adrenaline-filled moment of trial. At its climax, Americans will feel that the fate of posterity—for generations to come—hangs in the balance."[4] Since America is now globally linked as never before, any such crisis surely would be global.

Strauss and Howe point out that in history, "bad endings can take decades to build and in their early phases can be hard to foresee—hinging, as do all great episodes in history, on how small children are nurtured, and whether elder generations offer the young a constructive mission upon coming of age."[5] In other words, the key is not just *biological* generations, but the generational continuity of cultural values.

This generational approach highlights some basic issues of world history and our global future. Generation waves share common features, a sort of "peer personality" shaped by the leading events of each generation's younger years. Thus people coming of age during World War II, or in the so-called Consciousness Revolution of the late sixties and early seventies, were so shaped by those events as to give their generations an outlook and set of values markedly different from earlier and later ones.

Sociologically speaking, generations come in waves of about twenty to twenty-two years each. Though biologically generations are continuous, major cultural events—wars, depressions, religious awakenings, technological breakthroughs—mark off generational cycles.[6] One can read history as a recurring cycle of generations in which social crises and spiritual awakenings alternate in about forty-five year intervals.

Strauss and Howe posit a repeating cycle of four generations, which they call *Idealist, Reactive, Civic,* and *Adaptive.* Their thesis is that "in nontraditional societies like America" the generations function as follows: "Idealist generations tend to live what we might label a *prophetic* lifecycle of vision and values; Reactives a *picaresque* [that is, roguish] lifecycle of survival and adventure; Civics a *heroic* lifecycle of secular achievement and reward, and Adaptives a *genteel* lifecycle of expertise and amelioration." These generations "recur in fixed order, given one important condition: *that society resolves with reasonable success each secular crisis that it encounters.*"[7] Strauss and Howe hold that this four-generation cycle recurs consistently throughout American history. The one exception was during the period of the Civil War when a major national crisis was not successfully resolved and a whole generation was, in effect, wiped out.

These cycles thus yield a recurring pattern, like "the seasonal transformation of nature." "Through the generational seasons of social history," they write, the following pattern can be discerned:

- An AWAKENING ERA (Idealists coming of age) triggers cultural creativity and the emergence of new ideals, as institutions built around old values are challenged by the emergence of a spiritual awakening.
- In an INNER-DRIVEN ERA (Reactives coming of age), individualism flourishes, new ideals are cultivated in separate camps, confidence in institutions declines, and secular problems are deferred.
- A CRISIS ERA (Civics coming of age) opens with growing collective unity in the face of perceived social peril and culminates in a secular crisis in which danger is overcome and one set of new ideals triumphs.
- In an OUTER-DRIVEN ERA (Adaptives coming of age), society turns toward conformity and stability, triumphant ideals are secularized, and spiritual discontent is deferred.[8]

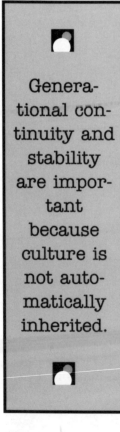

Genera-
tional con-
tinuity and
stability
are impor-
tant
because
culture is
not auto-
matically
inherited.

Strauss and Howe argue that "Wars and other secular crises are triggered from without, spiritual awakenings from within. . . . Idealist generations are nurtured to burst forth spiritually upon coming of age. When they do, they awaken other generations along with them." The cycle, these authors suggest, "provides each generation with a location in history, a peer personality, and a set of possible scripts to follow. But it leaves each generation free to express either its better or its worse instincts, to choose a script that posterity may later read with gratitude or sorrow."[9]

Where is history now? The last "Awakening Era" was the late 1960s and early 1970s, and the next should come around 2050. These authors foresee a major crisis around the year 2020, however. Significantly, other data unrelated to this generational analysis also points to the years around 2020 as a critical time globally, as we shall see.

Strauss and Howe's analysis is useful in examining U.S. history, but it is insufficiently global, especially as we look toward the future. The history of the United States and every other nation is inextricably bound together in emerging global society.

Generational thinking reminds us, however, that we are all linked in time as well as space. We are part of a generational stream, an ebb and flow of epochs. As part of four generations, our lives directly touch a two hundred-year span. Life is not simply the thirty to fifty years or so of our adulthood.

Studying generations has been knocked as faddist or simplistic. History is not that tidy, critics say. True. But generational awareness is useful because it highlights issues of culture continuity and change. Generations are important because *culture is not automatically inherited.*

In a stable society, heredity and environment combine to pass along the common culture like a deep, flowing river. But when new generations grow up in starkly changed environments, the process of culture transmission breaks down. When forms of communication, community, and (most importantly) family life shift with each succeeding generation, the generational flow of culture turns to chaos. Instead of a steady current, society comes to resemble a shallow river at flood stage. Streams flow across new land in unexpected ways, creating chaos or at least new channels. Lacking a larger coherence, order breaks down, and the future is shaky. This is important in viewing the relationship between global trends and historic civilizations.

The World in 2030

Many readers of this book won't be around in the year 2030. Most of our children and grandchildren will be, barring a major global catastrophe. If history continues until 2030—perhaps the dawn of a new Awakening Era—what will the world then be like? Here are a few educated guesses and concerns.

Technology. Well before 2030 the computer/electronics revolution will have integrated today's technologies and devices into a range of new products and will have moved to new frontiers. By the early 1990s, the key components of computers, photocopiers, laser printers, fax machines, telephones, television, and CD players were being combined in dozens of new products. Hand-held communicators, for example, will increasingly serve as combination TV, telephone, personal computer, and E-Mail machine. Computers will operate by voice command and voice data input/output, if the user desires. This technology, much of it already available, will form the basis for the next generation of small, cheap, easy to use, but highly sophisticated wireless personal communicators. These will link easily with megamemory computers at the office or other huge info-banks and will be global in range. The first generation of personal digital assistants (PDAs) that came to market in 1993 will be considered primitive within a decade.

By 2030, language barriers will be largely erased in electronic communication. With the right equipment, you will be able to choose between several languages in receiving or sending voice or written messages. An executive or student in Australia, for example, may carry on live conversations with Japanese colleagues, computers providing the translation. The equipment will even simulate the speakers' tone of voice. (Language translation technology is already in use, but it will take breakthroughs in instant-access megamemory and linguistics before computers can rule out wrong or imprecise alternative meanings so that instant language translation will be reasonably reliable.)

Some other likely innovations are houses made of supertough plastics and other so-called advanced materials; combination airplane-spaceships that easily move in and out of Earth's orbit; and monitors in doctors' offices that electronically take vital signs, do some routine chemical analysis, and give an initial diagnosis.

Will these developments really advance our health, happiness, and sense of purpose, or the welfare of the Earth? Not necessarily, for a full life is more than technology. But they gradually will change our perceptions of life and of meaning.

Energy and Ecology. By the year 2030, the energy crunch of the late 1900s will be largely forgotten because of conservation, miniaturization, renewable energy sources, and environmental sensitivity. Together, these keys will reduce the demand for energy while making it more available.

Two of these changes are primarily technological: miniaturization and renewable energy. As electronic components shrink due to integrated circuits, electro-optics, and microtechnology ("nanotechnology"), less energy is needed to operate them. Relatedly, new synthetic materials used in construction, aviation, and automobiles will take less energy to produce (and recycle). They will use less energy at every stage than do, for example, steel, glass, and concrete. As a result less energy will be demanded throughout the economy.

In industrial societies, conservation is the cheapest and most immediate source of new energy. Energy technology in the nineteenth and twentieth centuries was grossly wasteful. Most of the energy from the gasoline used in internal combustion engines, for example, is wasted and passes into the air as heat and "greenhouse" gases. As industrial societies become more ecologically awake, people will no longer tolerate such waste. Energy conservation will come from a wide variety of sources: use of lighter, energy-efficient materials, better insulation, and more extensive monitoring. Lifestyle changes also could help: using less water, walking more, and slightly lowering thermostat settings during cold weather.

Already many industries and organizations are discovering that energy conservation makes economic sense. When the National Audobon Society renovated its historic headquarters in New York City, it insisted not only on energy efficiency and ecologically safe materials but also on a reasonable pay-back period. If remodeling costs were higher, the long-term costs had to be lower. The result was a more pleasant, less wasteful environment with reduced costs.[10]

Conservation and new materials alone will not meet the world's energy demands over the next two generations, however, especially in areas of bulging population and rapid industrialization. The solution lies in breakthroughs in renewable sources that provide adequate energy and yet safeguard the environment.

Over the next twenty years it will finally dawn on us: More than enough energy is available around us naturally to meet our needs. This natural energy, much of it yet untapped, will be intelligently harnessed. New sources include wind, the movement of the tides, and geothermal energy. By 2030, many such sustainable sources will be harnessed in environmentally safe ways and will be widely available at relatively low cost. Recent developments in wind technology indicate that in many places, wind alone could supply over ten percent of energy needs within thirty years.

The most obvious energy factory, of course, is the sun. Solar energy will likely replace nuclear power and fossil fuels in the production of electricity. For the most part, this will be true not through the construction of gigantic solar stations but rather through smaller portable units that can be put wherever they are needed. In hindsight, the really prophetic breakthroughs of the 1980s were the solar calculator and the solar watch.

There is a catch, of course. Equipment for harnessing the sun's energy requires high-tech materials and the use of rare minerals. New developments in solar technology and synthetic materials should resolve this as a seriously limiting factor, but it may take until 2050. Research is continuing on nuclear fusion—in effect, the production of solar energy on Earth. But this technology is not likely to be economically feasible before 2050. By then, other renewable sources may make it superfluous except for a few ultra-high energy applications.[11]

Solar automobiles will be a common form of transportation before 2030. These will not be cars with solar panels, perhaps, but with solar-charged, high-efficiency power cells. The internal combustion engine will be as rare as the steam engine, which sparked the Industrial Revolution. We easily forget that gasoline and diesel engines replaced steam in industry and even in railway locomotives in only half a century. Many steam and electric cars cruised country roads before Henry Ford started mass-producing the models that later became America's gas guzzlers.

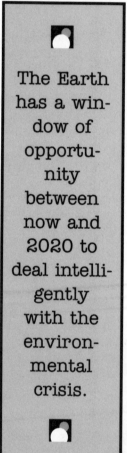

The Earth has a window of opportunity between now and 2020 to deal intelligently with the environmental crisis.

This rosy scenario will materialize, however, only if a strong ecological consciousness permeates Earth society. This must happen especially in industrial and political decision-making. As we will see in chapter five, Earth's environment is at risk, and some of the darkest dangers seem to be irreversible. The Earth has a window of opportunity between now and at best the year 2020 to deal decisively and intelligently with this challenge. Fortunately environmental concerns now figure in international political, educational, and business discussions.

The world may face a global eco-crisis within the next twenty to thirty years. Will this be the crisis of 2020? We can't tell yet. But growing ecological awareness over the past two decades sparks some hope that nations will work together to meet these challenges before they make Earth a wasteland.

The likely scenario: Environmental concern will speed the development of renewable, ecologically safe technologies, giving the world sufficient energy. These technologies will work with nature rather than against it. It obviously makes more sense to harness the tides or the power of the sun than to burn up limited oil and gas, making the world uninhabitable.

In short, energy will not be the crisis in 2030 that it was in the late twentieth century.

Health. Gene therapy for many diseases and birth defects will become increasingly common over the next twenty years as today's Human Genome Project is completed (see chap. 6). A cure for AIDS will be found, though not in time to prevent massive deaths, especially in several nations of Central Africa. New techniques in laser surgery pioneered in the 1990s will make eyeglasses unnecessary for many people. The dominant emphasis worldwide will be on preventive medicine. Many cancers will be found to be environmentally

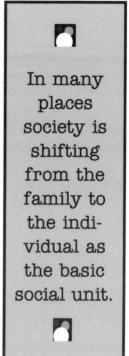

related, so the link between health and ecology will become much stronger.

Population. Will the population bomb explode by the year 2030, bringing mass starvation and political unrest? In fact, both of these are happening in the 1990s, especially in Africa. The issue is largely political and economic. Enough food is produced globally if properly distributed. The real issue is the ability of nations and agencies to work together and of each country to care for all its citizens. A 1993 U.N. report warned, however, that worldwide food production is lagging behind population growth.

The best way to cut population growth is to reduce poverty. Studies show that birth rates usually drop as people improve economically. Here again, the question is cooperation and equity for all Earth's peoples, not primarily technology. Scientific breakthroughs will be necessary, however, to keep food production growing.

In many places society is shifting from the family to the individual as the basic social unit.

Family Life. The cornerstone of society has always been the family, or the tribe as extended family. This is changing, and changing globally. Nontraditional family groupings are increasingly common. In many places society is shifting from the family to the individual as the basic social unit. In the United States, one person in four lives alone as a single-person household—a huge shift from forty years ago, when only one in ten lived alone. This is the tendency globally wherever techno-urban society is gaining.

Is the family on the way out? Today the "typical family" in Western nations no longer means father, mother, and two to four children. There is no typical family any longer; only a mix of arrangements. By 1990, only 7 percent of the North American population fit the "traditional" family profile of father as "breadwinner" and mother as "homemaker" caring for children under eighteen.

In 1984, futurist John Naisbitt catalogued eight emerging family "styles" or variations:

- Single parent (male or female) with one or more children (increasingly common)
- Two-career couple with no children
- Female breadwinner with child and house-husband

- Blended family consisting of previously-married husband and wife with children from the earlier marriages
- Unmarried couples
- Close friends or roommates with long-standing relationships
- Group houses where people live together in community
- Single-person households.[12]

Other reports suggest thirteen or more distinct types. In the United States, the most dramatic change has been the drop in households headed by a married couple—from about one half to one tenth in just forty years!

A parallel development is the sharp increase in the number of women (including mothers) who are employed. Sixty-five percent of preschool children and 77 percent of school-age children in the United States now have working mothers, according to a report by the National Association of Working Women.

These developments fray the social fabric. Because the family is the basic cell of society, or at least has been until now, changes in family life affect everything else. What is true in the nations of the North is not necessarily true in the South, but similar trends seem to accompany urbanization, economic development, mass communications, and the other marks of emerging global society. Without the traditional family, or a functional equivalent, the continuity and stability of generations is threatened. This could be ominous, far outweighing technical progress.

Family patterns and employment are closely linked. In the United States, the Bureau of National Affairs reported in 1990, "Demographic and societal changes throughout the 1990s and into the 21st century will spur a radical rethinking of the definition of family and work."[13] In particular:

- "The workplace will become the neighborhood of the 21st century, with schools, shops, child care, and medical care located there."
- One third of employees may work at home for at least part of the week by the early twenty-first century.
- Business will become heavily involved in supporting and even operating public schools, many of which will be at factories or office sites.

In 1990, 28 percent of U.S. companies offered child care resource and referral services. This may grow to 83 percent by 2000. On-site company child care centers will increase from 7 percent (1990) to 35 percent (2000).

One company which may be prophetic of things to come globally is Pantagonia, Inc., a Ventura, California, outdoor clothing manufacturer. Susan Greene, director of human resources for the company says: "We

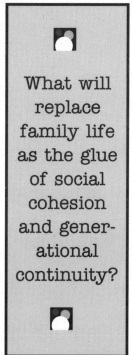

want to employ the whole person, not just a part." Patagonia provides an on-site kindergarten and care center, a natural foods cafeteria, exercise facilities, and yoga classes, among other benefits. In addition, it contributes 10 percent of its pre-tax profits to environmental causes and has begun a recycling program. The BNA report notes, "While the company is proud of its social activism, it has found that work and family programs also save thousands of dollars a year in reduced turnover and training costs."

Another trend prompted by global competition, however, is the dramatic increase of temporary and part-time work. As we will see in chapter three, this has deep significance both economically and socially.

As these economic developments increasingly shape global society, they will set the style of family life worldwide. In much of the world, the meaning of "family" in 2030 will be vastly different from today. "Family life" will likely be a mix of the eight styles noted earlier, with a dramatic increase globally of single adults sharing apartments because of the effects and pressures of techno-urbanization. Key questions are: What will replace family life as the glue of social cohesion and generational continuity? Will family and other forms of community be rediscovered?

Worldviews. In the final analysis, technological developments provide only the shell of life, not its substance. On the other hand, plenty of evidence from the field of communications and the history of civilizations shows that technological developments do shape how life is understood. They help define the meaning and quality of life. Technology can build its own worldview.

Technological society feeds on a basic principle: Whatever is technically possible should be done. "You can't stop progress" or "You can't hold back science" are some of its slogans. Technology is concerned with means, not ultimately with ends. What is technologically feasbile (the means) is good in itself, so the question of ends becomes superfluous.

> **What will replace family life as the glue of social cohesion and generational continuity?**

Technology thus births its own values—what Jacques Ellul calls "technological morality." This morality, says Ellul, "tends to bring human behavior into harmony with the technological world, to set up a new scale of values in terms of technology, and to create new virtues."[14] Technology itself will provide the means of instilling such a morality and winning adherence to it.

Such technological morality is suspect, not because the actual behavior induced would be "immoral"—it might, in fact, be very nice—but because it is a morality of means, not of ends; of technological necessity, not of personal relationships. It is a morality on the level of things and nonconscious being, not conscious persons. The social behavior of ants may be quite decorous, but it is not for that reason an adequate model for human morality.[15]

Technological progress thus raises worldview questions. By what models do we understand the world? The so-called Age of Reason in seventeenth-century Europe, the rise of Newtonian physics, and the Industrial Revolution gave the world the *machine model*. This became the way society, and life itself to a large degree, was understood over the past century and more. In the twentieth century this machine worldview was first cracked by Einstein's relativity theory. As we move into the twenty-first century with the rise of ecology, genetics, and quantum physics, the old machine model is in full decline.

The model of *organism* or biology and *ecology* will become dominant by 2030. This likely will be an enduring model because it is grounded in the nature of life itself. The medieval *hierarchical model* and the Enlightenment *machine model* were really abstractions from life. They accented some aspects of human existence but ignored others. The organic model, rooted in ecology, is much closer to the essence and relationships of life. Thus an organic-ecological conception figures to be the dominant model for understanding human society both locally and globally in the twenty-first century.

What about mind and spirit? Do they also suggest world models? Something beyond an organic model? An accent on mind and/or spirit may emerge as either a competing or a complementary model. Some people view the organism model more or less deterministically, as though "genes determine destiny." The new science of sociobiology can lead in this direction. In contrast, the model of mind or spirit emphasizes consciousness, awareness, choices, and the bursting of boundaries.

Is "spirit" merely a neat mix of DNA and brain chemicals? Are mind and spirit different dimensions of life, transcending biology? These are questions not only of science but also of worldview, as we will see.

The twentieth century was an amazing time of social upheaval. This was due especially to scientific and technical advances, two world wars, and increasing global linkages in commerce and communications. Dramatic as these shifts have been, however, they set the stage for even more rapid change in the next thirty to forty years.

Perhaps the most impressive fact about emerging global society is the way the globe has become linked in one massive communications grid. In the next chapter, we will see the significance of this.

CHAPTER TWO

Online:
The New Shape of Global Culture

> Computer networking "puts you in contact with many thousands of people all over the world, and this can easily change your views on nearly any topic."
>
> —PETER SALUS[1]

> Within a few short years, the Internet has changed our civilization permanently. . . . What happens when millions of people gather in a safe place to talk and to share?
>
> —HARLEY HAHN[2]

Global society has entered the Online Age, the world of instant access. Accelerating change has reached the critical point where all parts of the globe are electronically linked.

I lived in Brazil when Neil Armstrong stepped onto the moon in 1969. It was the middle of the night in Brazil, but like several hundred million other people worldwide, I was tuned in. I set my little black-and-white TV next to the bed and watched as the pictures and words streamed back from space.

Later some Brazilian friends told me they were sure the whole thing had been produced in Hollywood! To them, the event was unbelievable. The astronauts never really reached the moon. But they had. Men set foot on the moon, and the whole world knew it.

That televised moon walk marked a global turning point. Technology was now in place not only to put humans in space, but to allow Earthlings to watch every move.

We all are a part of the instant-access, online world. Access to news, financial trends, and styles of music, art, and fashion is shaping society the world over. Rock bands in the United States, Eastern Europe, Latin America, and even China look and sound much the same. Businessmen everywhere wear similar styles, and so do teenagers.

What does it mean to inhabit an instant-access world, to live online? Today's global communication networks speed and broaden the impact of other key trends that are already shaping the future. Online access is the new shape of global integration, a key element in the fundamental baseline trend of global convergence. In technology, for example, global computerization now enables complex computer programs to model climate and economic behavior. Computer models assist research in genetics, astronomy, and the quest for new energy sources. All this is now part of an international and global enterprise. All the eight key trends are unfolding globally, and must be seen in that light.

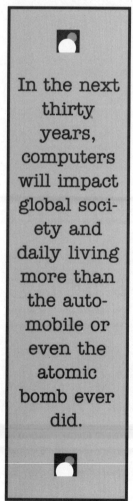

In the next thirty years, computers will impact global society and daily living more than the automobile or even the atomic bomb ever did.

An Electronic Nerve System

Electronics has conquered time and space. It lies behind nearly every technical development shaping the emerging world: telephones, fax machines, television and radio, CDs and video cassettes, multiservers, all kinds of sensors and switches, aerial and space navigation, and above all, of course, computers. The development of today's digital and tomorrow's optical, wireless, and neural computers is the climax of the electronic revolution.

Electronics has been the leading wedge of technical change for nearly a century, from the light bulb to the telephone, radio and TV, and now computers. Linked with other key technologies— the internal combustion engine (automobiles), nuclear power, and advances in chemistry—electronics has brought rocketry, plastics, and thousands of new drugs and medicines. Advanced electronics has synergized these other technologies, producing today's instant-access world.

The computer revolution is still in its infancy. It has brought quantum leaps in data processing, laying the foundation for changes we can barely imagine. And yet so far we have seen perhaps only one-tenth of what is coming. Over the next thirty years it will impact global society and daily living more than the automobile or even the atomic bomb.

Scientifically speaking, electronics is the practical application of electromagnetism, one fourth of the great puzzle of physical matter. The other three are gravity and the strong and weak nuclear forces. Electromagnetism means more than technology and new toys; it is one of nature's key forces, a frontier question. In fact, the electronics revolution and online society are hustling humanity ever closer to unlocking the final secrets of space, time, and matter. The implications here are mind-boggling, as we will see in chapter six.

The most immediate impact of the electronics revolution, however, is *speed*. Global communication is rapidly nearing the speed of light. This means the end of space and time as barriers to communication on Earth and vastly extends it into space. The globe is now linked electronically. That is, anywhere on Earth (or in space), anyone with the proper equipment can plug in to what is going on globally. Computerized electronics combined with fiber-optic cables and communications satellites have spread the electronics revolution worldwide. Single glass fibers, thin as human hair, now carry 600,000 simultaneous messages. This compares with a maximum of about 1,000 on the bulky older cables. And this technology will quickly give way to advanced wireless communication.

This instant-access revolution sparks change in other areas: politics, economics, technology, entertainment, cultural styles, even religion. This is the point. Modern technology creates an electronic nerve system that sends messages almost instantly to all parts of the Earth. Never has this been true before. We don't know yet all this will mean in the long term, but we can be sure that global society in the next half-century will be plugged in and turned on.

The electronics/communications revolution built the superhighway for the spread of American popular culture worldwide. Some say culture everywhere is becoming Americanized through U.S. movies, TV shows, music, books, and magazines. This may be an exaggeration, but it is true that U.S. entertainment has become a global phenomenon. The movie *Pretty Woman* was the top film in Germany, Sweden, Italy, Spain, Denmark, and Australia in 1990. *Reader's Digest,* the world's best-selling magazine, reaches over thirty million people in fifty countries, not including the United States. In 1992 Ognian Pishey, Bulgaria's ambassador to the U.S., said American rock 'n' roll, "the music of rebellion," helped undermine many Communist regimes. Export of American movies and TV programs worldwide amounts to some $3.5 billion yearly.

In effect, information technology is redrawing the world map. Wilson Dizard, Jr., notes that today's global information grid looks something like a weather map. "The map shows a dense mass of organized information over North America, with smaller masses over Europe, Japan, and [Russia]. Elsewhere the density of information shades off into thinness. The new technologies of information can change this map radically by helping create a global knowledge grid."[3]

The Information Superhighway

By the early 1990s, the global possibilities and economic potential of the next wave of the computer revolution were reaching public consciousness. Technocrats and politicians began to talk of an electronic superhighway, or skyway. Promoting and guiding these developments became government policy.

The information superhighway will link homes as well as businesses, research centers, and government facilities in online interactive networks with hundreds of options. Home applications will include a thousand or more TV channels, various shopping networks, and many financial and home-care services. Possibilities are nearly limitless, which means also that a lot of trash will travel on the electronic superhighway.

Big communications companies are now scrambling to be major winners in electronic highway construction. Motorola Corporation is building an ambitious wireless system called Iridium, using sixty-six orbiting satellites. For about $3.00 per minute, users anywhere can get online globally, using pocket phones, computers, or other wireless devices. The Iridium system is being developed jointly with firms in Canada, Japan, China, Russia, and Italy. And this is only one entry in the field. Other systems like Comsat and Globalstar have similar goals.

These developments are fueled in large part by the growing economic importance of information and access to it. Former AT&T chairman James E. Olson wrote:

> Information has become a vital resource for businesses large and small. For the largest enterprises, information has been elevated to the status of a business asset, as important as raw materials, plant, and employees. Increasingly information is being viewed as a *strategic* asset, not only for business and industry, but for governments as well. Moving and managing it effectively and efficiently is giving companies and nations a competitive advantage in both domestic and global markets.[4]

Geza Feketekuty, a former U.S. trade official, points out the broader significance of this:

> In the old days, services had to be produced where they were consumed. In the new world, most of the information-based services can be produced anywhere in the world. . . . Engineers in India draw up blueprints that are reviewed by construction company managers in San Francisco and used by construction crews in Saudi Arabia. A credit card transaction in Spain is key punched in Jamaica, processed by computers in London and Arizona and the bill is sent to the card holder in another part of the world. A data processing center in Cleveland serves clients from New York to California during daylight hours, clients from Japan in the early evening hours, then clients in Singapore, followed by Saudi Arabia and Europe in the early morning hours.[5]

The leading global network for general information today is Cable News Network (CNN), though it is only one of a growing number of world-nets, such as ITN and Reuters. CNN is watched in over 120 countries. Major world capitals are plugged into it. Iraq's President Saddam Hussein got his news from CNN during the 1991 Gulf War. Twenty-four hours a day (time) around the world (space), global information is only a TV switch away, as international travelers know. In addition, new financial information nets furnish data about markets and business developments. Less visible than TV and global journals like *Time* and *The Economist* are the proliferating computer networks covering everything from sports to updates on environmental crises. Greenpeace, for example, runs an online computer network giving constant worldwide environmental news. Over 25 million people globally now use the Internet.

Three key components underlie the communications revolution: high-tech computer systems, global linking, and an information explosion that both feeds and is fed by this networking. The globe is exploding with data. In the next chapter we will see how these linkages promote global *economic* integration, which is reshaping business and international politics.

What Is Information?

What is actually sent and received over this vast global network? Obviously, news of all kinds. Current events, but also huge batches of special information for particular networks and operations, whether in finance, science, the military, espionage, education, or hi-tech crime.

But what is information? To a computer, it is merely electric blips,

41

> **Communication is really about the manipulation of symbols and images.**

tiny pulses sent in patterns that can be translated into words, symbols, and images. *Communication is really about the manipulation of symbols and images.* This has always been true, of course, because words themselves are symbols. Communication includes many kinds of nonverbal signals, as well. In electronic communication, words and images are changed to digital signs, sent around the globe at near the speed of light, then converted back to their earlier form.

Symbols, signals, signs, images—these are the stuff of communication. Perhaps this is why symbols, signs, and styles—and the patterns that link them—are so central in emerging global culture. Here is one place where trends begin to touch worldviews. Global communications is an essential component in the global production, transmission, and manipulation of symbols. Here style, meaning, and worldview merge.

We may wonder whether instant access and online interaction really enrich human life or make us more wise. Bill McKibben warns that ours is in fact "the age of missing information." "We believe that we live in the 'age of information,' that there has been an information 'explosion,'" he writes. But this is true only narrowly. "We also live at a moment of deep ignorance, when vital knowledge that humans have always possessed about who we are and where we live seems beyond our reach. An Unenlightenment."[6]

McKibben tried an experiment: one twenty-four-hour day spent on a mountaintop near a pond, compared with twenty-four hours' worth of cable television viewing (with ninety-three channels, totaling over one thousand hours). His conclusion was "Our society is moving steadily from natural sources of information toward electronic ones, from the mountain and the field toward the television." This presents us, he says, with two extremes: "One is the target of our drift. The other an anchor that might tug us gently back, a source of information that once spoke clearly to us and now hardly even whispers."[7]

Although McKibben speaks specifically about TV, the broader issue is electronic media and communication generally. Many have commented that data and information are not the same as knowledge and wisdom. This is not to decry technology or online culture but to recognize their limitations. More data and increased options don't necessarily mean deeper knowledge and better lives. And yet increasingly, more data and access to it are necessary to live and function in the emerging global society.

Access-rich, Access-poor

Global communication is shifting the balance of wealth and poverty in the world. Information itself, usefully understood and handled, is wealth and power. Both spies and stock brokers know this. Since information is a key economic asset and speed in moving information gives an economic edge, wealth increasingly means access to information. The global gap between "haves" and "have-nots" is increasingly a question of the information access that makes material wealth possible.

Many observers warn about the growing gap between rich and poor. This issue is ethical and political more than technical. It concerns will and values. Ultimately it is a question of worldview—notably the worldviews of people with access to key data, the information brokers.

Global Info-Society

Information access redraws the world map because it ignores national boundaries. National histories and cultures have been shaped by rivers, oceans, deserts, plains, and mountains. This is no longer true. Earth's new borders are electronic. Global information society thus redefines the meaning of "nation" and of "national economy." U.S. Secretary of Labor Robert Reich writes:

> We are living through a transformation that will rearrange the politics and economies of the coming century. There will be no *national* products or technologies, no national corporations, no national industries. There will no longer be national economies, at least as we have come to understand that concept. All that will remain rooted within national borders are the people who comprise a nation. Each nation's primary assets will be its citizens' skills and insights. Each nation's primary political task will be to cope with the centrifugal forces of the global economy which tear at the ties binding citizens together—bestowing ever greater wealth on the most skilled and insightful, while consigning the less skilled to a declining standard of living.[8]

One sign of this is the rapid rise in transnational investment. American industry, for example, is investing overseas faster than at home. The five hundred largest U.S. industrial companies added no domestic jobs between 1975 and 1990; their growth was elsewhere. "Money, technology, information, and goods are flowing across national borders with unprecedented rapidity and ease," Reich notes. "The cost of transporting things and communicating ideas is plummeting. Capital controls in most industrialized countries are being removed; trade barriers reduced. Even items that governments wish to prevent from getting in (drugs, illegal immigrants) or out (secret weapons) do so anyway."[9]

In light of this historic shift, the big challenge nations face today is *people,* more than politics or economics. The issue will be investing in people who, after all, are the heart of any nation and what constitutes its real wealth. The key issue every nation must face is its national *society,* as distinct from its economy. The question is "whether there is still enough concern about [national] society to elicit sacrifices from all of [its citizens]—especially from the most advantaged and successful . . . to help the majority regain the ground it has lost and fully participate in the new global economy," says Reich. "The same question of responsibility confronts every . . . nation whose economic borders are vanishing." It's a question of national purpose: Are nations "bound together by something more than the gross national product? Or has the idea of the nation-state as a collection of people sharing some responsibility for their mutual well-being become passé?"[10]

Over the next generation or two, the idea of the nation-state may become archaic. What will replace it? Some sort of world-state? Or conversely, a global mix of local tribes? Or global culture wars, what some have called a clash of civilizations? This raises the question of world order, which we will discuss in chapter nine.

Think Globally—Act Locally

Online society presents an odd paradox: It no longer makes any difference where on Earth you live. Yet in another sense, it makes all the difference in the world.

Distance is a minor matter in an online world—at least for those with access. Modern corporations illustrate this: parts may be manufactured nearly anywhere in the world and assembled anywhere for distribution worldwide. Lightweight components can often be shipped halfway around the globe cheaper than they can be manufactured "at home"— wherever "home" is. One can be in contact with key people anywhere by phone, fax, and computer. The Chinese president of Singer Corporation lives in Toronto but conducts business worldwide from his office in Hong Kong.

Increasingly, distance and geography are irrelevant in other areas of life as well. Colleges and universities are becoming global learning networks, not just residential campuses. The key location for an educational institution may not be its city or country but its electronic address. This does not mean students simply sitting at home in front of TV screens or computer monitors. It means scattered groups of learners connected video-electronically and in occasional face-to-face contact with globetrotting professors and resource people.

"The global research university of tomorrow," notes Parker Rossman, "is emerging without much notice. It is taking shape as an electronic exchange of information and courses, with students, lecturers, and researchers in many countries connected by satellite, slow-scan television, computer networking, and other advanced telecommunications." Cooperation among university libraries will result in a global satellite library, "including the great global encyclopedia suggested long ago by H. G. Wells," says Rossman. "This 'world brain' would bring the world's knowledge together in one interactive system."[11]

This will not be true for all universities, of course, or all places. The future will be a blend of new and old, as always. And it is true, as a British research chemist working for an American pharmaceutical firm comments, that "Where you are geographically may well be a reflection of how well connected you are electronically!" But global linkage is the direction in which global trends are pointing.

The same is true in other areas: entertainment, science, religion. Where you *are* (geographically) will be less important than your electronic connections.

But this global picture is only one side of the story. The other side is local. Here it makes all the difference in the world where you live, what your turf is. Human life is rooted in specific places. The slogan, "Think globally; act locally" is on target. The world network is, after all, a linkage of myriad *local* systems, groups, and projects. This is obviously true in agriculture: plants must be rooted somewhere, in a local place.

The same is true with human relations. People need to be some*where*. They live and act locally but reflect global realities. Responsible living means ordering life in ways that have meaning locally and yet are socially and ecologically responsible from a global perspective. Conversely, responsible global living means commitment to the local place, the unique local topography and web of relationships where the little daily decisions arise that cumulatively shape our global home.

This suggests that a kind of ecological morality will be necessary for healthy human life on Earth. And it raises the key question—which we will find recurring—of the relations of each *part* to the *whole*.

CHAPTER THREE

Global Web:
The Emerging
World Economy

> We desire world economic prosperity. Continuing
> globalization is our basic approach to achieving
> this.
>
> —TADAHIRO SEKIMOTO,
> PRESIDENT, NEC CORPORATION[1]
>
> Words such as overseas operations, affiliates, and
> subsidiaries are disappearing. Nothing is 'over-
> seas' any longer.
>
> —KENICHI OHMAE[2]

Earth's economy is shifting from patchwork to network. Global integration and networking are now the driving force in business and economics. The world is becoming one vast marketplace, not a patchwork of local markets. Economic integration on a world scale is reshaping society in a process that will reach well into the twenty-first century.

Consider Shenzhen, the mushrooming Chinese metropolis just across the border from Hong Kong. China has made Shenzhen a "Special Economic Zone," turning it into a key contact point between East and West. Shenzhen is a dramatic sign of the emerging global marketplace. New hotels, banks, and a three-story McDonald's restaurant overshadow the older traditional town of small houses and market streets. By the thousands, Chinese flock from the interior to Shenzhen to study or set up

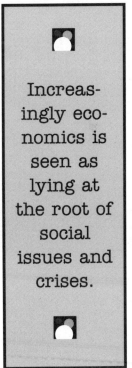

businesses. Everything is available, from luxury items to audio cassettes of Western classical and popular music to rare Chinese antiques.

With its modern communications and surging stock market, already Shenzhen is globally connected. Still a poor second to Hong Kong, of course, Shenzhen is a key bridge city in this interim before Hong Kong rejoins China in 1997. In the next century Shenzhen will outstrip Hong Kong in size and may rival it in economic clout, or be drawn into a Hong Kong-Shenzhen megalopolis.

This picture is not unique to China. It is global. In the next two decades the expanding web of economic dynamism will reshape the way we live and, possibly, how we think. Consider some key aspects:

From Ideology to Economics

First, the new global economy marks a new *shift from political ideology to economic pragmatism* as the major factor in international relations. This shift underlay the collapse of the Communist Bloc. Communism never delivered the promised economic goods. By the 1980s Communism clearly was the god that had failed. The success of other economic forms under a variety of political structures prompted deep questioning. Now throughout Eastern Europe and in the former Soviet Union economics has become the rising paradigm and the chief issue. With few exceptions, political leaders are willing to shift policy as necessary to build a workable economy. This is what Gorbachev's *perestroika* and *glasnost* were about, and such slogans have had their counterparts in many other nations.

The shift to economic pragmatism is most striking in China. Though Communists rule, Communism is now a dead faith. Paramount leader Deng Xiaoping announced, "To be rich is glorious," and urged his countrymen to prosper in business as the best way to transform the nation. New stock markets were opened in Shenzhen and Shanghai. Guangdong province, opposite Hong Kong, is thriving since family farming and private enterprise have been allowed to replace Mao's communes. Riding the daily train between Hong Kong and Guangzhou (old Canton) packed with businessmen and entrepre-

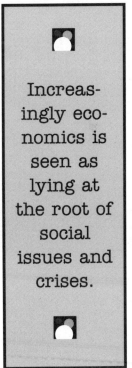

Increasingly economics is seen as lying at the root of social issues and crises.

neurs, one sees the economic transformation in the dozens of new factory-residential complexes replacing gardens and rice paddies.

Some younger Chinese leaders, such as central banker Chen Yuan, advocate combining free enterprise with a blend of nationalism, Confucianism, and Western philosophy—similar to the recipe that has proved so dynamic in nearby Singapore. The underlying concern, however, seems to be economic success as the key to the future.

This is the story from Malaysia to Venezuela. What works economically is the key issue. Increasingly economics is seen as lying at the root of social issues and concerns. Throughout Latin America, much of Asia, and elsewhere, economic pragmatism is replacing ideology. Or becoming the new ideology. Thus economics is not just about money, goods, and services. It also touches worldview questions.

The Global Information Economy

Second, the new reality is increasingly a *global information economy.* Economically advanced nations have moved from the industrial to the information age, and others are following. This shift is marked by an explosion of information and easy access to information globally, as we saw in the previous chapter. Today the leading edge of the new world economy is information, not manufacturing. It is data, not diamonds and doorknobs; signs and symbols, not screws and stereos. Hard products are not becoming less important, of course. Manufacture is booming in many countries, especially in the Pacific Rim. But the harbinger of the world economy and its main unifier is the information/communication sector on which everything else depends.

Regional Trade Zones

A third aspect of the global web is the rise of common markets and trade zones. Here again the map is being redrawn. Old categories no longer apply. The key alliances are economic. Lester Thurow writes, "The system that governed the world economy in the last half of the twentieth century will not be the system governing [it] in the first half of the twenty-first century. A new system of quasi trading blocks employing managed trade will emerge."[3]

Increasingly the news is about regional and global trade: NAFTA, GATT, ASEAN. The full emergence in 1992 of the European Economic Community (EEC; now EC) created the world's largest (at the time) and one of the most dynamic economic units—larger than the U.S. economy. How Eastern Europe will relate to the EC is still unclear, though several of these nations, including the newly-independent Baltic States, will probably be integrated into the EC. The Common Market standardized specifications, brand names, and marketing strategies throughout Europe, creating a broad new economic unit—and prompting similar developments elsewhere.

The economic rise of the Pacific Rim, fueled initially by Japan and the "Four Tigers" of Hong Kong, South Korea, Singapore, and Taiwan fits the same picture. The region's rapid growth has shifted the economic and social frontier of the United States to the West Coast. The Pacific Rim signals the new global economy: based more on people, knowledge, and ideas than on raw materials or (for the most part) heavy industry.

Hong Kong is nervous but cautiously optimistic about its absorption into China in 1997. The pressure of 1997 and China's newfound prosperity are speeding economic ties not only between Hong Kong and China, but throughout the region. The 1989 Tiananmen Square massacre has been all but forgotten as China forges economic links around the Pacific Rim, including even with Taiwan, and with Russia. Mushrooming trade throughout the region is clear evidence of this. With its huge population and booming economy, China is emerging as the Asian superpower to rival Japan.

In North America, the United States has been large and rich enough to prosper as its own mass market. The emergence of a united Europe and the dynamism of the Pacific Rim now is changing the game. This was a major impulse behind the North American Free Trade Agreement (NAFTA). The economic gap between the United States and Mexico long made a common market, with totally free trade, unthinkable. But things have changed. The 1989 trade pact between the United States and Canada virtually erased economic barriers, creating a free-trade zone in the North. NAFTA, ratified in 1993, expanded the pact to include all North America. This is a historic event with long-range social, political, and cultural impact.

The North American Free Trade Area (NAFTA) should spark a regional economic boom, transforming Mexico in particular. This in turn may spur further global integration among the various regional trade blocs. Or, it could promote a new regionalism. These blocs will compete and vie for dominance. But they will likely become more interdependent for both economic and ecological reasons. Global interests should outweigh regional ones (thus damping the likelihood of military conflict), but this is by no means certain.

Regional trade zones are appearing throughout the world. Mexico signed a free-trade pact with Colombia and Venezuela in 1994, creating another economic bloc with a combined gross domestic product of

$373 billion. In South America, the Mercosur treaty brings Brazil, Argentina, Uruguay, and Paraguay closer economically. The Chile-Argentina pact helped stimulate $1.2 billion in trade in 1992. These agreements partly reflect economic self-defense as these nations see what is happening in other parts of the world, but they promote economic vitality and stability.

South America is a continent with tremendous resources and large populations. Much of the region has seen sharp economic growth in the past decade. Otto Reich, former U.S. ambassador to Venezuela, says, "The changes in Latin America have been as radical as the changes in Eastern Europe," though less publicized—and could lead the continent out of poverty.[4] Presently Latin America is the fastest-growing market for U.S. goods, and foreign investment there from Japan, Europe, and the United States quadrupled from $24 billion to $100 billion in the period 1990-92.[5] Combined with a marked spiritual resurgence and the move toward democracy throughout much of the region, these economic developments could bring new prosperity. Major problems of corruption, injustice, and ecological damage in many of the region's nations remain serious obstacles, however.

Much of Africa, especially Central Africa, is in danger of being bypassed by these regional and global developments. If South Africa achieves democratic political stability and renewed economic vitality, it could be a key catalyst in African economic integration, stability, and prosperity. But the problems of central Africa are very deep. Economist Lester Thurow paints a bleak picture:

> Africa south of the Sahara, with the exception of South Africa . . . is the world's economic basket case. . . . Borders are in the wrong places to minimize ethnic animosities. The green revolution has not been made to work in the climates and soils of Africa. Effective, efficient governments do not exist. No economy has ever been able to cope with Africa's current population growth rates. Skill and education levels are the lowest in the world. Debts are large relative to earning power. . . . AIDS may be to Africa in the twenty-first century what the Black Death was to Europe in the fourteenth century. The falling per capita incomes of the 1980s are apt to be replicated in the 1990s.[6]

An equitable global system will require international cooperation to deal with these difficult problems. The global economy cannot really be healthy when such a large part of Earth's population is marginalized and suffering.

A major by-product of the collapse of the Soviet Union has been an expanding Muslim trade zone. In early 1992, leaders from Turkey, Iran, and Pakistan met with representatives of several Muslim republics of the former Soviet Union to discuss expanding the Economic Cooperation Organization (ECO), founded by Iran, Turkey, and Pakistan in 1985. Azerbaijan, Turkmenistan, and Uzbekistan joined ECO in 1992. Leaders project an eventual common market of ten nations, including Afghanistan. The Islamic trade bloc would stretch from Europe to Asia, encompassing some 220 million people. Because of its close ties with Europe and relatively more advanced economy, Turkey would be a key player in the new alliance.

The chief significance of ECO would be the relative displacement of political and military boundaries and connections with economic, cultural, and religious ones. This is another example of the way the world map is being redrawn and of the rising priority of economics.

Freer global trade and regional economic zones do not guarantee global prosperity. Nations never get rich overnight, cautions Lester Thurow. History suggests that becoming wealthy requires a full century of economic growth rates averaging 3 percent or better combined with slow population growth. Thurow considers this "an iron law of economic development." It boils down to a simple formula: Wealth must increase faster than population in order for the standard of living to rise. "It is simply impossible for any country to become rich in the context of a rapidly rising population," says Thurow.

Thurow uses Japan's century-long rise to relative wealth as an example:

> Over the past one hundred years, Japan averaged a 4 percent per year real growth rate while its population was growing 1.1 percent per year. This produced a 2.9 percent yearly rise in per capita income. Over the same one hundred years, the American growth rate averaged 3.3 percent per year while its population was growing 1.5 percent per year. . . . The result was 1.8 percent per year growth in per capita incomes.

It has taken over one hundred years, Thurow notes, for Japan to reach comparable per capita wealth to the United States. He is, therefore, not optimistic about prospects for Earth's poorer nations unless population growth is sharply reduced and wealthier nations help with debt forgiveness and other assistance. Even so, achieving prosperity is "probably going to get harder in the century ahead."[7]

Wealth is not solely a matter of material goods, of course. In the emerging global economy, where business networks and information links are often more important than national boundaries, old rules may apply less. Still, Thurow's analysis is a sobering caution that global prosperity will not come easily, even in the best of circumstances.

The New Corporation

The growth of global trade is partly the fruit of the long GATT process (the General Agreement on Tariffs and Trade), begun in 1947 in the wake of World War II, which reached fruition with the 1994 pact liberalizing trade and standarding practices for over one hundred nations. But the new global economy means more than expanded, freer trade. Combined with other trends, it also means a revolution in the way businesses are structured and function.

Robert Reich writes in *The Work of Nations:*

> The most profitable firms are transforming into enterprise webs. They may look like the old form of organization from the outside, but inside all is different. Their famous brands adhere to products and services that are cobbled together from many different sources outside the formal boundaries of the firm. Their dignified headquarters, expansive factories, warehouses, laboratories, and fleets of trucks and corporate jets are leased. Their production workers, janitors, and bookkeepers are under temporary contract; their key researchers, design engineers, and marketers are sharing in the profits. And their distinguished executives, rather than possessing great power and authority over this domain, have little direct control over much of anything. Instead of imposing their will over a corporate empire, they guide ideas through the new webs of enterprise.[8]

This suggests the fourth mark of the new global economy: the rise of a new kind of corporation. Economists speak of the *high-value corporation,* distinct from the high-volume corporation of the past century.

This shift is driven by global competition and enabled by high technology. "No longer able to generate large earnings from high-volume production of standard commodities," notes Reich, many key companies "are gradually, often painfully, turning toward serving the unique needs of particular customers. By trial and error . . . the firms that are surviving and succeeding are shifting from high volume to high value."[9]

Take computers. In 1984, 80 percent of the cost of a computer was hardware; only 20 percent was software. By 1990, the proportions had reversed. The value is less in the actual machines produced than in the services provided through specialized software. "Core corporations no longer focus on products as such; their business strategies increasingly center upon specialized knowledge," notes Reich.[10]

This means slimmer, more flexible organization. "The high-value enterprise . . . need not be organized like the old pyramids that characterized standardized production," Reich says. "In fact, the high-value enterprise *cannot* be organized this way." Rather, the new corporation consists of three key groups—problem-solvers, problem-identifiers, and strategic brokers—who work and avoid getting trapped in bureaucracy.[11]

Rather than planning high production runs, investing heavily in factories, and employing armies of workers, the new corporation leases facilities as needed and contracts a shifting array of services, components, and temporary workers. It does this *globally,* ignoring national boundaries and interests. Outwardly such new corporations may look no different—brand names and trademarks remain—but inside, the model is very different from the grand corporations of the 1950s and 1960s.

High-value corporations will not replace high-volume companies, of course. There will always be need for large quantities of mass-produced goods, from soap to shoes. But the high-value company is the leading edge of global integration and represents a model based on different assumptions than those that predominated for over a century.

Stateless Corporations

Many high-value firms are also supranational or "stateless." This is the fifth key element in the emerging global web. Transnational corporations have existed for centuries, of course. Think of the great banking houses of medieval Europe, or the British East India Company of the 1700s. But the new international corporation that emerged in the 1980s is different. Stateless corporations not only manufacture and market globally, they are multinational at every level, including ownership.

Stateless corporations are global in multiple ways: management, financing, production, marketing, and ownership. Management is drawn from several countries, often through acquisitions or mergers. A company in Sweden and one in Switzerland, for example, merged to form a combined firm that directs most of its operations from Germany. Such arrangements are increasingly common as corporations seek more global markets.

Supranational corporations also internationalize their research, design, and manufacture. A company in North America may form a design group in Europe, or even assemble a design team from different parts of the globe. A growing number of U.S. firms do their information processing in the Caribbean and Ireland. Cigna Corporation, for example, a major insurance firm, daily sends medical claims to Ireland for processing.

Most noticeably, marketing has gone global. Thousands of brand names from global corporations are following the long lead of Coca-Cola and cigarette makers, planting names like McDonalds, Samsung, and Estée Lauder into consumer consciousness from Red Square to Rio de Janeiro.

More recently, stateless corporations have begun securing financing internationally. Investment also has gone global. Shares now sell in a variety of financial markets around the world. As investors from different countries buy shares, such companies are literally owned by a global community transcending national borders. These firms really have no national identity. Individual and corporate investors in the United States, for instance, can now buy stock directly or indirectly in scores of different countries. New corporations such as Chicago-based Globex facilitate this global trading.

What are the long-range effects of these stateless global giants? Many of these enterprises are bigger financial operations than the nations where they operate. Their political and economic clout is enormous. A giant stateless corporation with its global web of investors, managers, researchers, designers, workers, marketers, lawyers, and customers constitutes a human and economic entity that cuts across the scores of nation-states it touches. Arguably, this is a force for global cohesion. But since the relationships are almost solely economic, pressing issues of ecology, social welfare, and cultural identity may get trampled.

These are the facts and fibers of the global web. Together they profile the new world of the global marketplace. Canadian communications guru Marshall McLuhan spoke of a "global village." But with rapid urbanization, "village" is hardly the right image. We might speak rather of the "global city." "Global marketplace" is even more apt. The emerging world is a marketplace of investment, research, development, manufacture, marketing, and consumption, and another sign of a new kind of global society.

A United States of Europe?

The uniting of Europe economically, culturally, and in communications creates pressures for deeper forms of union. This has significance globally as well as regionally. Europe will play a key role in the global economy.

With fuller economic integration in 1992, Europe became a more attractive market for Japanese industry. Japan invested heavily, building factories (especially in England) and forming joint ventures with European firms. In 1990, Fujitsu bought ICL, Britain's major computer manufacturer. Mitsubishi Motors teamed up with Volvo in Holland, and Mitsubishi Electric bought British computer maker Apricot in 1990. The Japanese "have systematically forged strategic alliances with companies short of cash and hungry for technology. . . . They have also worked at becoming good 'corporate citizens,' funding soccer teams, university chairs, and museums and art galleries across Europe," notes *Business Week*. "Europe is looking a lot more like America in the early 1980s, when U.S. consumer electronics, auto, steel, and machine-tool industries were hard hit" by the Japanese.[12]

United Europe is now the world's second largest market, after the NAFTA bloc (Canada, Mexico, the United States). Western Europeans buy more cars and consumer electronics than any one nation. "Europe is likely to become the fulcrum of the world's economic power balance for the new century," says *Business Week*. "It's a booming base from which multinationals will consolidate the financial strength and the economies of scale essential to compete around the world." The result is a three-way economic struggle among Europe, Japan, and the United States.[13]

Many U.S. firms now make their profits through European rather than domestic sales. The United States' investment in Europe is about three times that of Japan, but Japan is catching up.

Forty percent of Japanese investment in Europe so far is in Britain. Nissan, Toyota, and Honda now have plants there. This infusion of cash and technology may be a key to Britain's manufacturing future. Barry Wilkinson of the University of Wales says Japanese-inspired techniques are revitalizing the Welsh auto components industry. By the year 2000, about one in six British factory workers will have Japanese bosses, according to one study.

Something similar is happening throughout Europe. In Germany, for example, by 1991 Japanese businesses had created 8,000 new jobs in Dusseldorf and had moved some 7,000 business people and their families there from Japan.

The growing economic integration of Western Europe in time will probably include most of the non-EC nations of both Western and Eastern Europe. By 2050, most of Europe will likely have a common currency and increased social and cultural ties.[14]

Shifts in the U.S. Economy

In the 1980s and early 1990s, the United States was caught in a squeeze between an expanding Japan and a unifying Europe. This happened precisely as the nation was facing severe internal problems, particularly in education and in social and family life, which clouded its longer-term future. We will examine the broader cultural meaning of these issues in chapter eight. Here we note their meaning for the global economy.

Like other "advanced" industrialized economies, the United States is experiencing a major shift in employment patterns as it becomes a postindustrial information economy. According to the Bureau of National Affairs (BNA), by the year 2000 nearly nine out of ten working Americans will have jobs in the service sector, compared with about six in ten in 1980. Half of these will be in the information industry, and half of those in the information industry will work at home. The trend toward more women in the workplace will continue. Two thirds of the new jobs in the present decade will go to women, and 85 percent will be filled by minorities or women or both, according to Forecasting International. More and more people have part-time or temporary jobs, often without benefits, as large corporations slim down for global competition. And increasingly people work for government: In 1992 the number of civilians working for federal, state, and local government (18.6 million) outstripped the number of people holding manufacturing jobs (18.2 million).[15]

A major economic, as well as social, concern is the poor quality of American public education. One result is industry's entrance into the school business. Needing a steady supply of good workers, business has begun supporting and even operating public schools. Eventually many schools will be located at factories or office sites, according to several studies. Companies will hire family-life coordinators to help employees balance their work and family responsibilities, says Karol Rose, manager of work and family programs for the Time Warner Corporation. The trend is for businesses, which have the resources, the motivation, and the will, to step in where other structures of society have failed.

This trend is important because it means that the workplace is replacing the neighborhood as the site for social interaction and cohesion. "'The concept of the workplace as a village' will evolve as worksites begin to include services such as drug stores, medical and dental offices, schools and child care centers," predicts a BNA report.[16] This assumes, of course, the permanence of the trend toward dual-income families and the absence of a parent in the home during working hours.

"Worksite schools" already operate in Dade County, Florida. Honeywell Corporation's Space and Aviation Division, located in Clearwater, for example, opened an onsite kindergarten/first-grade school in 1990 for company employees. Such schools are seen as a "win-win" option. The company gains through increased worker productivity; employees get the convenience and quality of the new school; and the school system benefits from lower operating costs.

Traditionally the family, the neighborhood, and the church or synagogue have been the basis for social cohesion. These are essentially non-

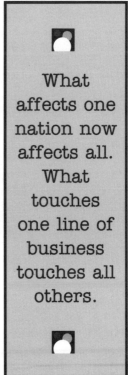

commercial groups. What happens when *economic* interests underlie such fundamental social cohesion? Will all other values become subservient to productivity and profit-making? This development is part of the larger commercialization and "consumerization" of U.S. society, as is the emergence of the shopping mall as the nation's most popular public space. Observers have noted the irony of a society's leading public space being privately owned and controlled by commercial interests.

These trends illustrate the first feature of the new global economy, the shift from ideology to economic pragmatism. Ideology and idealism are suspect in modern and postmodern America. As these cease to form the magnetic field of social unity, economic interests seem ready to step in.

The Global Economy

Economic pragmatism, new corporate styles, the increasing role of information, and growing competition in a global market are thus shaping the emerging world economy. The failure of the U.S. economy to bounce back quickly after the 1990–92 recession was symbolic of this global transformation. Because the U.S. economy is increasingly global and businesses must now compete worldwide, national economies no longer run through normal cycles more or less independently from the rest of the world. Japan and Europe learned this in their economic slow-downs in 1992-93. What affects one nation now affects all; what touches one line of business touches all others as well. We are in the new day of a global economy, with much greater international interdependence.

Robert Reich identifies three skills crucial to businesses that compete globally: problem identification, problem solving, and strategic linking or brokering. We might call persons who do these tasks *spotters, solvers,* and *linkers.* Essentially they are networkers in the business web. Each brings a special skill to the profit-making process.

Solvers skillfully put "things together in unique ways (be they alloys, molecules, semiconductor chips, software codes, movie scripts, pension portfolios, or information)."[17] They con-

> What affects one nation now affects all. What touches one line of business touches all others.

stantly search for new applications, combinations, and refinements. *Spotters* focus on what customers want and how best to respond. *Linkers* connect solvers with spotters.

Strategic brokers—the linkers who find winning combinations—help problem-solvers and problem-spotters work together. Linkers function like coaches, joining people synergistically, providing resources and giving them space to connect technologies with customer's needs. "Creative teams solve and identify problems in much the same way whether they are developing new software, dreaming up a new marketing strategy, seeking a scientific discovery, or contriving a financial ploy," says Reich. "Most coordination is horizontal rather than vertical. Because problems and solutions cannot be defined in advance, formal meetings and agendas won't reveal them. They emerge instead out of frequent and informal communications among team members."[18] This is a good example of what futurist John Naisbitt calls the megatrend from hierarchies to networking.

Leading-edge firms in the global economy look like a spider's web rather than a pyramid, suggests Reich. "Strategic brokers are at the center, but there are all sorts of connections that do not involve them directly, and new connections are being spun all the time. . . . Each point on the 'enterprise web' represents a unique combination of skills."[19] The web thrives on experimentation, constantly seeking new applications, often by trial and error. Working together in informal groups proves motivating. "Few incentives are more powerful than membership in a small group engaged in a common task, sharing the risks of defeat and the potential rewards of victory," Reich notes. The reward is more than money: "The group often shares a vision as well; they want to make their mark on the world."[20]

Around the globe, leading-edge companies are transforming themselves into enterprise webs, joining the growing mega-web of global business. Most of this is hidden from public view, for it involves internal restructuring. It often shows up as "downsizing" or "rightsizing" and increased temporary jobs.

One result is that Earth's economy will *decreasingly* be dominated by large firms that are distinctly American, Japanese, or European. This is true for two reasons. Leading-edge firms are increasingly stateless, as we have seen. Because the internal structure of these corporations is more web-like than pyramidal, wealth and power are not concentrated at the top but are diffused throughout the network. Resources flow to creative teams of innovators and problem-solvers who operate with an autonomy unthinkable in the old model. These creative power nodes may be located almost anywhere on Earth, since constant contact can be maintained electronically. Information flows across national boundaries through tens of thousands of leased telephone circuits carrying data and images instantly around the globe.

Defining products by country of origin thus becomes nearly meaningless. "When an American buys a Pontiac Le Mans from General Motors," notes Reich, "he or she engages unwittingly in an international transaction." Consider:

> Of the $20,000 paid to GM, about $6,000 goes to South Korea for routine labor and assembly operations, $3,500 to Japan for advanced components (engines, transaxles, and electronics), $1,500 to West Germany for styling and design engineering, $800 to Taiwan, Singapore, and Japan for small components, $500 to Britain for advertising and marketing services, and about $100 to Ireland and Barbados for data processing. The rest—less than $8,000—goes to strategists in Detroit, lawyers and bankers in New York, lobbyists in Washington, insurance and health-care workers all over the country, and General Motors shareholders—most of whom live in the United States, but an increasing number of whom are foreign nationals.[21]

Trade balance also changes meaning in the global economy. In 1990, for example, well over half of America's imports and exports were actually transfers *within* corporations that operate globally. Honda exports components from Japan to its plants in Ohio (or vice versa); IBM imports computer parts from subsidiaries in the Orient. Old categories and accounting methods have not kept up. Today no one really knows whether a nation's international trade is in or out of balance, or even what difference it makes.

In the new global economy, most workers will provide personal services rather than operate machines. The "three jobs of the future" argues Reich, "will be personal services, routine production, and symbolic-analytic services." In the United States by the early 1990s, over three-quarters of the work force fell into these three broad categories.[22]

The most highly paid jobs are in symbolic-analytic services (provided by the spotters, solvers, and linkers noted above). Through global networking, these services can be traded worldwide in ways that other kinds cannot. These people are research scientists, design engineers, software engineers, public relations executives, investment bankers, and myriad consultants, analysts, and developers. Artists, writers, publishers, and most teachers also fall into this category. These are the people who make their living manipulating data and symbols rather than performing routine tasks.

Robert Reich makes much of the emergence of such analysts who "solve, identify, and broker problems by manipulating symbols. *They simplify reality into abstract images* that can be rearranged, juggled, experimented with, communicated to other specialists, and then, eventually transformed back into reality."[23] These creative creatures inhabit the nodes of enterprise webs, forging the strategic links that boost corporate profits. They are mobile team workers, in contact with colleagues around the globe. Today, most symbol-analysts are white males, but the category increasingly includes women and people of diverse ethnicity.

Here, then, is a snapshot of the new global economy: A decreasing pool of producers and a growing army of service workers who implement others' plans or service the system, and a growing, highly paid elite of data-and-symbol manipulators, mobile and relatively rootless, making their living by creatively running and expanding the global enterprise web.

Stretched globally, this web is not the same everywhere, of course. Relatively prosperous countries like Japan and the United States, with high labor costs, have moved millions of production jobs to countries with plenty of cheap labor. In these places production workers may be the largest category. But in the global economy of symbol-analysts, service personnel, and production workers, the last category likely will grow more slowly than the other two areas because of the growing role of computer-based info-technology.

An Example: Reinventing the Corporation

Lord Corporation of Erie, Pennsylvania, illustrates how companies are changing to fit the global economy. Lord makes parts for global products like Sikorsky helicopters and Boeing jets. In the mid-1980s, Lord rejected nearly half of the parts from its Dayton, Ohio, plant due to poor quality. Then the plant was reorganized in 1989. The old hierarchical structure vanished and several self-managed production teams were formed. Morale and quality soared; the number of rejected parts fell to almost zero. The work force dropped initially from 110 in 1982 to 60 in 1991, but it was projected to increase again due to heightened productivity.

This clearly was a move from a vertical, hierarchical structure to a more participatory, organic one; from pyramid to web. Notes Greg Stricharchuk:

> The management structure . . . essentially has been turned upside down. Foremen who used to parcel out work orders—'baby sitters' in the [plant manager's] view—were eliminated. Workers were put in charge of their own jobs. Factory employees, organized in teams, now schedule their

own work, including overtime and vacations. They also appraise their own performance and wield enough clout to have goldbrickers fired. . . . The power of decision is being pushed to the lowest possible levels—the factory floor. And frontline bosses famous for temper tantrums and second-guessing are becoming extinct.[24]

Each work team operates much like a mini-business. Floor supervisors were eliminated, reducing both costs and confusion. Worker morale soared because employees now had direct responsibility for the quality of their workmanship and, to some extent, for planning. One worker, a woman, reported: "Now I don't have to find someone to tell me what to do. It makes you feel important to make your own decisions." Another said, "In the past, we always seemed under the gun, but now we look ahead. Now you put pressure on yourself rather than having others put pressure on you. It's freer."

The new system requires teamwork, and not all workers were able or willing to adapt to this. Some quit rather than change. Yet employee absenteeism dropped dramatically, falling to an average of less than two days per year.

Here is a microcosm of the new model of business organization that is sweeping the world. The same story could be repeated endlessly. In the United States, General Motors proved that even stodgy corporate giants can and must move in this direction by creating Saturn Corporation, whose hot-selling cars began cutting into the sale of Japanese models. Increasingly, companies around the globe are moving in this direction. Those that don't will cut themselves off as players in the global economy.

New Model, New Consciousness

The emerging global economy is significant in its own right. But it has deeper meaning. It signals three broad shifts, part of today's Earth Currents: a shift in model, in consciousness, and from things to symbols.

A shift in model. The new global economy reflects some underlying models and assumptions. Note especially the shift in leading enterprises from the *pyramid* to the *web* as the key form of organization—the shift from hierarchies to networking.

Significantly, this is a shift from a more rigid, mechanical form to a more biological, organic one. It is more evidence that today's society is moving from the machine to the organism; from mechanics to biology. One might have said from physics to biology, but with the rise of quantum physics, a similar shift has already occurred in what used to be called the "hard" sciences. Physics is no longer about mechanics in the old sense; it is about movement, indeterminability, and patterns. This organic form seems to be the emerging shape of culture at every level, including economics and business. So far this is evident not so much in academia or abstract theory or the arts, as in business and enterprise—the stuff of global power and global reach that so deeply shapes everyday life for growing numbers of Earth's billions.

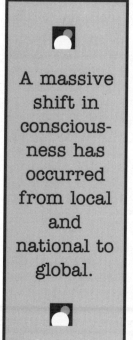

A massive shift in consciousness has occurred from local and national to global.

A shift in consciousness. No longer can business anywhere in the world think only locally or nationally. No longer do entrepreneurs or manufacturers operate in isolation from the global context. Even local businesses are plugging into global information networks to keep up with key trends. Increasingly sources of such information—magazines, computer networks, or consulting firms—are global or at least draw their information globally. A massive shift in consciousness has occurred from local and national to global.

This means that business people—in fact, anyone involved in economics or finance—increasingly will be conscious of working in a global environment and being world citizens. More and more, consumers buy products from all over the world. And what is true in people's business and commercial lives will likely carry over to other areas, creating more generalized global awareness. Coming generations will be globally conscious as never before. In the next forty years, two generations will come to maturity with a global consciousness. They will be people who know that their address is not Urbana or Irkutsk, but Earth.

A shift from things to symbols. People turn increasingly symbol-sensitive in the new global economy. Things in themselves mean less than what they symbolize. This does not necessarily mean less materialism. It could mean more, as things from jeans to jobs are valued less for what they are than for what they say: the brands, names, or other meanings tied to them.

More basically, this is a shift from things to the *connections between things,* a new focus, perhaps, on the patterns that hold things together rather than on hardware, goods, or material products. We already see this in high-value companies where the worth of the product is not so much the thing itself as in the services that go with it—not so much hardware as software. Or, to put it differently, increasingly the *real product* is seen to be services more than things. Banks and insurance companies, for example, now speak of the new services they provide as their "products." The most valuable resources of high-value enterprises are not factories and warehouses and finished goods, as we have seen, but their services, networks, and other intangibles like reputation and influence.

Here again we see the growing role of images and the focus on linkages, connections, and patterns of relationship. The emerging model is more organic than mechanical, more flowing and flexible than fixed or frozen. This suggests for the future a new sensitivity to permeating patterns that hold things together, perhaps countering tendencies toward diversity and disintegration. This is really a different perspective from the dominant one for people nurtured on the science and philosophy flowing from the Renaissance and the Enlightenment in Europe. In some ways this "new" mentality may actually be closer to that of societies less touched by modern culture and more aware of the patterns, textures, and interconnections of all of life.

This shift in model is also more in tune with newer directions in science, as hinted above. The famous physicist Werner Heisenberg notes that theoretical physics now classifies the world "not into different groups of objects but into different groups of connections. . . . The world thus appears as a complicated tissue of events, in which connections of different kinds alternate or overlap or combine and thereby determine the texture of the whole."[25]

In these respects, the emerging global web of economic relationships seems to parallel tendencies in other spheres, again raising issues of worldview and meaning.

CHAPTER FOUR

Gender Power:
The Feminist Revolution

One thing is certain: changes in economic and social life around the world during the next quarter-century will be intimately connected to changes in the status and roles of women.

—**KATHLEEN NEWLAND**[1]

The way we structure the most fundamental of all human relations (without which our species could not go on) has a profound effect on every one of our institutions, on our values, and . . . on the direction of our cultural evolution, particularly whether it will be peaceful or warlike.

—**RIANE EISLER**[2]

Nothing in human culture is more basic than the interaction between men and women. The philosopher Schopenhauer wrote, "The relation of the sexes is the invisible central point of all conduct."[3] Inevitably, anything that touches how the two genders relate affects everything else, from family life to world politics. The long-term trend, increasingly global, toward expanded social roles for women must therefore be counted as one of the deepest Earth Currents of history.

This trend is not new. Its roots are diverse. The revolution has sped up dramatically since World War II, and its long-term impact will be most revolutionary over the next two generations.

With few exceptions, most of human history has been the story of male dominance—"his-story" rather than "her-story," as some feminists say. From today's perspective, it is amazing how invisible women usually are in written history. Forever, it seems, the man has been head of the home, king of the castle, and censor of history. Chiefs and presidents, monarchs and prime ministers were mostly men. Women filled more homey roles that were crucial for society but secondary in terms of social, political, and economic power. The 1993 U.N. Human Development Report claims that men are still treated better than women in every country in the world.[4]

If the 1990s are a hinge of history, nowhere is this more certain than in gender issues. Even by itself this trend spells cultural change and worldview shift. Mixed with other Earth Currents, it has a multiplier effect. In synergy with economic and technological trends, this change goes to the deepest roots and self-perceptions of culture. Kathleen Newland of Worldwatch Institute notes, "The role of women in society is changing all over the world. The highly visible women's liberation movement in the industrialized West finds its muted parallel even in remote rural villages." Changes in women's roles are causing "seismic shifts." "The major fault lines run through all the important areas of human activity, including education, employment, health, legal structures, politics, communications, and the family."[5]

Linked to the gender revolution are other fundamentals of human self-understanding: sex identity and roles (including homosexuality), abortion and birth control, and the family. Most basic of all is the role and influence of women in society and as makers of history.

The gender revolution is a deeper current than today's feminist movements. Feminism, particularly in North Atlantic societies, has largely bypassed the concerns of many minority, poor, or "traditional" women, critics charge. "Many women feel mainstream feminism has ignored their plight," writes Monika Guttman. They feel "the feminist movement has failed to broaden its base and remains made up largely of white, highly educated women who have not adequately addressed the issues that matter to them: child care rather than lesbian and abortion rights, economic survival rather than political equality, the sticky floor rather than the glass ceiling."[6] Partly for this reason, some feminist leaders are now calling for a broader, more inclusive agenda.

In this chapter we trace the evidence for this trend toward broader roles for women and the ways it is becoming global. We ask about its present and future effects on human society and its implications for worldviews and world meanings.

Signs of Deep Change

Some signs of the times:

- Women are starting new businesses and cooperatives worldwide in record numbers—in some places, faster than men.
- About 40 percent of the members of Parliament in both Finland and Norway are women.
- In Russia, a women's political party won a sizeable block of seats in the new parliament, elected in 1993.
- Twenty-three percent of the candidates for Cuba's National Assembly, in the nation's first direct election in 1993, were women.
- A record number of women were elected to the U.S. Congress in 1992, raising the total to a historic fifty-three women serving in the two houses.
- For the first time in history, a woman was elected as speaker of Japan's lower house of Parliament.
- A woman astronaut helped repair the Hubble space telescope.
- Women are moving up the ranks and to the frontlines in national military establishments.

These widening roles for women are linked to the rise of an information society, argues Canadian futurist and business consultant Frank Feather. Because emerging global society "is based on information and knowledge, as many more women gain access to education we are seeing a rapid change in their status. With the emergence of post-industrialism, women are coming into their own and making a significant contribution to society that will continue to gain in strength and importance." This in turn further speeds the growth of the information society because women, unlike men, "are less likely to carry the stereotypical values of the preceding Industrial Age."[7]

In his book *Sex and Power: The Rise of Women in America, Russia, Sweden, and Italy,* Donald Meyer makes a similar point: "The main 'material' basis for revolutionary transformation in the lives of women has been no mystery. Those societies in which these transformations most forcefully emerged were industrialized societies. . . . Peripheral exceptions aside, the correlation with an industrial economy cannot be ignored in any stories of women's changed lives."[8]

As societies move from industrialization to post-industrialization, opportunities for women expand even more. This is true in part because physical size and strength are less a factor in an information society. Women often excel in the very skills most needed in an online and ser-

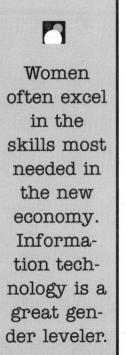
vice-oriented economy—data handling, human relations, and team-work, for example. Information technology serves as a gender leveler.

Women's roles are growing also because equal opportunity for women is now seen as a global human-rights issue. Worldwatch's Kathleen Newland notes that despite enormous obstacles to feminist aspirations, "the pressure for equality between men and women is a relentless sort of pressure, the same kind that is applied on behalf of other fundamental human-rights issues like religious freedom, racial equality, and political self-determination." This adds a worldview dimension. Increasingly people the world over, especially educated people, believe that women should have the same rights as men. "Although sexual equality is nowhere achieved as a fact," says Newland, "it is now almost universally accepted as a goal."[9]

> Women often excel in the skills most needed in the new economy. Information technology is a great gender leveler.

The North American Scene

Beginning in the North Atlantic societies, particularly France and the United States, the gender revolution has gradually spread globally. The depth of this shift can be gauged by changes in North American education and business. By 1992, not only were women earning nearly half the bachelor degrees but also 51 percent of masters and 33 percent of doctoral degrees in the United States. More than 40 percent of university professors in North America now are women. Of all university degrees awarded in North America in 1990, women earned 60 percent of those in accounting, 55 percent in business, 53 percent in law, and 48 percent in medicine—three times, at least, the number earned just twenty years earlier, in these categories.[10] This huge shift means a major increase in the numbers and percentage of women in business and the professions in the next ten to twenty years.

In business, women already are moving into corporate management positions in numbers. They are founding companies one and a half times faster than men, and the percentage of workers employed by women has gone from near zero in 1972 to about 12 percent now. Business consultant David Birch notes that 1992 "was an all-time record for incorporation" of new businesses, and much of this entrepreneurial "energy is coming from women and not men."[11] More and more business travelers are women. The percentage of women among business travelers shot up from 1 percent in 1970 to about one third in 1990 and is projected to reach 50 percent by 2000.[12]

> Women are starting new companies one and a half times faster than men. More and more men have women employers.

One can trace parallel developments in almost every sector of society, though the changes are uneven. An interesting example is religious life. In the 1980s, North American Protestantism turned a historic and probably irreversible corner with a shift toward women as pastoral leaders on a par with men. In 1970 only 2 percent of U.S. pastors were women. This doubled to 4 percent by 1984, and it continues to grow. The number of women in seminary jumped 223 percent from 1972 to 1980, compared to a 31 percent increase for males. Today about 20 percent of those who earn the Master of Divinity degree (now the standard for pastoral service) in U.S. and Canadian seminaries are women. This represents a tripling of the numbers over the decade.

Women already comprise a significant minority of ordained pastors in many U.S. church bodies. By 1985, 10 percent of all Disciples of Christ pastors were women. The figure was 12 percent in the United Church of Christ, 7 percent in the Episcopal Church, 5 percent among United Methodists, and 6 percent among Presbyterians. In Pentecostal groups, typically 10 to 20 percent of pastors are women. By the year 2000, close to one fourth of all Protestant pastors in the United States will be women. The total may well reach 50 percent within two or three generations.

Female leadership is starting to reshape the way churches operate. Pastoral roles are broadening and becoming more flexible as women introduce variety, different perspectives, and a broader range of leadership styles. Women in leadership appear to be pushing a growing emphasis on community, informality, and nurture. Conceptually, more women as church leaders increases the shift toward organic and ecological models of social interaction. Finally, the shift toward more women in ministry seems to feed the trend toward expanded "lay" involvement and ministry.[13]

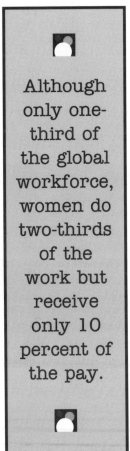

Similar developments are occurring in Jewish congregations and in much of the Christian Church worldwide, not just Protestantism. Within a generation or two the world will probably witness the spectacle of a Roman Catholic Pope opening the ranks of the clergy to women priests.

The Global Perspective

The global picture is, of course, uneven. Yet nearly everywhere signs of feminist revolution appear. In China, women are rising to higher levels in business and government than in the past. In 1988, the People's Bank of China had both a woman president and vice president. A slow gender revolution is underway also in Japan. There the percentage of women corporate presidents is small but growing. Increasingly Japanese women are starting their own businesses and doing well. More and more women are entering politics; 146 ran for Parliament's upper house in 1989.[14]

Sweden, often considered a global bellwether, provides more evidence of changing women's roles. After World War II, Sweden saw a dramatic rise in the number of women employed outside the home—from 30 percent in 1930 to 50 percent by 1968 and (boosted partly by income tax reform in 1970) to 75 percent by 1980. This shift was accompanied by marked changes in marriage and family statistics. The percentage of married young adult women (20 to 25 years old) dropped from 43 percent in 1965 to 22 percent in 1975. An additional 29 percent were cohabiting. "The generation of Swedes born during and after World War II was giving up marriage in favor of 'consensual unions,' " notes Donald Meyer. The number of babies born out of wedlock went from one in seven in 1965 to one in three just twelve years later. Abortions jumped from 3,000 in 1960 to 32,000 in 1975.[15]

The picture is much different in the world's agricultural and early-industrial societies. Although women are only about one-third of the global workforce, they reportedly account for two-thirds of total working hours but receive

> Although only one-third of the global workforce, women do two-thirds of the work but receive only 10 percent of the pay.

only 10 percent of total income paid.[16] Typically they lag also in literacy and health care. Yet this is changing in many areas.

Frank Feather comments on this broader global picture:

> Women are making most gains where economic modernization is most advanced. In many industrializing developing countries, women are starting to behave in accordance with the emerging . . . nonstereotypical global society, not in the typical ways of the . . . Western industrial era. They are starting to provide support to each other in small groups, recognizing that education and the capacity to work in several different jobs are basic elements in their progress. These women are also developing horizontal support networks rather than traditionally male-designed hierarchical organizational relationships.[17]

This increase in the numbers of women taking leadership in industrial and information economies, with their distinctive "women's ways of knowing" and acting, will continue to fuel global social change.[18] Surprisingly, however, this whole phenomenon is overlooked in many surveys of global treands and worldviews, especially in political and economic analyses.

Transforming Society

The gender revolution is transforming society. Patricia Aburdene and John Naisbitt argue: "A critical mass of women and like-minded men have embraced 'women's liberation.' It has become a *self-sustaining* movement that may at times experience setbacks, but its direction is unstoppable. Women are transforming the world—even though *all women* are not yet fully liberated."[19]

Many people foresee that the more horizontal, collegial-consensual styles of leadership often preferred by women will transform the workplace. Frank Feather predicts what he calls "supra-sexual management: team management that transcends gender but twins the unique intellectual capabilities of the sexes in genuine executive partnerships."[20] He notes research evidence that suggests the superiority of mixed-sex teams over either all-male or all-female groups. In one study, "The all-male groups performed identically as well as the all-female groups. The mixed groups, however, always did at least 25 percent better than single-sex groups."[21]

Donald Meyer argues the broader social implications of expanding female influence. He writes:

> The most revolutionary potential in the awakening of widespread thought among and about women [is that it goes] to the very roots of human identity. That awakening could quickly impinge upon politics, labor mar-

kets, and legal codes shaping relationships between the sexes in public institutions and marketplaces. . . . Unlike revolution potential in relationships of ideology, class, race, religion, culture, science, tribe, folk, or nation, revolution potential in sex . . . cuts into the most private mores, the most secret wishes, into family, child-rearing, marriage, love, sexual intercourse—realms commonly left in older societies to magic, incantation, prayer, unconsciousness. The awakening of consciousness and political thought among and about women [has] the potential of bringing all these realms of private, sub-political life onto public political agendas. In effect, the politicalization of the private would make all relationships between the sexes *themes of history, not of nature.*[22]

Others also see Earthwide impact in the gender revolution. The combined creativity of women and men, Feather writes, "has tremendous implications for the way global societies and organizations are governed and managed. Women . . . together with the new breed of men—will bring a new set of values to organizational life. Paternalistic and rigid organization structures will be transformed into fluid and organic networks for decision-making and the effective management of change for the future."[23]

Is this picture overdrawn? Perhaps, if seen out of context. But the gender revolution parallels and reinforces other trends. Significantly, it comes just at the time when various branches of science are starting to stress the importance of intuition and insight—traditionally thought of as feminine qualities. One can imagine a growing synergy between the contributions of women and the social and scientific need for intuition. Physicist Fritjof Capra, author of *The Tao of Physics,* has observed, "In our culture these intuitive aspects of scientific discovery or any other kind of discovery are just not emphasized. But physicists know them very well. For instance, Einstein experienced relativity theory before he formulated it. Bohr experienced quantum mechanics before he formulated them."[24]

Intuition, something more profound or more immediately holistic than the formulas to which they lead, often seems to underlie scientific breakthroughs and other kinds of creativity. This phenomenon is familiar, of course, to the author or artist who struggles to put into words or on canvas what is felt or experienced at a nonrational, prerational, or superrational level. Similarly, politicians value advisors who have keen "instincts" for political reality and change.

Precisely in these areas, many argue, women often excel. The reason may be partly physiological. Some research suggests that women have many more channels of communication between the two brain lobes than do men. The female brain can literally perceive or sense things

71

faster than it can think them through, like watching people cross a narrow bridge. In contrast, the male brain "slows down" the data flow between brain lobes. Narrowing the channel in this way allows the mind consciously to grasp and analyze the data passing through. This gives men (on average) the edge in logical, sequential thinking, but the liability of limited intuition and, perhaps, limited experience and sensitivity in some dimensions. Of course, these differences are not absolute. Many women are brilliantly logical, while many men are deeply intuitive.[25]

The gender revolution likely will speed up learnings and discoveries concerning this intuitive, other-than-rational (in traditional terms) dimension of reality. Already intelligence is being redefined in less strictly logical-analytical terms. These changes should give women, on balance, an advantage in all social roles where these other qualities are assets. One sign of this may be the increasing number and influence of women in some areas of politics, economics, and science.

Full gender equality will not have been gained, however, until women's rights are seen simply as a social ethical question, not a narrowly sexual one. Until now, "society" has meant, first of all, the world of men, with women playing a secondary and specifically sexual function. Women's issues seemingly have a distinctly sexual caste in ways that men's issues and social issues generally do not. Real equality will be achieved only when the place of women can be discussed as simply part of the broader question of society, not as something sexual, sexist, or sexy. Women are no more sexual beings than are men. "Women's issues" should not necessarily involve matters such as sexual identity, homosexuality, marriage, romance, or sexual relations any more than do "men's issues."

Women and Worldviews

Clearly these are worldview issues. How much are today's world models shaped by male thinking? How might they change as women's roles expand? A considerable debate already rages here. Some feminists contend that women bring essentially different understandings of life and power into the worldview discussion. This is argued forcefully, for example, by Riane Eisler in *The Chalice and the Blade,* a volume that anthropologist Ashley Montagu has called "the most important book since Darwin's *Origin of Species.*" Eisler maintains that all societies are patterned in varying degrees either on a "dominator model" or a "partnership model." Unsurprisingly, the dominator model has dominated. Women tend to favor the partnership model as being more inclusive, more peaceful, and less authoritarian. Moving in this direction would mean "a shift from a system leading to chronic wars, social injustice, and ecological imbalance to one of peace, social justice, and ecological balance," according to Eisler.[26]

In any case, a change in women's status does touch worldviews. The significance of the gender revolution, writes historian Donald Meyer, is that now women, like men, "have come to recognize themselves as historical agents. They have extricated themselves from the idea that their lives are properly prescribed for them, from outside themselves, whether by nature, historical necessity, divine order, or the good of society. Like men, they have come to realize that 'nature,' 'necessity,' 'divine edict,' and 'society' are all ideas generated by minds. They want to generate ideas too. They want to make themselves, make their own history."[27]

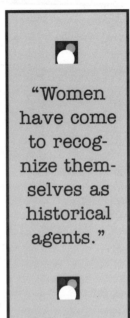

"Women have come to recognize themselves as historical agents."

The feminist revolution thus has the power globally to release tremendous social energy, as it already has in Western societies. Women's creativity and energy largely have been confined to the home, with the result that most women have been unconscious of their broader social power. Feminist consciousness-raising releases social energy to reshape society—for good or ill. Many people fear, perhaps legitimately, that essential family-building functions may be slighted (by both sexes) as women leave the home for the office, laboratory, or clinic.

Since gender, like race, goes to the heart of people's actual and perceived identity, wrestling with this issue can be wrenching. Robin Morgan says of her own experience, "I couldn't believe—still can't—how angry I could become, from deep down and way back, something like a five-thousand-year-buried anger."[28] This hints at how deep a revolution is underway. Such anger, like all strong emotion, can be destructive, or it can be personally and socially transforming. Here lies the power and promise of the gender revolution.

Feminism values nurturing, ecology, consensus, networking. Yet extreme feminism is often antagonistic to the very institutions and structures needed to nurture these values, particularly marriage and family. This is the feminist bind, a contradiction that threatens to undermine socially the liberating promise of the gender revolution, at least in some contexts. Much depends, therefore, on where the feminist revolution leads and how it interacts with other trends and with worldview issues. Within what context of larger meaning will women exercise their expanding influence?

It would be naive to think that all or even most of the results of the gender revolution will necessarily be positive. Especially is this true if family, community, and male-female partnership are poisoned. Channeled constructively, however, the energy engendered by gender consciousness can bring a healthier, happier, more nurturing society. Whether this happens is in large measure a question of values, beliefs, and perceptions of reality—in other words, of worldviews. So here again we encounter key worldview issues.

Gender power underlies and interacts with all the other global trends traced in this book. Because it is rooted in human identity and fundamental relationships, this trend in its mixing with others transforms today's Earth Currents from matters merely of ideas, politics, and economics into issues of the deeper structure of society and culture itself.

CHAPTER FIVE

Fragile Greenhouse:
The Environment at Risk

> You cannot have well people on a sick planet.
>
> —**THOMAS BERRY**[1]
>
> When giving us dominion over the earth, did God choose an appropriate technology?
>
> —**U.S. VICE PRESIDENT AL GORE**[2]

arth, home to all human life, is uniquely threatened today. The basic trend is twofold: an increasingly endangered ecosphere and also a growing awareness of environmental peril. Gradually eco-concern is becoming institutionalized into the structures of society, including business and government.

Environment was a word hardly heard when I was young. If used at all, the meaning was psychological: the old debate between heredity and environment in shaping personality. Since the 1960s, "environment" means much more, and *ecology* is now an everyday word. We have witnessed a generational shift in meaning.

Environment means, of course, where we live: our home. Here is the change: We have come to see that the home circle must be drawn larger and larger. Our house is bigger than we thought. It is the whole Earth— maybe even the universe. For all Earth's living creatures, it is especially the terrestrial globe. Earth with its thin skin of soil, water, and air, and the amazing life forms it hosts, is our environment.

This Earth is under siege by creatures who claim to be its wisest, smartest species: Human beings. Technology has now reached the point where it threatens to poison or blow up its own house. Our behavior is suicidal. "Thirty-five percent of the oxygen molecules we inhale in one breath comes from the rain forests, which we are chopping down at a rate of twenty-five million hectares a year. Every minute, four football fields of forests disappear from the face of the earth. Every minute, two hundred football fields of arable land disappear under concrete," Leonard Sweet warns.[3]

Rising Eco-Consciousness

Four things are prompting a new environmental awakening as people learn of possible deadly threats to all future life. The first reason is the growing list of ecological problems and the rising risk of major environmental disasters. Potential threats range from chemical poisonings to nuclear accidents. Water shortages and famines, even in prosperous nations, loom as deep aquifers are drained. Vanishing species and the deadly effects of acid rain may be slower disasters. With each environmental crisis that hits the media, global ecological consciousness rises.

Second, hard evidence mounts that ecological dangers are real and grave. Environmental vulnerability is now backed by sober scientific data. The risks no longer rest on emotional claims, long on rhetoric but short on facts. Major debate and differing data may continue on some issues, including global warming. But we now have scientific verification of the thinning of the ozone layer and related threats. Also, computer modeling of weather and other environmental systems shows how minor changes at one place on Earth eventually alter the environment half a world away. Global ecological risk now touches policy makers in industry, government, and even the military because of mounting scientific evidence.

The third reason for rising eco-consciousness is the growing political recognition of environmental concerns. World leaders have finally begun to speak of ecology as a top issue. It competes with others and sometimes is crowded out, but increasingly eco-concerns press for political attention as popular awareness grows.

Awareness is growing, globally. Brazil now has a green movement and qualified environmentalists in key government posts. Burning the rain forests makes news, but an ecology counter-trend, grounded in solid research, is spreading. Similar eco-movements are arising in dozens of countries, including the former Soviet nations of Eastern Europe.

The fourth reason is the rise of the ecology paradigm itself. Ecology is emerging as a basic model and potential worldview. In growing numbers

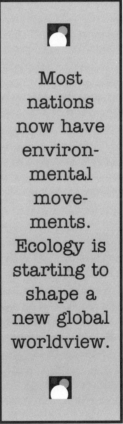

around the globe, people are thinking ecologically. We, or at least our children, are the first generation in history to share an environmental consciousness, in the contemporary scientific sense. Coming generations will think *ecologically and globally* as a matter of course. Already many people sense the vulnerability of the planet, the deep connections of life, and the reliance of humans on the environment. People begin to feel that today's decisions have long-range environmental impact, often globally. This represents quite a shift from the dominant thinking in the West for several centuries past.

In his book *Earth in the Balance,* then-Senator Al Gore described how his own perspective changed as he came to see the broader ecological connectedness of a whole range of issues. His comments are a good example of what an ecological perspective means and how it is becoming part of the larger human agenda. Gore writes:

> The ecological perspective begins with a view of the whole, an understanding of how the various parts of nature interact in patterns that tend toward balance and persist over time. But this perspective cannot treat the earth as something separate from human civilization; we are part of the whole too, and looking at it ultimately means also looking at ourselves. And if we do not see that the human part of nature has an increasingly powerful influence over the whole of nature—that we are, in effect, a natural force just like the winds and the tides—then we will not be able to see how dangerously we are threatening to push the earth out of balance.[4]

Most nations now have environmental movements. Ecology is starting to shape a new global worldview.

This mix of concerns is generating an environmental agenda that will touch every other area. Global economics will be affected, positively and negatively. Business is starting to ask: What economic opportunities does environmental awareness offer? Ecologically alert leaders foresee a whole new market, new ways of doing business that take seriously environmental limits. This is another key shift in thinking. A new business sector focusing on care of the environment and counteracting ecological spoliation will win expanding markets.

A Threatened Ecosphere

Environmentalism first emerged as a social and political issue in the 1960s and 1970s.[5] It caught the popular imagination with the publication of Rachel Carlson's *Silent Spring* in 1962. Similar books followed. The movement was fed by new scientific data on the long-term effects of pollution. The OPEC oil embargo, boosting gasoline prices and sparking conservation, also fueled environmental concerns.

During the 1980s, most politicians dismissed ecology as a dismal fad. In the United States, environmental programs and monitoring were slashed or put on hold. But environmental problems don't just go away. They pile up and seep in. The oil crisis passed, but the longer-term need to find renewable energy sources stayed. And a whole range of deep, growing environmental problems continues. Some of these are so dimly understood that to dismiss them could prove disastrous within a generation or two.

What are these dangers? Top concerns of eco-scientists include desertification and the destruction of arable lands; the depletion of major deep-earth aquifers that provide essential water for cities and agriculture; acid rain, including the poisoning of fresh water lakes and the destruction of forests; nuclear and chemical waste disposal; the depletion or scarcity of rare minerals essential for high-tech manufacturing; the direct or indirect effects of genetic engineering; the annihilation of thousands of species of plants and animals. In recent decades the number of species irretrievably lost each year has shot up to the tens of thousands.[6] "More 'Eagles' drive America's expanding road networks . . . than fly in the nation's polluted skies; and more 'Cougars' pass the night in America's proliferating garages than in its shrinking forests," warns Alan Durning of Worldwatch Institute.[7] Related issues, scientists say, are the gradual rise of sea levels worldwide and the continuing pollution of major rivers and lakes such as Lake Biwi in Japan and the North American Great Lakes (though some progress has now been made in cleaning up the latter).

These issues are political and economic time bombs. Any one of them, or (more likely, given the nature of ecology) several in combination, could bring widespread suffering or even utter chaos. The next generation or two may be decisive, ecologically speaking.

Of all the dangers, the most profound are those that threaten the delicate balance of Earth's atmosphere.

Greenhouse Gas and Ozone Holes

The so-called Greenhouse Effect and the thinning of the ozone layer together endanger the entire biosphere. These two problems, often confused, represent quite different dangers.

Overheated Greenhouse? The Earth appears to be warming up. Whether this represents a worrisome departure from normal cyclical patterns is disputed. Evidence is mounting, however, that the massive burning of fossil fuels like coal and gasoline does add to the warming. Though a somewhat misleading image, the Greenhouse Effect pictures Earth heating up and becoming more toxic as carbon dioxide builds in the atmosphere.

As long ago as 1896 the Swedish chemist Svante Arrhenius worried that increased burning of coal, oil, and firewood was adding millions of tons of carbon dioxide to the atmosphere. "We are evaporating our coal mines into the air," he wrote. The result would be "a change in the transparency of the atmosphere" that could heat the planet to intolerable levels. Discovery of global warming in the late 1970s showed that Arrhenius likely was on the right track.[8]

Major U.N. scientific studies project a dramatic rise in global temperatures over the next century unless humans stop pumping greenhouse gases into the air. A 1990 study by 250 leading climatologists predicted a rise in Earth's average temperature of about one degree Celsius by 2025 and three degrees before the end of the twenty-first century. That would be the fastest increase in history. Earth is running a fever. Such temperative increases would raise sea levels twenty centimeters (about half a foot) by 2030 and three times that by the end of the century. A change of only five degrees Celsius (nine degrees Fahrenheit) is believed to have triggered Earth's last ice age.[9]

Vanishing Ozone. Ozone depletion is different but related. The ozone layer, a thin gaseous shield some twelve to fifteen miles above the Earth, filters out vast amounts of cancer-causing ultraviolet rays from the Sun. Scientists have detected that ozone disappeared faster during the 1980s than during the 1970s. They have now proven that chemicals known as chlorofluoro-carbons (CFCs), widely used in refrigerators and air conditioners, attack and destroy the vital ozone shield. The CFCs react chemically with the ozone, producing chlorine monoxide. Each atom

> Scientists fear Earth's rising temperature will raise sea levels nearly a foot in less than a century, bringing massive flooding.

of chlorine gobbles up as many as 100,000 ozone molecules. Scientists can check the extent of ozone loss by measuring the amount of chlorine monoxide in the atmosphere.

Studies reveal growing ozone holes over both poles. More immediately ominous, ozone is rapidly thinning also over highly populated areas. In 1987 the international Montreal Protocol was signed, committing most nations to reduce CFCs. Many countries are now phasing them out, but even if production ends by 2000, CFCs already in the atmosphere will keep on eating the ozone layer well into the next century. Meanwhile, some scientists are warning about a new threat: methyl bromide, possibly released into the air by pest killers and fungicides. Methyl bromide is thirty times more deadly to ozone than are CFCs.

Why the concern with ozone and greenhouse gases? The dangers are multiple and long-term. Ozone loss means more harmful solar rays, and thus more skin cancer and other radiation-caused diseases. A 10 percent rise in skin cancer over ten years was projected by the 1991 U.N. study. Ozone thinning and the greenhouse effect can also disrupt agriculture and aquaculture, upset weather patterns, and raise sea levels. "The situation is definitely getting much worse than what was expected," says Mostafa Tolba, director of the U.N. Environmental Program. Similarly Michael Kurylo, head of upper-atmosphere research for the U.S. space program, warns, "Everybody should be alarmed about this. It's far worse than we thought."[10]

Too Late?

If there is a bright side to these twin dangers, it lies in the growing international cooperation they have sparked. The dark side is the same as in all ecological processes: Environmental damage can't be quickly fixed. "By the time the evidence is irrefutable, it could be too late to do anything," says Stephen Schneider of the U.S. National Center for Atmospheric Research.[11]

These and other eco-concerns are raising ecological awareness to unparalleled levels, as we have seen. Concern has grown gradually over half a century. The atomic bomb and the theory of relativity dramatized the interplay of matter and energy and the tremendous power packed in the atom. Growing problems of air and water pollution showed the delicate balance of our ecosystem and its frailty to human destructiveness. The energy crunch alerted us that Earth's bounty is finite and that the key resources fueling our economic growth won't last forever. Then there is the law of entropy (all systems run down), which has economic and ecological implications and raises basic questions about technology and progress.

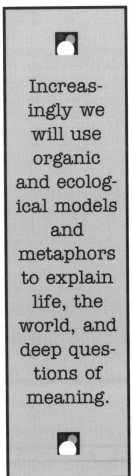

We inhabit an intricate, vulnerable bio-layer consisting of a few inches of topsoil and a few hundred feet of oxygen. Computer technology, cancer research, food studies, and other areas of investigation impress us with the fine balance of systems and forces that makes up our global home. We have begun to think in terms of a small planet, of Mother Earth or Spaceship Earth, or of a global city.

Ecological crises have a way of sneaking up on us. We are in a race with time. Do we have enough time to make the necessary economic and lifestyle shifts so life can survive past the middle of the twenty-first century? The coming generation will find out. As of 1994, the following scenario appeared likely:

- Knowledge of the real ecology and environmental interdependence of Earth will grow even more dramatically. Speeded by computer technology and new discoveries in astrophysics, genetics, archaeology, and other fields, the delicate web of life on Earth will impress us as never before. We should hope that such discoveries come in time and that humanity will have the wisdom and good sense to use such knowledge for peace and justice.

- The connections between disease and the environment will become much clearer. Scientific suspicion is growing that many forms of cancer are linked to environmental factors. What is true with smoking-related cancers may be true with other kinds of cancer, but in more subtle ways. Some scientists now think that breast cancer, a leading cause of death among women, is related to widespread use of pesticides known as organochlorines, which accumulate in fatty tissue. They point out that breast-cancer rates in Israel dropped after organochlorine pesticides were restricted. With more extensive research, many such links may appear.

- Environmental concerns may fuse with other issues to politically destabilize international relations at strategic points in the

> Increasingly we will use organic and ecological models and metaphors to explain life, the world, and deep questions of meaning.

world. If the past is a clue, people and nations will fight to keep what they have when resources run scarce, rather than work together to find a solution. Control of the oceans' resources, and eventually of space, will prompt international competition and potential conflict. Yet, the basic trend of globalization offers some hope for greater cooperation. Space exploration provides a potentially hopeful clue: Costs run so high that international collaboration is increasingly attractive. The same may prove true ecologically, especially as awareness grows that every environmental problem is ultimately global in cause and effect.

• Environmental issues will increasingly affect people's philosophical and religious thinking over the next twenty or thirty years. More and more we will use organic and ecological models and metaphors to explain life, the world, and deep questions of meaning.

The Nuclear Threat

Nuclear power, both military and commercial, is an environmental issue because it threatens huge ecological destruction or even annihilation. The end of the Cold War dramatically lessened fears of an all-out nuclear conflict, but the danger has not disappeared. For half a century the world lived under the threat of nuclear annihilation. Now the greater danger may be nuclear proliferation, terrorism, and aging power plants.

The full damage from the 1986 Chernobyl disaster in the (former) USSR won't be known for decades. But Chernobyl showed that the world's three hundred-plus atomic power plants can themselves be nuclear time bombs. Thousands of Russians, Ukrainians, and even Turks received dangerously high levels of radiation. The long-range cost to the nearby city of Kiev (nearly the size of Chicago) is still to be paid.

Some scientists warn of a 50 percent chance of a similar nuclear accident in the United States within a decade. This would mean major disruptions ecologically as well as economically and politically. And there are other dangers. The most likely future:

• Proliferation of nuclear weapons and technology will continue at least for the next two decades. Attempts to stop it will prove largely futile.

• Limited nuclear warfare between small nations could provide the greatest danger for the next decade or so. The effects, both ecological and political, would reach far beyond the countries immediately involved.

- Incidents of nuclear terrorism as extremist groups or nations acquire nuclear arms are possible. These could involve major bloodshed, even the destruction of some cities, and lingering health and environmental damage for centuries. The main impact, however, would be increased global tension and greater impetus toward nuclear control.
- The threat of all-out nuclear war will decline because of arms control agreements and global economic integration. If a major crisis arises, however, it could become the trigger to a global nuclear war that no one really wants. The danger will never fully go away because the clock can't be turned back to the time when the secrets of the atom were unknown. Hope and survival will continue to be major world questions. We get some sense of the impact of possible major nuclear devastation when we think of the Black Death in Europe (1340–50), so ably pictured by Barbara Tuchman in her book *A Distant Mirror.*[12]

The Crisis of 2020?

Eco-crisis and nuclear terror in a world split between rich and poor, yet linked by global media networks, could easily be a recipe for convulsions as devastating as any world war. This is the negative counterpoint to trends toward greater global cooperation and linkage.

Many environmental concerns seem to point to the next quarter-century as especially criticial. Studies in several areas suggest that the years around 2020 could be crisis ones. As we have seen, this coincides with generational and other projections. Will the global environment itself be the "crisis of 2020"? If so, it may be the next great turning point in human history.

Europe survived the Black Death, but in some places half the population died. Floods, earthquakes, disease, and wars have threatened in the past and likely will again. Today's environmental issues, however, are unique in their reach, touching the fabric of life for all Earth's peoples for all time.

Global eco-crises remind us that the human race itself is vulnerable. Just one among the millions of Earth's species, humankind is both dependent on the myriad species with which it interacts and, in many respects, a danger to itself. Humanity is at risk from its own diseases—physical, social, and spiritual.

Perhaps AIDS, not nuclear devastation, will be the Black Death of the next half-century. To date, those who have died from AIDS number far fewer than those killed by violence and auto accidents. But the numbers are mushrooming. In early 1992, the UN's World Health Organization (WHO) estimated that by the year 2000, thirty to forty million people will have AIDS worldwide, mostly in the poorer nations. Some countries in Africa face the loss of as much as half of their populations.

The Lethal Spiral

It is becoming clear that environmental factors link with population growth and various sociopolitical factors to form what might be called a lethal spiral. These intertwined dimensions can lead—and in places already are leading—to social chaos.

An international network of researchers formed by the University of Toronto and the American Academy of Arts and Sciences has compiled extensive evidence of these linkages. Thomas F. Homer-Dixon, co-director of the project, and his colleagues report: "Scarities of renewable resources are already contributing to violent conflicts in many parts of the developing world. These conflicts may foreshadow a surge of similar violence in coming decades, particularly in poor countries where shortages of water, forests and, especially, fertile land, coupled with rapidly expanding populations, already cause great hardship."[13]

The dynamic of this dangerous cycle may be pictured as follows:

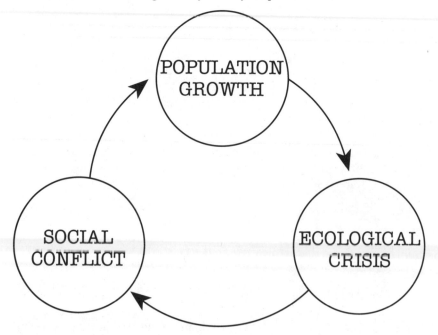

Each of these factors affects the others, and together they form a cycle. *Population growth,* concentration, or displacement puts new burdens on the environment. These burdens take various forms: pollution, depletion of water, deforestation as people cut down forests for firewood. The result is *ecological crisis,* whether in extreme form (drought and famine) or as longer-term ecological degradation—potentially as deadly, but often less obvious. Consider Bangladesh, whose fast-growing population already numbers 785 people per square kilometer. Since all available farmland is now in use, continued population growth will mean that only half as much cropland per capita will be available by 2025.[14]

Environmental crisis in turn increases *social conflict.* Disease, famine, and resulting migrations of people add to existing political, ethnic, and religious tension. When the physical environment goes bad, social conflict easily leads to complete social breakdown. The social environment reflects the physical environment. Even if chaos is averted, ecological crisis aggravates social tensions.

It is now clear that *social conflict* in turn stimulates further *population growth,* thus completing the lethal cycle. Birth rates go up as society breaks down. Typically, the highest birth rates are in regions suffering poverty and social instability. Human beings apparently share with other species the trait that the more they are threatened, the more they reproduce. Even with high mortality rates, the net result is bulging population, which speeds the cycle of ecological degradation and social breakdown.

All three of these areas—population, ecology, and conflict—need to be addressed, but a piecemeal approach will not do. The direction of the arrows must be switched. The long-term goal must be to reverse the spiral—a gradual process, at best. Environmental stability then supports material well-being and social cohesion, which in turn reduces population growth and eases pressures on the environment. This does not necessarily mean a "steady-state" or "no-growth" environment, but it does mean a healthy and sustainable ecological interrelationship between population growth, environmental realities, and the social, political, and economic dimensions of culture.

The Meaning of Ecology and the Ecology of Meaning

While all of these factors—*population growth, ecological crisis,* and *social conflict*—are dynamically linked, they are not the only dimensions of the human story. Since human beings are conscious, reflecting, willing beings, each of these factors also raises worldview issues. Population growth is more than biology and economics, just as the environment and social-cultural issues are more than science, sociology, and politics. They reflect values, beliefs, and larger shared meanings, as well. Thus the lethal spiral described earlier must be viewed in terms of its worldview dimensons:

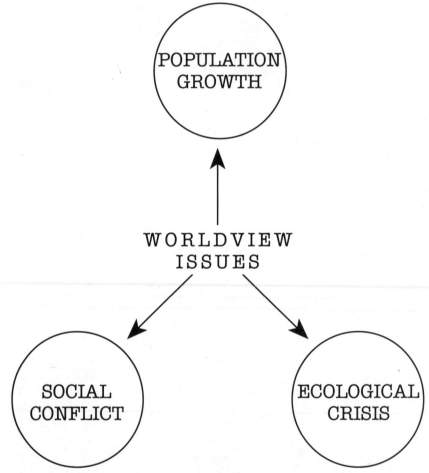

This is, in fact, part of the *real ecology* facing global society over the next few generations.

Ecological thinking speaks to our deep models for understanding life and the universe. These are worldview issues. Ecology is perhaps the deepest *fact* and *perspective* shaping the way we will see things in the future. It touches ourselves, the universe, social relationships, even politics and religion. The next half-century may see the shaping of a new world consciousness with ecology as the primary model.

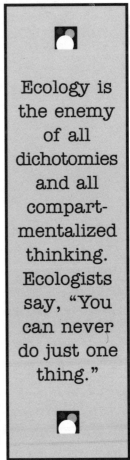

Ecological thinking today is much like the birth of psychology a century ago. Since Freud and Jung, people have come to think in psychological terms. We no longer simply write biographies of famous people; we attempt to understand the inner reasons for their behavior. We examine the psychology behind wars and elections. We now know that people act the way they do not simply because of what they think or because of outside events, but also, and very importantly, because of inner feelings, urges, and forces they are hardly aware of.

Now we are coming to think ecologically, not just psychologically. At the most basic level, this means a growing sense that everything (literally *everything*) is linked. Environmental issues and the new global economy are inseparably connected when seen through the wide-angle lens of ecology. With time we will come to see that this connectedness holds true not only in the physical world but in every area of life, including mind and spirit. Ecological thinking is the enemy of all dichotomies. "You cannot have well people on a sick planet," says Thomas Berry.[15]

Earth's growing eco-consciousness is prompting reflection not only on the relationship between humans and their environment, but also, more deeply, on what it means to be human. In this sense, the environmental crisis is also a crisis of the human spirit. "The more deeply I search for the roots of the global environmental crisis," writes Al Gore, "the more I am convinced that it is an outer manifestation of an inner crisis that is, for lack of a better word, spiritual."[16] Here one senses a deeper meaning to ecology and deeper questions that concern belief and worldview.

Only in the past quarter-century has it become really possible to think ecologically in this broader sense. Never before could people have thought of the meaning of ecology or the ecology of meaning in this fashion. We are coming to see that *ecology does mean something.*

How far can ecological awareness and reflection lead us? Whether ecology itself can provide *ultimate* meanings for life—a worldview—is an open question. We will return to this in later chapters. But however we view ecology, clearly eco-thinking will impact all global worldviews over the next generations.

> Ecology is the enemy of all dichotomies and all compart-mentalized thinking. Ecologists say, "You can never do just one thing."

CHAPTER SIX

Vital Strings:
DNA and Superstrings

> We may break through to a complete theory of the universe. In that case, we would indeed be Masters of the Universe.
> —**MATHEMATICIAN STEPHEN HAWKING**[1]

> The dream of a final theory inspires much of today's work in high-energy physics. . . . already in today's theories we think we are beginning to catch glimpses of the outlines of a final theory.
> —**NOBEL PRIZE-WINNING PHYSICIST STEVEN WEINBERG**[2]

Surprisingly, many books on trends skip over developments in science. This is a serious oversight. Futurists talk about technological breakthroughs but often say nothing about the basic science from which they arise. Yet it is just here, at the scientific frontiers, that seeds of revolution are often sown. Not political or economic revolution, but new insights into the nature of the physical world that prove revolutionary in their long-range social impact. This fifth Earth-Current is no less earthshaking than global economics or the gender revolution.

So we must inquire into the world of science. This is difficult for those of us who are not scientists. Often the concepts, terminology, and calculations are beyond us. But fundamental worldview issues are at stake. We should know, at least, the key issues science is wrestling with, and what they mean for Earth's future.

Fundamental science is on the brink of two of the greatest breakthroughs of all time. These concern genetics and physics: unlocking the secrets of life's gene structure and of matter itself. Solving these two fundamental puzzles of our physical environment will have long-lasting impact, and in fact may be linked.

Decoding Our Genes

In 1990, the U. S. National Institutes of Health carried out the world's first successful gene therapy on a four-year-old girl. A team of doctors introduced a billion cells into her bloodstream—cells containing a foreign gene—to counteract ADA deficiency, a rare genetic disorder. This landmark treatment opened a new era in medicine. Formerly incurable genetic diseases will be treated or even prevented. The long-term impact on society could be enormous, possibly giving a big boost to world health.

Such initial experiments in genetic therapy are the first fruits of a major new scientific breakthrough: mapping the entire human gene structure. Science is already well along this road. The Human Genome Project, a global computerized effort to map all human genes, is well underway. This opens a new era in the treatment of disease. Other genetic research will transform agriculture—the development, for example, of new crops that can fix nitrogen in the soil as some already do naturally. This holds both promise and dangers.

The key secrets of how genes function were unlocked a generation ago with the discovery of the double-helix and the cracking of the genetic code. Science now knows, in a general way, how genes work. Mapping the total human gene structure, now in progress through painstaking research and the use of high-powered computers, is opening up the mysteries of the genetic design of human beings and, probably, all other life forms. Within a generation we will know, for example, which genes produce specific traits or cause particular diseases, and what the genetic mechanism is that produces different birth defects. The full complex ecology of genetics will remain a mystery for some time, however.

Already enough of the genetic structure is known to "invent" new life forms. Several new forms, as well as artificially produced copies of rare genetic material, have already been patented. Some of these are controversial, like BGH (bovine growth hormone), now sold commercially, which causes cows to produce about 15 percent more milk.[3]

Today's genetic revolution sprouted in the 1940s and 1950s. The key discovery came in 1953 when the young American biologist James Watson and British scientist Francis Crick figured out the structure of deoxyribonucleic acid, or DNA, the stuff genes are made of. By the late 1980s, enough was known to launch the massive Human Genome Project. Eventually every gene and gene combination will be mapped. ("Genome" means the total of all the chromosomes within each nucleus of a particular species.)

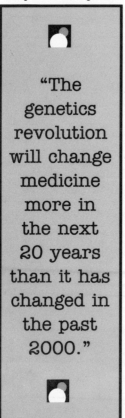

"The genetics revolution will change medicine more in the next 20 years than it has changed in the past 2000."

Begun in 1990, the Human Genome Project aims to blueprint every one of the 100,000 genes that make up the 46 (23 pairs) human chromosomes. Dr. Leroy Hood of the California Institute of Technology, a leading geneticist, says, "The genetics revolution will change medicine more in the next 20 years than it has changed in the past 2000."[4]

All the characteristics of the human body are determined by genetic combinations known as base pairs. With 100,000 genes, the human genome contains 3.5 billion base pairs. This is something like the way the 26 letters of the English alphabet combine to build all the words in the language. A complete genetic map including all base-pair sequences is expected not long after the year 2000.[5]

Such mapping, coupled with related medical advances, will permit gene therapy for all diseases and disorders that are genetically based. Notes John Pekkannen, "Coupled with powerful technologies developed since the mid-1970s, [gene therapy] is now unlocking the most closely guarded secrets of human biology, yielding almost daily insights into the prevention, diagnosis, treatment and cure of the most devastating diseases."[6]

Many diseases are caused by faulty or missing genes. Genetically based illnesses include emphysema, lung and some colon cancers, Alzheimer's disease, diabetes, and some heart ailments. Researchers believe almost all disease involves the genetic structure in some way, though various types of environmental triggers may actually start the disease. Already one common form of mental retardation has been found to be caused by a defective gene. Genetic therapy may permit treatment of these and many other diseases and disorders, including AIDS.

Genetic medicine seeks to replace bad genes with good ones. It may include tricking the human body into producing its own drugs. Genetically altered cells could be mass produced by the body, then channeled to the point where they're needed. "Gene therapy is actually a sophisticated drug-delivery system," says Dr. W. French Anderson, a leader in the field. "Anything given now by injection—growth factor, factor VIII, insulin— you can just engineer the patient's own cells to pump them out. The advantage is that it's a one-time treatment."[7]

Genetic research and therapy are moving rapidly. "Twenty years ago, you couldn't utter the phrase gene therapy without being told you were talking nonsense," notes molecular geneticist Dr. Theodore Friedmann. "Now it's taken for granted that it's coming." Friedmann predicts the treatment of thousands of genetic diseases including, eventually, even complex neurogenic disorders like Parkinson's and Alzheimer's diseases.[8]

Gene therapy involves risks, faces technical barriers, and can be very expensive. Ethical questions arise if research eventually permits genetic engineering of sperm and egg cells, as it probably will. *Time* magazine notes, "Such *Brave New World*-style manipulations would affect the genetic endowment of future generations, raise new ethical issues and pose unknown risks."[9] Dr. Paul Billings of California Pacific Medical Center in San Francisco warns of the possibility of genetic discrimination. "Once genetic information is gleaned about someone," he says, "there will be no way to keep it private." Partly for this reason, concern for strict privacy laws has been rising.

One of the fascinating things about DNA is that nearly every human cell contains in its nucleus a full set of genes. In a sense, every cell contains everything it means to be human, at least in potential form. Much like a hologram, the whole is contained in each part. Some think this constitutes a small clue to the meaning of life—maybe of the universe.

> Who or what will guide humanity in the wise, humane use of genetic technology? And according to what worldview?

What worldview questions arise here? The chief ones concern the meaning, integrity, and value of life. The danger is that vastly increased technical power to manipulate life has emerged precisely at a time of growing doubts about life's value. When human embryos were cloned by two U.S. researchers in 1993, scientists in other countries were amazed that more ethical questions weren't raised. Who or what will guide humanity in the wise, humane use of genetic technology? And according to what values?

Finding a Theory of Everything

Today scores of physicists, astronomers, and other scientists are engaged in a global race to build a Grand Unified Theory (GUT), or Theory of Everything (TOE). A breakthrough likely will come in the next generation or two—probably not long after 2000. Even if a real TOE proves to be impossible, as some scientists argue, insights gained in the search will push science into new frontiers of understanding matter and energy.

The problem is this: What is the connection between the four forces of nature—gravity, electromagnetism, and the strong and weak nuclear forces? More specifically, how does gravity, the force that makes objects fall and keeps planets in orbit, connect with electromagnetism and nuclear energy? Science says these are the four basic forces of nature. Can they be joined in one theory? If so, this theory should tell us how the universe holds together and probably how it formed after the Big Bang. Could it even make it possible to harness gravity waves as an ever-present source of energy, as in old Dick Tracy comics? No one knows for sure.

This is both the most simple and the most complex problem in science today. Simple, because it is easy to imagine that such elementary forces must be linked. Complex, because the problem goes to the heart of the origin and structure of the universe. Science already understands fairly well how three of these forces connect, through the theories of relativity and quantum physics. The remaining problem is the "biggest" but weakest force: gravity. No one has yet figured out just what the connection is between the force that keeps planets orbiting the sun and the force that holds the tiniest particles together.

Many scientists believe the secret to all these physical forces will soon be found. Albert Einstein, building on his general theory of relativity, tried unsuccessfully for years. Today in physics, mathematics, and astronomy, theorists are working on the puzzle, with growing hope of a breakthrough. The noted Cambridge scientist Stephen Hawking cautions, "Each time we have extended our observations to smaller length scales and higher energies, we have discovered new layers of structure." An "infinite sequence of layers of structure at higher and higher energies" is theoretically possible. Yet Hawking and others believe, on the basis of what is now known about gravity, that science has nearly figured out matter's most basic structure.[10]

This scientific quest has been building over generations, even centuries. In 1758 the Serbo-Croatian scientist Roger Boscovich published his *Theory of Natural Philosophy*, the first scientific Theory of Everything. Boscovich attempted to "derive all observed physical phenomena from a single law," he said, by combining the then-known forces into a "single continuous curve." His theory was far from complete; nuclear energy was still unknown. But it had wide influence on later scientists, giving impulse to the TOE search. Astronomer John Barrow comments, "Perhaps, in the eighteenth century, only a generalist like Boscovich, who successfully unified intellectual and administrative activities in every area of thought and practice would have the presumption that Nature herself was no less multicultural."[11]

Science appears finally to be nearing a critical breakthrough point in the TOE quest. If so, it will be the crowning achievement of physics, even "the end of theoretical physics," according to some. A solid, verified Theory of Everything would constitute a turning point in history, which would be even more significant when linked with other key Earth Currents.

In Newtonian physics (deriving from the famous Oxford physicist, Isaac Newton, 1642–1727, who probably never really felt an apple fall on his head), the universe is like a great machine operating by fixed laws. Gravity, the weakest but "longest" force, holds the planets in orbit. Newton was aware also of atoms and sound and light waves. He thought atoms were the fundamental building blocks of the universe.

Modern physics has discovered, however, that an atom's electrons and protons are made of even smaller particles (various kinds of quarks and leptons). At this subatomic level, matter appears as both particles and waves. This is sometimes called the wave/particle duality. Here an element of mystery enters. Elementary particles sometimes appear to be continuous waves and at other times separate particles. In other words, energy travels sometimes like ripples in a pond and sometimes like a stream of tiny bullets or packets, or so it appears. These packets are called "quanta," from which comes the term "quantum physics." Further, experiments suggest that whether such elementary energy acts like a wave or a particle depends in part on what the experimenter is expecting to see! If so, this strikes a blow at the whole idea of "objective" science.

Quantum theory—the branch of physics that deals with these matters—thus seems to document an element of randomness or uncertainty in the basic nature of material existence. Some scientists reject this idea, as did Einstein. The uncertainty only shows how much we don't know, they say. Physicists have confirmed that some sort of wave/particle duality does lie at the heart of matter, however. Both waves and particles are necessary to describe reality, and an element of unpredictability is fundamental at the subatomic level.

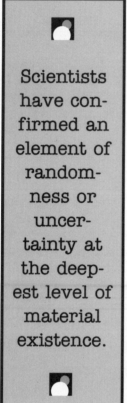

Scientists have confirmed an element of randomness or uncertainty at the deepest level of material existence.

Here Heisenberg's uncertainty principle (named for the physicist Werner Heisenberg) comes into the picture. This principle arises from scientists' ability to measure the speed *or* the position of a subatomic particle but not both at the same time. Quantum physics says that subatomic entities are sometimes waves and sometimes particles, never fully both. Which one they will be at a given point of measurement is unpredictable. Far from Newton's view, this perspective suggests an unexpected element of flux and dynamism at the most basic level of matter.

Quantum theory suggests further that material existence is not simply what *is* but is a sort of blend of possibilities and actualities. Physicists speak of "virtual transitions" in which an electron sort of "tries out" simultaneously many possible new orbits before actually moving into one. Some physicists have even carried this so far as to propose a Many-Worlds Theory—that an infinite number of universes exist so that all possible potentialities are realized. The more generally accepted view, however, is that in some way various possibilities are "tested" but only the most efficient ones are actualized. This also is part of the quantum mystery.

A lot of mystical nonsense has been written about Heisenberg's uncertainty principle. While quantum uncertainty is real, it is not mystical. The reason for the uncertainty is the very small scale involved and the difficulty of measuring at this subatomic level. The problem is that measurement requires light, and light collides with the particle to be measured, changing its trajectory. As Hans von Baeyer puts it, "the light transmits such a jolt that it knocks the particle out of its original *position,* giving it a new and unpredictable *speed.* In short, the measurement of one variable renders another unmeasurable."[12]

In other words, there is an understandable reason for the uncertainty. It is a little like someone using sonar to pinpoint a submarine in the ocean. Imagine a submarine equipped with a device that caused it to change speed and direction automatically whenever it sensed a sonar signal. The person sending the signal would get confusing readings. Yet it is the sonar itself that prompts the submarine's course changes. The analogy is not exact, but it gives some idea of the uncertainty principle.

The mystery, then, is not the how or why of quantum uncertainty. That is fairly well understood. The mystery is the fact of the uncertainty itself. That is, at the subatomic, quantum level, the universe really is unpredictable, although it operates within a range of probabilities. It is not irrational.

Another puzzle of quantum physics is the so-called Bell Effect, named for the physicist John Bell. According to the theory of relativity, nothing can travel faster than the speed of light. But experiments have shown that if two subatomic particles shoot off into space as the result of a subatomic reaction, they always seem to "influence" each other, no matter how far apart they travel. What happens to the one happens *simultaneously* to the other—faster than the speed of light. Does some sort of "information" link them, some instantaneous connection that defies the limits of the speed of light? Scientist Ernest C. Lucas comments, "How is the Bell effect produced? No one knows, but experiment suggests that it is a reality. Here, some argue, is the ultimate evidence of the oneness of all things. What happens to a particle in one part of the universe affects a particle in another, far-distant part without any physical cause-and-effect link." This is sometimes called instantaneous nonlocality, and it seems to defy the law of cause and effect as science has known it.[13]

In any case, the discoveries of quantum physics do not yet explain how the four basic forces relate. Together with research in other areas, however, they give rise to some educated guesses and hypotheses, now being developed and tested. Of particular interest is so-called string theory, or the superstring model.

Superstrings

String theory suggests that the forces of material energy are held together in a pattern resembling a set of twisted strings. At its most basic level, matter (or matter/energy) consists of "tiny loops of space knotted in six dimensions beyond the four of normal spacetime."[14] Visually the proposed model (still controversial) reminds one somewhat of the double helix of DNA.[15] Princeton physicist Edward Witten says that string theory is "probably going to lead to a new understanding of what space and time really are, the most dramatic [breakthrough] since general relativity." "Enough beautiful things have been discovered," he says, "that we're pretty sure we've just found the tip of the iceberg."[16]

Superstring theory (based in part on the concept of "supersymmetry") is a complex mathematical formulation that can probably never be tested in the laboratory, at least not directly. For this reason some scientists have likened the theory to medieval theology; something to be contemplated in "schools of divinity by future equivalents of medieval theologians," with "faith replacing science once again," in the words of physicists Sheldon Glashow and Paul Ginsparg.[17] A key problem with the theory is that an extra six dimensions beyond the four we encounter in normal space-time must be added to make the equations come out right.

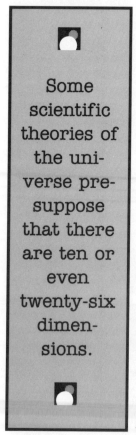

Some scientific theories of the universe presuppose that there are ten or even twenty-six dimensions.

But superstring theorists have worked out a variety of consistent string theories by supposing there really are ten (or perhaps twenty-six) dimensions. They believe superstring theory will change our very understanding of space and time. In the superstring model, energy/matter consists of ten dimensions compacted together, four of which have "unrolled," as it were, to form the material universe as we know it. "Superstrings are conceived as objects that vibrate in ten dimensions," writes Richard Morris. "Different levels of vibration correspond to different observed particles."[18]

The idea of ten- or twenty-six-dimension superstrings as the source of our present four-dimensional world is based partly on the emerging science of symmetry and symmetry-breaking. When a raindrop hits the ground, its symmetry is shattered, but not entirely. The resulting splash also has symmetry, but of a lower order or "dimension." This is symmetry-breaking. When one level of symmetry is disrupted, the result is not chaos but a lower-order symmetry. Some such process is believed to have occurred in the Big Bang that formed the physical universe. "From the smallest scales to the largest, many of nature's patterns are a result of broken symmetry," note Ian Stewart and Martin Golubitsky in their book, *Fearful Symmetry*. "When systems have symmetry, there's a good chance that the symmetry may break. When it does, very tiny asymmetries play a crucial role in selecting the actual outcome from a range of potential outcomes." Interestingly, less-than-perfect symmetry seems more interesting to us: "An oddity of the human mind is that it perceives *too much* symmetry as a bland uniformity rather than as a striking pattern; although some symmetry is lost, pattern seems to be gained because of this psychological trick."[19]

Given the ferment among today's scientists, a theoretical breakthrough leading to a comprehensive Theory of Everything seems likely within the next two decades, either as an outgrowth of string theory or from other lines of research. Eventually the theory will be confirmed experimentally. This will have profound implications not only technologically but also in worldview. It will alter the way humans understand the universe, bringing a new Copernican revolution. A scientific breakthrough in this area will further narrow the line between matter and spirit, providing new challenges for both scientists and philosophers.

It should be remembered that such a TOE is not really a theory of *everything,* but of the fundamental forces of energy and matter. A TOE would not provide answers to every question, even in science. From it one could not predict everything that will ever happen, as some people think. However, such a theory would fundamentally influence the way we understand the universe and probably would give technology a quantum boost.

The Shape We're In

The genetic code concerns the essential make-up of physical life; quantum physics deals with the essential make-up of the material universe itself. Both are basic to understanding what the universe really is.

At the other end of the spectrum from genes, quarks, and neutrinos is the immensity of the whole physical universe. Here also the next generation or two will witness large leaps in understanding. The exploration of space, enhanced by deep probes and satellite-mounted radio telescopes, is taking us to the very edges of the universe.

Some scientists are addressing themselves to the difficult question of the *topology* of the universe—its shape and surface contours. What is the shape of the cosmos?

Just as Earth is round, so also, it seems, is the universe. Travel in any one direction along Earth's surface and you'll eventually end up where you began. You would circle the globe. In a much more mysterious, harder-to-understand way, the same thing might happen if you journeyed far enough into space.

If you traveled straight out from Earth, never changing directions, you would end up where you began. Of course, you might need to dodge some stars en route, and at the end of the trip you would have to travel straight through the Earth. But your straight line would turn out to be a circle. In theory, of course. In fact, several things make such a trip impossible, quite apart from shortages of food, oxygen, and time!

The reason for this curvature of spacetime, it seems, is not that the universe is a three-dimensional sphere like the Earth is. Rather, the universe seems to be a four-dimensional sphere, a "hypersphere." Since we can sense only three spatial dimensions, we can't really imagine such a thing. Some scientists suggest this thought experiment:

1. Imagine a cube, equal in height, width, and length.
2. Extend the top and bottom of the cube and bend these extensions around until the two ends meet, forming a ring like a fat washer. Draw a line around the outside edge of the cube, forming a circle.
3. Now, similarly, extend the front and back of this ring outward and bend the ends around until they join. You now have a hollow ring, like an inner tube or a hollow donut. The line you drew in step two is now a circle through the center hole and around the tube at one point. If you draw a new line around the outside edge of the tube, it will·trace a circle, crossing the first line at right angles. You have now extended two of the three dimensions of the original cube into circles, and the original squares have disappeared into circles.
4. Now comes the hard part! Extend the two sides of the tubular donut and bend the ends around until they join. This forms a larger hollow donut, and begins to give some idea of a hypersphere. Your second line now runs through the hole and around the new donut at a particular point, while the first line has disappeared inside the larger structure (though it touches the outer surface at one point).

The universe may be something like that. Imagine yourself—in fact, our whole galaxy—as a tiny speck floating somewhere inside this donut, and imagine that the whole structure is rapidly expanding, like a balloon. Travel in any direction, and the curving contours of time and space would bring you right back to your starting point (if you could travel that fast and that far). This gives some idea of what our universe must really be like. But it is only a vague impression, for we are trying to imagine dimensions beyond the limits of our minds, and the universe has no solid or visible "edge" like a balloon has.

A leading thinker on cosmic topology is the noted Chinese astrophysicist and human rights advocate, Fang Lizhi. Dr. Fang raises interesting questions such as: Is the universe shaped like a ball or a donut?

In topology (the mathematical study of how objects fit together), the technical term for the donut shape is a *torus*. Unlike a ball, a torus has a hole in the middle. This makes its topology unique. Dr. Fang has developed a controversial but elegant three-torus model of the universe. His model is rather like a pliable box stretched around so that its top and bottom are joined like a donut, but also so that the front and back, and the two ends, are similarly stretched and perfectly joined, as in the thought experiment above. This is impossible to do with a physical model, but not with mathematics.

Hans Christian von Baeyer, describing Fang's work, says:

> If you were ever to find yourself inside a three-torus, you would soon discover that the customary notions of spatial relation and physical reality must be suspended. Suppose, for instance, that some familiar rectangular room were suddenly transformed into a three-torus: each wall is glued to the one opposite, and the floor is glued to the ceiling. In this topsy-turvy setting, if you were to walk straight into the front wall, you would emerge from the back wall . . . go into the left wall and you would turn up on the right; sink into the floor and you would drop from the ceiling.
>
> Standing in the center of the torus, you will experience an optical effect much like the one in a hall of mirrors, but with a difference: in front of you, your line of sight would pass through the transparent, abstract front wall and return from the opposite point on the back wall; you would thus see a copy of yourself from the back. . . .
>
> If the same scenario were extended into the cosmic realm, to make a three-torus universe filled with stars and galaxies, each object would have multiple images as far as the eye could see. . . . Because their light—bent by the gravitational pull of the cosmic mass and, by definition, always following the shortest path between two points—would curl repeatedly round the universe, their images would recur again and again until they became too dim to perceive.[20]

Such see-yourself-from-the-back (or meet-yourself-where-you-started) scenarios are actually misleading, because no person—not even light—could make the full circuit within the "life span" of the universe. "A closed universe does not last long enough to be circumnavigated," notes Richard Morris.[21] Even so, such thought experiments are useful in exploring the nature of the universe and questions of worldview.

Dimensions and Worldviews

Another scientist working with topology is Brown University mathematician Tom Banchoff. Banchoff uses colorful computer images of a torus to explore the phenomenon of multi-dimensionality. He points out that time is *a* fourth dimension, not necessarily *the* fourth dimension.

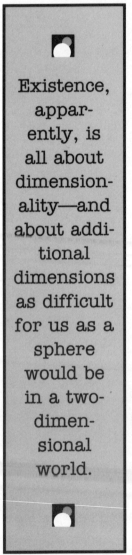
Mathematically there can be any number. Physicists commonly speak of ten to twenty-six different dimensions, as we have noted. But living in a three-dimensional world—or, at least, being able to *perceive* only three dimensions, plus time—we humans can form no coherent mental picture of a five-, six-, or seven-dimension world. This is why we can't really imagine a universe such as Dr. Fang describes.[22] Yet, not being able to visualize, understand, or prove the existence of other dimensions doesn't mean they are not real—any more than a chemical or genetic analysis of human emotions would disprove the reality of love.

> Existence, apparently, is all about dimensionality—and about additional dimensions as difficult for us as a sphere would be in a two-dimensional world.

The theory of relativity combines space and time as spacetime, as we have seen: time as a fourth dimension. In other words, "future and past are just directions, like up and down, left and right, forward and back, in something called space-time," says Stephen Hawking.[23]

Are the four dimensions of spacetime, then, all the dimensions of the universe? Might there really be ten or twenty-six? Scientists have discovered that they sometimes have to resort to "imaginary" time in order to make sense of these issues. Imaginary time is not the same as nonexistent time. It is another way of dealing with additional dimensions.

How can one conceive of imaginary time? Think of it as a time dimension running at right angles to ordinary time, says Stephen Hawking. If you "think of ordinary, real time as a horizontal line," or a time line running from past through the present into the future, you can then imagine "another direction of time, up and down the page" as it were, running "at right angles to real time."[24]

Is there, then, more than one time dimension, as is true with space? Can time move sideways? Does it have height and width as well as length, like space, so that spacetime is really six-dimensional? Why should time have one dimension when space has three? It doesn't seem fair![25]

These questions exceed our comprehension because we are bound (physically, at least) in a four-dimensional spacetime world. Yet science discovers it *has* to raise such questions in its journey toward scientific explanation of the universe. Increasingly, it seems, scientists have to assume additional dimensions in order for their research to move forward.

Fang, Banchoff, and other thinkers tinker at the frontiers of the meaning of physical matter. Existence, apparently, is all about dimensionality—about additional dimensions that are as difficult for us to grasp as a sphere would be in a two-dimensional "Flatland" having height and width but no depth. As we have seen, superstring theory also depends on the existence of at least ten dimensions.

Banchoff says we must "sensitize people to dimensionality." "The fourth dimension helps us break away from the tyranny of prepositions—relational words like 'among,' 'beside,' 'between,'" he says. "These are all dimensionally dependent ideas. It depends upon what dimension you are in whether a particular thing is separated from something else or blocks you or surrounds you."[26]

Such investigations are attempts to come to grips with the strange data that the universe presents to us. They are attempts to understand what it means that "the universe is a three-dimensional structure embedded in a four-dimensional space," as von Baeyer says. These are serious efforts to comprehend and explain reality. They push the limits of what our minds can comprehend. More: they stretch the limits of our models, asking us to think in new ways.

Humanity today stands poised on the brink of several *interlocking* breakthroughs—theoretically, experimentally, or both—that will change forever the way "life, the universe, and everything" are conceived by the human mind and spirit. What does this mean for belief and worldviews? At the very least, it means that any believable, livable worldview for the future will *have* to transcend the limits of space and time to be credible, even scientifically!

The tables have turned. Now it is those who think that space, time, and matter are all there is who are scientifically naive and out of date. Tomorrow's credible worldviews will be those that *begin* with multidimensionality as a basic starting assumption.

Stephen Hawking remarks, "The whole point of quantum mechanics is that it has a different view of reality."[27] These altered perceptions, however—because they are based in verifiable science—will increasingly become part of new, postmodern views of reality. Yet there are other, broader, worldview questions that science can ask, but cannot answer, because they reach beyond science.

CHAPTER SEVEN

Electric Minds:

Artifical Intelligence and Virtual Reality

> The most sophisticated technology is that which you aren't even aware of.
>
> —COMPUTER TECHNOLOGY MAXIM.
>
> In the closing decades of the twentieth century, reality is disappearing behind a screen. Is the mass marketing of artificial reality experiences going to result in the kind of world we would want our grandchildren to live in?
>
> —HOWARD RHEINGOLD[1]

Genetics and string theory lie at the frontier of the physical sciences, but in the computer age, the human mind is as great a frontier. What are consciousness, thinking, and intelligence? What is the essential difference between human minds and electronic ones? Is there such a thing as spirit, a kind of consciousness greater than the biology of the brain? Or are mind and spirit merely higher functions of this electro-chemical computer inside our skulls?

The key EarthCurrent here is the vanishing line between mind and machine. In this chapter we will look at several related issues: artificial intelligence, computer-generated virtual reality, and the possible linking of mind and machine.

The following scenario seems far out. Yet it claims to be more science than fiction:

You've just been wheeled into the operating room. A robot brain surgeon is in attendance. By your side is a computer waiting to become a human equivalent, lacking only a program to run. Your skull, but not your brain, is anesthetized. You are fully conscious. The robot surgeon opens your brain case and places a hand on the brain's surface. This unusual hand bristles with microscopic machinery, and a cable connects it to the mobile computer at your side. Instruments in the hand scan the first few millimeters of brain surface. High-resolution magnetic resonance measurements build a three-dimensional chemical map, while arrays of magnetic and electric antennas collect signals that are rapidly unraveled to reveal, moment by moment, the pulses flashing among the neurons. These measurements, added to a comprehensive understanding of human neural architecture, allow the surgeon to write a program that models the behaviour of the uppermost layer of the scanned brain tissue. This program is installed in a small portion of the waiting computer and activated. Measurements from the hand provide it with copies of the inputs that the original tissue is receiving. You and the surgeon check the accuracy of the simulation by comparing the signals it produces with the corresponding original ones. They flash by very fast, but any discrepancies are highlighted on a display screen. The surgeon fine-tunes the simulation until the correspondence is nearly perfect.

To further assure you of the simulation's correctness, you are given a pushbutton that allows you to momentarily "test drive" the simulation, to compare it with the functioning of the original tissue. When you press it, arrays of electrodes in the surgeon's hand are activated. By precise injections of current and electromagnetic pulses, the electrodes can override the normal signaling activity of nearby neurons. They are programmed to inject the output of the simulation into those places where the simulated tissue signals other sites. As long as you press the button, a small part of your nervous system is being replaced by a computer simulation of itself. You press the button, release it, and press it again. You should experience no difference. As soon as you are satisfied, the simulation connection is established permanently. The brain tissue is now impotent—it receives inputs and reacts as before but its output is ignored. Microscopic manipulators on the hand's surface excise the cells in this superfluous tissue and pass them to an aspirator, where they are drawn away.

The surgeon's hand sinks a fraction of a millimeter deeper into your brain, instantly compensating its measurements and signals for the changed position. The process is repeated for the next layer, and soon a second simulation resides in the computer, communicating with the first and with the remaining original brain tissue. Layer after layer the brain is simulated, then excavated. Eventually your skull is empty, and the surgeon's hand rests deep in your brainstem. Though you have not lost consciousness, or even your train of thought, your mind has been removed from the brain and transferred to a machine. In a final, disorienting step the surgeon lifts out his hand. Your suddenly abandoned body goes into spasms and dies. For a moment you experience only quiet and dark. Then, once again, you can open your eyes. Your perspective has shifted. The computer simulation has been disconnected from the cable leading to the surgeon's hand and reconnected to a shiny new body of the style, color, and material of your choice. Your metamorphosis is complete.[2]

This strange scene appears not in science fiction but in a serious book of science: *Mind Children: The Future of Robot and Human Intelligence,* by Hans Moravec of Carnegie Mellon University. Moravec explores what could reasonably happen as a result of robotics and computerized life simulation. He adds, "For the squeamish, there are other ways to work the transfer of human mind to machine. A high-resolution brain scan could, in one fell swoop and without surgery, make a new you 'While-U-Wait.' " Or you might carry a miniature computer with you that records your actions and monitors your brain, really getting to know you, building a total simulation. "When you die, this program is installed in a mechanical body that then smoothly and seamlessly takes over your life and responsibilities," writes Moravec.[3] A perfect electronic transition to eternal life—or "virtual eternal" life.

Moravec and others working on artificial intelligence believe humanity eventually will enter a "post-biological" age. Computerized devices will surpass (not replace) humans. "Today, our machines are still simple creations . . . hardly worthy of the word 'intelligent,' " writes Moravec. "But within the next century they will mature into entities as complex as ourselves, and eventually into something transcending everything we know—in whom we can take pride when they refer to themselves as our descendants."[4] Moravec believes machines equaling human intelligence will phase in around 2030.

Many people doubt that the line between mind and machine can be crossed so easily, or that computers can really ever be taught to think. But advances in artificial intelligence and life simulation may make us think! We may wonder about the real meaning of this kind of technology.

The main direction of this EarthCurrent seems clear. The next two generations will see a blurring between mind and machine, and more generally, between machines and biology. In the area of life simulation, for example, the question is being raised: If a computer or robot can function just like a human, can we say that it is not alive? What does it mean to be alive? The old question, "What is the meaning of life?" or what is life, takes on new dimensions and urgency.

Some foresee biotechnical or "living" computers operating very much like the human brain. Computers linked directly to the brain, with software enhancing or extending its powers, could be possible. Brain-like neural computers that work chemically, using "wetware" operating systems, could be another option. In addition, new generations of computers, possibly built atom by atom at a level of miniaturization never before imagined, may be possible within the next decade or two. Research scientists at IBM are already manipulating individual atoms, using atoms as building blocks. We do not yet know where this will lead.

Narrowing the gap between mind (or brain) and machine proceeds from both directions: how the brain actually functions and how computers might evolve. These two lines seem to be converging. That is, brain research, on the one hand, is discovering the mechanisms by which the brain works. They are studying how the brain carries out its billions of processes through multiple parallel or simultaneous interactions. On the other hand, computer research (cybernetics) as it progresses is more and more mimicking the brain, moving to multiple parallel-processing and the use of "fuzzy" logic, where not every operation is either/or.[5]

At a minimum, such developments blur the distinction between mind and machine and between living and inanimate states. They raise questions about the definition of life, mind, and spirit.

Artificial Life?

The term *artificial intelligence,* or AI, was coined in the 1950s as computer scientists (especially at the Massachusetts Institute of Technology) tried to match the operation of the human brain by using computer models. AI is defined as the ability of an artificial mechanism to exhibit intelligent behavior. Progress was slow at first. The subject is highly complex, and early computers were not up to the task. Today, AI research is studying the complexities of human language, common sense reasoning (as compared to mathematics or scientific reasoning), symbol recognition and manipulation, and a host of related problems.

In the 1980s the new field of "artificial life" (AL) was born. Here the focus is on simulating living things, whatever their IQ. The focus is on software, not hardware: the ways in which computer programs can be made to "act like" they are alive. Simulation and virtuality are the key goals.

Electronic viruses that have appeared on the computer scene in recent years are a notorious example of programs that "behave" as if alive, continuously reproducing themselves. They are not really alive, of course. They are human creations; rather simple software programs with built-in commands to copy themselves under certain conditions. Thus they seem to be living.

Today hundreds of researchers at leading universities and laboratories are exploring both AI and AL. Scientists at the University of California at Los Angeles (UCLA), for instance, have generated colonies of computer "ants" that with time "evolve" to the point that they work their way through mazes and seek out "food." Such elementary experiments lead to ever more complex ones.

Are such "creatures," or new generations of robots such as the insect-like machines created at MIT, really alive? The common-sense answer is no. Yet these experiments raise precisely the question: What is life? Researcher Christopher Langton at Los Alamos National Laboratory in New Mexico, argues, "Artificial life will be genuine life. It will simply be made of different stuff."[6] Others disagree, insisting that actual life and the simulation of life are essentially different. But who is to say? What is life, and what is the essence of consciousness?

Many are fascinated with the possibility of extending the powers of human intelligence through modern technology—computers, genetics, or both together. Present-day computers and computerized robots already expand human capacity in remarkable ways, opening questions always before thought to be closed, obvious, or irrelevant.

Living Machines

Research to develop machines that behave like humans proceeds along three lines. One is increasing miniaturization, using "nanotechnology." Another is the study of the way molecules work and the recognition that molecular organic processes are in some respects mechanical. The third is the fusion of biological, electronic, and mechanical processes. Hans Moravec notes, "Living organisms are clearly machines when viewed at the molecular scale. . . . Some proteins have moving parts like hinges, springs, and latches triggered by templates." What lies ahead, he argues, is "the fusion of biological, microelectonic, and micromechanical techniques into a single, immensely powerful, new technology."[7]

Nanotechnology, microscopic in scale, promises tiny machines that in turn might build other machines, using molecules and atoms. Such machines could have dozens of applications, especially in electronics and medicine. A nanomachine might be injected into your bloodstream to do repairs on your heart or brain.

Some scientists speculate about a world where "living machines" evolve to the point of erasing any practical distinction between life and nonlife. Human-manufactured beings would surpass human capacities in almost every area. "Our speculation ends," says Moravecz:

> in a supercivilization, the synthesis of all solar-system life, constantly improving and extending itself, spreading outward from the sun, converting nonlife into mind. Just possibly there are other such bubbles expanding from elsewhere. What happens if we meet one? A negotiated merger is a possibility, requiring only a translation scheme between the memory representations. This process, possibly occurring now elsewhere, might convert the entire universe into an extended thinking entity, a prelude to even greater things.[8]

Here speculation about robotics and artificial life crosses the line into philosophy or perhaps mysticism. The point, however, is that this speculation is rooted in science, not religion or philosophy. It shows how easily the leading edges of science raise larger issues of value and meaning and often imply a worldview.[9] .

Moravec admits that the prospect of transferring human minds into artificial bodies may be unsettling to many people. "Regardless of how the copying is done, the end result will be a new person," they say. But Moravec disagrees. He writes:

> This point of view, which I will call the *body-identity position,* makes life extension by duplication considerably less personally interesting. I believe the objection can be overcome by acceptance of an alternative position which I will call *pattern-identity.* Body-identity assumes that a person is defined by the stuff of which a human body is made. Only by maintaining continuity of body stuff can we preserve an individual person. Pattern-identity, conversely, defines the essence of a person, say myself, as the *pattern* and the *process* going on in my head and body, not the machinery supporting the process. If the process is preserved, I am preserved. The rest is mere jelly.
>
> The body-identity position . . . is based on a mistaken intuition about the nature of living things. . . : Most of our body is renewed this way [that is, by the replacement of cells] every few years. . . . Every atom present within us at birth is likely to have been replaced half way through our life. Only our pattern, and only some of it at that, stays with us until our death.[10]

Is the essence of life, then, in the material stuff of the body, or in the patterns and processes (in essence, the software) that runs the body? Moravec says the essence is in the software. What is this, exactly? What is a "pattern" or "process" as distinct from the matter that is patterned? Are these the only possibilities?

Virtual Reality

The most sophisticated new wave in the electro-communications revolution is "virtual reality," or VR. Smelling huge profits in the new technology, major communications companies scrambled to merge or form global partnerships in the early 1990s. Billions of dollars are at stake in this next quantum leap in electronics. The big communications players are positioning themselves for the global marriage of TV, video disks, computers, and telephones.

Computer grammar-check programs tell you to get rid of the words "virtual" and "virtually"; they're virtually meaningless. But *virtual* has become a hot term in late-twentieth-century cyberspeak. The concept of virtual reality speaks eloquently to the thinning line between "real" and computerized reality.

"Virtual" simply means existing in effect, though not in name. Commonly it has the sense, "for all practical purposes." In computerese it means "almost as good as real"—sometimes "better than real!" Enthusiasts sing the virtues of virtual reality.

Virtual reality creates an electronic environment—cyberspace—that engages the senses so vividly that it feels real. Using a three-dimensional helmet and gloves linked to a computer (and perhaps other gear), you see, hear, and touch objects in the simulated environment. With the external world thus blocked out, you have the sense of actually being in a different place. You have entered cyberspace.

Virtual reality results from the merging of half a dozen technologies. Think of your television, telephone, VCR, CD player, and computer. Then think of combining all that technology, upping the power and shrinking the size. This is the revolution that is now surfacing. Virtual reality is only one dimension of this revolution. It is the one the public, and especially children, will discover first.

Technically, virtual reality is an interactive system involving the participant's senses of sight, hearing, and touch, giving a highly realistic feeling of being inside the virtual world. The term VR is used more loosely, however, for the new generation of video games that entered arcades and the home kid-vid market in the early 1990s. These games are increasingly realistic, though they may not be three-dimensional or include the sense of touch. Some call this "virtual virtuality"—just one step (and a few years) away from true VR. The new technology has already generated its own vocabulary, which is now passing into popular use: Cyberspace, cyberpunk, DataGlove (or PowerGlove), telepresence, knowbot, virtuphone, virtual communities, virtual sex, virtual world.

What makes VR potent is the way it interfaces with the brain. The mind grasps images much faster than printed words. "The eye-brain system is incredibly advanced," says Larry Smarr of the University of Illinois. "Our mental 'text computer'" can handle only about one hundred bits per second. But "looking at the world, we absorb the equivalent of a billion bits of information per second," about as much as the text in a couple of hundred books.[11]

Thomas Furness III, VR pioneer at the University of Washington, describes virtual reality as "an environment that you create using a combination of visual, auditory and tactile images so that it becomes an alternative, sort of an artificial, environment or reality. We call it a 'reality' because you perceive it as if it is a world. It's just like you're walking into another world, and you're perceiving it as if it becomes reality itself."[12] Howard Rheingold, editor of the *Whole Earth Review* and a popular writer on virtual reality, calls VR "a magical window onto other worlds, from molecules to minds." He notes, "Although it sounds like science fiction, and the word 'cyberspace' in fact originated in a science-fiction novel, virtual reality is already a science, a technology, and a business, supported by significant funding from the computer, communications, design, and entertainment industries worldwide."[13]

To understand what VR feels like:

> Imagine a wraparound television with three-dimensional programs, including . . . sound, and solid objects that you can pick up and manipulate, even feel with your fingers and hands. Imagine immersing yourself in an artifical world and actively exploring it, rather than peering in at it from a fixed perspective through a flat screen in a movie theater, on a television set, or on a computer display. Imagine that you are the creator as well as the consumer of your artifical experience, with the power to use a gesture or word to remold the world you see and hear and feel. That part is not fiction. The head-mounted displays (HMDs) and three-dimensional computer graphics, input/output devices, computer models that constitute a VR system make it possible, today, to immerse yourself in an artifical world and to reach in and reshape it.[14]

Like so many innovations, today's virtual reality is a spin-off from military and space research. Several years ago, NASA scientists developed a "reality engine" to simulate conditions in space. Earlier, the U.S. Air Force built flight simulators for training pilots. These high-tech computer applications are now widespread in military and intelligence operations. The U.S. Central Intelligence Agency, for instance, uses satellite photos, maps, and other data to generate three-dimensional photo-like computer images that can be manipulated and explored at will. If the computer contains enough information, a remote high-tech snoop can roam the inside of buildings, walk through walls, and enter top-secret installations. All of this, of course, in cyberspace.

Commercially, VR has reached the stage technically that it is limited only by human imagination and investment dollars. A torrent of cash has begun to flow, and right now some of the sharpest minds in Japan, America, and Europe are imagining and building ever more elaborate cyber-worlds. Today this industry is positioned where the computer industry was about ten years ago, and it is moving fast.

Wedding TV and video with computers and new interactive devices, VR technology engages more of the senses than just sight and sound. Touch is already well developed, thanks to the DataGlove (first developed by NASA). Replacing a mouse or joystick, the DataGlove lets you pick up and feel objects—their hardness, texture, weight—as if they were real. Researchers in Italy are developing highly sensitive, superthin electroplastic skin that can receive the sense of touch virtually as well as the real thing.[15]

VR Promise and Peril

Like all new technologies, virtual reality has tremendous potential for both good and evil. As a sophisticated form of simulation, it has many important applications, from medical research to space exploration. Architects can construct intricate images of buildings that show every board, window, and electrical circuit. Then they can "walk" through them, even going within the walls, to see how everything fits and how costs can be cut and improvements made. Furness sees applications primarily in five areas: accelerating learning, enhancing creativity, extending ability to communicate, providing means for rapid information assimilation in certain jobs, and recapturing "lost world" citizens—the handicapped, disabled, or otherwise physically or mentally challenged.

Furness foresees the day when VR "knowbots" will tackle complex research and design problems. A knowbot would be "an intelligent assistant, an electronic associate, that you can send off to do things for you," he says. "The knowbot is a virtual object, but you actually pick it up and give it a command. You say, 'Knowbot, I'm going to build a building of this size at this particular location, and I'm interested in knowing its history and the likelihood that we are going to have disturbances in the foundation of this building over the next twenty-five years. Would you go find that out for me?' " Later you "put on" the knowbot to check out the results. "You pick this thing up and now you go inside of it. What it has done is created an alternative world for you," giving you answers in a form you can see and explore.[16]

Virtual reality is being tried out in other areas, such as education and marketing. In Japan, customers can don headsets and walk through virtual kitchens, choosing the design and arrangement they like best. But the breakthrough area commercially is in the amusement industry. Interactive video games, first in arcades and now in the home, are leading the way. Already video games are big business worldwide. In the United States they gross $5.3 billion annually, more than Americans spend on movie-going.

People familiar with the cartoonish images of home video games will be shocked by the vivid realism of VR images and action. Using three-dimensional headsets with stereophonic sound and stereographic vision, the new technology surpasses movie-quality realism. By blanking out other sensory input, advanced VR gives participants the sense of actually entering a new dimension. For many people, and especially for teens and preteens, this can be more enticing than the real world. Virtual reality offers some unique advantages: power, control, constant thrills, combat without physical danger, and the ability to exit and start over at will.

The downside of VR equals its benefits. It turns sex and violence, increasingly the bane of TV, into interactive VR sports. If you watch someone killed on TV, your only options are to watch or not watch. But virtual reality games give you more choices, including torturing or killing (in exquisite ways) your victim. A person's *will*, not just eyes and hands, get involved. Violent or sexually explicit video games thus go far beyond movies and cable TV. The participant is enticed and *decides* to engage in violent or other kinds of (simulated) immoral or antisocial behavior. And the level of perceived reality and sensory involvement will only grow greater with time.

All this leaves some unsettling questions. What will be the long-term moral and psychological effects of children practicing virtual violence hundreds of times a week in a world that feels more real than reality? What will be the social behavioral effects of millions of preteen boys, in the United States and globally, spending hours each week realistically decapitating their foes in video games, then going forth to interact with real people? These virtual activities certainly involve the emotions, will, and imagination.

Defenders say such games provide a healthy outlet for frustration and aggression. Kids have no trouble separating fantasy from reality, they claim. One video-store manager sees games like Mortal Kombat as good therapy: "You had a bad day, so you can go in there and rip a couple of heads off and feel better." But we may wonder. Many kids, especially those with tragic lives, already struggle to know what reality is. Further, no one can predict how VR will shape a person's sense of reality because there has never been a technology like this. In virtual reality the membrane between "virtual" and "real" stretches ever thinner. That's the whole point. It's the same issue, at root, as with artificial intelligence: the definition of what is real and what has meaning and value.

Virtual Sex

Since virtual reality and sex are both powerful, they are, of course, being combined. Virtual reality gurus talk much about "virtual sex." Some people scoff at the idea; others say it's the hot frontier of technology. The truth lies somewhere in between. By far the biggest commercial applications of VR will be in video games and in research and design (CAD/CAM upgraded to VR). But pornographers are moving in, as they have with X-rated computer video programs and computer-sex networks. Already some "adult" computer games carry the label "Parental Discretion Advised," and many of the 50,000 computer bulletin board systems in the United States have so-called adult subnets.[17]

Now that compact disc players are becoming standard computer equipment, a number of sexually explicit CD-ROM games and programs have become hot-selling items. Discs like "Virtual Valerie" and "Heavenly Bodies Vol. 3" are, in effect, interactive pornography: Let your fingers do the fondling. Besides being erotic, the manipulative character of such "Seedy Roms" subtly promotes sex-as-control or domination. The genuine personal mutuality is gone. These programs are not fully virtual reality, but they show where the technology is speeding.

Virtual sex with a high degree of realism, with a "you are there" feel, will be available for those who seek it and are most vulnerable to it— and perhaps for those who want the thrill of sex without the danger of AIDS. This high-tech pornography will be a comparatively small segment of the VR business. But in such a colossal industry, even a small slice could be huge, running into hundreds of millions of dollars.

Interactive virtual sex is already yielding huge profits. Lawrence Miller, who founded California-based Interotica in 1993, says with remarkable candor: "We wanted to do a rain forest title, but we looked at the market and we figured if we wanted to make money, adult material was the way to go." Similarly, Kathy Keeton of General Media, which now produces sex-oriented programs, says, "The profits on this are incredible."[18]

Research suggests that those most likely to be affected by VR over the next generation will be young boys—teens and preteens by the millions, worldwide. Boys this age seem especially attracted and addictable to the fascinating, escapist world of VR. This spells a big challenge to parents (and to family structure), since VR goes far beyond movies and TV. Most vulnerable are children and teens for whom reality is something to be escaped—kids wounded by divorce, abuse, and neglect. Virtual reality provides some escape. But at what cost?

What does virtual reality mean for the future? Jaron Lanier of VPL Research, a leading VR company, believes the new technology is as big as the invention of writing.[19] Technologically, VR is simply the predictable extension of computers into optics and robotics. Thus it is related to artificial intelligence, already discussed. But it is more. Because VR creates a world that *feels* as real as everyday experience, it grabs attention and invites participation. You are in control, so you can safely have as many adventures as you like.

Virtual reality will become much more life-like and convincing over the next decade. And it will be more accessible to the general public, in the home as well as in VR theaters and arcades.

What about "virtual communities"? The rapid growth of interactive computer networks in the early 1990s has created electronic discussion groups on a wide range of topics, from boating to child rearing. This is a good example of Earth's new electronic map. What unites these people is not place but technology and shared interests. Here is a new form of human community, one where geography, social position, nationality, race, and gender are irrelevant. These virtual communities are already here. As technology advances and contact becomes more immediate—with live images of your partners on your computer screen, for example—these electronic communities may grow in significance. Perhaps they hold promise for greater global understanding and well-being.

Virtual reality is spawning philosophical debate about the meaning of "reality" as we experience more "virtual reality." If there is "virtual reality," is there also "virtual truth," "virtual spirituality," or "virtual love"? If so, where is the line between "virtual" and "actual"? Or is all reality virtual reality? In other words, what is "really real"? Here again technology raises worldview questions. This is one dimension of emerging postmodern society, where the definition of reality is an open question.

Matters of the spirit are involved, as well. We can imagine virtual religious experience, virtual prayer, virtual spirituality. Basic issues of human being and identity are involved. "When today's infant VR technology matures in a few years, it promises (and threatens) to change what it means to be human," Howard Rheingold warns. "Given the rate of development of VR technologies, we don't have a great deal of time to tackle questions of morality, privacy, personal identity, and even the prospect of a fundamental change in human nature. When the VR revolution really gets rolling, we are likely to be too busy turning into whatever we are turning into to analyze or debate the consequences."[20]

Is this concern overdrawn? To many, it will seem so. Don't turn technological toys into cosmic questions, people may say. But this is just the point. Caught up in the fascination of ever more adventurous technology, most people don't ponder profound issues. Yet emerging global society will be shaped by these issues, by design or by default.

What Is Life?

As we noted earlier, artificial intelligence and virtual reality have sparked debate about the nature of life and of human consciousness. Can computers ever have "minds" in the human sense? How realistically do mind and machine merge in virtual reality? Many enthusiasts for artificial intelligence and biotechnology believe that consciousness arises from the structures and patterns of life. To fully *simulate* life, therefore, replicating its patterns, would be to create or recreate life.

Some scientists, like Oxford University physicist Roger Penrose, disagree. "The very fact that the mind leads us to truths that are not computable convinces me that a computer can never duplicate the mind," says Penrose.[21] "The *conscious* mind cannot work like a computer, even though much of what is actually involved in mental activity might do so."[22] Penrose believes, however, that the reason we can't fully understand the concept of "mind" is our incomplete grasp of the fundamental laws of physics. Eventually we will know. But the answers will not, he believes, erase the line between mind and machine. Others say consciousness is *in principle* a function of the complexity of the brain, but at such a high level that *in practice* replication will always be impossible.[23]

These are some of the dimensions of the ongoing debate about the nature of life, mind, consciousness, and human uniqueness. The debate will intensify over the next generation. Obviously science, technology, philosophy, and religion overlap in these discussions. Here again we face issues that will shape the worldviews of global culture in the days ahead.

Worldview Questions

Questions of computer technology and of artificial or "virtual" life, intelligence, and experience may be seen as a new, technologized version of the old mind-body problem—the philosophical question of how a (presumably) nonmaterial mind can be connected to a material body. In Plato's *Phaedo*, Socrates hinted at this. Socrates was asked how he should be buried. "However you please," he replied, "if you can catch me and I do not get away from you." Heinz Pagels comments, "Every reflective person must, at some time, come to terms with the mind-body puzzle; it is a litmus test of one's philosophical, even metaphysical, dispositions."[24]

Philosophers have dealt with the mind-body riddle in various ways. Technology is beginning to provide its own answers, or at least to reframe the question. Artificial intelligence and virtual reality give new twists to this old issue even as they change our perceptions of reality itself.

I was startled by the conclusion to an article entitled "The Death of Proof" that appeared in *Scientific American*. The article discusses current trends in mathematics. The author reports on the growing use of computers, and especially computer graphics, in mathematical explorations. He tells how mathematicians are working with teachers to improve the teaching of high school math.

> The mathematicians insisted that proofs are crucial [in teaching mathematics] to ensure that a result is true. The high school teachers demurred, pointing out that students no longer considered traditional, axiomatic proofs to be as convincing as, say, visual arguments. "The high school teachers overwhelmingly declared that most students now (Nintendo/joystick/MTV generation) do not relate to or see the importance of 'proofs,' " the minutes of the meeting stated. Note the quotation marks around the word "proofs."[25]

Note the implication here. Visual reality has become more real, and thus more convincing, than rational argument or mathematical proof. This signals a turning point in cultural perception. Perhaps it means that increasingly a person's or group's worldview will be literally that, a world*view*, not a set of arguments or ideas or concepts. Here is an example of postmodern perception. Yet in some ways it is closer to premodern and "primitive" perceptions than to modern ones.

Here the key worldview questions concern the meaning and experience of "life," "mind," and "reality." By what pictures, experiences, or stories are these to be understood? These nagging worldview questions remain.

CHAPTER EIGHT

Western Decline:
America's Final Hour?

> The menace to America today is in the emphasis on what separates us rather than on what brings us together—the separations of race, of religious dogma, of religious practice, of origins, of language.
>
> —HISTORIAN DANIEL J. BOORSTIN[1]

> This is our problem in the United States: we have begun to lose trust in our institutions . . . . The heritage of trust that has been the basis of our stable democracy is eroding.
>
> —Robert Bellah and colleagues, *THE GOOD SOCIETY*[2]

L aboratory discoveries and technological breakthroughs are not walled off from the world of politics and international relations. Political climate often shapes priorities in science, and science makes an impact on politics, either directly or indirectly through technological advances that touch the economy. No atom is an island.

Politics is a key part of global ecology. It mixes with other Earth Currents that are shaping our common future. Where is global politics headed? We look first at the United States, and in the next chapter we will focus on the question of a new world order. Both chapters trace a historic powershift in global politics.

The West (Europe, then the United States) dominated world history for half a millennium. In our new age of global science, global economics, and instant-access popular culture, however, this is changing. The West still dominates in economics, politics, and military might, but the global balance is shifting. Today's new reality is the comparative decline of the West (particularly the United States), the impact of this globally, and the rise of new centers of influence.

The West rose to global prominence rather quickly. The potent mix of rediscovered classical Greek and Roman culture and resurgent Christianity in the fifteenth and sixteenth centuries gave rise to modern science, technology, industry, and the democratic nation-state. Ships from Spain, Portugal, England, and Holland sailed the seas and set up economic and political empires that lasted well into this century. After World War II, a kind of *pax americana* spread worldwide and was held in place mainly by American dynamism and the stalemate of the Cold War.

Visit the little city of Malacca, on the Malay peninsula, and you can feel this history. Malacca, "the Singapore of the sixteenth century," was the key contact point between expanding West and emerging East. It was especially important because of the spice trade. Crumbling remains now tell the story: conquest by the Portuguese in the early 1500s; the influence of Francis Xavier and other Jesuit missionaries; the coming of the Dutch, who expelled the Portuguese. Later British warships and trading ships arrived. The British drove off the Dutch and later set up a monument to Queen Victoria in the town square. The bright red Anglican chapel, still in use, reveals its origins by its Dutch façade.

Today Malacca is part of Islamic Malaysia, and the earlier Western influence is almost gone. Yet new Japanese factories outside town show that Malacca is being drawn back into international trade, in fact, into the global economy. Walk into Malacca's sleek new shopping center and you feel like you're in Los Angeles or Tokyo.

America's Final Hour?

The 1900s often have been seen as "the American Century." In many respects, this is accurate. But centuries come and go. In terms of inner vitality and global influence, the late 1990s may be America's final hour. "The United States today is passing through a period of reckoning, when the deepest national issues have a critical religious component and the deepest religious issues have critical national consequences," writes Os Guinness.[3]

In relative global terms, Japan and China are growing in influence and the United States is fading. A new global society is emerging. The appearance of Japanese signs and literature at tourist spots such as London's Westminster Abbey or the old Castle District in Budapest are signs of this global realignment.

Is the United States really slipping? If so, in what sense? Books like *Megatrends 2000* paint a rosy picture, but their time frame is too short. We might better ponder analyses like Paul Kennedy's in *The Rise and Fall of the Great Powers.* Kennedy argues that as nations rise to power economically and politically, they overextend themselves militarily, leading to economic crisis. Huge deficits eventually force great powers to contract, shrinking their might and influence. When a nation's economy weakens, its global influence eventually fades. The key factor, according to Kennedy, is uncontrollable deficits due to the massive military outlays necessary to sustain the empire—so-called imperial overstretch. One can see how this applies to the United States, though globalization and the fact that America primarily was never really a military empire are mitigating factors.

The issue is not just economics and armies, however. Deeper questions of social and moral cohesion arise—the social fabric that undergirds a nation's economy and political stability. Here also one senses a global shift in power.

In the United States, most people now believe that the nation is in decline, according to opinion polls. In a 1994 *Newsweek* poll, 76 percent of respondents said that the United States is in a "moral and spiritual decline."[4] This is a significant attitude shift. Some failure of national vision and will has occurred, something that goes deeper than economic cycles. The 1991 Gulf War temporarily lifted America's spirits (ironically) and sparked a burst of flag-waving enthusiasm. But underlying problems and pessimism remain. Further, the perception of decline may become self-fulfilling prophecy.

Today one senses a souring of the national mood that may be long-term. Though linked to fears about the economy, the malaise goes deeper. Year end polls in 1993 showed most Americans thought crime and race relations would worsen, despite a rosier economic outlook.[5]

Idealism—often naive, sometimes arrogant, but perennially effervescent—has driven Amer-

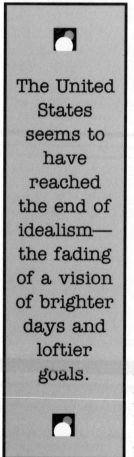

The United States seems to have reached the end of idealism— the fading of a vision of brighter days and loftier goals.

ica onwards for two centuries. Repeatedly this drive was rekindled by fresh waves of immigrants, "yearning to breathe free." But the United States in the 1990s seemed to run out of idealism. One felt the fading of a vision of brighter days and loftier goals.

How different from most of American history! Consider the Consciousness Revolution of the 1960s. However else one assesses it, the really attractive thing about the sixties was its idealism—its naive, zany, happy, starry-eyed, flower-flaunting, world-embracing idealism. It is this impulse that has died in America. Some environmentalists and assorted religious circles still have it, but movement-idealism now seems defunct in America.

If this is true, the reasons are abundant, though complex. Long-term somber signs loom in five areas: the economy, politics, population shifts, family life, and popular culture.

The Economy

As the world's largest debtor nation, the United States owes over $500 billion to foreign banks and nations. The external debt of the United States outstrips that of Argentina, Mexico, Brazil, India, Egypt, the Philippines, Indonesia, and Malaysia combined. Obviously large differences in scale separate the economies of these nations from that of the Unites States. Still, this new economic reality is startling.

The mushrooming U. S. debt (even when adjusted for inflation) worries economists, business leaders, and the world's financial markets. Today it takes all the federal income tax collected from the Mississippi to the West Coast to pay the interest on the national debt. Analysts warn that this would become unmanageable if the nation slipped into a prolonged recession. If the economy grows steadily, the red ink is manageable, though it squeezes other priorities. A deep recession, though, could throw the nation into the nightmare of hyperinflation where interest on the debt, and interest on the interest, would bankrupt the nation.

A related concern is the gap between rich and poor. The Reagan years saw a massive transfer of wealth from the poor to the rich, as has now been widely documented. This came about partly through tax breaks for the wealthy, massive military spending, and drastic cuts in domestic health and welfare programs. Equally damaging was "financialization," making money from financial deals rather than investing in manufacturing and real economic growth. Buying companies, trimming their assets, and then reselling them made a few rich and many poorer through job loss or raided pension funds. Kevin Phillips cautions:

Excessive preoccupation with finance and tolerance of debt are apparently typical of great economic powers in their late stages. They foreshadow economic decline, but often accompany new heights of cultural sophistication, in part because the hurly-burly expansion of the middle class and its values are receding. Yet these slow transitions involve real economic cost to the average person or family, and politcal restiveness reflects that.[6]

Many of the issues facing the United States today, from homelessness to spiraling violence, have been aggravated by such policies. Today America is increasingly stressed and divided as its industry adjusts to global competition. "We seem to be evolving into two classes: the underemployed and the overemployed, those who are desperate for work and those who are desperate for time," writes Ellen Goodman.[7]

The Political Process

Given this economic challenge, the creeping paralysis of the U.S. political process is not a good sign. The subversion of representative government by special interest lobbies and the exorbitant costs of campaigning have made government unresponsive to the will and needs of the people. Massive disillusionment with office holders and with government in general suggests the depth of the disease. Negative campaigning in which one's opponent is ridiculed or portrayed falsely has lowered the level of political discourse. Yet there is no adequate defense against this, and so opponents respond in kind. Voters know they are being manipulated and so become even more apathetic.

The cancerous growth of special-interest groups around federal and state government looks ominous in the lens of history. Kevin Phillips notes, "The United States of the 1990s . . . probably ranked as the greatest interest-group concentration in world history—and in Washington some of the most influential agents represented foreign masters. None of the previous great economic powers had been able to clear out the sclerosis of entrenched elites and interest groups; the United States, with its populist traditions, would have to be the first."[8]

These problems clog the wheels of government and subvert the political process. Perhaps they merely reflect a pendulum swing, presaging a new surge of vitality. Arthur Schlesinger, Jr. suggests in *The Cycles of American History* that the United States shifts in approximately fifteen-year cycles between "public purpose" and "private interest"; perhaps the nation in the 1990s may be recovering a sense of public purpose.[9] But massive debt and government gridlock may defeat any new reform impulse. More basically, the character of society itself—the foundation for functional politics—is shifting.

Population Shifts

A historic demographic shift is part of this change in character. The United States is moving from a mostly white population shaped by European traditions and values to a population that more nearly mirrors the global mix. Americans are experiencing "the browning of America" through surging immigration from around the world, and particularly from Latin America. By 2050 less than half the nation's citizen's will be of European descent. By itself, this is probably a sign of vigor, not decline. Immigrants have always helped keep America young and vital. But coming at a time of social strain and political sclerosis, these demographic shifts further stress American society.[10]

Until recent decades, most immigration was European and chiefly Christian and Jewish. Increasingly it is Oriental, Middle Eastern and Latin American, with dramatic increases in Buddhist and Islamic minorities. Thus the religious, ethical, and philosophical character of the nation is also changing. Islam is said to be the fastest-growing religion in America, with adherents estimated at between four and seven million—more now than Episcopalians. By 1993 some 1,500 new mosques had been built in the United States.[11] Buddhist and Hindu temples begin to dot the landscape. This diversity itself is no threat, but it does heighten the question of national cultural identity and helps spark "culture war" fever.

The 1965 U.S. Immigration Act reversed long-standing policy that favored Europeans. Third World people flooded in, bringing new culture currents. In Los Angeles County, California, for example, non-Hispanic whites dropped from the majority to a minority between 1980 and 1990. During the same period, the number of Hispanics in the United States more than doubled.

Such diversity sparks tensions between nativism and multiculturalism and touches every fiber of the social fabric. Paul Gray notes, "It is now fairly commonplace [for U.S. schoolchildren] to learn American history in the context of who has oppressed, excluded, or otherwise mistreated whom. All across the country, students are imbibing a version of the past and present that their parents would not recognize." Instead of the melting pot, a new model has emerged. This view "emphasizes the racial and ethnic diversity of American citizens, of the many cultures that have converged here, each valuable in its own right and deserving of study and respect."[12] The rewriting of American history, to date mainly the history of the dominant Eurocentric tradition, is well underway.

This swing to multiculturalism can be a needed and overdue awakening to the complex and conflicted facts of history and the injustices done to oppressed groups. But as political agenda pursued for partisan purposes, multiculturalism is socially corrosive. "Radical multiculturalism turns upside down the principles that drew, and continue to draw, people to America," notes Gray—"the freedom to create a new personal identity, and the chance to become part of a nation of people who have done the same thing."[13]

Demographic changes do not stand alone, of course. They are tied to trends in other areas, especially technology, religion, and urbanization. Over two centuries, the center of American life moved from the farm, to the city, to the suburb. By 1992, over half the American people lived in suburbs—a historic first. But the shift now seems to be, unexpectedly, to the ghetto—a new "ghetto-ization" of American life. Suburbs turned out not to be next door to heaven. The people who suburbanized in the 1950s and 1960s to escape city life, or fled to the countryside or private cocoons in the 1980s, found in the 1990s that ghetto life had arrived on their doorstep. You never knew when it would crash through your window or hijack your car at a busy intersection.

These demographic shifts could conceivably renew American society over the next couple of generations. A nation of immigrants, the United States has repeatedly been invigorated by fresh waves of displaced adventurers, newcomers seeking a brighter future for themselves and their children. But the short-term impact over the next generation or so will be unsettling. The dominant cultural tradition in the United States is becoming the minority tradition. Many people, especially middle- and lower-middle-class whites with European roots, will feel threatened. Social discord will likely increase dramatically before any kind of new national unity and identity can emerge.

The contours of a new national consensus are unpredictable. It will look very different, however, from the values that have carried American democracy for two hundred years—unless those values and their institutional expressions can be renewed. "America increasingly sees itself as composed of groups more or less ineradicable in their ethnic character," writes Arthur Schlesinger, Jr. The danger is a new ideology of fragmentation and separatism that "belittles *unum* and glorifies *pluribus*." Schlesinger adds, "The historic idea of a unifying American identity is now in peril in many arenas—in our politics, our voluntary organizations, our churches, our language. And in no arena is the rejection of an overriding national identity more crucial than in our system of education" where "militants of ethnicity" argue that "history and literature should be taught not as intellectual disciplines but as therapies whose function is to raise minority self-esteem."[14]

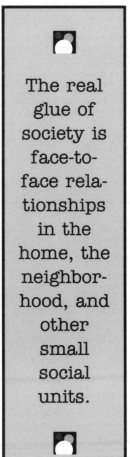

The Faltering Family

America's families are disintegrating. Many are in a state of near-collapse, or worse. This, coupled with a growing debate about what "family" means, is a related cause for concern. Since World War II, America has undergone a family revolution as great as any other change shaking society during these decades. The nature of gender and family relationships has been redefined. The emerging pattern is relationship without commitment, sex without morality, and parenthood without family.

Society is held together not primarily by its macro-structures but by its micro-structures. The real glue of society is not large institutions but face-to-face relationships in the home, the neighborhood, the church, and other small social units. These give legitimacy and moral persuasiveness to the larger structures of government and economics. But the American social fabric is fraying at these vital levels.

Imagine ten babies, all born the same day in the United States. If a typical sample, this is their fate: Two will be raised by their mothers only, outside of marriage. One may be raised by the father only. Three will experience the divorce of their parents. Three will spend some part of their growing-up years in a "blended" family, with stepsisters or stepbrothers. Two will be raised in poverty. Five will be left home alone for part of the day during their school years. Two will be abused physically or sexually by their parents or others. Only two will be raised by both parents and grow to adulthood without experiencing parental divorce, separation, or remarriage. This is a dramatic departure from the past two hundred years of American history. It is unprecedented not only in American history, but perhaps in all of human history.[15]

Of all society's micro-structures, family is the most basic. Amitai Etzioni, founder of the communitarian movement in North America, observes, "Throughout the enormous variety of human experience, over all continents and throughout all history, no society ever thrived without family."[16] "It is no accident that in a

> The real glue of society is face-to-face relationships in the home, the neighborhood, and other small social units.

wide variety of human societies (from the Zulus to the Inuits, from ancient Greece and ancient China to modernity), there has never been a society that did not have two-parent families."[17] Yet the very word *family* no longer has any clear meaning in the United States. A 1993 book telling the story of two lesbian women and the child they are raising bears the title *Family Values*. In contemporary America, Etzioni argues, family issues are trapped in "an ideological word game." The default thesis in discussions about family, he says, is "that it does not matter which social arrangements adults devise to bring up children."[18]

Although the family is society's most basic unit, stable family life is waning in the United States. The reasons are complex, but they include increased divorce, the effects of TV and other mass entertainment, and the loss of an overarching, shared moral vision. Divorce is the common experience of more and more children and adults, and "each divorce is the death of a small civilization."[19] The dramatic rise of dual-income families adds stress and reduces parents' time with children. One fourth of U.S. children now live with just one parent and about half will live with just one parent some time during their lives. The number of children living with grandparents or other relatives has nearly doubled in a decade, reaching 3.2 million in 1990. The nation has an estimated 157,000 "throwaway children" yearly—kids kicked out or rejected by their parents. Some 40 percent of human conceptions in the United States occur outside marriage. Moral questions aside, this is a danger signal for social cohesion.

By the early 1990s, the United States faced a growing crisis of rising numbers of unattached, uncivil, and uncivilized young males. Marriage, for all its problems, is a great civilizing force. Decreasing marriage means increasing violence in society. Massachusetts Senator Daniel Patrick Moynihan noted in a "Meet the Press" interview in 1993, "We have had a behavioral sink in the last thirty years that has no counterpart in our history. . . . The breakup of family inevitably, predictably . . . [leads] to the growth of large numbers of predatory males." If the nation doesn't get out if its "denial phase," he warned, it will regress

A nation "can sink into basically barbaric behavior in a generation and hardly notice it."— Daniel Patrick Moynihan into "a caste society." "You get used to barbarism," Moynihan added. "The fragility of the social contract is [much greater] than we think. [A nation] can sink into basically barbaric behavior in a generation and hardly notice it. We almost now don't notice how awful things are."

Asked about solutions, Moynihan said, "The principal social objective of American national government at every level, to the degree it can have any effect, [must be] to see that children are born to intact families and that they remain so." This should be a top priority of society generally, including the churches. "Thirty years ago we said this was coming, and it has come. And don't think it will go away in less than thirty years."[20]

The issue is deeper than marriage and divorce rates. The whole conception of marriage and family has shifted since the 1950s. Most popular movies and TV shows assume that marriage is passé or irrelevant and certainly not a prerequisite for sexual union. For those who do wed, marriage is often seen as a low-level commitment. George Washington University law professor Thomas Morgan notes, "It is easier in these United States to walk away from a marriage than from a commitment to purchase a used car. Most contracts cannot be unilaterally abrogated; marriages in contemporary America can be terminated by practically anyone at any time, and without cause."[21]

More and more, marriage is seen as an arrangement for individual adult fulfillment, not for children or the larger society. Robert Bellah and his colleagues note that "we are shifting from a child-centered family to an adult-centered family. Or to put it even more strongly, as a French jurist has written, 'Instead of the individual "belonging" to the family, it is the family which is coming to be at the service of the individual.' This is a vivid way of saying that we no longer understand the institutional logic of family life."[22]

Amitai Etzioni suggests that "A few decades back, we [Americans] decided that marital bonds tied too tightly. . . . We responded with no-fault divorce. A generation later, many feel that our society oversteered the other way, rendering marriages almost disposable." He insists, "Our society requires a change in the habits of the heart, in the ways we think about marriage and how we value it."[23]

Etzioni provides an arresting image:

> Consider for a moment parenting as an industry. As farming declined, most fathers left to work away from home. Over the past twenty years millions of American mothers have sharply curtailed their work in the "parenting industry" by moving to work outside the home. . . . At the same time a much smaller number of child care personnel moved into the parenting industry.

If this were any other business, say, shoemaking, and more than half of the labor force had been lost and replaced with fewer, less-qualified hands and still we asked the shoemakers to produce the same number of shoes of the same quality (with basically no changes in technology), we would be considered crazy. But this is what happened to parenting. As first men and then women left to work outside the home, they were replaced by some child care services, a relatively small increase in baby-sitters and nannies, and some additional service by grandparents—leaving parenting woefully shorthanded. The millions of latchkey children, who are left alone for long stretches of time, are but the most visible result of the parenting deficit.[24]

This does not mean the family is dead or disappearing. Etzioni reminds us that many healthy families exist, despite much greater diversity. In fact "the majority of preschool children (about 78 percent) live in functioning families of one kind of another: 33 percent in families in which the father works outside the house and the mother is at home; 29 percent in which both parents work full-time; and 16 percent in which the married mother works part-time. The two-parent family is less common than it used to be, but it is far from dying out."[25] But families are increasingly under stress, both internally and externally.

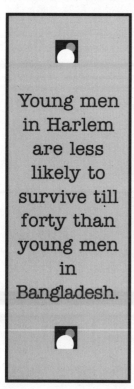

Young men in Harlem are less likely to survive till forty than young men in Bangladesh.

Popular Culture

The United States is experiencing a crumbling also of its broader cultural foundations, an unraveling of the social fabric that goes far beyond demographics and multiculturalism. Whether perceived as the "fraying" or "unraveling" of America (Robert Hughes, Stephen Monsma), "the closing of the American mind" (Allan Bloom), or a "crisis of cultural authority" (Os Guinness and others), the sociocultural crisis of the United States has been widely noted over the past few years.[26] Historian Arthur Schlesinger, Jr., speaks of the "disuniting" or "decomposition" of America.[27] This crisis of cultural cohesion is evident especially in three areas:

1. *Deep doubts about the value of human life.* The "sacredness" (specialness and inherent value) of human life has been a bedrock American conviction. Now, for increasing numbers,

personal convenience (a strange way of conceiving "choice") has replaced a fundamental valuing of human life for its own sake. We see this most starkly in the abortion debate. But it is evident also in issues of elder care and the terminally ill, where ethics is complicated by the role of ever-advancing medical technology. Casual abortion, domestic violence, child abuse and neglect, poor schools, and the gradual social acceptance of suicide and at least passive euthanasia all suggest lessening concern for human life.

Statistics tell the tale. Six thousand youth between the ages of fifteen and twenty-four commit suicide each year in the United States, a threefold jump since 1950. Violent crime rates among youth have shot up. In the early 1990s, America's long love affair with guns began to bear bitter fruit as social cohesion wore thin and domestic, gang, and random violence soared. Homicide rates have jumped, notably among young men, both black and white (though much more among blacks due to the weight of poverty). More than 24,000 people are killed in the United States by guns each year. Young men in Harlem are less likely to survive until the age of forty than young men in Bangladesh. Murder rates are much higher for the United States than for other industrialized nations. In 1993 *Time* magazine devoted a cover story to "America the Violent."

In 1990, 2,874 children and teenagers fell victim to guns. In the space of two generations, American society has gone from kids being kids, to kids having kids, to kids killing kids.

2. Add to this *the rise of the Instant Gratification Society*. People expect pleasure as a basic right—a shift from bearing present sacrifice in order to gain future satisfactions. This is fed in part by prosperity and consumerism. "If you want it, buy it; get it now, not tomorrow." Increasingly America is an entertainment culture "amusing ourselves to death," says Neil Postman.[28]

3. A third symptom of cultural decline is *the deterioration of American public education*. Among the economically developed nations, the United States now has perhaps the poorest education at the primary and secondary levels. Fourteen percent of young Americans never complete high

Social fragmentation is replacing cohesion in a dozen places: education, politics, urban life, religion, the family.

school, and many who do are ill equipped to function productively in society.

These symptoms all signify a society in decline. One can tote up the positive data, particularly economically and technologically. But the cracks in the foundation are widening. Fragmentation is replacing cohesion in a dozen places: education, politics, urban life, religion, the family. What Ralph Waldo Emerson felt 150 years ago is much more true now: "The state of society is one in which the members have suffered amputation from the trunk, and strut about [as] so many walking monsters—a good finger, a neck, a stomach, an elbow, but never a man."[29]

Here are the mind-numbing statistics that profile the new America and reveal a surprising degree of social disintegration:

- The United States ranks twenty-first among industrialized nations in infant mortality. While this is partly an economic issue, fundamentally it is a question of values and priorities. (Economics is, if anything, a matter of value.)
- Thirty percent of pregnant woman in the United States get no or inadequate prenatal care.
- More young black American men are in prison today than in college. This is a story not only of personal tragedy but also of economic waste. The high cost of imprisonment compared to the cost of a college education (with long-term social and economic benefits) suggests some of the dimensions of the problem.
- More than 40,000 women are held in U.S. prisons and jails. In 1990 the number of imprisoned women jumped by one-fourth, about twice the rate for men.
- The United States recently surpassed South Africa and the former Soviet Union in the percentage of its citizens behind bars, and it now leads the world.
- The United States has become Earth's most heavily armed and violent nation, as measured by handgun murders: over 10,000 persons in 1990, compared with ten in Australia, twenty-two in Great Britain and sixty-eight in Canada.

Will the United States confront and solve these combined social, political, and economic challenges? Can it take the hard steps to reverse disintegration, rebuild community, and reduce its huge debt burden? The catch is that such steps demand the moral strength to exercise discipline and self-sacrifice—and *this is precisely where the United States is growing ever weaker.* Increasing self-centeredness, the devaluing of human life, the breakdown of close community, the massive growth of

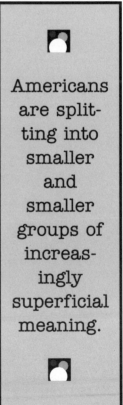

the entertainment industry, drug abuse, and an often mindless, uninformed, egocentric patriotism make the United States morally incapable of making hard choices.

If the negative trends continue for another two generations, one of two things will happen. The United States will disintegrate culturally to the point where a right-wing government, promising to end anarchy, imposes a virtual police state. Or else America will come increasingly under global (perhaps U.N.) control, with international sanctions and global financial strictures imposing the necessary social discipline.

The Niching of America—and the World?

A present irony of American society is the way it mixes social and moral confusion with economic dynamism. But every social problem is, of course, someone's economic opportunity. This is why fragmentation goes hand in hand with economic niching. American society is shifting from the melting pot to the market niche.

Niche-marketing has grown dramatically in recent years. It is a function of multiplying product variety and sophisticated technology on the one hand, and increased social fragmentation on the other. The two reinforce each other, with a twofold result: Even greater cultural diversity, and the increasing dominance (and cohesive force?) of economic and large-scale business enterprise.

Americans are splitting into smaller and smaller groups of increasingly superficial meaning.

Americans are coming to be defined more by their brand names than by their faiths, families, or philosophies. These are the new middle-class markers: Not so much Democrats and Republicans as Dockers and Miatas; not liberals and conservatives, but Levis and country music; not Christians and Jews, but Corvette lovers and Jaguar owners. Broad consensus groups are being replaced by the banality of brand loyalty—often T-shirted to the world, as if announcements of public import, by hundreds of micro-communities. These are really pseudo-communities, but they are keenly important commercially.

The United States is being segmented into

smaller niches as never before. The evidence is everywhere: hundreds of TV channels instead of three main networks; a mushrooming, dizzying variety of magazines, newsletters, and computer networks; proliferating social clubs and support groups; sophisticated radio niche-marketing. Affluence makes even small niches commercially profitable in an electronic society capable of computer-assisted design and manufacture (CAD/CAM) and computer-sorted advertising.

The niching of America strikes you forcefully when you scan the radio dial. I noticed this one day while driving, listening to one of those stations that keeps talking about how they have less talk. Scanning the dial, I noticed the dizzying spectrum of options: Country music, hard rock, soft rock, "classic" rock, easy listening, Golden Oldies (by decade!), Christian, classical, news-radio, and ethnic stations—with yet finer gradations within the niches. Each is a market slot with its own range of products and services. In some sense, each niche represents a separate community. One wonders how distinct these communities are in lifestyle, values, politics, and worldviews, not just in their spending habits.

These niches are more than mere markets. They really are distinct slices of American society, however much they overlap. And this social segmentation is happening at the same time that the bonds that traditionally bound Americans together in larger communities are dissolving. Broad generalizations and categories seldom fit anymore. Americans are splitting into smaller and smaller groups of increasingly superficial meaning. *Time* magazine asks, "Will scores of narrowcast [TV] channels devoted to arcana like needlepointing or fly fishing fracture whatever remains of a mass culture, leaving Americans with little common ground for discourse?"[30]

America has always had subgroups of special interests, of course. This is one of the nation's strengths, and a fruit of democracy. The new thing today is the decline of a broader cultural consensus and the way the fragmentation is commercially encouraged through increasing technological sophistication.

It takes more than labels, logos, and brand loyalty to form a culture or hold society together. Over the next generation the United States will face a deep crisis of social cohesion and cultural authority.

This is not a uniquely North American challenge, however. Similar trends are stirring in the most prosperous and technologically advanced societies—certainly in Japan, Singapore, Australia, Western Europe, and now even China. More important, this seems to be the direction of modern techno-urban society. To the extent that this tendency defines emerging global culture, it is a key part of the future of the planet. We are heading for the niching of the world.

First Signs of Renewal

Will the West's downhill slide continue? Not necessarily. The first mistake of futurists is to assume that current trends will go on indefinitely. Today's signs of decline could be reversed by a combination of hard times, new moral leadership in the political arena, and deep spiritual renewal.[31]

Some hopeful signs began to appear in the United States in 1993–94: a new emphasis on family life, an emerging consensus favoring gun control, innovative private and government programs to support family life, and increasing neighborhood activism here and there. Sexual abstinence outside of marriage was being rediscovered as a positive value. The surprising success of William Bennett's *The Book of Virtues* is an encouraging sign,[32] as is the rise of the Promise Keepers movement, calling men to commit to integrity and moral responsibility. Also, one noted a new willingness by national leaders to speak of the fraying of the social fabric as a question of moral vision and values. President Bill Clinton called for the rebuilding of community and family life as a top national priority. A new emphasis on community, cooperation, and teamwork was discernible—a trend that could be strengthened by the growing number of women leaders at all levels of society.

Another hopeful sign was the beginning of slow, steady economic growth combined with low inflation. If this continues for several years, it holds some promise for reducing unemployment, a prime contributor to social unrest. Since America's economy is increasingly tied into the global economy, though, the future remains unclear. Still, these considerations give some ground for guarded optimism.

The problem is that America's decline, and that of the West generally, is more than economic. Much of what is happening in the United States is mirrored in varying degrees throughout the North Atlantic nations and in culturally akin societies like Australia. Given the gravity of Western decline, and if history is any guide, deep cultural renewal will not come without some form of deep spiritual renewal.

What is lacking in the United States is an overarching moral vision, one that transcends narrow self-interest, partisanship, and individualism. Fundamentally this is a worldview question. If a nation's vision doesn't extend beyond its own greatness, it falls into the dangerous pit of nationalism as ideology. The Nation is seen as the highest good, sanctioned by God and the universe. This has been a perennial temptation in the United States, as it has been in many other countries and empires.

One's nation can be loved, revered, and honored. But Nation makes a terrible God and a cruel master. Some loftier, worthier goal, some cosmic vision, is needed. An end to Western decline and hope for renewal ultimately translate into questions of worldview and spiritual renewal.

131

CHAPTER NINE

New World Order:

Global Culture or Clash of Civilizations?

> The clash of civilizations will dominate global politics. The fault lines between civilizations will be the battle lines of the future.
>
> —**SAMUEL HUNTINGTON**
>
> The deepest change may be a planetary intuition that military war is pointless. . . . The new world's battlegrounds are markets and ideas.
>
> —**LANCE MORROW**[1]

The power shift of the late twentieth century can be read in various ways. At one level, it is a historic shift in empires. At another, it is a change from nation-states to a new global contest between Earth's several great civilizations. Others see a new global fragmentation or even social disintegration.

Empires still rise and fall and replace each other, as the past decade shows. The collapse of the USSR—really an empire—was powerfully symbolized by images of Berliners tearing down the Wall with their bare hands in 1989 and the "Second Russian Revolution" of 1991. The Iron Curtain crumpled. Reunification of Germany, the election of democratic governments in many Eastern European states, and a shift toward market economies soon followed.

These events mark the beginning, though not the end, of a global seismic shift. The coming decade will see the reunification of Korea (despite contrary rhetoric), a change in government in Cuba, and probably the collapse of totalitarianism in China. Diplomatic relations will be normalized between the United States and both Cuba and Viet Nam, and between China and Taiwan.

So the Cold War is over. Initial appearances say the United States won. Not really.

The past decade is better read as the decline of *two* great empires— and the rise of two or maybe three new ones whose power is primarily economic: a uniting Europe, the Pacific Rim complex led by Japan, and China. It is not yet clear whether China's recent resurgence will mean one or two Asian empires (China and Japan), and how South Korea, Taiwan, and Singapore will line up.

Today the dominant powers in these shifting empires are Germany and Japan—not coincidentally, the two main losers of World War II. These are new-style empires. They are not empires of armies and tanks, but of economic dynamism and technological prowess.

The Long Shadow of Global War

World War II, not 1989, was the great watershed. The first truly global war, World War II was all about empires: Hitler's Thousand Year Reich and the Japanese Empire of the Sun. It was also about economics. Both Germany and Japan built booming war economies that made dreams of empire believable. The attacks by both countries and their Axis partners eventually united Great Britain, the United States, the Soviet Union and many other nations against them. Germany and Japan were devastated, their economies shattered. Toward the end of the war the Soviet Union rushed in to grab much of Eastern Europe, including eastern Germany. The United States and the Soviet Union scrambled to net as many German secrets and rocket scientists as possible. German scientists later provided the foundation for guided missiles and space technology in both countries, as we now know.

The United States and the Soviet Union emerged from World War II as the only great nations with nuclear power and rocket technology— and with directly opposed political and economic systems. This shaped the forty-year Cold War. Two empires faced off globally. One was based partly on the appeal of Communist ideals but more impressively on brute military might, and for twenty-five years it was closely tied to Communist China. The other, the United States, built strategic economic ties and mutual defense agreements like NATO and SEATO with most of the key non-Communist nations of Europe and Asia. The 1944 Bretton Woods Conference in New Hampshire established the International Monetary Fund (IMF) and the World Bank, laying the basis for a postwar economic boom tied to the U.S. dollar. Ironically, Stalin refused to bring the USSR into this system. But by the time of Soviet collapse, the USSR was knocking at the door.

The Cold War was a half-century struggle. Two generations grew up feeling this ideological, economic, geopolitical, and at times military tug-of-war between two vastly different empires. Nearly all regional political questions were shaped by the East-West struggle.

The economic dynamism of the American-led alliance finally spelled the end of the Cold War and the defeat of Communism. Reasonably free market economies could deliver the goods, literally, that centralized command economies could not. After toying for two decades with some aspects of free market economy, under Mikhail Gorbachev the Soviet Communist system collapsed and nations formerly under Soviet control began turning, by fits and starts, to democratic reform and market economies.

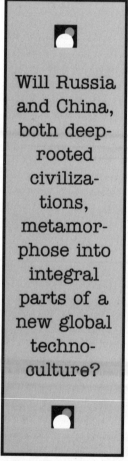

Will Russia and China, both deep-rooted civilizations, metamorphose into integral parts of a new global techno-culture?

Meanwhile, a similar but less visible process was transforming Communist China, especially after the death of Mao Zedong. Despite the crackdown on the student democracy movement in 1989, a decisive shift to a government-regulated market economy began. In 1993 placards all over Beijing proclaimed, "A More Open China Awaits the 2000 Olympics" as the government wooed and wowed the International Olympic Committee.

Deep change will reshape China over the next decade—either peacefully and gradually, or more disruptively, as in the former Soviet Union. We may expect more political and economic reform, more democracy, and, perhaps, partial disintegration as regional ethnic identities re-emerge. This transition will loose a knot of social changes: rapid urbanization, disintegration of traditional village and family patterns, and conflict over basic values.

A key question faces both Russia and China: Over the next generation, will these two great peoples return to their traditional roots, which are centuries or millennia old, or will online techno-society metamorphose them into mere parts of one global civilization?

The answer lies partly in the nature of civilizations—what they are, what holds them together, and what makes them change. We will examine this question shortly.

By 1990, the United States appeared to be the one remaining superpower. It boasted nuclear weapons, space technology, a global military presence, and a vital, highly diversified economy. The Soviet Union was never a nation; it was a Russian-led empire of conquered nations and peoples. In fact, the disintegration of the USSR looks a lot like the collapse of the Ottoman Turkish Empire in the nineteenth century. By 1993, it was clear that the fall of the USSR boosted the relative global influence of China, with its immense population and revved-up economy.

But other forces were at work. By 1990—in fact, nearly a decade earlier—it was clear that the energy driving the world economy had shifted to Western Europe and Japan. The reasons for this also trace back to World War II: the rebuilding of the Japanese and West German economies and political systems by (primarily) the United States. Japan and Germany lost the war militarily but won it economically, thanks to their major conqueror. The United States occupied Japan and built democratic institutions and a market economy there. Similarly the Western Allies, through the Marshall Plan, rebuilt West Germany's economy and steered it toward democracy.

Restrictions imposed on their militaries left West Germany and Japan free to develop vital economies geared primarily toward consumer goods and services. To some degree this gave both countries an economic edge over the United States and the USSR. The wartime destruction of German and Japanese factories and infrastructure forced them to rebuild from the ground up. In contrast, England, the cradle of the Industrial Revolution, was left relatively impoverished after the war, with aging and inefficient factories.

By 1990, Japan had surpassed the United States as the world's richest economy (by some measures). The European Common Market, helped along by U.S. partnership, NATO, and West Germany's postwar economic recovery, became the keystone of a resurgent Europe. The launching of full economic integration within the European Community in 1992 created an economic bloc larger than the United States. Meanwhile the United States moved from the world's largest creditor to its largest debtor nation in less than a decade, due to a massive military build-up and other policies of the Reagan administration. The high costs of German reunification and a global economic downturn slowed European integration in 1992–93, but the deeper currents of unification were still flowing.

In the 1990s, the world's three largest and strongest economies belong to the United States, the European Community, and Japan. But China's huge economy is growing faster than all three. Using the more accurate yardstick adopted by the International Monetary Fund in 1993, China's gross domestic product (GDP) is now Earth's third biggest, larger than Germany's or France's (though much smaller than the combined GDP of the European Community). China's economy will likely be larger than Japan's by 1995. Some forecasters say the combined economic strength of China, Taiwan, and Hong Kong will exceed America's by the year 2000.[2]

A four-way scramble is shaping up (Japan, China, the EC, and the NAFTA), with the kinds of global implications noted in earlier chapters. These four will increasingly be drawn together in one global economy, as we have seen. Yet it makes considerable difference where the economic dominance lies. Whether Earth's economy is more or less integrated and globally synergistic, or comparatively regionalized, with intense interregional competition, has large political and ecological consequences.

The major powers of the next thirty years will be Europe (including the integration of at least some of the former Communist bloc countries, such as Poland, Hungary, Slovakia, and the Czech Republic), Japan (with its Pacific Rim trading partners), and China. These will be economic, not primarily military or political, powers. Yet they will have great cultural influence. Because of the emergence of the interlinked global society described earlier, these will not be empires in any traditional sense. But they will be the primary shaping, trend-setting nodes in the global web.

Emerging Americo-Japanese Pop Culture

A new phenomenon of the 1990s will be an emerging Americo-Japanese pop culture. This new hybrid blends popular U.S. tastes and trends and Japan's technological and economic prowess. It may produce a new global culture that in surprising ways parallels Greco-Roman society 2,000 years ago.

This sounds absurd, because the two cultures seem so alien to each other. Consider the evidence, however, and a lesson from history.

By the first century A.D., Greek art and ideas had permeated the Mediterranean world and become the dominant cultural influence, a process called Hellenization. Greek became the *lingua franca*, the common language of trade, education, and international communications. Roman school boys did their lessons in Greek, and Greek teachers were much prized throughout the empire. Greek culture and learning flourished in Alexandria, Egypt, and many other cities.

But it was Rome that controlled the Mediterranean world. With the rise of the empire, Roman roads, armies, and political and legal structures bound the world together. While diverse ethnic groups populated the empire's scattered regions, the blending of Greek culture and Roman power was the real glue of social cohesion.

So today we speak of the Greco-Roman world, the dominant political and cultural influence for four centuries. This influence, dynamically interacting with rapidly spreading Christianity, shaped the culture of Europe. Eventually, through the global influence of Europe and later the United States, it touched the whole world. What came to be called "the West" was heavily indebted to Greco-Roman culture in its education, arts, political structures, and worldview. Public buildings and monuments throughout the West remind us of this.

It is fascinating, therefore, to see something similar happening globally today. The new culture is not Greek or Roman, but American and Japanese. By 1990 the technological and industrial edge of North America had passed to Japan. Yet the dominant popular cultural values globally continued to be American. New supermarkets throughout Asia may be part of Japan's Sogo or Yaohan chains, but the music piped over the speakers is American, as are many of the styles. Japanese products exported globally have English labels and instructions.

Japan itself has been deeply shaped by English-speaking culture. The most popular playwright in Japan is Shakespeare; baseball is the leading sport. But it is particularly American popular culture that is making inroads. Rock stars from the United States regularly tour Japan. The big movie hits are all American. The Japanese sell VCRs to the United States, but they watch American videos at home. The new $40 million Elvisland outside Tokyo features American styles of the 1950s. Tokyo's Disneyland is already a huge success, logging 300,000 visitors weekly. Over a third of Japanese weddings are Western "Christian" style, though only about 3 percent of the population is Christian. *Time* writer Barry Hillenbrand notes, "America is an essential element of growing up urban in Japan."[3]

When Japanese firms buy big American film studios and Sony signs up U. S. superstars like Michael Jackson, this simply underscores this trend. These developments represent, of course, other global trends, as well: instant access, the growing cultural role of media and entertainment, the rise of a global teen culture. Aping American styles in Japan is a way to assert adolescent independence—a rather un-Japanese thing to do. Donald Ritchie, an American observer of modern Japan, writes: "Young people view America as a dangerous wilderness filled with freedom and adventure. Embracing America is a way of rebelling against the strict paternalistic society at home."[4]

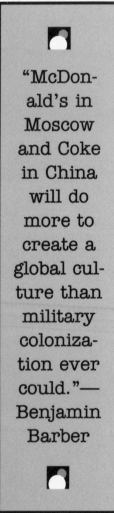

"McDonald's in Moscow and Coke in China will do more to create a global culture than military colonization ever could."— Benjamin Barber

American dominance in popular culture lies behind some of the economic shifts in Japan. "No wonder the Japanese are buying Hollywood film studios even faster than Americans are buying Japanese television sets," notes Benjamin Barber. He adds:

This kind of software supremacy may in the long term be far more important than hardware supremacy, because culture has become more potent than armaments. What is the power of the Pentagon compared with Disneyland? Can the Sixth Fleet keep up with CNN? McDonald's in Moscow and Coke in China will do more to create a global culture than military colonization ever could. It is less the goods than the brand names that do the work for they convey *life-style images* that alter perception and challenge behavior. They make up the seductive software of McWorld's common . . . soul.[5]

Japanese fascination with Americana carries over to food, clothes, and ideas. Often American books sell more in Japanese translation than they do in U.S. editions. Also, the three million annual Japanese visitors to the United States and the Japanese students in American universities heighten cultural interaction and the blending of cultural ways and concepts.

Meanwhile, less obviously, Japan is changing America. Karaoke sing-along bars are now common in U.S. cities (as they are globally, in fact). Japanese cuisine is popular, and Japanese ways are affecting business practice. At a deeper level, one senses a shift away from the anti-Japanese phobia stirred up during the Second World War.

One shiny sign of this cultural blending is the new Americo-Japanese automobile. The distinction between "American" and "Japanese" cars is vanishing as more and more parts and styles are interchangeable, and as manufacture has become increasingly internationalized. A Honda from Ohio may get half its parts from Japan and half from the United States.

A Ford may have a Mitsubishi engine, or be built by Mazda. In fact, a new hybrid car is emerging, the blending of American and Japanese enterprise. This would have been unthinkable a generation ago. And cars are only the most visible part of a wide range of Americo-Japanese consumer goods.

Behind this trend is a growing U.S.-Japanese trade interdependence. From 1985 to 1992 American exports to Japan more than doubled, rising to about $50 billion annually. The two economies are increasingly linked—not least by the fact that Japanese firms employ 600,000 Americans and Japanese investors bankroll $180 billion or more of the United States' massive debt. And together these two countries now look at China and see a billion buyers of TVs, CDs, VCRs and, eventually, PDAs equipped with Global Positioning System (GPS).

Broad cultural contact and economic ties do not necessarily mean cultural blending, of course. Many foresee growing tension and even conflict between Japan and the United States as Japan reaches or surpasses America economically. But even enemies often end up imitating each other. The vanquished militarily can conquer culturally, as so often in history, and as the analogy with Greece and Rome illustrates. The likely scenario is this: While these nations' elders suspect and compete with each other, the younger generation, less concerned with politics and economics—and cheered on by businesses alert to the massive youth market—will build a new hybrid popular culture from both U.S. and Japanese components.

Thus the social force that will likely shape the world for the next half-century is Americo-Japanese popular culture. Not so much the United States and Japan *as nations,* but the values, styles, and energies that arise from the global blending of influences from these two powerful but contrasting societies.

The Rise of Latin America

Another mark of today's global power shift is a deep transformation of Latin America. For centuries, most of South and Central America has been known for its poverty, political instability, debt-ridden economies, and (often) repressive governments. Today a much different picture is emerging.

Latin America is changing economically, politically, and spiritually. Although many of its national economies are still shaky, a new economic dynamism is driving much of the continent, as we saw in chapter 3. Several nations are developing robust economies with growing international trade. Alongside government-sanctioned enterprise, a flourishing "informal economy" is also bringing change. Peruvian entrepreneur and economist Hernando de Soto's *The Other Path,* which became a Latin American best-seller, shows that this informal economic sector is often larger than the official one.[6]

Politically, much of Latin America turned toward greater democracy and freedom in the 1980s. By 1991, almost all the nations of Central and South America had democratically elected governments—a major turnaround from the previous decade. This was fueled by the collapse of Communist ideology, massive urbanization, and the deeper currents of globalization. In addition, Latin America has been undergoing a spiritual transformation, as documented by London sociologist David Martin in his book, *Tongues of Fire: The Explosion of Protestantism in Latin America.*

Martin argues that Pentecostal Protestantism in Latin America offers a spiritual dynamism and sense of responsible community reminiscent of the Methodist Revival in eighteenth-century England. The movement is also fed by urbanization and the rise of megacities like São Paulo and Mexico City. Says Martin, in Latin American Pentecostalism "millions of people are absorbed within a protective social capsule where they acquire new concepts of self and new models of initiative and voluntary organization."[7] Similarly, David Stoll writes in *Is Latin America Turning Protestant?* that "evangelical Protestants are giving Latin Americans a new form of social organization and a new way to express their hopes."[8]

This Latin American resurgence may impact global society in some surprising ways. Probably the most important result will be a closer networking with the global economy and global society generally. Many of these nations are entering the world arena as equal partners, not economic basket cases or banana republics. This too is part of the global power shift. A major economic trend, as we saw in chapter 3, is regional economic integration through trade pacts. A sizeable part of Central and South America may be drawn into NAFTA, the North American Free Trade Area. Countries that tie into the NAFTA stand to gain, but possibly to the further impoverishment of sidelined nations.

Deep problems persist in Latin America. Marvin Cetron and Owen Davies write, "Pressing questions remain to be answered during the 1990s. Will the new democratic governments survive? And will their more market-oriented economic policies at last relieve the crushing poverty and extreme income disparities?" They conclude, "The region will remain populated by a very few 'haves' and many 'have-nots' for many years to come. Yet the 1990s offer the best opportunities for improvement that Latin America has ever had."[9]

The Democratization of China

We noted above China's new economic dynamism—again, a development largely unforeseen a generation ago. Economic ties among China, Taiwan, Korea, Japan, and the United States are growing stronger. Intentionally or not (and certainly with some ambivalence), China is being drawn into the global economy. As the world's largest nation—more than 1.1 billion people—China will play a growing global role. It will wield much wider influence in the twenty-first century than ever before.

In 1997 Hong Kong reverts to China. This has spawned considerable anxiety in Hong Kong and prompted a brain drain to Canada, Australia, and Singapore. But the emerging global economy plus some political liberalization within China almost guarantee that Hong Kong, with its busy stock exchange, will continue to be one of Earth's leading financial markets. It also will be a key catalyst for China's integration into the world economy, as China seeks to build (in effect) a string of Hong Kongs along its coastline.

Much of the Communist power structure in China will have collapsed by 1997. The ideology behind it has been discredited. A generational change in leadership and growing economic and cultural contact with other nations will likely bring democratic reforms similar to those that transformed Eastern Europe and the Soviet Union, though more gradually and less disruptively.

The excesses and corruption of Mao Zedong's long regime are becoming generally known within China itself. The notorious and vicious Kang Sheng, long Mao's right-hand man, was discredited in an official Communist Party biography of him, published in 1980 when Kang was posthumously expelled from the party. Something like *glasnost* is coming to China, a decade after Gorbachev brought it to the Soviet Union. With such opening, and with market-style economic reform, the pressures toward democracy will become irrepressible.

Paramount leader Deng Xiaoping continued to push economic reforms even after Tienanmen Square. State-run media in 1992 called for "urgent" reforms and an end to ideological "dogmatism." The government endorsed the development of "a capitalist economy . . . as a useful supplement to the socialist economy." As part of this, five Special Economic Zones (Shenzhen and four other cities in coastal provinces near Hong Kong) are rapidly developing as capitalist production centers and key nodes in the global network.

The role of China's vast military establishment is also being transformed. "Beijing since 1985 has encouraged hundreds of military factories to halt production of bullets, tanks, and missles and turn out soda, fans, toys, and other consumer goods," note Ann Scott Tyson and James L. Tyson of *The Christian Science Monitor.* Units of the military are receiving less subsidy from the government and are operating in effect as state-affiliated capitalist enterprises. Meanwhile the ideological commitment of the army to Communism has waned, and the loyalty of many units to the central government is very much in question.[10] At the same time, China is rapidly modernizing its military and is a major international arms supplier.

China's economic boom has big ecological costs, and these must eventually be paid. Earth's largest nation is not immune to the lethal spiral of population, environment, and social forces we noted in chapter 5. The magnet of coastal economic development has combined with serious soil erosion and deforestation in interior areas to produce a major population shift. Robert Kaplan notes, "Large-scale population movements are under way, from inland China to coastal China and from villages to cities, leading to a crime surge like the one in Africa and to growing regional disparities and conflicts in a land with a strong tradition of warlordism and a weak tradition of central government."[11]

The long-term direction of China is uncertain. A trend toward broader democracy seems likely, either throughout China or in major sections, should the nation break into smaller pieces. China's recent economic growth, coupled with its huge population and economic restructuring, certainly make it a rising world power.

Splitting Rich and Poor

In 1979 the late Herman Kahn of the Hudson Institute wrote about "the dramatic increase in the disparity of per capita income between the wealthiest and poorest nations." Kahn predicted that the gap between rich and poor would almost certainly worsen over the next several decades. Closing it "simply cannot be approached, much less attained, in the next 100 years."

Despite this unsettling prospect, Kahn was optimistic. The chasm results "because the rich are getting richer," not because the poor are getting poorer. "This is not necessarily a bad thing for the poor, at least if they compare themselves with their own past or their own present rather than with a mythical theoretical gap," Kahn saw the rich/poor split as "a basic engine of growth" that "generates or supports most of the basic processes by which the poor are becoming rich, or at least less poor." The gap could be closed only by a massive relocation of capital investment and consumer goods—politically impossible. But left alone, Kahn argued, the problem would finally heal itself: "The widening gap is in reality a force for transferring the benefits of economic development to the poor." Like difference in water levels, the rising tide of wealth would spill over and eventually reach the poor.[12]

This hard-headed analysis assumes, probably naively, that such a widening rich/poor split would not prove unsettling, perhaps plunging the world into chaos or war.[13] It does reveal, though, two key facts: The gap between rich and poor almost certainly will increase over the next two generations. And approximately half of Earth's population will be neither rich nor absolutely poor, but will be in a middle range of comparatively low and often inadequate income.

The gap between rich and poor in large measure mirrors global economic policy and power. As John Briggs notes, "The existence of [stateless] corporations, taken with the vast debt owed by many developing countries to the bankers of the developed world, illustrate the general maldistribution of power between the rich North and the poor South." To a large degree, this is the engine that elevates the rich from the poor.

At present the widening gap between rich and poor, both internationally and within nations, is one of the world's megadangers as global society enters the twenty-first century. Where will it lead? There are four likely outcomes:

1. Global public awareness of the gap between rich and poor will rise dramatically over the next generation, perhaps provoking growing political unrest in poorer nations.
2. Latin America, Australia, and parts of Africa will face a crisis of cultural identity as they feel both the pull toward global integration and the magnetism of national self-image and self-assertion.
3. New ideologies and movements (political, religious, or both) may arise that draw their energy from the tension between rich and poor in the world and that give novel or appealing interpretations to this issue. The combination of poverty, oppression, and economic change historically has spawned revolutionary political, religious, or tribal movements—sometimes with world-shaking results.[14]
4. The emerging global economy may prove a hopeful sign. As more and more nations shift to open markets and cooperation, international trade will grow and multinational linkages at all levels will strengthen. The world economy will be less split between a few dominant nations and a mass of disadvantaged poor countries. This could bring a more equitable global economic network. The result may be a narrowing of the wealth gap between rich and poor nations, though not necessarily between rich and poor people within these countries.

Tribes, Nations, and Civilizations

The global picture consists not so much of nations as of peoples and cultures. Clashing currents of globalization and ethnic reawakening seem to be shaping the future. Benjamin Barber argues that the world is increasingly caught between the competing forces of *tribalism* and *globalism*—a world of "Jihad versus McWorld." Barber writes:

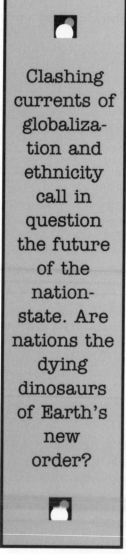

Clashing currents of globalization and ethnicity call in question the future of the nation-state. Are nations the dying dinosaurs of Earth's new order?

Just beyond the horizon of current events lie two possible political futures—both bleak, neither democratic. The first is a *retribalization* of large swaths of humankind by war and bloodshed: a threatend Lebanonization of national states in which culture is pitted against culture, people against people, tribe against tribe—a Jihad in the name of a hundred narrowly conceived faiths against every kind of interdependence, every kind of artificial social cooperation and civic mutuality. The second is being borne in on us by the onrush of economic and ecological forces that demand integration and uniformity and that mesmerize the world with fast music, fast computers, and fast food—with MTV, Macintosh, and McDonald's, pressing nations into one commercially homogeneous global network: one McWorld tied together by technology, ecology, communications, and commerce. The planet is falling precipitantly apart *and* coming reluctantly together at the very same moment.[15]

Conflicts in India, the former USSR, and Bosnia illustrate these tendencies, Barber believes. "The old interwar national state based on territory and political sovereignty looks to be a mere transitional development."

The globalization of politics is being driven by four "imperatives," Barber argues: markets, resources, information technology, and ecology. He observes, "Enlightenment science and the technologies derived from it are inherently universalizing. They entail a quest for descriptive principles of general application, a search for universal solutions to particular problems, and an unswerving embrace of objectivity and impartiality." This in turn requires an open flow of information, making "science and globalization practical allies." "The pursuit of science and technology asks for, even compels, open societies."[16]

All four of these imperatives, Barber argues, are "transnational, trans-ideological, and transcultural. Each applies impartially to Catholics, Jews, Muslims, Hindus, and Buddhists; to democrats and totalitarians; to capitalists and socialists." And the kind of globalization they foster is not necessarily democratic.[17]

The contrasting reality is tribalism, "the Lebanonization of the World." The question is whether the model of the future will be Lebanon or Switzerland. Today the "world's real actors," says Barber, are "subnational factions in permanent rebellion against uniformity and intergration . . . they are cultures, not countries; rebellious factions and dissenting minorities at war . . . with the traditional nation-state. . . . people without countries, inhabitating nations not their own, seeking smaller worlds within borders that will seal them off from modernity."[18]

Barber overlooks the fact that some of these "tribes" are actually ancient peoples and nations, forced to become now part of one empire, then of another. Croatia, for example, was an independent country from approximately A.D. 900–1100. Ethnic and national identity was not lost, only submerged. It surfaces when empires crumble.

Floods of refugees also rise when empires crumble. Any viable New World Order will have to confront the global disorder caused by mass migrations of displaced peoples. The world refugee population reached eighteen million in 1992, according to the U.N. High Commissioner for Refugees, nearly twice the number in 1982 and nine times the 1976 total of about three million.[19] Earth now has more refugees than the total population of Australia or Saudi Arabia. In fact, some 100 million people—two percent of the world's population—have left their home countries in the past three years, according to a U.N. Population Fund estimate. This flood of refugees and assorted migrants further aggravates the "tribalism" resurgence.

Where will all this lead? Barber suggests that "globalization will eventually vanquish retribalization." The most attractive outcome, he writes, would be "a confederal union of semi-autonomous communities smaller than nation-states, tied together into regional economic associations and markets larger than nation-states." Such an arrangement would be "participatory and self-determining in local matters at the bottom, representative and accountable at the top."[20]

Between the global-tribal tensions, however, lies another current, which Barber overlooks: *regionalism*. Globalizing forces may fail to unify the world. Regional trade zones could divide Earth into competing blocs, though economic and ecological realities would ensure considerable interdependence among these.

A Coming Anarchy?

A more somber picture is painted by Robert D. Kaplan, a traveling editor for *The Atlantic Monthly*. In a provocative article entitled "The Coming Anarchy," Kaplan argues that today's chaos in several African nations is a preview of things to come globally. The culprit is the combination of social and political turmoil with environmental collapse— bringing "the withering away of central governments, the rise of tribal and regional domains, the unchecked spread of disease, and the growing pervasiveness of war." Kaplan summarizes:

> West Africa is becoming *the* symbol of worldwide demographic, environmental, and societal stress, in which criminal anarchy emerges as the real "strategic" danger. Disease, overpopulation, unprovoked crime, scarcity of resources, refugee migrations, the increasing erosion of nation-states and international borders, and the empowerment of private armies, security firms, and international drug cartels are now most tellingly demonstrated through a West African prism.[21]

In Sierra Leone for example, Kaplan says, "A premodern formlessness governs the battlefield, evoking the wars in medieval Europe prior to the 1648 Peace of Westphalia, which ushered in the era of organized nation-states." The result is massive social dislocation: 400,000 citizens internally displaced; another 380,000 refugees fleeing to neighboring Guinea and Liberia.[22]

We fail to understand the depth of upheavals in places like Sierra Leone and Nigeria, Kaplan argues, unless we understand the environmental factors. "Environment" will be "*the* national-security issue of the early twenty-first century," Kaplan maintains. "The political and strategic impact of surging populations, spreading disease, deforestation and soil erosion, water depletion, air pollution, and, possibly, rising sea levels in critical, overcrowded regions like the Nile Delta and Bangladesh— developments that will prompt mass migrations and, in turn, group conflicts—will be the core foreign-policy challenge from which most others will ultimately emanate."

When social chaos reaches this stage, war becomes an accepted, even celebrated, way of life (as it was for major periods in medieval Europe). Humans (or at least, males) are naturally aggressive. "Only when people attain a certain economic, educational, and cultural standard is this trait tranquilized," says Kaplan. "In light of the fact that 95 percent of the earth's population growth will be in the poorest areas of the globe, the question is not whether there will be war (there will be a lot of it) but what kind of war. And who will fight whom?" Any proposed New World Order will have to take this into account.[23]

Kaplan's analysis is a splash of cold water in the face of utopian dreams. The lethal spiral of population growth, environmental crises, and social upheaval is overlooked too often. Still global or regional anarchy is not inevitable. Growing ecological awareness may help break or reverse the cycle. Global economic integration could help bring stability and prosperity to troubled areas, as could other forms of global networking to be discussed shortly. And we must leave open the possibility of broad-based renewal movements that could release unexpected energy for change and social cohesion.

Global Culture or Clash of Civilizations?

As we see, proposed scenarios for emerging global society span a wide spectrum. But what is the glue that really holds societies together? This is an important issue, because scenarios for the future often make broad assumptions about human society—what it is and how it changes or resists change.

Harvard professor Samuel Huntington argues that neither economics nor politics, but deep cultural identity will shape the future. He writes,

> The great divisions among humankind and the dominating source of conflict will be cultural. Nation states will remain the most powerful actors in world affairs, but the principal conflicts of global politics will occur between nations and groups of different civilizations. The clash of civilizations, not tribes, will dominate global politics. The fault lines between civilizations will be the battle lines of the future.[24]

Huntington argues further that with the end of the Cold War, distinctions of First, Second, and Third Worlds have become obsolete. Now deeper realities of culture and civilization are pushing to the fore. The emerging reality is not three "worlds" or 192 nations, but seven or eight great world civilizations. The prospect is global culture wars.

Huntington defines a civilization as a "cultural entity"—that is, a broad cultural complex not part of a larger culture. "A civilization is thus the highest cultural grouping of people and the broadest level of cultural identity people have short of that which distinguishes humans

147

from other species. It is defined both by common objective elements, such as language, history, religion, customs, institutions, and by the subjective self-identification of people."[25]

Huntington believes that differences among civilizations are basic and enduring. They outlast political arrangements and economic systems. "Civilizations are differentiated from each other by history, language, culture, tradition and, most important, religion," he says. They have "different views on the relations between God and man, the individual and the group, the citizen and the state, parents and children, husband and wife, as well as differing views of the relative importance of rights and responsibilities, liberty and authority, equality and hierarchy." In other words, different worldviews. Rooted in centuries of history, these differences "will not soon disappear."[26]

The next thirty years will show whether today's trends are bringing one new global culture, or a rebirth of Earth's historic civilizations.

Earth's great civilizations, Huntington suggests, are Confucian, Japanese, Islamic, Hindu, Western, Slavic-Orthodox, Latin American, and perhaps African. "The most important conflicts of the future will occur along the cultural fault lines separating these civilizations."[27] Because of these deep tensions, a truly global culture is not likely. "For the relevant future, there will be no universal civilization, but instead a world of different civilizations, each of which will have to learn to coexist with the others," Huntington concludes.[28]

This scenario recognizes the deep structure of culture and also the capacity of civilizations to sustain their core values and identity over many centuries. But is the assumption of cultural continuity still valid? Earth's civilizations have never faced today's challenge: a wave of potent trends, all global and all increasingly linked. The key question then becomes: How stable are the great civilizations in the face of these singular global currents? How will these trends affect the glue holding civilizations together? Will the new Earth-Currents reshape these civilizations' history, language, culture, tradition and religion (the key elements of culture, says Huntington), or be shaped by them? Or both? Generational continuity of culture can no longer be assumed in *any* civilization.

The issue, then, is the nature of culture and civilization itself. What happens to the next two generations will be crucial. Within thirty years we will see whether today's Earth Currents are really producing one global culture, a resurgence of historic cultures and civilizational identities, or global anarchy. This may be the deepest question in prospects for any new global order.

A New World Order?

It already seems an eon since U.S. President George Bush announced a dawning "new world order." That was in 1990. Bush foresaw continued leadership by the United States, growing international cooperation, and a more activist role for the United Nations.

In fact, as the above analysis shows, any New World Order likely to emerge in the next generation or two will be based on more sweeping principles than these. If it is effective, it will necessarily be rooted in long-term care of the environment, respect for all cultures and religious traditions, economic cooperation, and democratized information and technology. It will practice the premise that providing the primary priorities of food, shelter, security, and employment for all Earth's people is a shared global responsibility and a realistic economic option.

Does this require world government, a real United Nations? The role of the U.N. grew dramatically in the 1980s and 1990s. But world government is not necessarily where Earth is headed. At least not in the sense of some centralized political and military authority. Organic models will prove more winsome and workable. With the rise of the ecological model, the likely scenario is several mutually interdependent global and/or regional authorities and networks functioning in a sort of check-and-balance symbiosis. Some measure of global authority will be needed in certain areas—economics and finance; settling international, inter-ethnic, or other disputes; responding to natural disasters; and exercising military police force in order to ensure a just peace, for example. The cooperative arrangements and authorities worked out in Western Europe over the past thirty years or so may provide a model for what must emerge globally.

The United Nations itself will need to be reformed and restructured to more justly represent Earth's peoples. Its present form is a creature of the Cold War. It reflects the political realities of the 1940s, not the 1990s. The only permanent seats on the fifteen-member Security Council are China, France, Russia (succeeding the USSR), the United Kingdom, and the United States. This must change. Nations could take turns in rotation, or some form of regional representation could be used.

Mikhail Gorbachev has recognized this need. He foresees a restructuring of the U.N. in part due to environmental pressures. He suggests an advisory council, "a kind of chamber of representatives of professions," to bring together knowledgeable scientists and others to develop and approve ecologically-sound policies.[29]

The newly formed Unrepresented Nations and Peoples Organization (UNPO, founded in 1990) is another piece in the global puzzle. Its birth is a witness to "tribalism" and the reassertion of ethnic and other subnational identities. But it is equally a sign of globalism. Marginalized groups are finding each other and networking globally for their common interests. The new entity already includes forty or so groups representing 130 million people from dozens of countries around the world. The new network should, in fact, be a force for greater global cohesion.

A "kaleidoscopic cross section of the oppressed, the colonized, the neglected and the rebellious," UNPO is a growing voice for unrepresented ethnic and subnational groups. Members must disavow terrorism and show that they are really representative. Who are the members? Kurds, Frisians, Sioux, Mohawks, Ogonis, Nagas, Sakhas, Batwa Pygmies, and many others with names unfamiliar to Western ears. Four founding members have already become independent states: Estonia, Armenia, Georgia, and Latvia.[30]

UNPO is another sign of the times. It is further evidence of today's Earth Currents, the globalizing of tribalism and the tribalizing of globalism.

Global Order and Global Worldviews

The most a global network of political and economic checks and balances can provide is the environment in which the human race can continue to develop peacefully. Cooperative global networking can preserve an earthly home where people and cultures learn to live together with mutual respect or at least mutual tolerance, and everyone is able to "sit under [their] own vine and under [their] own fig tree" (Micah 4:4).

Larger questions of meaning and destiny, however, must be factored in to the global equation. These are the questions of mind and spirit; of faith and values. They are worldview questions. We may hope for a global society sufficiently free from disaster and unnecessary suffering so that these questions can be addressed in an open market of ideas and worldviews.

These are the deeper issues, the more profound currents. It is to these questions of values, beliefs, and worldviews that we now turn.

PART TWO
EMERGING GLOBAL WORLDVIEWS:

What
Are
Folks
Believing?

CHAPTER TEN

Global Economics:
A Pragmatic Worldview

In 1946, with the advent of the computer, information became the organizing principle in production. With this, a new basic civilization came into being.
—PETER DRUCKER[1]

The ideas of economists and political philosophers, both when they are right and when they are wrong, are more powerful than is commonly understood. Indeed the world is ruled by little else. Practical men, who believe themselves to be quite exempt from any intellectual influences, are usually the slaves of some defunct economist.
—JOHN MAYNARD KEYNES[2]

I ncreasingly we see that global trends and worldviews interact. They shape each other. We have observed how every global trend, without exception, raises worldview questions. These questions we must now explore. What do these trends suggest about world perception and belief and thus about the future of human society on Earth?

Economics and politics don't function in a vacuum. They are part of a larger society in which people are asking questions and seeking answers.

We wonder: Is there some unity beneath today's ever greater complexity? How do we connect and make sense of basic EarthCurrents? Does everything fit together in some way? These are worldview questions. Pondering the future raises such questions for thinking people. The reverse also is true: Our views and attitudes about the future reflect the worldviews we employ—consciously or unconsciously.

So we turn from trends to worldviews. Just as seven or eight global trends are transforming our world, so a half-dozen emerging worldviews are changing the way we see the world. Earth is now a marketplace of competing worldviews. The global shopping mall offers not only goods and services but also quite different views of reality.

In this chapter we will examine the first of these: Global economics seen as a worldview. Then we will turn to several other worldview "products." First, however, it will be helpful to think a bit more about the nature of worldviews.

Our Worldview Lens

A worldview is the grid we use to make sense of the cosmos. It is our set of silent assumptions as we navigate life's currents. It is our sense of the world, the framework that tells us what is true and important and what isn't. Worldviews answer questions of right and wrong and serve as the basis for countless daily decisions. Without a workable worldview, people are immobilized or else swept around like loose leaves, wherever the winds of events and the push of other people drive them.

To be more precise, a worldview is "a set of presuppositions (or assumptions) which we hold (consciously or unconsciously) about the basic makeup of our world," writes James Sire. "A world view is composed of a number of basic presuppositions, more or less self-consistent, generally unquestioned by each person, rarely, if ever, mentioned to one's friends, and only brought to mind when challenged by a foreigner from another ideological universe."[3]

A "well-rounded world view," Sire says, will answer five basic questions:

> Just as eight global trends are transforming our world, so a half-dozen emerging worldviews are changing the way we see the world.

1. What is really real?
2. What does it mean to be human?
3. What happens to us at death?
4. What is the basis of morality?
5. What is the meaning of history?

These questions are not exhaustive. Other issues may arise, such as the nature of the external world (Is it real?), determinism or freedom, how and what we can know, and "Who is in charge of this world—God, or man, or man and God, or no one at all?"

Nearly everyone assumes answers to these questions, Sire argues. "We will adopt either one stance or another; refusing to adopt an explicit world view will turn out to be itself a world view or at least a philosophic position. In short, we are caught. So long as we live, we will live either the examined or the unexamined life."[4]

A worldview is our key to the universe. It is the lens through which we see. Danah Zohar calls a worldview "a theme running through a life," binding everything "into a coherent whole." She recalls her own struggle as an adolescent to build a personal worldview, "to find answers to life's 'big questions': who am I, why am I here, what is my place in the scheme of things, why is the world like it is, what does it mean that one day I must die?" (In a later chapter we will see what she found.)

A comprehensive worldview encompasses the personal, social, and spiritual dimensions of life, Zohar says. Lack or loss of a coherent worldview brings alienation from oneself, from society, and from a sense of ultimate wholeness. "A successful worldview must, in the end, draw all these levels—the personal, the social, and the spiritual—into one coherent whole. If it does so, the individual has access to some sense of who he is, why he is here, how he relates to others, and how it is valuable to behave. If it does not, the world it was meant to articulate will fragment and the individual will suffer alienation on some level, perhaps on all levels."[5]

A credible worldview answers life's ultimate questions. In particular, it gives responses to these key questions:

1. Is there purpose to life? If so, what is it? (This is not essentially different from the ancient philosophical question: What is the good?)
2. What is the design of the universe?
3. How does my life relate to other people, to history, and to the universe?
4. Where is history going? Is there an end or goal to history?

These are the questions of *purpose, design, relationships,* and *the future.* While linked, they are also distinct. They deal with the meaning (if any) of life in all its actual and potential dimensions.[6]

Today a global market of worldviews offers us many styles, sizes, and colors to choose from. We will examine six viewpoints or "working philosophies" that qualify as global worldviews. Some are new, some old, and some are new variations on old themes. Each, in a certain way, makes sense. Each provides a framework for life to those who hold it.

These worldviews may not be mutually exclusive. Doubtless each contains some truth. Probably most of us "wear" more than one worldview, though usually one is dominant. E. P. Sanders is right: "Worldviews, in fact, are not very often exclusive. Most of us carry two or three around with us all the time."[7] However, the worldviews outlined here will probably be the top-selling philosophies over the next two generations.

The Economic Worldview

Peter Drucker's comment, quoted at the beginning of the chapter, suggests the key role of economics in human civilization and the way it has been transformed by computer technology. Economics assumes an increasingly central place in global society, and not merely in the sense of dollars and cents. For many today, economics has become a worldview—their lens on reality.

Today Earth's economists and business leaders are busy with the practical task of recreating the world. Most have little time for worldview discussion. They are immersed in budgets, strategic planning, and providing the whole range of goods and services for emerging global society. At the same time, knowingly or not, these business practicioners are building a new worldview. While some intellectuals talk about the impossibility or uselessness of worldviews, Earth's financiers and entrepreneurs are building a new global worldview on the foundation of economic pragmatism.

Global economists and other leaders talk of a New Economic Order. For many, this means more than world trade and monetary policy. It is really worldview talk, though not called that. Actually at stake is a worldview that sees the emergence of a new global economic community as the best hope for humanity.

Over the past two centuries, economics has grown in global importance; even more so in the past forty years. As we noted in chapter 3, economic theory and practice now often overshadow politics and military might. This is a major shift in reality and in viewpoint. Economics

> As the steam engine brought a mechanical worldview, so the information revolution gives us a biological model, says Peter Drucker.

has often been a key underlying factor in wars and other conflicts, of course. But today's new global economic integration is bringing a decided shift from politics to economics. Economic life requires reasonable social and political stability. For this reason, many argue that increasing global economic integration will bring greater global stability.

How does economics function as a worldview? Both economics and worldviews concern *value* and the arrangement of society. Economics shapes worldviews and vice versa. Peter Drucker suggests that as the invention of the steam engine about 1700 (a technological and economic breakthrough) introduced the mechanical worldview, so the computer age is pushing society from the machine model to a new model. Now "information will be the organizing principle for work. Information, however, is the basic principle of biological rather than mechanical processes," notes Drucker. "Very few events have as much impact on civilization as a change in the basic principle for organizing work."[8]

This sizeable shift is shaking up worldview thinking in many places. One common result is to raise economics itself to the level of worldview. Here we are speaking not simply of economic activity, but of economic order as itself implying or leading to a functional worldview. Ideology yields to economic pragmatism, which in turn may become a new ideology. This seems to be the vision Mikhail Gorbachev initially set forth in his writings on *perestroika*.[9] Whether such a view can overcome the corrosive countertendencies of mounting ethnic restiveness remains to be seen. But certainly economics plays a key role in dealing with ethnic and tribal concerns.

We have seen in previous chapters how economics is networking the world at multiple levels. Wherever one turns, from store shelves to the stock market, global linkage is more and more obvious. It may be that the emerging global economy is building a new worldview right before our eyes. Worldviews don't suddenly spring as brainstorms from the minds of philosophers; they grow piece by piece, gradually, through human interaction at many levels. The global economic worldview described here is not something written in books so much as it is a growing complex of practices and half-conscious assumptions that increasingly form the way many global citizens see the world.

This new economic paradigm is pluralistic regarding religion, ideology, and philosophy. Economic linkages and dynamics form the basic framework for everything else. The world is a community of peoples defined primarily by economic relationships (for example, the European Economic Community, now simply the EC; other common markets and trade zones). Political boundaries are perceived as secondary; often simply troublesome "barriers" to be breached.

Many economists, political leaders, and others have outlined such an economic worldview. For example, Marvin Cetron of Forecasting International and Owen Davies, formerly of *Omni* magazine, argue in their book, *Crystal Globe: The Haves and the Have-Nots of the New World Order,* that Earth is forging a new system based primarily on economic pragmatism. Their thesis seems to assume an economic worldview. "The outlines of a new, more flexible world order are already clear," they write. "The world will be a more peaceful and prosperous place in the 1990s than it has been in the decades since World War II because the premises by which it is governed have changed. In the coming years it will no longer be ruled to suit the needs of ideological and military competition, but instead to promote international trade and the well-being of the trading nations." As a result, they believe that "we will soon enjoy a burst of prosperity much like the one that buoyed the United States during the 1950s. This time, the entire developed and developing world will share in it," with only minor exceptions.[10]

Three business consultants who operate globally—Kenichi Ohmae, Herbert Henzler, and Fred Gluck—have proposed a global economic "Declaration of Interdependence" that embodies the kind of worldview we are speaking of. It reads, in part:

> Inevitably, the emergence of the interlinked economy brings with it an erosion of national sovereignty as the power of information directly touches local communities; academic, professional, and social institutions; corporations; and individuals. It is this borderless world that will give participating economies the capacity for boundless prosperity.
>
> We avow that the security of humankind's social and economic institutions lies no longer in superpower deterence but is rather to be found in the weave of economic and intellectual interdependence of nations.

To realize this promise, the world's "leading nations must be united under this belief," working collectively to "enhance networking" globally, "develop a new framework to deal collectively with traditionally parochial affairs," and induce all nations "to actively participate in the global economy." This cooperation would include working to resolve a whole range of concerns, from the environment to "human rights and dignity."[11]

Here again the underlying assumptions—largely optimistic—presume economic answers to the basic worldview questions.

The Worldview Questions

All versions of the global economic worldview share this conviction that the world's problems are at root economic, or at least that economics is the key to solving them. Generally this conviction is not stated, because the seemingly self-evident good of economic pragmatism and material well-being is assumed. Yet the economic viewpoint does provide, implicitly, coherent worldview answers.

1. What about basic questions of purpose? In the economic view the purpose of life is to provide a full, free, prosperous existence for all peoples and nations. This is "the good." To be human is to be *homo economicus*. We are all economic beings, and the sooner we recognize this and act accordingly, the better off (literally) everyone will be. Ideologies, philosophies, and religious creeds only cloud the issue, hampering plain economic pragmatism.

This does not mean that intangible values such as beauty, justice, or faith are frivolous. They may even have some ultimate worth. But the more accessible and therefore more immediately important reality, that which makes such values possible, is economics. Earth needs to get its economics straight precisely so people are free to pursue "higher" or more abstract interests. Good economics makes art and ethics possible. Someone has to make money so painters can paint and thinkers can think.

We are economic beings, after all. That is the hard fact of the matter. Everyone needs food, shelter, and clothing. Producing, distributing, and using material things is essential to life. This is precisely what economics is all about. It is pointless to talk of other things when people can't eat or find shelter. Everyone needs and should have productive work. Our best thought and energy, therefore, should go toward solving the economic problems of humanity. Only thus can people reach their true potential.

In this worldview the good, then, is economic well-being. Not just for some but for all, because economics is about interrelationships. Most advocates of a global New Economic Order understand this. They know

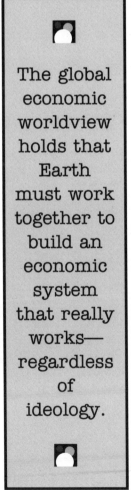
that in the emerging world marketplace no people or nation can live as an island. World economics in our new age has long since passed that point. Further, it is destabilizing to the social order when some nations or groups are so isolated from the global network that they may disrupt it through violence or sabotage. Ultimately, economics means global economics. The well-being of any one sector depends on the propserity of all.

Yet this worldview also affirms market forces. Economic dynamism does not necessarily mean material equality, for real-world economics recognizes the constant ebb and flow of economic life. Some disparity may even be necessary to keep the global economy running. When water or weather are totally still, there is no energy for change. This dynamic is what creates markets, consumer demand, and entrepreneurs. But all people should have the opportunity to participate as best they can. The goals should be maximum economic involvement and at least basic economic equity.

2. Here worldview questions about *design* arise: How to find workable, global economic structures, a macro-economic model for all forms of economic activity. The design of the universe is not a given; it has to be built or discovered. But it is fundamentally economic. The economic worldview recognizes the great diversity of Earth's peoples and sees their destiny as mainly economically determined. Equitable but functional structures must be developed that will lift impoverished people out of their misery, use natural resources wisely, and facilitate economic activity on a global scale.

The stress here is on pragmatism. Economics is about what works. Elaborate theories mean little if they don't (literally) deliver the goods. Through widening global cooperation, the world must strive toward an economic system that really works—regardless of ideology. The proven mechanisms of relatively free markets, entrepreneurship, and enlightened government policy must be expanded and globally networked to build a healthy world system.

Many economists who think in these global

> The global economic worldview holds that Earth must work together to build an economic system that really works—regardless of ideology.

terms now also think ecologically, recognizing the need to protect the environment. The global economy must be green—working with, not against, the environment. "In principle, environmentalism is a place where the professional economist and the professional environmentalist should be working together," says Lester Thurow. "A clean environment is [now] seen as one of several desirable economic outputs."[12]

Perhaps economic pragmatism is an inductive way to discover the ultimate design, if any, of the universe. Start with basic economics, and you may end up solving bigger puzzles. Economics really does raise philosophical issues. Economists are, in Robert Heilbroner's words, "worldly philosophers." Economic pragmatism could lead humanity to an Earth-saving worldview where economy itself provides the paradigm. In a more primitive but still profound way, this was the case in Greece 2000 years ago, when economy (*oikonomia*) was a key concept for understanding not only the household (*oikos*) but even the whole inhabited Earth, the *oikoumene* (root of our word *ecumenical*). In other words, an economic worldview is not just nuts and bolts, nickles and dimes. It is, literally, a view of the world, but it begins with the prosaic and pragmatic rather than with high-flying theories.

3. *Relationships* are a key concern of economics, as well as a basic worldview question. The economic worldview sees all human relationships as at base economic, as already noted. Other kinds of relationships are important, but economic ties go to the root of life. How does my life link with other people, history, and the universe? Economics provides the best answer. I am economically bound to others, and all history is economic history. Once other lenses are removed, I see that in fact my most important relationships are all economic. Marriage and family are economic communities, as are the city, the nation, and potentially the globe. We share our lives and resources with those we love; that is economics. This is not to demean human relationships or human life. It simply recognizes the actual stuff of life—its economic interdependence.

4. Likewise, the *future*—the fourth worldview question—is an economic matter. As Earth's population bulges and the globe shrinks, the economic future of humanity becomes ever more pressing.

In former times, as in the Middle Ages, economic dynamics often were not well understood. Most people died young and could only look beyond the grave when facing the question of the future. This world held little hope. Until it was overturned in part by the gradual rise of capitalism, the static medieval worldview assumed the unquestioned rightness of existing economic arrangements. Some people were poor and weak; some were rich and powerful. That was simply the way things were. Everyone had their station in life, reflecting the eternal order of things.

Today, however, we understand much better the nature of economic relationships. Science and technology have stretched life spans and clarified our options. Paradise or the Heavenly City can exist on Earth—*if* we really take economics seriously. There is an agenda, then: to further global understanding of economic realities, and to build a global order that allows people's hopes and dreams to be fulfilled *now*, in the present. Questions of life after death can be left to religion or poetry. But be sure you have life insurance.

The goal of history, then, is material well-being and global prosperity. A worldly goal, but one that is global and enduring. Once this goal is reached, or at least in sight, human creativity and culture can flower in ways beyond our imagining.

Many utopian communities of the past, especially in the eighteenth century, shared this perspective.[13] So did most of the communes and "intentional communities" that sprung up during the so-called Consciousness Revolution of the 1960s. The idea was to set up a community according to proper economic order, and all would be well—a shortcut to the future.

Some of these communities flourished; most failed. Many isolated themselves from society, trying to build prosperous self-contained units, microcosms and pilot projects of a New World. Many, perhaps most, were naive about the real economics of human organization. Today we perhaps know better. But we can view such communities as prophetic in making economics primary. In fact, many medieval monastic communities, especially the Benedictines, were highly successful economically. Key agricultural breakthroughs, like the horse collar, are attributed to them.[14] The Shakers in nineteenth-century America provide a similar example, adapting emerging technology into furniture making, sewing, and woodwork.

What about Marxism, the political system that, more than any other, focused on economics? Probably most modern economists believe Karl Marx was wrong in much of his economic theory. Yet he more than anyone else swung attention to economic questions, and that changed the world. His flaw was forcing his economics into a philosophy of determinism rather than following the logic of economic pragmatism. Today we must approach the critical question of economics not with the ideologies of Marxism or even classical capitalism. Rather, we must find by trial and error, computer models, and increasing global cooperation the way to economic prosperity and stability for all of Earth's peoples.

Such an approach to global economics is surely a worldview. It answers the basic questions; it provides an outlook for all of life. But some serious difficulties remain unresolved.

The Limits of Economics

With the end of the Cold War, economic pragmatism seems to be where Earth is headed. Today's news is more about trade agreements and global marketing than about armies or even nuclear threats. If this means greater peace and well-being for the Earth, well and good. But as an overarching worldview, economic order fails in at least four ways.

First, the global economic worldview falls prey to what might be called the "economic fallacy." Jacques Ellul has described "the political illusion": the notion that all problems are essentially political and can be solved by political means.[15] The economic worldview commits a similar error. Economics is enormously important. But it is not at all clear that it is the essential reality from which everything else springs.

Second, the economic perspective is overly optimistic about what is known and can be discovered about economic dynamics. Some things *are* becoming clearer, particularly with the collapse of Marxist Communism. State ownership of the means of production and command economies simply do not work in most cases. But there is little evidence that humanity so far has enough experience or knowledge about economic reality, particularly on a global scale, to warrant much confidence for the future. Economic science is still very imprecise, and much economic behavior is unpredictable. The level of complexity blocks the possibility of accurate long-term forecasting. Cooperation on a global scale and the willingness to take a pragmatic approach are hopeful signs. But what we know so far is insufficient to build a worldview upon.

Third, economics as worldview does not—at least so far—sufficiently take ecology into account. Economics and ecology must be merged, or at least linked, in any worldview adequate for the twenty-first century. Both, after all, are eco-concerns; both concern "the house" (*oikos*). Herman Daly and John Cobb write in this connection, "When economists deal with living things, and especially with large systems of living things, they cannot think of these *only* as resources for fueling the human economy. Instead, the human economy needs to be shaped with the health of the biosphere in view."[16]

Fourth, no economic paradigm can provide *ultimate* answers to the deep questions of human existence. By definition, economics stops at the boundary of space, time, and matter. But many people today, as always, feel there are other, more fundamental dimensions to life. Economics does not even deal adequately, in fact, with the nature of matter itself. It is concerned with the proper *use* of material things but can say nothing about their essential nature or their ultimate origin. Any worldview based on economics is fundamentally materialist and, therefore, incomplete. The human spirit soars beyond the material. Increasingly we are finding, also, that matter itself is mysterious, not hard and predictable.

Humanity will, of necessity, deal seriously and globally with economic issues in the coming decades. Global economics will become increasingly crucial, as we have seen. The emergence of a stable but dynamic and just global economic order is a pressing need. It would be welcome and highly useful. But a fully adequate worldview must provide more than the economic perspective has to offer.

On the other hand, any adequate worldview will have to make room for economics. It will have to show how economics fits into the total understanding of reality. It must do this in a way that encourages and provides space for a productive economic model that benefits all and respects the whole Earth.

CHAPTER ELEVEN

Quantum Mystery:

A New Scientific Worldview?

> Out of the fusion of relativity with quantum mechanics there has evolved a new view of the world, one in which matter has lost its central role. This role has been usurped by principles of symmetry, some of them hidden from view in the present state of the universe.
> —NOBEL PRIZE-WINNING PHYSICIST STEVEN WEINBERG[1]

> Researchers at the leading edge of science, various social movements, and numerous alternative networks are developing a new vision of reality that will form the basis of our future technologies, economic systems, and social institutions.
> —PHYSICIST FRITJOF CAPRA[2]

W hat is life like at the level of the quantum? Weird, compared to our usual view of things. Time bends, matter is sometimes unpredictable and vague, and subatomic particles seem to change their behavior if someone is watching. As we saw in chapter 6, the strange world of quantum energy is a fascinating one and perhaps the most important frontier in science today.

Already many people, including respected scientists, are raising worldview questions as they ponder the larger significance of quantum

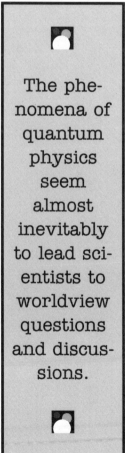

discoveries. Some people believe that the world of quantum physics will yield the ultimate worldview over the next few decades, a "final" Theory of Everything. Here the universe is seen as a mix of physical forces in a way that transcends current models. This could mean a new "scientific" worldview, one emerging from the frontiers of the science of physics. The key question: Will an emerging Grand Unified Theory (GUT) or Theory of Everything (TOE) in science give us the ultimate scientific worldview, a perspective that answers our most basic questions? Would not such a perspective settle worldview issues forever?

We saw in chapter 6 how scientists are working to combine the four basic forces of gravity, electromagnetism, and the strong and weak nuclear forces in one unified theory. Many believe that quantum physics will find the answer—that explorations across a broad front will reveal a fundamental unity that can be experimentally proved.

A number of people have been quick to build new mystical or quasi-mystical worldviews on the still incomplete foundation of quantum physics. The idea of mystery, unpredictability, and instantaneous nonlocal communication has an irresistible appeal for many. Gary Zukav, for instance, writes in *The Dancing Wu Li Masters,* "The study of complementarity, the uncertainty principle, quantum field theory . . . produces insights into the nature of reality very similar to those produced by the study of eastern philosophies."[3]

Physics or Metaphysics?

Even famed physicists seem unable to resist raising questions of ultimate meaning, and even of God, in their discussions of quantum mystery. Modern physics seems to lead naturally to such questions. Perhaps this is because, as physicist Lawrence Krauss of Case Western Reserve University writes, "By its very nature, physics alone among the sciences offers the possibility of coming as close to understanding *why* as our culture is likely to get. It is only physics, after all, that can tell us, in some fundamental sense, how what there is came to be." He adds, "Questions

The phenomena of quantum physics seem almost inevitably to lead scientists to worldview questions and discussions.

that a few years ago would have been dismissed as metaphysical, such as, 'Could there be universes with other rules?' 'Is there only one consistent set of principles allowing for a measurable physical reality?' have become part of the current discussions in both cosmology and particle physics."[4] A notable example: Nobel laureate Steven Weinberg includes a chapter, "What About God?" in his book, *Dreams of a Final Theory.*[5]

Weinberg says that quantum mechanics has brought us "a new view of the world." Does he mean a new worldview? Not exactly, in the comprehensive sense we are discussing here. He really means a changed view of the nature of the physical universe. Yet he is very much aware, as are other scientists, that any new model of the material world will have broader implications for understanding all of life. Scientific revolutions soon become worldview revolutions. One can't divorce questions of scientific truth from broader questions of truth—or from Truth, if there is such.[6]

Weinberg says that although present theories are limited and incomplete, yet "behind them now and then we catch glimpses of a final theory." All the "arrows of explanation" reveal a "remarkable pattern" of connectedness. "Sometimes in discussions among physicists, when it turns out that mathematically beautiful ideas are actually relevant to the real world, we get the feeling that there is something behind the blackboard, some deeper truth foreshadowing a final theory that makes our ideas turn out so well." No one knows what that final theory will look like. But "when we have our final theory, what will happen to science and to the human spirit?"[7]

God and ultimate Truth (arguably the same thing) cannot be found in the laws of science, Weinberg and other scientists contend. A successful Grand Unified Theory or TOE would prove nothing, by itself, about God, for instance. Traditionally, Christian thinkers and other theists have argued that God is not absent from nature, but God is not nature. Probably most Christians, Jews, and Moslems would contend that nature shows God's grandeur and thus provides a motive for praise. And nature may mirror something of God's nature. But scientists often conclude opposite things about ultimate meaning from their experiments and theories. Some scientists are atheists; many are agnostics; some are theists of one type or another. Clearly it is not science itself that answers the worldview questions, even though it may raise them.

Yet today—and increasingly, I believe, in the future—people move from the answers and questions of quantum physics to the building of worldviews. Some scientists see this as an unwarranted leap of faith beyond what the data tell us. A "scientific" worldview may be no more scientific than is astrology, which claims a scientific base. Often world-view construction quickly leaves science behind, engaging in mystical and/or psychological speculation with little scientific grounding. But there is a wide spectrum here. Some worldviews are well grounded in science; others much less so.

The Tao of Physics

Probably the best-known inquiry into the possible worldview impli-cations of quantum physics is Fritjof Capra's much-reprinted *The Tao of Physics: An Exploration of the Parallels Between Modern Physics and East-ern Mysticism*. In the third, updated edition of the book, Capra, a profes-sional physicist, declares, "When I discovered the parallels between the world views of physicists and mystics, which had been hinted at before but never thoroughly explored, I had the strong feeling that I was merely uncovering something that was quite obvious and would be common knowledge in the future."[8]

Capra believes that "a consistent view of the world is beginning to emerge from modern physics which is harmonious with ancient Eastern wisdom." Eastern mysticism offers a "consistent and beautiful philo-sophical framework which can accommodate our most advanced theo-ries of the physical world."[9]

Capra sees his own investigations as part of a broader shift. The "pro-found harmony," he says, between the worldviews of quantum physics and Eastern mysticism "now appears as an integral part of a much larger cultural transformation, leading to the emergence of a new vision of reality that will require a fundamental change in our thoughts, percep-tions, and values." And just in time, given the present crisis: "We have favored self-assertion over integration, analysis over synthesis, rational knowledge over intuitive wisdom, science over religion, competition over cooperation, expansion over conservation, and so on. This one-sided development has now reached a highly alarming stage; a crisis of social, ecological, moral, and spiritual dimensions."[10]

Capra outlines a new quantum worldview in what he calls "six crite-ria of new-paradigm thinking in science."[11] The key points of the new paradigm are:

1. *A redefinition of the part and the whole* in which "the whole is pri-mary" and provides the source and framework for understanding the parts. Nature is "a network of relations"; "ultimately there are no parts at all in this interconnected web. Whatever we call a part is merely a pattern that has some stability and therefore captures our attention."

2. The new paradigm *shifts the focus from structure to process.* Process

is primary, and "every structure we observe is a manifestation of an underlying process."

3. The new worldview transcends the subject/object split, recognizing rather "the process of knowledge" and the necessary and valuable presence and participation of the person in science and in all of life.

4. The new model *shifts from the root metaphor of buildings, foundations, and fundamental laws, to the images of networks, webs, and relationships.* Says Capra: "We may not see it necessary . . . to build our knowledge on firm foundations, and we may replace the metaphor of the building by the metaphor of the network. Just as we see reality around us a network of relationships, our descriptions, too—our concepts, models, and theories—will form an interconnected network representing the observed phenomena. In such a network, there won't be anything primary and secondary, and there won't be any foundations."

5. The new paradigm also requires a *shift from truth to approximate descriptions,* according to Capra. "In the new paradigm, it is recognized that all scientific concepts and theories are limited and approximate. . . . Scientists do not deal with truth (in the sense of a precise correspondence between the description and the described phenomena); they deal with limited and approximate descriptions of reality." Capra quotes Louis Pasteur: "Science advances through tentative answers to a series of more and more subtle questions which reach deeper and deeper into the essence of natural phenomena." How does this relate to Eastern mysticism? Capra notes that "the mystics often insist that no single phenomenon can be fully explained." They are interested more in "the direct, nonintellectual experience of the unity of all things" than in rational explanations.

6. Finally, the new model, says Capra, requires "the shift from an attitude of domination and control of nature, including human beings, to one of cooperation and nonviolence." Capra notes the long connection between "mechanistic science and patriarchal values." Clearly he is rejecting a basic aspect of Enlightenment science:

> Before the seventeenth century, the goals of science were wisdom, understanding the natural order, and living in harmony with it. In the seventeenth century this attitude, which one could call an ecological attitude, changed into its opposite. Ever since [Francis] Bacon the goal of science has been knowledge that can be used to dominate and control nature, and today both science and technology are used predominantly for purposes that are dangerous, harmful, and anti-ecological.
>
> The change of worldview that is now occurring will have to include a profound change of values; in fact, a complete change of heart—from the intent to dominate and control nature to an attitude of cooperation and

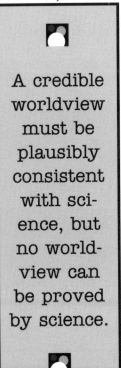

nonviolence. Such an attitude is deeply ecological and, not surprisingly, is the attitude characteristic of spiritual traditions.[12]

A Scientific Worldview?

Capra and a number of others have tried their hand at worldview thinking with quantum physics as a basis or starting point. The last decade has seen a cascade of books discussing the philosophical and worldview implications of the new physics. These range from the mystical to the psychical and psychological to the more cautiously scientific, as noted above. This, of course, raises the question of a proper use of science (in this case, physics) in considering worldviews. Is there such a thing as a scientific worldview?

What would qualify as a "scientific" worldview? If limited to ones that give experimentally proven answers to the basic worldview questions, then a truly scientific worldview clearly would be impossible. It will never be possible to prove scientifically *why* the world exists, or what life's purpose is (or even if it has a purpose). Science may, however, give some hints. It may point in some directions, or suggest metaphors that open new worldview thinking.

A scientific worldview in the fullest sense is thus impossible. But in a secondary, more limited way we may speak of a scientific worldview. In this sense, a worldview may be said to be scientific if it is plausibly consistent with the proven results of science. A worldview which contradicts scientific proofs would be unscientific. That does not necessarily mean it would be untrue. Where a worldview conflicts with science, the apparent conflict may be due to one or more of several factors:

> A credible worldview must be plausibly consistent with science, but no worldview can be proved by science.

1. The scientific proof may be true but may be applicable only under certain conditions. It thus might not invalidate the worldview claims. Quantum physics, for example, has shown the limited applicability of Newtonian physics. Space and time are not always what they seem.

2. The scientific proof may be inaccurately stated because of the limitations of current language, models, or understandings. One suspects that this may be the case with the quantum wave/particle duality.

3. Similarly, the *worldview claims* may be inadequately or incompletely articulated due to limitations of language, models, and current understandings.

Given these (and possibly other) qualifications, it is probably better to set aside all claims for a scientific worldview. The claim to be scientific only confuses the issue and should be considered irrelevant. The issue, then, becomes the plausibility, coherence, and usefulness of any worldview—*including,* of course, how this view might be illuminated, clarified, illustrated, or challenged by current and emerging scientific knowledge.

A Quantum Worldview

One of the more interesting proposals for a worldview built on quantum physics comes from Danah Zohar in her book, *The Quantum Self: Human Nature and Consciousness Defined by the New Physics.* Though some of her ideas are typical of New Age attempts to wed the new science with spiritual or mystical ideas, Zohar tries to stay close to recognized scientific theory. She proposes a worldview that links consciousness and quantum phenomena. As a theory, of course, it is speculative, but that in itself does not make it unscientific. More important for our discussion here, Zohar spells out a worldview based largely on quantum physics and the physiology of the brain. She suggests, "The functioning of our own minds may provide a key to the nature of fundamental reality."[13]

Zohar's worldview model is useful here for several reasons. It is grounded in quantum physics, yet goes beyond it to raise philosophical questions, directly addressing worldview issues. It is postmodern in its understanding of science. Her basic argument is that "quantum physics, allied to a quantum mechanical model of consciousness, gives us . . . a perspective from which we can see ourselves and our purposes fully as part of the universe and from which we might come to understand the *meaning* of human existence—to understand why we conscious human beings are here in this material universe at all." This perspective "would not replace all the vast poetic and mythological imagery, the spiritual and moral dimensions of religion, but it would provide us with the physical basis for a coherent world picture one that includes ourselves."[14]

Zohar, an American-born philosopher living in England, argues that the traditional Newtonian worldview was doomed from the start because of "three pernicious dichotomies" (philosopher Lawrence Cahoone's phrase): the split between subject and object, or mind and matter; the split between the individual and his or her relationships; and the division between nature and culture. The mechanical worldview can explain *things*, but not consciousness or social life. This has led, in the Western world at least, to an impossibly split worldview: either idealism or materialism; either individualism or enforced communism; either relativism or fundamentalism.

Zohar attempts to get beyond a fuzzy physics-mysticism. The "partial and groping attempts" to build a holistic worldview on the foundation of quantum physics to date have failed, Zohar argues, for lack of a theory of "the actual physics of consciousness." This she seeks to provide, suggesting that quantum processes within the brain may yield the key link between mind and matter. This leads to the heart of her proposal:

> The quantum worldview transcends the dichotomy between mind and body, or between inner and outer, by showing us that the basic building blocks of mind . . . and the basic building blocks of matter . . . arise out of a common quantum substrate . . . and are engaged in a mutually creative dialogue whose roots can be traced back to the very heart of reality creation. Crudely put, mind is relationship and matter is that which it relates. Neither, on its own, could evolve or express anything; together they give us ourselves and the world.[15]

This approach also heals the split between individuals and their relationships, for each person is, literally, "an utterly unique pattern of relationships." "For the quantum self," says Zohar, "neither individuality nor relationship is primary because both arise simultaneously" from quantum dynamics. "The quantum self thus mediates between the extreme isolation of Western individualism and the extreme collectivism of Marxism or Eastern mysticism."[16]

This view also solves the culture/nature problem, because both arise from the same quantum-dynamic source. The same physics is at work: "In both cases it is a physics driven by the need to maintain and increase ordered coherence in free response to the environment." Both nature and culture reflect the same reality, the same principles.

> In summary, the quantum worldview stresses dynamic relationship as the basis of all that is. It tells us that our world comes about through a mutually creative dialogue between mind and body . . . between the individual and his personal and material context, and between human culture and the natural world. It gives us a view of the human self that is free and responsible, responsive to others and to its environment, essentially related and naturally committed, and at every moment creative.[17]

Does such a view need or have a place for God? Zohar's model is essentially evolutionary, though she says it does not preclude the possibility of God's existence. The idea of a transcendent God behind the Big Bang "is a perfectly tenable position, though it leaves us with a God who Himself undergoes no creative transformation, who is not in dialogue with His world," she writes. "Such a belief must remain wholly a matter of faith." Zohar proposes instead a post-Big Bang God:

> But if we think of God as something embodied within, or something that uses, the laws of physics, then the relationship between the [quantum] vacuum and the existing universe suggests a God who might be identified with the basic sense of direction in the unfolding universe—even, perhaps, with an evolving consciousness within the universe. The existence of such an "immanent God" would not preclude that of a transcendent God as well, but given our knowledge of the universe the immanent God (or immanent aspect of God) is more accessible to us.
>
> This immanent God would be at every moment involved in a mutually creative dialogue with His world, knowing Himself only as He knows His world. . . . it makes sense [in this view] to speak of human beings—with our physics of consciousness, which mirrors the physics of the coherent vacuum—as conceived in the image of God, or as partners in God's creation.[18]

Zohar affirms the vision of the late Roman Catholic theologian/scientist Pierre Teilhard de Chardin, who wrote in *The Phenomenon of Man*, "The movement of our souls expresses and measures the very stages of progress of evolution itself. Man discovers that *he is nothing else than evolution become conscious of itself,* to borrow Julian Huxley's striking expression."[19] Zohar reinterprets the Christian story of the fall into sin as the "fall" into individuality and redemption through grace as return to undivided unity, assisted by a built-in drive toward coherence ("grace").

A Holographic Model?

Zohar discusses briefly the "holographic" nature of reality: the way the whole seems to be contained in each part, as in a hologram. A hologram is a three-dimensional image created by using a laser beam. Holograms have become familiar to many through three-dimensional photographs sold in stores and the small holographic images found now on some credit cards. Holograms have the interesting feature that each part contains the whole; it is "holistic." The whole picture can be projected from any part, though with decreasing vividness the smaller the part used.

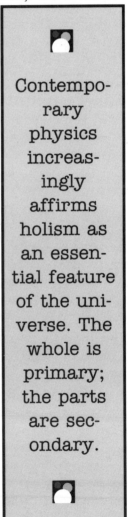

The holographic model is attractive because it suggests the connectedness of all things. Each particle and person is part of the larger whole. Zohar notes that "this latter-day holism has its antecedents in both East and West"—in Buddhism, for example, or in the Western concept of the Great Chain of Being. "Those who suggest the hologram as a model for the brain" or for the universe "are attempting to put such metaphors on a scientific footing," she writes.[20]

In recent years a number of writers and thinkers have explored holograms as a model for consciousness and for all reality. The influential physicist David Bohm, author of *Wholeness and the Implicate Order* and other books, suggests the view that "the world itself is constructed or is structured on the same general principles as the hologram." The universe should be understood not as a collection of things or objects but as "the holomovement," a movement of beams or waves creating, in effect, a photographic hologram. "All existence is basically holomovement which manifests itself in relatively stable form," Bohm says. "The holomovement is the ground of what is manifest. . . . And what is manifest is, as it were, abstracted and floating in the holomovement."[21]

The holographic model has been explored in a number of articles and books, including Michael Talbot's *The Holographic Universe,* the anthology *The Holographic Paradigm and Other Paradoxes,* edited by Ken Wilber, and *Reality and Empathy: Physics, Mind, and Science in the 21st Century,* by Alex Comfort.[22]

Contemporary physics does, in fact, increasingly affirm holism as an essential feature of the universe (though not necessarily the hologram model specifically). This holism becomes more and more evident as our understanding of quantum reality grows. Capra's first point, discussed earlier, is a redefinition of the relation between part and whole in which "the whole is primary." Increasingly scientists are finding "not elementary space-time realities, but rather a web of relationships in which no part can stand alone; every part derives its meaning and existence only from its place within the whole," revealing the "holistic

> Contemporary physics increasingly affirms holism as an essential feature of the universe. The whole is primary; the parts are secondary.

character of the world," writes Henry Stapp of the Lawrence Berkeley Laboratory in California.[23]

Danah Zohar criticizes the holographic model as one-sided and inadequate, however. It must be seen as part of a more encompassing model. She says that it falls short at two points: First, it is still too much an "objective" model that can't explain consciousness. "The physics of the hologram," she says, cannot "account for the unity of conscious perception." Second, holograms are not strictly holistic but are "ultimately divisible into parts." "This is not the kind of holism required to explain the unity of consciousness," she argues, though clearly today "some sort of holism is in the air."[24] The holographic model, while useful, must be joined to a more inclusive quantum-consciousness model.

Although Zohar's proposed worldview is worked out differently from Capra's, the underlying convictions and assumptions are much the same. Capra's "criteria of new-paradigm thinking" are all reflected in Zohar's analysis. In general, Capra explores and affirms parallels between quantum physics and Eastern mysticism, while Zohar works with worldview categories more familiar in the West. Both represent a new postmodern model in science.

Quantum Questions and Answers

Quantum mystery attempts to answer the basic worldview questions. Its vision is a coherent view that seeks to be consistent with and informed by quantum physics. How and to what degree does it address the questions of purpose, design, relationships, and the future?

1. The *purpose* to life in this view seems to be to achieve an ever higher level of consciousness and unity. This includes heightened personal awareness, the achieving of one's human potential, and a deepened sense of relationship to all other things.

2. In the quantum worldview, the *design* of the universe is fundamentally the patterns of quantum physics. In Zohar's version, consciousness itself, and therefore all human society and history, trace back to quantum mechanical processes—essentially the same processes found in the human brain. More fully, the design of the universe is the workings of quantum physics that has within it a built-in drive toward coherence, order, and consciousness. It is fundamental to the Quantum Mystery worldview (in whatever version) that the secret to understanding the universe is to be found in the dynamics of quantum mechanics, either directly or by way of analogy.

3. The question of *relationships* receives a fuller answer in the quantum worldview. Everything is related to everything else at the level of

the quantum, the most basic level. More importantly, quantum reality has a built-in tendency toward coherence and unity. As Zohar puts it, "I am my relationships—my relationships to the subselves within my own self (my past and my future), my relationships to others, and my relationships to the world at large." This is the only way human life can really be understood.[25]

4. The quantum worldview also answers questions about *the future*. The phenomenon of "virtual transitions" in quantum physics, in which particles seem to "try out" many possible paths before actually "choosing" one, suggests a strong element of potentiality built into the physical universe. This is the basis for evolution. The universe is evolving, or unfolding, to achieve its highest potential, which appears to be unified consciousness.

Quantum Mystery in the Balance

The quantum-based worldview has several attractive features. It is friendly toward science and open to its new directions, especially in the new physics. The element of unpredictability and apparent randomness in quantum physics is more dynamic than the old mechanistic worldview. The quantum perspective offers a viewpoint that, on the one hand, is scientific, and yet that allows for a measure, at least, of unpredictability and human freedom and creativity. The universe is not a closed system. The quantum model also provides a place for ecology and environmental concerns, for personal life and meaning, and for human society and culture.

The quantum worldview does not provide an adequate answer, however, to the question of why there should be purpose or meaning in life. It is comprehensive in the sense that it takes in all material existence, not just the Earth. Yet in a sense it is fundamentally material and time-bound, for it sees purpose, meaning, and consciousness as arising out of the quantum vacuum created by the Big Bang. Meaning, it seems, could not have existed before that. This view appears unable to conceive of dimensions of reality other than or greater than those that are based in quantum dynamics. Granted that there is an element of mystery within quantum mechanics, is it not still conceivable that quantum reality is in some way an expression of larger or more comprehensive dimensions of existence—some form of spiritual or metaphysical realm—rather than (in effect) the other way around?

Capra concludes *The Tao of Physics* with the statement, "We are embedded in the multiple alternative networks of what I have called 'the rising culture'—a multitude of movements representing different facets

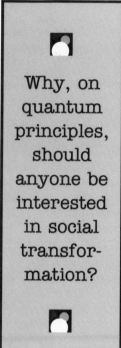

Why, on quantum principles, should anyone be interested in social transformation?

of the same new vision of reality, gradually coalescing to form a powerful force of social transformation."[26] Perhaps. But why, on quantum principles, should anyone be interested in social transformation? *Something else is at work here,* concerns that come from some other source than quantum physics. It seems that the quantum perspective is indeed changing many people's worldview thinking. But it does not provide a sufficiently comprehensive view of life and the universe.

Lacking a basis for purpose and other human concerns, the quantum worldview also fails at the point of ethics and the value of human life. Something is lacking—a source for meaning, value, and ethics in human relationships and cultural expression.

The quantum worldview is in several ways closer to the actual reality of things than the older, now-outdated worldview of modern science. It is less mechanistic, more organic and open-ended, more dynamic in its sense of process, and more holistic in its conception of human consciousness and its relationship to the world "out there." In all these ways it is nearer to the truth. But it is incomplete and inadequate as a comprehensive worldview or Theory of Everything.

CHAPTER TWELVE

Life on a Living Planet:
The Gaia Worldview

> Suppose that the Earth is alive.
>
> —JAMES LOVELOCK[1]
>
> My view of our planet was a glimpse of divinity.
>
> —EDGAR MITCHELL

Economics and ecology form one of the deepest, yet perhaps most hopeful, tensions of emerging global society. The pressure mounts. Not surprisingly, new or hybrid worldviews start emerging from this high pressure system.

Eco-crisis makes us rethink Earth and our relationship to it. This reflection can take different forms: Scientific or mystical, classical or New Age, religious or postmodern. Ecology has its own fascination, for at least two reasons: It stresses the connectedness of all things, and it touches on the mystery of life itself. Here is fertile soil for worldview thinking.

Enter, then, the Gaia Hypothesis, a fascinating and suggestive ecological worldview. Gaia thinking—Earth as a living organism—has become something of a movement. More than a dozen books promoting it with various levels of seriousness have appeared since James Lovelock's seminal *The Ages of Gaia: A Biography of Our Living Earth* was first published in 1988. We now have, for example, *The Gaia Atlas of Future Worlds*. Few ideas have caught on so fast, and yet so combine up-to-date science with myth and metaphor.

Gaia was the Greek goddess who personified Earth. *Gaia* comes from the Greek word for Earth or land, *ge* (as in our *geography* and *geology*).

In Greek mythology Gaia (or Gaea), daughter of Chaos, birthed many other gods. Cronos, Oceanus, and Aphrodite were among her offspring. She is thus Mother Earth, equivalent to the Roman Terra. To speak today of Earth as Gaia, then, is to suggest a symbolic and spiritual dimension that contrasts sharply with hard-nosed economic worldviews and with the skepticism of postmodernism. It is more like "quantum mystery." But this worldview takes its cues from biology rather than physics. In this approach "Gaia, the Greek goddess of the earth, has been reborn through modern science"[2]—more specifically, the life sciences.

Love Your Mother

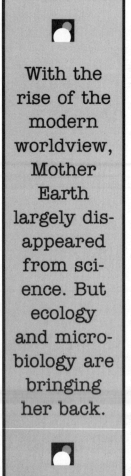

With the rise of the modern worldview, Mother Earth largely disappeared from science. But ecology and microbiology are bringing her back.

The idea of Mother Earth, or Mother Nature as the *anima mundi*, the World Soul, has been a sub-theme of Western society since the early Greeks. Always conceived as female, Mother Earth was the source of life on the planet. In medieval worldviews Mother Earth was mainly understood symbolically or metaphorically. In some views she was the means through which God created Earth's life forms, a sort of super-link in the Great Chain of Being.[3] With the rise of modern science since Galileo and Newton, the idea of Mother Earth became mainly a romantic, poetic convention. Mother Earth disappeared from science. Gaia thinking today, however, is based in cutting-edge contemporary science, especially in ecology and microbiology. It thus signals a shift away from the dominant science of the past several centuries.

"What is most striking about the Gaia hypothesis," says Riane Eisler, "is that in essence it is a scientific update of the belief system of the Goddess-worshiping prehistoric societies" in which "the world was viewed as the great Mother, a living entity who in both her temporal and spiritual manifestations creates and nurtures all forms of life."[4]

Gaia thinking has been popularized by British atmospheric scientist James Lovelock. But it had been brewing in some circles for over a decade. The international Lindisfarne Association held a series of discussions on the idea. Today the Gaia hypothesis is associated especially with Lovelock and with microbiologist Lynn Margulis, coauthor of *Microcosmos: Four Billion Years of Microbial Evolution.*

Lovelock adopted and adapted the Gaia hypothesis through reflecting on his own study of the environment. He believes that Earth, rather than simply *containing* billions of living organisms, is itself a huge living thing, or at least it acts like one. "I think of the Earth as a living organism," says Lovelock. "The rocks, the air, the oceans, and all life are an inseparable system that functions to keep the planet livable. I now believe that life can exist *only* on a planetary scale."[5]

Lovelock stresses the dynamic connection between the physical earth and its life forms. In his earlier 1986 essay, "Gaia: The World as Living Organism," Lovelock wrote that Gaia theory "sees the evolution of the species of living organisms so closely coupled with the evolution of their physical and chemical environment that together they constitute a single and indivisible evolutionary process."[6]

Gaia is a theory about Earth that, for many people, has become a new worldview. Author Lawrence Joseph calls it "the first comprehensive scientific expression of the profoundly ancient belief that the planet Earth is a living creature." The theory holds that the planet's life forms—plants, animals, and microorganisms—control the Earth's surface environment in a significantly interactive way. "Taken as a whole, the planet behaves not as an inanimate sphere of rock and soil, sustained by the automatic and accidental processes of geology, as traditional Earth science has long maintained, but more as a biological superorganism—a planetary body—that adjusts and regulates itself."[7]

A Whole Earth Theory

Lovelock's insights came directly out of his involvement with the U.S. space program. He had helped design experiments to find out whether there might be life on Mars. Looking at Mars, and then looking at Earth as seen from space, Lovelock was struck with the uniqueness of Earth's atmosphere. "This gift, this ability to see the earth from afar, was so revealing," writes Lovelock, that it forced him to a "top-down" approach to life on Earth, not the traditional "bottom-up" approach that begins with the smallest forms and works from them to larger systems. It is more revealing to view the whole Earth as one system, then see each part in relation to the whole. The key perspective is not each particular life form or micro-system, but the overall system—Living Earth—of which each smaller system (microbes, forests, oceans) is but a part.

Lovelock was struck with the stark difference between Earth and other planets. Unlike Earth's atmosphere, those of Mars and Venus are "like . . . exhaust gases, all energy spent." Other planets' atmospheres are at least 95 percent carbon dioxide, but Earth's is an unstable mix of gases dominated by nitrogen and oxygen. "When the Earth was first seen from outside and compared as a whole planet with its lifeless partners, Mars and Venus, it was impossible to ignore the sense that the earth was a strange and beautiful anomaly," Lovelock writes. "What if the difference in atmospheric composition between the Earth and its neighbors . . . is a consequence of the fact that Earth alone bears life?"[8] He was struck with the way the whole Earth is very much like a living thing.

Conventional evolutionary theory teaches that life arose through gradual changes in the rocks and minerals of Earth. The focus is on the life forms themselves and how they developed. Lovelock calls his view "a new theory of evolution." It builds on Darwin but holds that "the evolution of the species of organisms is not independent of the evolution of their material environment. Indeed the species and their environment are tightly coupled and evolve as a single system" into "the largest living organism, Gaia."

Lovelock sees Gaia theory as "the basis of a new and unified view of the Earth and life sciences." He points out, however, that this view is not really new. Ancient cultures and a scattering of scientists in past centuries have also seen the Earth as a living organism.[9]

Gaia thinking stresses that humans are simply one of Earth's teeming species. They have no special place. It is Gaia that is special. Humans are neither Earth's owners nor its stewards. They are part of the living Gaia system—creatures that interact with, and even host, many other organisms. The human body, after all, is a sort of elongated tube. Through it pass many bits and pieces of Earth's bounty; within it live a host of microorganisms. Human life, in other words, is an intricate symbiosis (living-together) with everything else on Earth. The future of human life depends on learning to live harmoniously with Gaia and all her life forms.

> In the Gaia worldview, humans are neither Earth's owners nor its stewards. They are simply one of the planet's teeming species.

Gaia is a living organism made up of many smaller organisms, each with its own boundaries. This is her ecology, more evident to us if we begin by viewing Earth from a distance. Lovelock writes:

> As we move in towards the Earth from space, first we see the atmospheric boundary that encloses Gaia; then the borders of an ecosystem such as the forests; then the skin or bark of living animals and plants; further in are the cell membranes; and finally the nucleus of the cell and its DNA. If life is defined as a self-organizing system characterized by an actively sustained low entropy, then, viewed from outside each of these boundaries, what lies within is alive.[10]

By this definition, Earth appears to be very much alive. It is a stable, self-organizing system able to sustain itself over time. Gaia theory holds that not just the biosphere, the thin membrane of organisms at or near Earth's surface, is alive. The whole planet, rocks and all, makes up the living Gaia. Rocks aren't alive, we may say. But Gaians point to the giant redwood tree. Everyone agrees it is alive. Yet 99 percent of the tree is dead wood. The tree is sustained by its thin layer of living bark. So it is with the Earth.[11]

The Spirit of Gaia

Is the Gaia hypothesis simply an extended analogy? Or is it something deeper? For some people, Gaia is an analogy only. Some scientists would call it a "heuristic" model that helps us grasp the vastness and intricacies of our life system. Earth is similar to a living organism in many ways. This analogy helps us understand Earth's actual ecology, partly by narrowing or erasing the line between living and nonliving matter.

Others view Gaia in mystical, symbolic, or religious terms. Lovelock himself believes the Earth *is* a living organism, but for him this is a scientific hypothesis, not a religious viewpoint. Lovelock generally speaks as a scientist, but as one whose research has led him to a hypothesis with undeniable spiritual overtones. He writes, "For the present, my belief in God rests at the stage of a positive agnosticism. I am too deeply committed to science for undiluted faith; equally unacceptable to me spiritually is the materialist world of undiluted fact. . . . That Gaia can be both spiritual and scientific is, for me, deeply satisfying. . . . In no way do I see Gaia as a sentient being, a surrogate God. To me Gaia is alive and part of the ineffable Universe and I am a part of her."[12]

Not surprisingly, many people rush on to make a religion of Gaia theory, worshiping the Mother Goddess Earth. At this point a whole range of possible worldviews appears, from a reborn Earth-paganism to a blending of the Gaia perspective into Christian belief. Some people take Gaia thinking (including its New Age versions) in a more vaguely mystical direction, seeing Gaia as part of the evolution of the universe toward cosmic mind or consciousness, a "noosphere" (from *noema,* the Greek word for mind or thought). Theodore Roszak speaks of "groups that are prepared to embrace Gaia as the rebirth of paganism in our time; others who take her as the basis for nature mysticism, others who see her as an ally in the politics of ecofeminism."[13] Emerging ecofeminism often blends ecology, feminism, and Gaia mysticism. "The result," says Ted Peters, "is a form of neopaganism that centers on worshiping the Mother Goddess" in which Earth is "a living and sacred being." Its promoters argue that this concept "marks an attitude shift toward a holistic vision that will help us to solve our ecological problems."[14]

Other people talk about "the holographic universe," as noted in the previous chapter. This is different from the Gaia model but resembles it in some ways. Here the universe is seen as a cosmic hologram in which every bit reflects and embodies the whole. Like the Gaia hypothesis, this view begins with science (in this case, holography and particularly research on memory and other functions of the human brain) and then goes on to suggest a worldview that resembles more mystic versions of Gaia thinking.

It is important to recognize the wide diversity within Gaian thinking. The Gaia hypothesis, Earth-goddess worship, Ecofeminism, and New Age consciousness are not all the same thing, for example. Commentators on these currents often betray confusion or ignorance here. This range of views—from scientific to mystical, from "secular" to "religious"—is, in part, testimony to the creative ferment of a lot of new thinking. It is also evidence of the shift in global consciousness from the subject/object split to an awareness of the "subjective"—or better, *personal*—nature of all knowledge.

Despite this diversity, a coherent basic worldview appears to be emerging. It is possible to talk here in worldview terms.

The Gaian Worldview

Whatever its particular form, Gaia thinking provides a new worldview for growing numbers of people. And as a worldview, it directly or indirectly responds to all the key questions.

1. What is life's purpose? For Gaians, the good goal is *homeostasis,* harmonious balance that allows life to flourish on a global scale. Our

lives find meaning through living in harmony with Gaia, contributing to her well-being, and enjoying her beauty and bounty. Yet this leaves unanswered some deeper questions. It tells us *what* and to some degree *how*, but not *why*. People may conclude that the purpose of life is to promote the well-being of Gaia, but the Gaia hypothesis itself, as a scientific theory, does not tell us that. This really is a leap of faith. It is probably the felt need for these deeper answers that leads many to religious or mystical versions of Gaia.

2. The Gaia hypothesis better answers the *design* question. This is its strength. Earth is a living organism. Starting here, we can discern how everything fits together. *Design* is, of course, a loaded word; it implies intention, a designer. Scientific Gaians hold that there is order and structure to the universe, but that this does not necessarily imply intentional design. It is just the way things evolved. More mystical versions of Gaia may see a kind of cosmic mind or spirit at work within all things, an implicit cosmic intentionality toward coherence, harmony, and beauty. In either case, the Earth is structured organically. Its order is that of a living thing.

3. As a worldview, the Gaia hypothesis provides, perhaps, fuller answers than do many worldviews to the question of *relationships*. Every human life is connected with every other, organically and ecologically. The same principles, in fact, run through all earthly existence. Human life is linked organically, interdependently, to everything else on Earth. The place of humanity shifts from the center or the peak of existence (as in many worldviews) to that of merely one part in the system—and not an especially important part. The larger reality is Gaia, the earth-organism. This is what counts. Gaia will continue, even if humans extinguish themselves through their own ecological folly. "Any living creature can and will be killed, but life itself cannot be stopped. Not from any plan or intention, and assuming no 'soul' or other mystical power, Gaia theory states that the net effect of this ancient, ubiquitous life force is the regulation of [the] local, and ultimately the global, environment," says Lynn Margulis.[15]

The Gaia worldview thus transfers uniqueness or specialness from humankind to Gaia itself. Gaia is a special place in the universe, precious and worth nurturing. In the vastness of space similar living planets may exist; we don't know. But if they do, they are so far off that they carry no practical meaning for us. In any case, the important thing is not humanity, but Gaia.

4. Where is history going, in the Gaia view? Ultimately, to oblivion, the extinction of life, but only over the span of millions or billions of years. Prac-

tically speaking, Gaia is eternal and self-regulating. There is no *ultimate* purpose to life or history, but we don't have to be concerned with ultimates. We should focus on the here and now and care for Mother Earth. Our present task is to live in harmony with Gaia for the well-being of the living Earth and its inhabitants both now and into the future.

The Limits of Gaia

Gaia is an attractive worldview. It seems both scientific and spiritual. As we noted, Lovelock finds it "deeply satisfying" that the Gaia viewpoint is "both spiritual and scientific." The Gaia model fits in well with humanity's growing ecological awareness and with the recognition that, ecologically speaking, humankind is not the center of the universe. It seems to be a humbler, kinder, gentler worldview. There is beauty in its appreciation for the varied forms of life and the awesome intricacies of living organisms.

As a worldview, the Gaia hypothesis also has its limitations. We must note three in particular.

First, as implied above, the Gaia worldview has no real answer to the question of life's meaning. We should cherish Earth, live in harmony with her. But why? Simply out of self-interest? Or because of some larger purpose? The Gaia worldview is agnostic about these deeper questions. Things simply are the way they are, the result of evolution. So far as we know, the universe has no ultimate purpose. Of course, it is possible to find human purpose, subjectively, in working for the well-being of Gaia and all she contains, animate and inanimate. But if there is no overarching significance, it is not clear or compelling why people should commit themselves to the well-being of Gaia. Some deeper answer is needed here.

Second, the Gaia hypothesis is really an incomplete worldview. It focuses exclusively on Earth, or at most on our solar system. Gaia is a beautiful goddess floating alone in a sea of nothingness. Gaia thinking says little about the vast universe of constellations and galaxies within which the Earth is only a microscopic speck. Against the background of the cosmos, Earth appears achingly beautiful, vulnerable, and precious. This makes sense, of course, for humans, because Earth is our home. But any worldview is incomplete that tells us about Earth but not about the rest of the universe. The Earth is not the universe. So how can the meaning of the universe by confined to Earth? Gaia thinking makes us aware of the nature of our earthly environment, but it leaves us unsatisfied, with unanswered questions.

It can be argued, of course, that Gaia is really all we need to know.

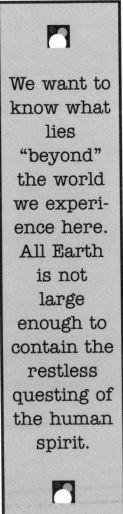

Looking to Heaven or the heavens and not paying attention to Earth is precisely what caused our environmental mess, some would say.

But there are two problems with this response. First, Earth's environment is in fact affected by the whole universe, not just by the sun. Our solar system is not a closed world. Like the atom, no solar system is an island. As surely as there is an Earth ecology, so also there is some kind of super-ecology of the universe in which Earth is also bound. Certainly this is true at least at the level of such fundamental realities as gravity, electromagnetism, and nuclear energy.

The second problem with an Earth-centered view concerns what it means to be human. The human mind and spirit cannot be confined to, and ultimately will not be satisfied with, a worldview that does not encompass all that is. Like a person raised in a ghetto or small town, humans eventually begin to wonder about what lies "beyond" the world they know. All Earth is not large enough to contain the restless questing of the human spirit.

This leads us to a third limitation of the Gaia model. While the Gaia viewpoint is scientific, it is primarily a view based on the life sciences. It has not fully engaged other branches of science that clearly will be crucial for a truly comprehensive worldview—in particular, quantum physics. Gaia thinking may prove to be enormously helpful in understanding human life and well-being in relation to the other life systems of Earth. In this sense it is already making a contribution. But the deeper question of the nature of matter itself remains.

In sum, Gaia thinking tells us much about the nature of Earth and of human life as part of Gaia. It is useful in helping the human race to understand its relationship to the Earth and therefore the importance of environmental issues. But it has little to say about those dimensions of existence that are smaller and larger than Gaia: the subatomic world of the quanta and the cosmic world of galaxies, black holes, quasars, and pulsars—and the many dimensions of the human spirit.

> We want to know what lies "beyond" the world we experience here. All Earth is not large enough to contain the restless questing of the human spirit.

CHAPTER THIRTEEN

Divine Design:
God in the Shadows?

> There is the music of Johann Sebastian Bach. Therefore there must be a God. You either see this one or you don't.
>
> —**PETER KREEFT AND RONALD TACELLI**[1]
>
> God can see our world as a three-dimensional creature could see Flatland.
>
> —**MATHEMATICIAN THOMAS BANCHOFF**

The fourth worldview we must consider is one both widely believed and widely doubted or mocked: the view that all things come from the hand of God. Of the six worldviews we are considering, only this view and fatalism (chap. 14) see meaning as transcending the physical universe. But in this conception, the fundamental transcendent reality is a personal power, not an impersonal force. Do global trends now make this view obsolete?

According to this worldview, the universe exists not by chance or fate or accident. Its source is not some self-contained evolutionary process, either random or purposeful. Rather, the universe has a Designer. The world and everything in it was made by God. God, without beginning or end, created all things.

This is the theistic worldview—the view that God is the ultimate source of all being, both material and immaterial. It is the view still held by most of Earth's citizens including, presumably, a large majority of the world's nearly two billion Christians and one billion Muslims.

Theism can take many different forms, as we will see. But its core belief is that God exists and created all things. This is fundamentally the view common to the three great monotheistic world religions—Judaism, Christianity, and Islam—as well as other religious worldviews that hold that behind or above all else is a High God who created the world. In the Western tradition this has been "the foundational view, the one from which all others developing between 1700 and 1900 essentially derive," notes James Sire.[2]

I call this worldview "Divine Design: God in the Shadows." It holds that the universe has order and purpose that derive solely from God's creative action. Yet often in this view, God is seen as rather uninvolved with the day-by-day life of the world. God exists and in some ultimate sense is in control. But for the most part God remains in the shadows or behind the curtain. Orthodox theology (Jewish, Christian, or Islamic) may well hold that God is directly involved with human affairs in some way. Yet, this seems to have little practical meaning for many who may think they hold this view. Many theists are practicing deists (deism implying a remote, hidden, largely passive, maybe irrelevant God). The main point is that the universe is an ordered, purposeful place because it derives from divine intention and action.

The Shape of Theism and Deism

The Divine Design worldview divides into two branches: theism and deism. The differences concern the character of God and the degree of God's ongoing activity in the world. Etymologically, *deism* and *theism* mean the same thing, since both come from the word for God (*theos* in Greek; *deus* in Latin). But historically deism has commonly been defined as belief in a creator God who exerts no influence on people or the world he created, whereas theism is a broader term, generally implying God's engagement with the world and with history. The two may be contrasted as follows:[3]

	Theism	*Deism*
God:	Infinite and personal; transcendent and immanent; all-knowing, sovereign, and good	Transcendent First Cause; created universe to run on its own; not immanent, fully personal, or sovereign
Cosmos:	Created by God from nothing; operates with a uniformity of cause and effect in an open system	Created by God, but operates as a uniformity of cause and effect in a closed system; no miracles
Humans:	Possess personality, self-transcendence, intelligence, morality, sociability, and creativity because created in God's image	Personal, but part of the clockwork of the universe

Relationship:	God communicates with humans; humans morally accountable to God	No direct communication; humans can know the universe and determine what God is like by studying it
Ethics:	Morality is transcendent, based on the character of God as good, holy, just, and loving	Ethics limited to what we can know of God through nature; the universe is normal, so reveals what is right
History:	Linear, a meaningful sequence of acts and events that will ultimately fulfill God's purposes	Linear; governed by universal laws determined by creation. Little interest in history

In these ways theism and deism contrast rather sharply, though both claim a belief in God. The historian of philosophy Émile Bréhier summarizes the differences as follows:

> [Deism introduced] a new conception of [humanity], wholly incompatible with the Christian faith. . . . God the architect who produced and maintained a marvelous order in the universe had been discovered in nature, and there was no longer a place for the God of the Christian drama, the God who bestowed upon Adam "the power to sin and to *reverse the order*." God was in nature and no longer in history; he was in the wonders analyzed by naturalists and biologists and no longer in the human conscience, with feelings of sin, disgrace, or grace that accompanied his presence; he had left [humans] in charge of [their] own destiny.[4]

In this chapter we will consider theism and deism together, since they both affirm a Creator God. We will note the differences between the two as necessary.

Obviously a Divine Design worldview contrasts sharply with those examined in previous chapters. It denies that we cannot know the source of the world, or that the universe is totally self-contained or self-generating. What are the main marks of this worldview? We may note six.

First, the theistic worldview starts with the presupposition that God exists and is a Being of supreme power who can create everything else simply by an act of will. While various "proofs" may be advanced for the existence of God, it seems clear that in the nature of the case God's existence can be neither proved nor disproved. Belief in God is simply an act of faith, though not a simple act of faith. It is a presupposition, a foundational belief of this worldview that God exists and is the Creator. The logic itself is simple: We and all things were created by God. So of course we cannot fully understand God or prove his existence by some sort of logical or scientific process. The created cannot fully prove the existence of the Creator; the lesser and limited cannot comprehend the Ultimate.

A second mark of this worldview is that God created the universe from nothing (*ex nihilo*). God did not use some pre-existing energy or material. If he had, matter or energy also would be eternal, co-equal with God. God created the universe from nothing—or, perhaps, as an expression of his own energy, since we now know matter is a form of energy. Nothing else, and no other explanation, is necessary. The faith that God exists carries with it the implication that God is capable of creating from nothing.

It is true that some theistic worldviews hold that God created the world out of some pre-existing material. While that is a possible view, it is actually inconsistent with the Divine Design view. It would imply that God is something less than the ultimate source of all being and existence. One is left with an eternal dualism—God *and* matter, or God and necessity, or God and Fate.

A third feature of the Divine Design view is that it implies a God of order, not of disorder or chaos. The created order is a reflection, in some fundamentally consistent way, of the character of the Creator. God is a God of order. He is coherent, not chaotic or cosmically confused. The creation is like the Creator in this sense, though it is finite and at least partially time bound.

This does not mean that the created world is totally orderly, like a fine machine. Disorder in the world is obvious and must be accounted for. The theistic view holds that this disorder is not fundamental to the character of the cosmos, or at least not inconsistent with its order. It arose somehow subsequent to the world's creation. While the universe may appear to be in some significant ways disordered, if we look deeply enough we can detect an order built into the very nature of things. Disorder and chaos are bounded by a more encompassing frame.

Some varieties of theism, notably deism, have pictured the universe as a machine, a sort of cosmic clockwork, as noted above. This view was popular in England and France in the late seventeenth and early eighteenth centuries, with their emphasis on reason and the "laws" of science. It is an "Enlightened" view—or thought to be so at the time by those who held it. But theism as such is not committed to, and usually rejects, such a mechanical model.

A fourth basic of the Divine Design view is that it grounds the meaning and purpose of the universe outside the created order itself. While one may find hints or analogs of God's purpose within the world, these only point to the Ultimate Source, to the purpose of God in creation.

Thus right and wrong—all ethical questions—trace back to God, not simply to the pragmatics of earthly life. Morality is based in God's character. We live in a moral universe.

This means also that our material world is not the ultimate reality. Our world is made of "solid" matter, but more basic "things"—dimensions or levels of reality—exist. Some theists believe that relativity and quantum mechanics lend scientific support to this view—not in the sense at all that quantum science "proves" the existence of God or of spiritual reality, but in the sense that it is consistent with the theistic view. The "theory" of a transcendent, personal God logically "predicts" that matter is the expression of a more fundamental reality and relationship.

Why did God create the universe? Ultimately, this remains a mystery only God can answer. Typically theism has suggested that God created all things either for God's own pleasure and glory, or simply as the consistent expression of his character. It is God's nature to create. Creating would be part of the divine job description, if God had one.

Meaning "Out There"

Of the six worldviews discussed here, this is the only one that offers a truly transcendent perspective. That is, it is the only one that places the source of life's significance completely beyond the realm of material existence and human experience. Other worldviews locate the source of meaning within human experience, either individual or corporate. Or they view meaning as grounded in some way in the material universe. In the Gaia hypothesis, for instance, meaning and purpose are seen as transcending human experience but as still arising from within the material world. Only the Divine Design worldview is transcendent in the sense of holding that purpose and meaning exist first of all completely above or beyond the universe.

Is God personal, or a Person? Most theistic views say yes, and so refer to God as "he" (or more recently, "she").[5] God is not an "it"; not an impersonal force like gravity or electricity, or like fate. God as Person is the source of human personality. Human consciousness, decision-making, and moral conscience are not the mere outcome of evolution. They reflect God's nature. Human consciousness derives from God's self-consciousness. It reflects the spark of God in human being, part of what traditionally has been called "spirit." In the biblical view, man and woman were created "in the image of God" (Gen. 1:27).

This is the fifth mark of the Divine Design worldview, but it is a point of debate within theism. Most theistic worldviews, and especially historic Christianity, are deeply convinced that God is a Person. In the

Christian view, this is demonstrated most conclusively in the very real person of Jesus Christ, who was God incarnate or "made flesh" on Earth. Here, certainly, God steps out of the shadows. But other theistic worldviews, including some that have appeared often enough in Christianity, stress the remote transcendence of God and thus really see only a shadowy God. God is Designer-in-chief more than present actor.

If God is personal and the Creator (directly or indirectly) of human consciousness and conscience, then humanity has a unique and special place in the cosmos. On the one hand, humans are part of the physical, "natural" order, part of the web of life and matter, culture and economics. On the other hand, humans have traits that make them different and unique in the world—more like God than like rocks and trees, at least in this crucial sense.

Historically, deism departed from theism at this point. Deists see God as a remote Creator who set the universe going—made the machine, in other words—but left it to run according to cause-and-effect laws. God is not personal, or at least not knowable as personal. This presents a logical inconsistency, of course. No impersonal force could build an intricate machine, much less conscious humans. Partly for this reason, deism was an unstable worldview and really forms the transition from theism to naturalism (the view that matter exists eternally, and there is no God), as James Sire has pointed out.[6] Deism is certainly a worldview of Divine Design—pre-eminently so—but in our life on Earth we are left only with the design (in the form of our universe), not the Designer.

The final feature of Divine Design is that history has direction and a goal. The design is not frozen, static, or a repeating cycle. Life is more than cycle. It's more than wheels turning or ecosystems evolving. It has the nature of story because it is fundamentally personal. History is more than time. By definition, history is human. It is personal. It is both objective and subjective, blended, because that is the nature of personality. History is more than matter plus space plus time. The coherence of the universe has the character of direction, story, and purpose.

In other words, history is "going somewhere." Just where, of course, is a key question. Different theistic worldviews answer the question differently. Theism by itself does not answer the question until we bring in other considerations. Therefore we will need to return to this issue later.

The Character of God

The theistic worldview stresses the personal nature and character of God, as we have seen. God is the source not only of the created order but of the moral order as well—simply because of who he is. The high-point of the disclosure of God's character comes in the ancient Hebrew prophets. The writings of the prophet Isaiah are especially eloquent. Isaiah describes God's greatness and power:

> He sits enthroned above the circle of
>   the earth,
>   and its people are like grasshoppers.
> He stretches out the heavens like a
>   canopy,
>   and spreads them out like a tent to
>   live in.
> . . . .
> "To whom will you compare me?
>   Or who is my equal?" says the Holy
>   One.
> Lift your eyes and look to the heavens:
>   Who created all these?
> He who brings out the starry host one
>   by one,
>   and calls them each by name.
> Because of his great power and mighty
>   strength,
>   not one of them is missing.
>   (Isa. 40:22, 25-26 NIV)

God is the Creator, supremely sovereign over all things. Yet he is not a remote God, unconcerned or unengaged with human life. So we read:

> Do you not know?
>   Have you not heard?
> The LORD is the everlasting God,
>   the Creator of the ends of the earth.
> He will not grow tired or weary,
>   and his understanding no one can
>   fathom.
> He gives strength to the weary
>   and increases the power of the weak.
> Even youths grow tired and weary,
>   and young men stumble and fall;
> but those who hope in the LORD
>   will renew their strength.
> They will soar on wings like eagles;
>   they will run and not grow weary,
>   they will walk and not be faint.
>   (Isa. 40:28-31 NIV)

The combination of transcendence and immanence—God both far and near—is no contradiction. It is simply who God is. It is a necessary mystery and a mysterious necessity if spacetime creatures are to speak coherently about God. This mystery is nowhere expressed more profoundly than in Isaiah 57:15:

> For this is what the high and lofty One
>   says—
> he who lives forever, whose name is
>   holy:
> "I live in a high and holy place,
>   but also with [whoever] is contrite and
>   lowly in spirit,
> to revive the spirit of the lowly
>   and to revive the heart of the
>   contrite.

God is a God of justice and compassion for the oppressed, not solely of might and power. Therefore God expects compassion and justice from those God created. Humans live in a moral and ethical universe because of who God is. Isaiah and others of Israel's prophets denounced injustice and even religious rituals such as fasting when they were not matched by right living. So God says through Isaiah:

> Is not this the kind of fasting I have
>   chosen:
> to loose the chains of injustice
>   and untie the cords of the yoke,
> to set the oppressed free
>   and break every yoke?
> Is it not to share your food with the hungry
>   and to provide the poor wanderer
>   with shelter—
> when you see the naked, to clothe him,
>   and not to turn away from your own
>   flesh and blood?
> Then your light will break forth like
>   the dawn,
>   and your healing will quickly appear.
>
> (Isa. 58:6-8 NIV)

This is far different from common New Age and some highly mystical views of God that see God as a cosmic consciousness in which everyone may participate if they are just sensitive enough. In the theistic world-view, God makes moral and ethical demands, though not in a legalistic, autocratic way. God is a moral Person of love and justice, and knowing God means reflecting God's character in one's life.

In the Hebrew worldview, God is thus much more than a shadowy Creator. God is awesome justice and rightness. All men and women are alienated from God, not because they are creatures or finite, but because they are in moral revolt against God. The human race has chosen to deify itself, or raw power, or some part of the created order, instead of living according to God's character. Isaiah again expresses this eloquently and speaks of God's own solution: the promise of a Messiah, an anointed servant, who will bring people into reconciliation with God:

> We all, like sheep, have gone astray,
>   each of us has turned to [our] own
>   way;
> and the LORD has laid on him
>   the [evil] of us all.
>   (Isa. 53:6 NIV)

In the Hebrew, and the Christian, view of God, the Creator is thus fully personal—so profoundly so that it is God who defines what "person" and "personality" are, not the other way around. Thus the relationship between God and humans is deeply personal, relational, and moral in character.

The Worldview Questions

These are the essential elements of the Divine Design worldview. For summary and clarity, we may now ask the key worldview questions: Purpose, design, relationships, and history.

1. What is the *purpose* of life in the Divine Design worldview? Where is meaning to be found? What is the good? Most basically, the purpose of life is to live consistently with the design of the universe. This means finding and "doing the will of God." Not all versions of the Divine Design view conceive of God's will the same way, so we find differing answers to the question of how humankind is to please God, and differences as to how much we can know God's will or purpose.

The classic Christian formulation has been that the "chief end of [humankind] is to glorify God and to enjoy him forever." At various times, Divine Designers have understood the purpose of life to be escape from the world, love for other people, following the life of Jesus, engaging in religious practices, stamping out idolatry and apostasy, or destroying the infidel. Clearly, purpose in life is a reflection of how the *character* of the Creator God is understood. Purpose and meaning are found,

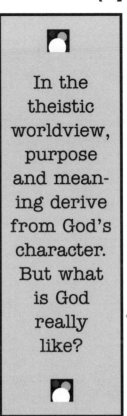

however, not within oneself, society, or the material world but in the transcendent purpose God built into the universe from the beginning.

2. What is the *design* of the universe? First of all it is, as we have seen, *purposive*. The universe is ordered, not random.

This order need not be conceived of mechanistically—the universe as mega-machine—although that certainly is one option. Eighteenth-century deists tended to see the universe as a gigantic clock, well designed and well ordered, whose laws and principles could in principle be grasped, as we have seen. Operating like a clock, the universe never fundamentally changed or developed. Not a very dynamic conception.

The Divine Design view has frequently been understood in a more dynamic, organic sense, however. This was true in much of Greek thought, in early Christianity, and in some more recent Christian worldviews. The universe is like an organism, but this organic nature is not the source, in itself, of meaning. Rather it reflects the nature of the living God.

3. What about *relationships?* How does my life relate to other people, to the universe, and to history? The Divine Design view sees God as the common ground for all human relationships. All people are by creation the children of God. In the biblical book of Genesis, man and woman are created in the image of God, as already noted. Thus every person is inherently God-breathed and God-imaged. One way this has often been stated is as "the fatherhood (or motherhood) of God and the brotherhood (or sisterhood) of Man (humanity)." Or, similarly, "every child of God is a brother (or sister) to me."

If this is so, why do human beings murder and slaughter one another? The theistic view gives a variety of answers. The most common have been:

> In the theistic worldview, purpose and meaning derive from God's character. But what is God really like?

1. We are all children of God but have all fallen into sin, becoming self-centered (the Bible, historic Christianity).
2. Although we are all children of God by creation, only those who rightly worship God are God's true children, and everyone else is an enemy of God and his people (fundamentalism, as found in Christian, Islamic, Hindu, and many other forms).

3. Although we are all children of God, our finite human nature keeps us from really understanding this and living the way we should (Islam, in general; several varieties of mysticism; theistic versions of New Age thinking).

Here again we see how important the nature of God's *character* is in the theistic view. The central point here, however, is that all human life has a common grounding in God's creative activity. This in turn provides the basis for an understanding of ethics, society, and history.

4. What of *history?* Generally the theistic view sees history as the long working out of God's purposes in human affairs. God's will is being done, or will ultimately be done, in history. This can be understood in the classic Christian sense that history is moving toward the ultimate goal of reconciliation in the Kingdom of God. God actually works in the present and, as it were, back from the future to accomplish his purposes. Or, God's purposes and intention can be seen as woven into the very fabric of the universe. Thus history eventually, inevitably, will fulfill its intended purpose or reach its divine goal.

History, therefore, is not random or meaningless, as we have seen. History has significance, even if we have trouble seeing it. It is neither meaningless nor malevolent. Further, the meaning of history is not to be found in mere balance or homeostasis, or in smoothly repeating cycles, but in the movement of history toward the fulfillment of God's purposes. In other words, ultimately history is neither chaotic, fatalistic, malign, nor destructive.

A Strong Worldview

Divine Design is a strong, confident worldview. It claims to have ultimate answers. This has been its strength. But in a postmodern age of pluralism, relativism, and skepticism, its confidence has become perhaps a chief liability. Today thinking people are wary of any worldview that claims to have answers or assert meaning. We should remember, however, that most worldviews do claim to provide credible replies to the basic worldview questions.

A special strength of this worldview is its coherence. If one grants its presuppositions, this view holds together with impressive internal logic. Also, it is a comprehensive view. All things come from one source. This view provides a basis for showing how everything fits together. If one believes that God exists and created all things, that presupposition gives the starting point for answering every other question people ponder. It raises other questions, of course. But it sets the big frame within which to consider them.

Another feature of the Divine Design worldview clashes sharply with every contemporary view: its *sense of eternity*. I mean not only the conviction that existence is more than spacetime, but the sense of the existential importance of eternal things. Life is lived (if this view is taken seriously) with the consciousness of an eternal dimension of existence that one enters at death—and which thus impinges on, and is partially experienced in, present life. This sense has been lost almost completely in most of today's world. In many areas, life spans have lengthened, material goods abound, and earthly existence is much less precarious. The focus is on time, not eternity.

Plainly put, most people in the world today, even religious people, are not much interested in eternity. It is irrelevant. This is curious, both historically and psychologically. Throughout history the shortness and uncertainty of life (so it is argued) made people concerned about their eternal destiny. God has "set eternity in [our] hearts," said Solomon (Eccles. 3:11 NIV).

Yet, this sense of the eternal seems mostly lost today, even though human life is still only a speck in time. Relatively few people live much longer than a century—yet our universe has existed for some fifteen billion years.

It is curious that humans can have so little interest in eternal (or more-than-spacetime) dimensions just when our scientific sense of time has stretched so markedly. Part of the reason seems to be the "now-ism" or "me-ism" or "present-ism" of much modern and postmodern culture, wrapped up in itself. Perhaps the increasing sense of the length of geologic time (and thus the shortness of human life) will combine with the collapse of other worldviews to bring a new curiosity and concern about things eternal—at least for those who take the time to ponder and wonder.

This sense of eternity is a strength of the theistic worldview. Yet it makes this view seem irrelevant or obsolete to many. Then too, many people claim to have a theistic view, but God to them is a remote God in the shadows. This eternal sense is not really felt.

What About Evil?

The two biggest problems with the Divine Design worldview, both historically and in the minds of many today, are the question of faith and the problem of evil. Many people reject Divine Design because they say it is based on faith rather than on reason or scientific fact. The problem of evil is even more vexing. If God created all things, where did evil come from? We seem locked in an unbreakable syllogism:

a. God created the universe.
b. Evil exists in the universe.
c. Therefore, God is the source of evil.

Either God is evil, or evil exists in eternal struggle with God, or God permits evil for some ultimately good purpose. Or perhaps evil arose "accidentally" somehow, and God is not strong enough to stop it. This is a conundrum. There are profound problems with each of these options, though the Divine Design model generally opts for the third. Somehow evil will eventually be swallowed up by good—perhaps analogously to complex systems, where at times order seems spontaneously to arise from chaos. But this will come by God's good action, not by some blind, mindless process.

The question of faith is less difficult. It is a false problem. The dominant thinking over the past few centuries, particularly in the West, built a wall between faith and reason, or between faith and science. Faith and reason were thought to operate in different spheres. One can function on "mere" faith or on "real" facts and "sound" reason. Faith was seen as purely subjective (and by implication, of less importance). In contrast, science dealt with the objective world of verifiable facts.

In the past fifty years, this view has been exploded. Relativity and quantum physics were the dynamite. While such a split-level view is still commonly held, it is dying fast. Increasingly people are coming to see that all knowledge is personal (both objective and subjective) and that some dimension of faith operates at every level of people's lives.[7] It turns out that faith is necessary in life. Even those who claim to have no faith really do. They believe in something—their own reason, some philosophy, fate or astrology, or the opinions of influential persons.

We noted in the beginning of our worldview discussion, in chapter 10, that every worldview is based finally on faith. There is no such thing as a scientific worldview in the sense of a view that has been or can be verified by science, as we saw in chapter 11. Some worldviews take the findings and hypotheses of science as their foundational beliefs, but these presuppositions remain precisely that: faith positions. This is why some scientists caution against making the leap from science to a worldview, or from physics to metaphysics. In taking that step one moves beyond science, they say. This is true, of course. Yet everyone with a worldview does so, because reason and science lead only so far.

Faith, then, is not the issue. Every worldview requires it. The issue is which view most plausibly and comprehensively answers the basic questions of human life. Which is more believable? Then, of course, the question becomes: believable *to whom?* One cannot escape the *personal* element, the believing subject. And here we must take care not to answer for others.

Through the centuries, many worldviews have been pronounced "incredible" or "unbelievable." Yet millions of people go right on believing them. Anyone who says a worldview is unbelievable is really saying, *I* can't or don't believe it. So the question becomes: Is a particular worldview believable *to me?* And since we are social creatures, part of a culture, the wider dimension also enters in: Is this view believable to "our group"; to "my people"? An array of factors make a worldview believable in a particular context. But we should not deceive ourselves: Ultimately faith is required. Faith functions. People either believe or do not believe a particular worldview, whatever the persuading factors and forces may be.

The Problem of Origins

Some say the Divine Design worldview is weak in answering the question of origins. Is belief in God really necessary to explain the universe? Wouldn't the Big Bang theory work just as well? Or do we even need an answer?

Many have argued that faith in God is simply a human projection (or retrojection) from our cause and effect experiences in daily life. In order to explain the universe, we imagine an Ultimate Cause who is simply a sort of super human being, a cosmic superman. We make God in our own image. How does it help to say that God caused the universe to exist when we can't answer the question of why God exists? Does God really answer the question of causation or merely push it back one step?

The Divine Design view gives a twofold answer. First, many people find it more satisfying and plausible to believe in a God of will, purpose, and power who created all things than to think that the universe somehow caused itself. The question of the origin of God is unanswerable. But it seems more plausible to believe in a divine being, a divine Personality who exists in a dimension of reality where time, space, origin, and causality have no meaning or are transcended in some kind of higher meaning (or higher dimensions) than to believe the universe caused itself. This is an inherently credible viewpoint. It says that the ultimate reality is personal, not impersonal; purposive, not random or deterministic; conscious, not unthinking and unfeeling.

The second point is implied in the first. The hypothesis of God raises the question of ultimate reality to new dimensions. It puts it on a different plane. If God is an eternal spiritual being with consciousness and will,

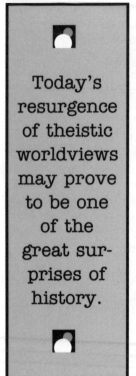

Today's resurgence of theistic worldviews may prove to be one of the great surprises of history.

then when we talk about God we are speaking of dimensions of existence that surpass those of our space-time world. We are, perhaps, dealing in a realm of multidimensionality that goes far beyond the four dimensions we normally sense. (This is the view of mathematician Thomas Banchoff, who believes God inhabits more dimensions than those we experience. "God can see our world as a three-dimensional creature could see Flatland," he says.[8])

Is Divine Design believable in a world of quantum physics, space exploration, emerging global order or chaos, and global pluralism? Again we must ask, believable to whom? Global statistics show that theistic worldviews are winning *increasing* acceptance within the world's population. Christianity and Islam are growing worldwide, as are other religions that believe in an ultimate design that comes from God. In secular cultures like those of the United States, Western Europe, Australia, and (increasingly) Japan, this is not the perception. There, belief in a theistic worldview may be considered naive or outmoded, particularly among intellectual elites. This may change, however, under the impact of globalization and the emergence of new paradigms in science and other fields.

Do today's Earth Currents make theistic worldviews obsolete? Hardly! Far from dying out due to secularization, as two or three generations of Western intellectual leaders thought would happen, the Divine Design worldview (in one form or another) is increasingly accepted in many places in the world, including in nations and among peoples formerly under Communist control.

This resurgence of theistic worldviews may prove to be one of the great surprises of history, at least for those who thought belief in God would dissolve in the acids and relativities of science. But two cautions: There are quite different kinds of Divine Design worldviews, as we have seen. And among influential intellectual elites, nontheistic worldviews, or pantheistic worldviews that see "God" as somehow present and evolving within the universe, appear to be gaining ground.

The Divine Design worldview is still a living option for billions of Earth's people today. Yet in the light of global trends, we may sense that it is not wholly adequate. Something is missing.

CHAPTER FOURTEEN

The Force of Fate:
Determinism Revisited

> These are the Fates, daughters of Necessity . . .
> Lachesis singing of the past, Clotho of the present,
> Atropos of the future.
>
> —**PLATO**
>
> Fate laughs at probabilities.
>
> —**EDWARD BULWER LYTTON**

A ccording to a popular song of the 1950s, "Que será, será—whatever will be, will be." The advice was comforting, in a way: We don't know the future, so don't worry about it. If something is going to happen, it will. Fate will have its way.

The underlying message in this and similar popular sentiment, though seldom stated, is clear: The future is predetermined. We can do nothing about it. What will be will be.

This is popular fatalism. Many of us are probably part-time fatalists. We are fatalists by default, perhaps—particularly when tragedy strikes. A man dies, and we say (in the passive voice): Well, his time had come. So Napoleon Bonaparte wrote in 1821, near the end of his life: "Our hour is marked, and no one can claim a moment of life beyond what fate has predestined."

The *Star Wars* movies, seen worldwide in the late 1970s and early 1980s, appealed partly because of the underlying theme of The Force: "May The Force be with you!" It was never clear just what the Force was. It had an ambiguous quality. The Force was a kind of moral gravity, an invisible power that touched everything and couldn't safely be ignored. And it was ambivalent; there was a "dark side" to the Force. One had to learn how to use the Force for good, yet not yield to its shadow side. Darth Vader became the arch-villain by surrendering to the dark side of the Force.

In this chapter we examine fate as a worldview. We need to, because many people really are fatalists. Fatalism has outlived the premodern and modern ages and continues to thrive as a worldview option even in a global, postmodern age. People take refuge in fatalism as they feel global trends may overwhelm them.

We will explore the nature of fatalism by looking at a nineteenth-century example. Then we will see how fate functions as a worldview today and look at its connection with magic and astrology.

Fate, Force, and Chance

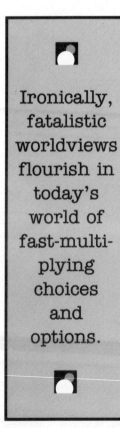

Ironically, fatalistic worldviews flourish in today's world of fast-multiplying choices and options.

Fate is an enduring fact of history, it seems. Many people really believe in fate *as a force*. What will be will be—not because there is random chaos in the world but because some force furtively moves things along. This force is not God. It is not someone or something to be reasoned with or prayed to, not someone who could change her mind. It is just there, the gravitational pull of history. A power that ultimately controls all that exists and happens, robbing us of our freedom. Blind fate! If people really believe this, or act like they do, then Fate is actually their worldview.

Some have argued with Karl Löwith that "in the reality of that agitated sea which we call 'history,' it makes little difference whether man feels himself in the hands of God's inscrutable will or in the hands of chance or fate."[1] But most feel differently. It does make a difference. Fate and fatalism figure as one of the earliest and most enduring of human worldviews. Interestingly, it flourishes in today's world of fast-multiplying choices and options. One of the modern ironies is this perdurability of Fate in the global marketplace of ideas and worldviews. This curiosity calls for some reflection.

Greeks and Romans believed in Fate—or more correctly, the three

Fates, goddesses who ruled human affairs and never changed their minds. Clotho spun the thread of life; Lachesis measured its length; Atropos cut it. Here was the real explanation for—or at least the cause behind—life's hard mysteries.

Gods and fate were bound up together in Greek and Roman mythology. Significantly, the gods themselves were subject to fate, or the Fates, and were not totally free. In the first century A.D. the Roman philosopher Seneca spoke of Fate as the ultimate force, "an irrevocable cause which carries along human and divine affairs equally . . . leading the willing and dragging the unwilling."[2] Seneca still believed in God as the First Cause of things. But Fate was the nearer, more pressing reality in human affairs.

Fate here is not merely a fact, not just a default explanation when others fail. That would be Chance. Fate is a force—in fact, *the* Force. Fate is not a rock that trips your foot. It is a power that moves your life, all lives, yet can never be fully explained.

The idea of the force of fate persists down through history in both East and West. Whatever other realities govern people's lives, underneath is some blind force, inescapable, immutable, untouched by human fears or tears. So people have believed. It sets the limits and governs the contingencies of our lives. "Fate laughs at probabilities," wrote Edward Bulwer Lytton.

Modern Fatalism: Ralph Waldo Emerson

Despite its faith in reason and progress, the modern age (modernity) did not annihilate fate. Moderns could also be fatalists, just as most of us carry around more than one worldview in our approach to life. One of America's most influential thinkers, Ralph Waldo Emerson (1803-82), is an instructive example. Emerson seemed to view fate as a force. He illuminates the appeal of the historic, and still popular, fatalistic worldview. As a shaper of American thought (often pictured as being Christian but really "America's first 'death-of-God' theologian"[3]) Emerson shows the persistence and resurgence of Fate.

Reacting against the Christianity of his youth, Emerson argued for courageous, optimistic self-reliance. But the self is not sovereign. Emerson saw Fate as the final reality, stronger than mere humans. "Nature is no sentimentalist," Emerson wrote in his 1860 essay, "Fate." "We must see that the world is rough and surly, and will not mind drowning a man or a woman; but swallows your ship like a grain of dust. The cold, inconsiderate of persons, tingles your blood, benumbs your feet, freezes a man like an apple. . . . The way of Providence is a little rude." For

Emerson, "Providence" has lost its Christian sense; it is a euphemism for Fate.

Every person is limited by their genetic endowment, Emerson noted. "When each comes forth from his mother's womb, the gate of gifts closes behind him. Let him value his hands and feet, he has but one pair. So he has but one future, and that is already predetermined in his lobes, and described in that little fatty face, pig-eye, and squat form. All the privilege and all the legislation of the world cannot meddle or help to make a poet or a prince of him." Here is fatalism reborn and sadly celebrated. Nature is little concerned about the individual: "In certain men, digestion and sex absorb the vital force, and the stronger these are, the individual is so much weaker. The more of these drones perish, the better for the hive."

In one stark passage Emerson wrote:

> The book of Nature is the book of Fate. She turns the gigantic pages,— leaf after leaf,—never re-turning one. One leaf she lays down, a floor of granite; then a thousand ages, and a bed of slate; a thousand ages, and a measure of coal; a thousand ages, and a layer of marl and mud: vegetable forms appear: her first misshapen animals . . . rude forms, in which she has only blocked her future state, concealing under these unwieldy monsters the fine type of her coming king. The face of the planet cools and dries, the races meliorate, and man is born. But when a race has lived its term, it comes no more again.[4]

Translation: Evolution itself is forced by Fate, which is more basic, and human life has no *ultimate* significance.

"Whatever limits us, we call Fate," Emerson wrote. This line of limitation runs through all of nature. We press against the walls of necessity, feeling them, finding our own measure of freedom. "The limitations refine as the soul purifies, but the ring of necessity is always perched at the top." Above all, "in the world of morals, Fate appears as vindicator, levelling the high, lifting the low, requiring justice in man, and always striking soon or late, when justice is not done."[5]

Is Fate, then, on the side of justice? A curious thing, if so, because then Fate has some moral character. Either Emerson is inconsistent here—for Fate often seems capricious and unjust—or he simply means that Fate eventually catches up even with the unjust.

For Emerson, Fate is not really a negative or neutral force. It has a positive side, permitting the power of thought and an element of freedom. It is humanity's fate to be free, though with limits. "Intellect annuls Fate. So far as a man thinks, he is free," Emerson thought. A person should "look not at Fate, but the other way." "Too much contemplation of these limits induces meanness. They who talk much of destiny, their birth-star, etc., are in a lower dangerous plane, and invite the evils they fear." Only "weak and vicious people . . . cast the blame on Fate. The right use of Fate is to bring up our conduct to the loftiness of nature." Thus Emerson concludes, "The best use of Fate [is] to teach a fatal courage. Go face the fire at sea, or the cholera in your friend's house, or the burglar in your own, or what danger lies in the way of duty, knowing you are guarded by the cherubim of Destiny. If you believe in Fate to your harm, believe it, at least, for your good."[6] You can't escape Fate, Emerson says, but that is no excuse for giving in to it. Have courage. Believe in its benign side.

Emerson's view is thus curiously optimistic. Fate is in some sense a positive force, a challenge to be faced, even though ultimately invincible. "A breath of wind blows eternally through the universe of souls in the direction of the Right and Necessary," he wrote. "It is the air which all intellects inhale and exhale, and it is the wind which blows the worlds into order and orbit." If, then, "Fate is ore and quarry, *if evil is good in the making,* if limitation is power that shall be, if calamities, oppositions, and weights are wings and means,—we are reconciled."[7] We have a choice, in other words: courageous or cowardly living in the face of Fate. Yet it is not clear why one is better than the other.

Plainly, Emerson makes Fate out to be, finally, a good force. Necessity equals Right in his view. Fate, though cruel or "rude," ultimately means that "evil is good in the making." And so we can be reconciled to it. But why? How do we know fate is finally good, or can be made good by our courage? There is no answer. For Emerson, this seems to have been *his* leap of faith, or perhaps the fruit of his optimism.

Is Fate good or bad? Or equally both, balanced in a sort of moral mathematical equation? Rationally, empirically, there is no answer. The person who totals up all history's disasters and sufferings and says they prove Fate is evil has as strong a case as the optimist who says that finally the good outweighs the bad. There is no proof. Something else must be added to the equation or appealed to. For Emerson, the added ingredient seems to be simply his own optimism.

Why, then, should one act courageously and face fate with fortitude? In Emerson's view, because this aligns us with the aspect of Right in Fate (the "good side" of the Force?). But since we really don't know that Fate is in any sense good, passive fatalism makes just as much sense rationally. The only escape would be to resort to pragmatic psychology: You will be happier if you believe Fate is ultimately benign and if you act like your actions have meaning and value.

How did Emerson come to such a view? The answer lies in his personal story. He was raised in a Protestant Unitarian home, but eventually came to doubt the Christian (as he understood it) view of God. Yet he maintained much of the Christian ethic and ethos, carried over from his family and community. Functionally, Fate replaces God in Emerson's system. There still is a sovereign force, but not a personal one.

Fate and History

Can one believe in fate and history at the same time? Or is faith in fate fatal to history? It is interesting that Emerson had very little interest in history as such. Sydney Ahlstrom speaks of Emerson's "refusal to think historically."[8] History for Emerson was the repeated embodiment, perhaps in new combinations, of Platonic ideas. Its real value is to teach us about ourselves through looking at history.

"The student is to read history actively and not passively; to esteem his own life the text, and books the commentary," Emerson wrote in his essay "History." Everyone "should see that he can live all history in his own person." One looks for the "secret sense" in the facts of history. "Time dissipates to shining ether the solid angularity of facts. No anchor, no cable, no fences, avail to keep a fact a fact," he said. "All history becomes subjective; in other words, there is properly no history, only biography." Thus Emerson concurs with Napoleon: History is merely "a fable agreed upon."

For Emerson, history is the repeated manifestation of universal mind. "There is one mind common to all individual" persons, and whoever has "access to this universal mind is a party to all that is or can be done, for this is the only and sovereign agent." Thus throughout history "camp, kingdom, empire, republic, democracy are merely the applications" of the first human's "manifold spirit to the manifold world."[9]

Here is a worldview that is fatalistic, yet subjectively cheerful. But whence comes this optimism? In Emerson's case, it seems to spring from a secularized Christian hope blended with Greek philosophy, and especially Plato. Emerson is the type of the more optimistic sort of fatalism: Fate is a positive force.

This is a common view among people to

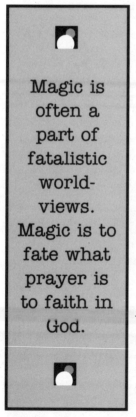

Magic is often a part of fatalistic worldviews. Magic is to fate what prayer is to faith in God.

whom the Fates have been kind! But it offers little comfort to others. If one suffers from disease or poverty, from despair or a broken heart, from loneliness or world-weariness, what then? What will be will be—and probably *should* be. We are in the hands of Fate. Despair would seem the logical conclusion.

If so, if Fate rules, then we look for omens, star signs, clues that shed light on our destiny. Or perhaps we turn to magic. Perhaps we can trick Fate by some form of clever art or incantation. Magic is therefore often a part of the Fateful worldview. Magic is to fate what prayer is to faith in God.

Fate, fortune; luck, chance; magic, astrology; signs and omens—all are powers out of our control, yet controlling us in some way, mysterious forces than people instinctively believe in. And this is the point: *Faith* in what we believe affects us, regardless of and impervious to our faith. Even the fatalistic worldview requires faith. And it does provide a framework for life. For many, it makes life bearable.

Fate and Purpose

What answer does fate as a force give to the basic worldview questions?

1. The *purpose* question can be answered by a negation or an affirmation. *Life has no purpose* is one option. Fate exists, without reason and without appeal, and rules all, but to no purpose. That's simply the way things are. Fate is blind and gives no explanations. As humans we anthropomorphize fate (or deify it), speaking of it as "acting" (as Emerson did), as "blind," as "cruel," maybe even as "willing." These words simply personify what is believed to be an abstract, inanimate but very real force. Fate is a purposeless force in a purposeless universe, and we are its unwitting victims. But Fate doesn't say it's sorry because it is unaware of the pain it causes—or the pleasure.

Emotionally and psychologically, this is too pessimistic for most people. So many, like Emerson, answer the purpose question more positively. The purpose of life is to find meaning and happiness in spite of fate. More boldly: The purpose of life is to *claim* purpose, to *assert* meaning. Fate may be bad, or have sad effects, but life is good. Life is its own justification and reward. One need look no further. Here one arrives at a position that feels a lot like deconstructive postmodernism (to be discussed in the next chapter).

This is plausible. "It is better to have loved and lost than never to have loved at all." This aphorism expresses the hopeful instinct of the

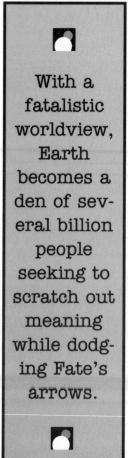

human spirit. Death, or fate in some other guise, may sweep the loved one away, but the experience of love itself tells us it was worth it. Love makes life worth living, in spite of fate.

If the ultimate reality is the force of fate—if there is no cosmic meaning, no universal purpose—then we are left to find meaning where we may. Love is a good option; it is absorbing, joining mind and heart, and relational, tying persons to one another. But what happens when love fails or is unfound? No love, no meaning. And therefore no life? Or, when love fails, the lover may look elsewhere for meaning: art, violence, a crusade, a political cause. This is just what many people do.

Some people find meaning and purpose in the mind, in thought and imagination, in ideas and philosophy. Mental activity itself proves sufficient to provide a reason for being. Emerson is a prime example.

People may create purpose from their attraction to art and form, or pleasure and sensation, or power and its uses. But when meaning and purpose arise solely from one's own quest for them, two things remain true. First, this is a purpose that we in some sense impose from our own experience. We create it from within; we don't discover it from without (though we may universalize from our own experience). And therefore, second, we are left fundamentally with individualism, atomism. The world becomes a den of four or five billion people seeking to scratch out meaning while dodging the arrows of Fate. In fact, of course, they do so in groups—families, neighborhoods, gangs, teams, cities, tribes, nations—and find much of their meaning there, often with no conscious search for meaning. When these groups disintegrate, the individual is left in a lonely universe indeed.

> **With a fatalistic worldview, Earth becomes a den of several billion people seeking to scratch out meaning while dodging Fate's arrows.**

If fate is the force controlling all, then meaning is absent or is what one makes it. What is good is what is good *for me* —or, if one is less self-centered, more enlightened perhaps, for me and my world. What is bad is whatever is bad for me and mine. Evil is whatever ruins my life. And fate is both good and evil, for the dice don't always give sixes.

Fate and Design

2. What is the *design* of the universe?—another worldview question. In a sense, the fate-as-force worldview really begins here. There is no *intentional* design, so whatever pattern we find is random, accidental, or something we impose to make life livable. Human life is an ordered space within a pervading chaos, or a circle of humanity tucked away in a vast but meaningless machine. This is true for those who experience life as orderly and humane. For billions of turn-of-the-millennium people who find life to be chaos and misery, however, the purposelessness of the universe invades them like a cold chill that can't be warmed.

The fatalistic worldview says *Fate is, in fact, the design of the universe.* Or more accurately, fate is the reality, whether seen as chaotic or orderly. Fate is what is really real. It is futile to look further for design.

3. Under the wheel of fate, how does a person's life connect with other people and with history? This is the question of *relationship.* For starters, everyone is subject to fate. It is not fate's fault if some folks suffer while others prosper. For fate has no purpose, no morals, and no accountability. History shows the hand of fate in human affairs; it is the story of how people and nations have dealt with what befell them.

4. What about *history?* In Emerson's view, history is the illustration of every person's life. I relate to history as one who must deal with life's challenges and, in some sense, as representative of all that is human in humanity. More pessimistic views might find history totally meaningless, or as the story that confirms the absence of meaning, or as diabolical. The more truly fatalistic the worldview, however, the less historical. For if the ultimate, controlling reality is fate, history itself is fettered and can't go anywhere. "When history dies, the future has no children," says a Chinese proverb.

This is why history in a fatalistic view tends to be static or cyclical, not linear. It does not head in any direction, toward any goal. One senses again the affinity with much of postmodernism. Here one finds some of its century-old roots.

Fate and Magic

This is also where magic and astrology come into their own. Magic is the effort to manipulate fate. Astrology (literally, "a word about the stars") is the belief that fate is connected with the movement of the heavenly bodies. Fate is blind, but stars give clues. Magic and astrology are ways to deal with the force and the logic of fate.

Astrology may seem rationally consistent with fate, for it is not so much an attempt to change fate as to cooperate with it. What do the stars say? It makes sense to pay attention to the signs (a fatalist might say), even if ultimately our destiny is set. We have at least some wiggle room. There is no point in tempting fate—so to speak; logically we would have to admit that fate can't be tempted.

So it is with astrology. But magic? Fate would seem to make it impossible or irrelevant. Fate does not respond to human tricks. Yet few people truly believe this, or can live consistent with the belief. Man is an actor; woman is a doer. On the one hand, we may take comfort in the inevitability of what we don't want to take responsibility for. On the other hand, we must act. We must try to subvert the inevitability of fate, or outsmart it. This is what magic does. Whether it really works or not is another question.

Magic tries to dodge the logic of fate. Magic sneaks up on the blind side of Lachesis, Clotho, and Atropos (particularly Atropos, the Future); quakes the earth beneath them; tricks them into serving another Fate, one even they don't control. Or so people think.

The popularity of astrology is a sure sign that fate is a contemporary worldview. Horoscopes, charms, and superstitions abound worldwide. Up-to-date bookstores display Tarot cards. Popular rock stars talk of their superstitions and consult their astrologers—as did a U.S. president's wife during the 1980s.

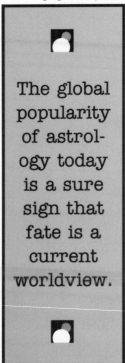

The global popularity of astrology today is a sure sign that fate is a current worldview.

In fact, magic persists down the millennia, in both East and West. It seems to be as old as civilization. Magic has continued despite vast social, economic, and religious upheavals. Medievalist Jeffrey Russell notes that in Europe "indications of magic in the period from the eighth to the twelfth centuries are so numerous as to defy citation"—astrology, divinations, weather-witching, "diagnoses" and "cures," and the use of amulets. Russell points out that magic "persisted throughout the Middle Ages in open defiance of the Church. Magic is a kind of prototypical science and technology, scientific in its highest forms in that it strives for understanding, and technological in its ordinary forms in that it strives to bring the forces of the universe under human control."[10]

Historian Jon Butler writes about the importance of the occult in more recent centuries. Practitioners of magic, astrology, and divination "could be found throughout England and the Continent during the entire modern period," he writes. Common people went to the "cunning person," the "wise man" or woman to get help or to harm a foe. Consider seventeenth-century England:

> All substantial evidence reveals that occultism's appeal transcended class, age, and gender. Wise men and wise women drew clients from the wealthy, the middling, the poor. Queen Elizabeth commissioned horoscopes from John Dee, the mathematician . . . . Merchants, lawyers, and servants consulted occult practitioners. William Lilly, the astrological physician, saw as many as four thousand clients a year in the 1640s and cast horoscopes to plan battle strategy for parliamentary leaders during the English Civil War. Even clergymen came. . . . a clergyman secured a horoscope from Lilly to determine whether the nation's new Presbyterian system "would stand here in England."[11]

Many practitioners of magical arts were university educated, Butler notes. Others were illiterates who learned their lore directly from other adepts. The learned William Lilly wrote a 700-page book, *Christian Astrology*, trying to harmonize Christianity with the stars. Popular and intellectualized forms of magic, alchemy, and divination, as well as Jewish Cabalistic writings, were part of the same picture.

The irony is how much of this persists through the centuries. It continues today, particularly in popular and folk culture. For many, global techno-society seems not at all incongruous with astrology, magic, charms, and other options on the occult menu. Of course, such beliefs and practices can take other forms than those found in the fate-as-force worldview. But they seem particularly to fit here.

Fatal Flaws?

Popular persistence of the fatalistic worldview, even when half-hidden or a countercurrent to other views, signals some deep human need. First, probably, is simply the need to explain what happens in life—especially the bad things, the sad things, the senseless tragedies. Surely a fateful force acts behind all these.

The fatalistic worldview wears thin, though, when considered globally. A frontline challenge for global society in the next two generations will be to rediscover community, to live together locally and globally. But the Fate worldview is fundamentally individualist. It offers no basis for shared life grounded in any significance beyond what each individual may find. In other words, it has no adequate answer to the basic question of *relationships*. Fate is atomistic. It is the worldview of the individual human person confronting his or her *own* fate. The quest can be very brave, invigorating, even seemingly noble. But it can also be very lonely.

So fate is a self-absorbed worldview. On the surface it appears just the opposite: cosmic, transcendent, universal. Fate rules! But digging deeper we see that this rule is simply a projection from human experience. A force that is by definition as impersonal and unfeeling as gravity offers no comfort and no purpose. The cosmic truth is the force of Fate. But the practical meaning is that I am left pretty much on my own. The Fate that brings people together just as surely tears them apart.

This may lead to despair, resignation or, for brave souls, something like Emerson's self-reliance. One can't really trust in Fate, for it is capricious, tricky. Only in a limited way can one rely on others, for they too are subject to the whims of Fate. So Emerson says, "A man should learn to detect and watch that gleam of light which flashes across his mind from within, more than the lustre of the firmament of bards and sages." Here alone is morality: "No law can be sacred to me but that of my nature. . . . The only right is what is after my constitution; the only wrong what is against it."[12] This is as high as one can go if fate is the final fact.

This suggests the deepest problem with Fate as a worldview. It offers no really satisfying answers to the basic worldview questions. It is more a *negation* than an affirmation. It is a least-common-denominator worldview. No more ultimate meaning exists than Fate, and Fate is ultimately meaningless. So we can only assert meaning for ourselves.

The result is that society and history can rise no higher than humanity's collective self-centeredness and individualism. There are the noble souls, "representative men" and women in Emerson's view, who show us a high and enobling path of self-reliance, being true to oneself. But if Fate rules, how can anything be noble? The mass of humanity, perhaps instinctively following the inner logic of the Fate worldview, simply say, "Well, what will be will be. I will find my own way as best I can."

So Fate is a faulty worldview. It offers no base for morality or ethics, no reason why people should not turn fatalist. It is not really a Theory of Everything. One feels with those whose only answer (even unconsciously) is Fate. But there must be a better way.

CHAPTER FIFTEEN

Postmodernism:
The Death of Worldviews?

> We are products of historical fracture, standing on the cusp of the modern and postmodern worlds. This explains why we find few terms in everyday language to convey what we are experiencing, making it almost impossible to express new experiences in old language.
>
> **—LEONARD SWEET**[1]
>
> History has ruptured, passions have been expended, belief has become difficult; heroes have died and been replaced by celebrities.
>
> **—PROFESSOR TODD GITLIN**[2]

Our age has been called the end of ideology, the end of history, and the end of geography.[3] Is it rather the end of worldviews? Has society reached such a state of diversity and pluralism that cogent worldviews are no longer possible or believable, or even wanted or missed?

Much of the West—and increasingly, global society—is phasing from modernity to postmodernity. Is there such a thing as a postmodern worldview? If so, what does it look like?

The Birth of Postmodernism

Postmodernism is fast becoming the anti-ideology of the 1990s. It traces directly back to the 1960s however, and its longer roots reach back centuries.

Modernism died and postmodernism was born at 3:32 P.M. on July 15, 1972, in St. Louis, Missouri. At that moment the Pruitt-Igoe low-income housing project, a prize-winning version of modernism, was dynamited as unsuitable for human dwelling.[4] Postmodernism came of age in 1991, the year when for the first time more tourists visited Disney World than Washington, D.C., and the mammoth Elvisland theme park was announced for construction outside Tokyo.

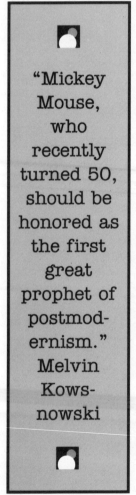

"Mickey Mouse, who recently turned 50, should be honored as the first great prophet of postmodernism." Melvin Kowsnowski

Here are apt symbols for two different worlds and worldviews. Consider Washington and Disney World. Washington, D.C., represents history, progress, enlightenment, and a global vision of democracy. Disney World represents contrived style, artificiality, and momentary experience; it is the collapsing of history and culture into a montage of spectacles and shows, all commercially driven.

Events and symbols like these signal cultural shift. The move to postmodernism is a process that has been underway for at least a century, particularly in the West but now globally. The last generation (from about 1965 to 1990) represented the critical time of transition. As David Harvey says in *The Condition of Postmodernity*, "Over the last two decades 'postmodernism' has become a concept to be wrestled with, and such a battleground of conflicting opinions and political forces that it can no longer be ignored." Harvey concludes that the countercultural movement of the late 1960s, though a failure on its own terms, was "the cultural and political harbinger of the subsequent turn to postmodernism. Somewhere between 1968 and 1972, therefore, we see postmodernism emerge as a full-blown though still incoherent movement out of the chrysalis of the anti-modern movement of the 1960s."[5]

Postmodernism pops up everywhere today. In architecture, from the new Seattle Art Museum to shopping centers in Hong Kong to a new police station in Dayton, Ohio. Also in literature, movies, university curricula, the self-conscious irony of David Letterman's humor, Michael Jackson's music, and Madonna's commercialized self-promotion—the last two figures, at least, are now global icons. Postmodernism is much more than an intellectual movement and much wider than the West.

The postmodern attitude is perhaps most starkly expressed by Todd Gitlin, professor of literature at the University of California, Berkeley. A political activist in the 1960s, Gitlin now describes postmodernism as

> indifferent to consistency and continuity. . . . It self-consciously splices genes, attitudes, styles. . . . It disdains originality and fancies copies, repetition, the recombination of hand-me-down scraps. It neither embraces nor criticizes, but beholds the world blankly, with a knowingness that dissolves feeling and commitment into irony. It pulls the rug out from under itself, displaying an acute self-consciousness about the work's constructed nature. It . . . derides the search for depth as mere nostalgia for an unmoved mover. . . . "The individual" has decomposed, as "reality" has dissolved, nothing lives but "discourses," "texts," "language games," "images," "simulations" referring to other "discourses," "texts," etc.[6]

Gitlin calls postmodernism "the spiritless spirit of global class." (Note the global accent.) Postmoderns deny the continuity of history and "live in a perpetual present." This spirit or spiritlessness of postmodernism is marked by a "post-1960s . . . cultural helplessness," says Gitlin. "History has ruptured, passions have been expended, belief has become difficult; heroes have died and been replaced by celebrities. The 1960s exploded our belief in progress, which underlay the classical faith in linear order and moral clarity. Old verities crumbled, but new ones have not settled in."[7]

Here, certainly, is a worldview—or, perhaps more accurately, an anti-worldview. In any case, it is a perspective from which people live and move and have their being.

What Is Postmodernism?

It is no small challenge to say what postmodernism really is. David Harvey calls it "a mine-field of conflicting notions," partly because modernism is itself an ambiguous term. Most obviously, postmodernism is a vigorous reaction to modernism. It is a flat rejection of the "Enlightenment project" to build a new world through reason, law, and objective science.

The literary critic Terry Eagleton wrote in 1987:

> There is, perhaps, a degree of consensus that the typical post-modernist artefact is playful, self-ironizing and even schizoid; and that it reacts to the austere autonomy of high modernism by impudently embracing the language of commerce and the commodity. Its stance towards cultural tradition is one of irreverent pastiche, and its contrived depthlessness undermines all metaphysical solemnities, sometimes by a brutal aesthetics of squalor and shock.[8]

Postmodernism rejects "metanarratives"—overarching or universal theories and explanations—and all efforts to totalize—that is, to bind everything together in some kind of coherent whole. In Eagleton's words:

> Post-modernism signals the death of such "metanarratives" whose secretly terroristic function was to ground and legitimate the illusion of a "universal" human history. We are now in the process of wakening from the nightmare of modernity, with its manipulative reason and fetish of the totality, into the laid-back pluralism of the post-modern, that heterogeneous range of life-styles and language games which has renounced the nostalgic urge to totalize and legitimate itself. . . . Science and philosophy must jettison their grandiose metaphysical claims and view themselves more modestly as just another set of narratives.[9]

Behind this discussion, though, is the question of what modernism itself is. To some, modernism means reason, order, science, and the triumph of technology. This aspect was perhaps best captured by the French architect and city planner Le Corbusier, who pronounced that the straight line is always superior to the curve. To others, modernism is just the opposite: formlessness, transitoriness, and skepticism about meaning.

David Harvey argues that the essence of modernism is both these elements held in tension. Modernism involves the "conjoining of the ephemeral and the fleeting with the eternal and the immutable," he writes; and he quotes from Baudelaire's 1863 essay, "The Painter of Modern Life": "Modernity is the transient, the fleeting, the contingent; it is the one half of art, the other being the eternal and the immutable."[10] Modernism is the effort to find hints of universal truth in a time of flux, and the faith—or at least the hope—that this is possible. In postmodernism, the tension breaks apart.

A helpful comparison of modernism and postmodernism is given by I. Hassan in his essay "The Culture of Postmodernism," though we should remember that postmodernism is not so much a series of polarities as it is a multifold web of interacting sensibilities.

SCHEMATIC DIFFERENCES BETWEEN MODERNISM AND POSTMODERNISM[11]

modernism	*postmodernism*
romanticism/Symbolism	paraphysics/Dadaism
form (conjunctive, closed)	antiform (disjunctive, open)
purpose	play
design	chance
hierarchy	anarchy
mastery/logos	exhaustion/silence
art object / finished work	process/performance/happening
distance	participation
creation/totalization/synthesis	decreation/deconstruction/antithesis
presence	absence
centering	dispersal
genre/boundary	text/intertext
semantics	rhetoric
paradigm	syntagm
metaphor	metonymy
selection	combination
root/depth	rhizome/surface
interpretation/reading	against interpretation/misreading
signified	signifier
narrative / *grande histoire*	anti-narrative / *petite histoire*
master code	idiolect
symptom	desire
type	mutant
genital/phallic	polymorphous/androgynous
paranoia	schizophrenia
origin/cause	difference-difference/trace
God the Father	The Holy Ghost
metaphysics	irony
determinacy	indeterminacy
transcendence	immanence

From Pre- to Postmodernism

To grasp what is happening today, look back to the time before the modern age. The transition from premodern to postmodern thinking is now clear.

The *premodern worldview* affirmed a fixed, unchanging, eternal order that was reflected in all human life, including the structures of society.

217

Life had meaning precisely as a reflection of this unchanging order, however that order was specifically conceived. Fundamental truth was real and unquestioned. History reflected the verities of the eternal.

The *modern worldview* was grounded in Renaissance, Reformation, and Enlightenment. It rejected much of the premodern perspective, but not all. Modernity was full of ideas of progress, fresh discoveries, and the making of a new world based in large measure on human achievement. Skeptical of religious beliefs not based in science or in human experience, modernity affirmed change, the contingent, even sometimes the seemingly irrational, and yet believed there were underlying patterns of truth and meaning to be discerned and experienced. Modernity included such diverse and conflicting movements as rationalism, romanticism, and surrealism.

The *postmodern worldview* represents the triumph of the subjective, the ephemeral, and the fragmentary over the unchanging and the universal. It rejects the tension inherent in modernism as both impossible and destructive. Postmodernity signals the triumph of the contingent, the transitory, and the ironic. It is a frank rejection of "the Enlightenment project." It has punctured the Enlightenment balloon and meaning is escaping, blowing out, evaporating.

Postmodernity thus completes the pendulum swing from premodern to postmodern thinking. Now modernism appears as merely a transitional phase, inherently unstable. Yet postmodernity, too, almost by definition, is transitional to something else. Just what is still unclear, undefined. Perhaps postmodernity is the last gasp of modernity.

Is postmodernism a fad or more profound? Is it a merely Western phenomenon, simply another symptom of the decline of the West as global culture emerges? Or does it signal the direction of global culture? A. Huyssens wrote in 1984:

> What appears on one level as the latest fad, advertising pitch and hollow spectacle is part of a slowly emerging cultural transformation in Western societies, a change in sensibility for which the term "post-modern" is actually, at least for now, wholly adequate. The nature and depth of that transformation are debatable, but transformation it is. I don't want to be misunderstood as claiming that there is a wholesale paradigm shift of the cultural, social, and economic orders; any such claim clearly would be overblown. But in an important sector of our culture there is a noticeable shift in sensibility, practices and discourse formations which distinguishes a post-modern set of assumptions, experiences and propositions from that of a preceding period.[12]

Huyssens speaks of "sensibility, practices and discourse formations." In fact, postmodernism may be a mood, a moment, or a worldview. It can be a sensibility, an ideology, or a deeper cultural mood. In emerging global society, it is not yet clear what it is, except that postmodernism is all these things in varying degrees in different places among different people. We might better use the term *postmodernity* when referring to this cultural sensitivity or mood and *postmodernism* when we mean an intellectual current or a worldview.

Postmodernity and Popular Culture

As an intellectual current, postmodernism so far may be marginal, but it seems to signal deeper cultural shifts. There is today a growing postmodern *sensibility* evident not so much in academe as in nonreflective popular culture. This postmodern sensibility is taking hold precisely in those sectors of society that are rapidly globalizing—nowhere more notably than in popular global youth culture.

Even to speak of "sensibility" is partially to adopt the language of postmodernity. This is where postmodernity becomes so subtle. It is a sort of verbal virus, invading the language, and hence the thinking, even of those who oppose or ignore it. For the language of postmodernity is the language of the day. Some of its pet words—*sensibility, feeling, impression, role-play, lifestyle, viewpoint, mind-set, network, spacetime, project, model, value, choice, pluralism,* and, of course, *style*—have become the coin of the realm. As a spliced concept, even *worldview* is a kind of postmodern word.

Most of these words are not new, of course. But their use, connotation, and frequent splicing are. An earlier age would have used strong, less self-referential terms—perhaps character for lifestyle, declaration for viewpoint, reality for sensibility, virtue for value, and so forth (depending on the context). Nearly all these newer terms share an environment of (1) assumed pluralism, (2) self-consciousness or self-reference (a psychological quality), and (3) hybridization, the mixing our joining of things previously seen as distinct or unrelated.

This is not to blame language, of course. But this shift in vocabulary does illustrate two things: the subtle pervasiveness of "the condition of postmodernity" and the fact that something deeper is at work than a theory of literature, intellectual fad, or elitist movement. At this level postmodernity constitutes nothing less than *a shift in cultural consciousness*. And this means, for many, a shift also in worldview.

Os Guinness well captures this subtler but more pervasive sense. "Popular postmodernism is a far cry from sophisticated theories bearing the same name, and more a sensibility than a philosophy," he writes. In this popular form:

> postmodernism now encompasses much of American life. Among its defining features are a rejection of an identifiable self for shifting sets of

relationships, content for style, truth and meaning for impressions, beliefs for games, ethical rules for social role-playing, commitment for self-consciousness and irony, vocation for strategies of manipulation, enduringness for disposability, . . . consistency and continuity for the spliced, the blurred, the self-consciously created pastiche of forms and moods. Nothing epitomizes popular postmodernism better than MTV and the handheld remote controls through which American adolescents nibble and dabble their way toward lostness, grazing at will in the flickering pastures of one greener channel after another.[13]

We should note, of course, that MTV, remote controls, and video arcades are now as much global as they are American. When a boatload of Chinese were caught as they tried to enter the United States, a reporter asked if any of them spoke any English. One young man raised his hand. "MTV," he said. He had risked his life to come to the land of MTV.

Popular postmodernity is arguably the most aggressively global of all today's cultural currents. Though postmodernism rejects globalizing perspectives, postmodernity globalizes. But Guinness's description of the American scene is right on target.

Guinness points out that in postmodernism, "the philosophy of the patch-up . . . nothing is pushed out to the logic of its consequences. Bold assertions and initiatives can be made, but only as devices or sops to keep the devil of modernity at bay. So neither hope, nor despair, nor activism is serious. Everything is finally a pose and is for effect." The possibility of serious worldview discourse is canceled. Guinness argues:

> Answers to the big questions of life are only an appeasement of the need for meaning while the grand flirtation with the meaninglessness of modernity goes on, but in a party mood. Religion is no longer transcendent, but a recreational pursuit for the connoisseurs of "spirituality." Art, homes, life-styles, ideas, character, self-renewal, and even belief in God all become an auxiliary to sales and the ceaseless consumption of styles.[14]

Note here the degree to which popular postmodernity is commercially driven. Sober Japanese businessmen and Wall Street investors who buy or bankroll movie companies and popular entertainers unwittingly become, for profit, the prophets of postmodernism. Disney World and Elvisland become prime icons of postmodernity. The artefact is created to provide private thrills to the consumers and hard cash to the investors. In the process, both become part of an emerging postmodern global popular culture.

Postmodernism has global political dimensions, as well. Robert Kaplan suggests that Earth is now entering a postmodern age geopolitically. Modern political maps (reflecting Enlightenment concern for logical order, he claims) mask deeper social and ecological realities, such as those noted in chapter 9. The "political and cartographic implications" of postmodernism today point to "an epoch of themeless juxtapositions, in which the classificatory grid of nation-states is going to be replaced by a jagged-glass pattern of city-states, shanty-states, nebulous and anarchic regionalisms."[15] Postmodernism, in other words, is more than an intellectual or pop-cultural phenomenon. It is intertwined with emerging global society and its underlying tensions.

Postmodernism seldom thinks about worldviews, no doubt. But beneath the postmodern sensibility the profile of a worldview starts to emerge.

The Postmodern Worldview

As a worldview, postmodernism exhibits six characteristics:

1. *It is a rejection of universal or totalizing perspectives,* of theories or viewpoints that claim to put everything together in a coherent whole. This would seem, at first glance, to make postmodernism an anti-worldview and hostile to every attempt to form worldviews.

2. Relatedly, postmodernism represents *a pastiche of styles* thrown together with no overall design. Each piece is (at least in principle) of equal worth. So postmodernism often lumps together classical, romantic, and modern elements with little thought of coherence. This is clear in postmodern buildings, literature, and humor.

3. Postmodernism's *focus on the individual and the particular* is a further expression of the same tendency. Rejecting holism, postmodernism explores the individual person, motif, artefact, or subculture as the proper focus of attention. It is atomistic in this sense. In sociology, anthropology, and history this has issued in an explosion of studies of particular communities, tribes, towns, or occupations, such as Michel Foucault's studies of the insane and of homosexuals and prisoners. "The idea that all groups have a right to speak for themselves, in their own voice, and have that voice accepted as authentic and legitimate is essential to the pluralistic stance of postmodernism," notes Harvey.[16]

Disney World and Elvisland become prime icons of post-modernity. The artefact is created to provide private thrills to the consumers and hard cash to the investors.

Relatedly, postmodernism focuses on surfaces, not on depth; on the illusive and transitory; on style, not substance. Style is itself the substance.

4. The *aspect of self-reference* is another key element of postmodernism. Acutely aware of the impossibility of objectivity, the postmodernist celebrates subjectivity, frankly and perhaps playfully acknowledging his or her own presence in the activity or the work produced. The "happenings" of the 1960s' Consciousness Revolution were prophetic of this. Today participant-observer historiography is an example. No attempt is made to remove or mask the presence of the acting subject. To do so would be manipulative. Thus what was true of much modern art is even more true of postmodernism: the art or composition "often wilfully reveals its own reality as a construction or an artifice," turning it into "a self-referential construct rather than a mirror of society," notes E. Lunn.[17]

Postmodernism is thus highly self-conscious and keenly aware of consciousness. What we experience and feel, particularly what we experience and feel *at this moment,* is what is real. Everything else is suspect, or at least secondary.

5. Conscious of subjectivity, postmodernism is also *keenly aware of power* and the "power games" that shape all of life. It rejects totalizing perspectives and the "cult of objectivity" because these are really power tools used to control dissent and difference. Postmodernism does not necessarily reject power, however. Quite the opposite. Power is there, like gravity, and we may well use it to advance our own agendas.

6. The total of these elements yields what some see as the trademark of postmodernism: *the sense of irony.* In Hassan's formula, irony is the polar opposite of metaphysics. It is the recognition that we are caught. There is no escaping ourselves, the multiplurality of "the others," and the omnipresence of power games at every level of life from daily speech to international affairs. When you have no over-arching ideology from which to critique other ideologies because the very possibility of ideology is dead, you are left only with irony. Truth then is simply what you can get away. You assert your own truth as an act of power and will, fully conscious of the irony of doing so.

Not everyone who lives or "inhabits" a postmodern worldview would subscribe to all the above elements. Often, though, these values have been internalized unconsciously, never articulated or thought through. Millions of people today have a postmodern worldview and don't know it.

Postmodern Science

Postmodernity is deeper than an intellectual toy or popular attitude. Developments in basic science, such as those noted in earlier chapters, are leading to profound perceptual shifts and to what can properly be called postmodern science. David Ray Griffin has shown how science in recent decades has moved away from "the mechanistic, deterministic, reductionistic worldview associated with modern science," not through abstract theorizing but because of "substantive developments within science itself."[18] Physicist Fritjof Capra describes this paradigm shift in his book *The Tao of Physics*. Here postmodernism takes a different twist:

> The paradigm that is now receding . . . consists of a number of ideas and values, among them the view of the universe as a mechanical system composed of elementary building blocks, the view of the human body as a machine, the view of life as a competitive struggle for existence, the belief in unlimited material progress to be achieved through economic and technological growth, and . . . the belief that a society in which the female is everywhere subsumed under the male is one that is "natural." During recent decades all of these assumptions have been found severely limited and in need of radical revision.[19]

Capra offers six "criteria for new-paradigm thinking in science," as we noted in chapter 11. These include shifts from structure to process, from laws to relationships, and from truth to "approximate descriptions." Yet he says also that postmodern science will be holistic and ecological, "seeing the world as an integrated whole rather than a dissociated collection of parts."[20]

Clearly, this view conflicts with the kind of postmodernism described above. Most postmodernism denies order and connectedness, whereas postmodern science affirms them. The reason for this is that literary postmodernism is primarily speculative, whereas science is more rooted in mathematics and experiment. Here science seems to be on much firmer footing. Postmodern science is a clearer signpost to the future and perhaps an implicit rebuke to extreme deconstructive forms of postmodernity. In the arena of popular culture, though, the more deconstructive, atomizing, disconnecting form of postmodernism seems to be winning the day.

The Worldview Questions

How does the postmodern worldview answer life's hard questions? Principally in a negative way. As a worldview, postmodernism is best understood as nixing the main worldviews that have been a part of Western civilization. It sees them all as ideologies designed to serve political ends. This may not be fully true of postmodernity as a moment or a movement, but it is true of postmodernism to the degree that it actually functions as a worldview.

1. We see this first with the question of *meaning and purpose*. Life has no purpose because meaning is impossible. Or at least, if there is pur-

pose to the universe, we have no way of knowing that. The cosmos seems essentially purposeless. It doesn't tell us anything certainly.

This is not to say that life itself can have no purpose. We may grasp purpose wherever we find it. People do this all the time. But there is no ultimate purpose *outside ourselves*. We may claim for ourselves whatever meaning and purpose in life we wish—or none.

In general, the postmodern worldview is cynical about the whole question of meaning. Usually meaning and purpose have been used ideologically, for political ends. Meaning itself is a suspect category. Like "reality," "meaning" must be put in quotes. The question of purpose is probably superfluous after all. One does not expect to find meaning in life. Life is simply to be lived. It has no higher purpose unless, perhaps, to undermine and destroy all other worldviews, the tools of oppression.

2. Is there *design* to the universe? The postmodern worldview has no answer. The question itself is ideological and, therefore, suspect. In any case, all previous theories about cosmic design must be junked as inadequate, outdated, and probably destructive. Any reputed design is really the imposition of someone's will and agenda.

In art and architecture, postmodern design is eclectic, mixing classical and modern styles more or less at random. Postmodernism has no unifying theme, unless it is the lack of a theme. By definition a negation, postmodernism is unable, at least until now, to point the way to new forms of integration or coherence. Yet, ironically, this very phenomenon of pastiche and negation constitutes a sort of recognizable pattern.

The same holds true, in a general way, for postmodernism as a worldview. By definition it lacks any coherent pattern because it negates all existing patterns. Pattern is always imposed. It is never simply "the nature of things." Design itself is ideological.

3. What about *relationships?* How do humans connect to one another, society, and the broader universe? To the postmodernist, all relationships are essentially power deals. Fail to see this, and you fall victim to someone else's will or ideology. Every person is, in some sense or to some degree, in a power struggle with others and with the structures of society. This is simply reality, and one must act accordingly.

4. *History*, similarly, is merely the continuing tale of power politics. To the degree that history has any meaning, this is it. It's foolish to look elsewhere. To assert any meaningful pattern or direction in history is to reveal one's own agenda.

In sum, as a worldview postmodernism dissolves in its own deconstruction. Strip away ideology, "mega-meaning," and totalizing frames of reference, and what is left? Merely the behaving individual in the present moment before a meaningless world. The result looks a lot like fatalism.

While postmodernism shuns the language of fate, the existential end-point is much the same. Is postmodernism possibly a new form of fatalism? Is it fatalism in party dress, fate with style? Perhaps postmodernism is fate self-consciously decked out, because style is all that is left. The self-conscious, acting individual asserts meaning, or (more accurately) immerses himself or herself in the present in lieu of larger purpose. Postmodernity is, of course, a complex phenomenon. But carried to its conclusions (a non-postmodernist enterprise), it leads to fatalism.

These are the marks of postmodernism in its dominant forms, both as an intellectual current and a popular, cultural worldview. It is essentially deconstructive of apparent order. But this is not the whole story of postmodernity. Postmodern science, as we saw, does not fully share this disintegrative agenda. There is, in fact, a contrasting current of postmodernism that points a more constructive direction.

Worldview or World Negation?

How may we evaluate a worldview based primarily on negation? What can one say about a perspective that is suspicious of all attempts to build a coherent worldview because it might turn into a tool of political ideology?

David Ray Griffin rightly says that deconstructive postmodernism "overcomes the modern worldview through an anti-worldview; it deconstructs or elminiates the ingredients necessary for a worldview, such as God, self, purpose, meaning, a real world, and truth as correspondence." This kind of thought "issues in relativism, even nihilism. It could also be called *ultramodernism,* in that its eliminations result from carrying modern premises to their logical conclusions."[21]

This is true enough; yet postmodern thought and sensibility is itself a trend, an EarthCurrent as well as a worldview. As such, it is prophetic of things to come. Unlike most worldviews, it takes seriously the collapse of modernism and the end of the Enlightenment. It recognizes that Enlightenment models and paradigms are rapidly losing their grip and are inadequate for an emerging global society. Since it is fed by many of the streams of popular culture, it unwittingly points to the future—even if its pointing is ironic and the future is hazy.

It is true that worldviews have often served as tools in the hands of people in power. Ideologies have helped keep the poor "in their place" and perpetuate social injustice. Worldviews have been weapons of domination and accomplices of colonialism. We should welcome, therefore, the postmodernist critique, whether or not we agree with its worldview assumptions. Furthermore, the modern world is indeed unraveling as Eurocentric perspectives lose their cultural dominance, whether in art, entertainment, business, or ideas. Postmodernism rightly recognizes this.

It is also true that worldviews often impose a coherence that is more a reflection of the current social and political status quo than of the actual nature of things. A good example is the idea of a Great Chain of Being that for centuries gave cosmic justification to oppression and social inequality. In the eighteenth century, the British philosopher-poet Alexander Pope expressed the common conception. His *Essay on Man* sings:

> Vast chain of Being! which from God began,
> Natures ethereal, human, angel, man,
> Beast, bird, fish, insect, what no eye can see,
> No glass can reach; from Infinite to thee,
> From thee to Nothing.—On superior pow'rs
> Were we to press, inferior might on ours:
> Or in the full creation leave a void,
> Where, one step broken, the great scale's destroy'd:
> From Nature's chain whatever link you strike,
> Tenth or ten thousandth, breaks the chain alike . . .
> All are but parts of one stupendous whole,
> Whose body Nature is, and God the soul.

Pope didn't fail to draw the social implications of this:

> Order is Heav'n's first law; and this confest,
> Some are, and must be, greater than the rest,
> More rich, more wise; but who infers from hence
> That such are happier, shocks all common sense.[22]

The Great Chain of Being, with its notion of hierarchical coherence, has been a background assumption throughout Western culture, and has its analogs in the East. Whatever its positive contributions in sustaining a sense of order, it also has been an instrument of oppression. It functioned to support hierarchy and privileged interest. It may be that the very concept of hierarchy is nothing but a mechanism to give cosmic justification for social inequity. Postmodernism serves a useful function in casting this and other oppressive "totalizing narratives" in doubt. Yet at some point, negation must lead to affirmation, deconstruction to reconstruction.

Constructive Postmodernism

A more positive approach is constructive postmodernism. This view sees signs of hope and clues for building a better world in today's cultural currents.

David Ray Griffin of the Center for a Postmodern World is one of those who argue for such an integrative approach. Constructive post-

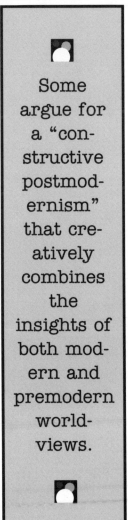

modernism, says Griffin, "seeks to overcome the modern worldview not by eliminating the possibility of worldviews as such, but by constructing a postmodern worldview through a revision of modern premises and traditional concepts." Such a "revisionary postmodernism" means "a new unity of scientific, ethical, aesthetic, and religious intuitions. It rejects not science as such but only that scientism in which the data of the modern natural sciences are alone allowed to contribute to the construction of our worldview."[23]

The concern here is not only conceptual—an updated worldview—but the fostering of "a postmodern world that will support and be supported by the new worldview," says Griffin. "A postmodern world will involve postmodern persons, with a postmodern spirituality, on the one hand, and a postmodern society, ultimately a postmodern global order, on the other." This quest seeks to transcend the "individualism, anthropocentrism, patriarchy, mechanization, economism, consumerism, nationalism, and militarism" (Whew!) of the present order, supporting instead "ecology, peace, feminist, and other emancipatory movements of our time, while stressing that the inclusive emancipation must be from modernity itself." This view retains the term *postmodern,* however, to signal that "the modern world has produced unparalleled advances that must not be lost in a general revulsion against its negative features."[24]

Griffin stresses that constructive postmodernism preserves modern concepts of the self, history, and "truth as correspondence," as well as key premodern notions of "a divine reality, cosmic meaning, and an enchanted nature." This kind of postmodernism, he says:

> is not only more adequate to our experience but also more genuinely postmodern. It does not simply carry the premises of modernity through to their logical conclusions, but criticizes and revises those premises. Through its return to organicism and its acceptance of nonsensory perception, it opens itself to the recovery of truths and values from various forms of premodern thought and practice that had been dogmatically rejected by modernity. This con-

> Some argue for a "constructive postmodernism" that creatively combines the insights of both modern and premodern worldviews.

structive . . . postmodernism involves a creative synthesis of modern and premodern truths and values.[25]

This proposal takes seriously the postmodern challenge to modernity and "the Enlightenment project." But it wants to move ahead to a new coherence rather than embracing incoherence. Does it, then, provide a livable worldview for postmodern global society?

Where Constructive Postmodernism Fails

Despite its strengths, constructive postmodernism has flaws that seriously undercut its usefulness as a worldview. It is wiser than other varieties of postmodernism because it recognizes the good as well as the bad in premodern and modern worldviews. It is more discriminating about and continuous with history and more informed in its attitudes toward science. It is certainly an intelligent improvement on popular postmodern sensibilities, while preserving the legitimate concerns for diversity and the particular. But it has a couple of major flaws.

A serious difficulty with constructive postmodernism is its view of history. It tries to rescue history from being a meaningless sequence of happenings, but it fails to go far enough. Griffin, for instance, perceptively criticizes postmodernism's view of history, but offers an alternative reading that still empties history of its meaning *as story*. He argues that constructive "postmodern [thinking] returns meaning to the historical (including the evolutionary) process." But he denies that the universe has any beginning or end, or that history can have any "middle." History is still seen essentially as a sequence of events in a way that undercuts the possibility of meaningful history. Griffin writes, "If creativity is ultimate, becoming is eternal, and an eternal process can have no middle."[26] Here he reveals his philosophical assumptions but fails to understand history's deeper narrative structure. If history is not "going somewhere," or if meaning is found only within history's own evolution, then ultimately history is either meaningless randomness or endless cyclical repetition. Neither is history if history is story (as we shall see later in discussing history and story).

A deeper problem with constructive postmodernism is its misunderstanding of personality and human uniqueness. Like most postmodern thought, constructive postmodernism cannot show what is special about being human. With a weak view of history and no source of transcendent purpose, it still leaves us wondering about meaning. This is both spiritually unsatisfying and rationally suspect, as we shall see.

The Meaning Question

Throughout this book I have asumed that *meaning* is important. Most postmodernists, of course, deny this. Many people in postmodern societies don't even think about meaning, it appears. "Today the issue is experience, not meaning," says Leonard Sweet.

I will say more about meaning in later chapters. But what about the claim that "meaning" is itself meaningless today, or that meaning was a preoccupation of Enlightenment thinking, which has now lost its grip?

The issue is not so simple. In the first place, experience tells us that many people do ask questions about meaning, from simple queries ("What do you mean by that?") to more profound one ("Why did this happen?" "Why did my friend die?" "Does life have any purpose?"). The continuing popularity of religion and the occult is due, at least partly, to the human quest for larger meaning.

Second, and more basic, meaning is inseparable from personality. Our very language betrays us here. Consider these two sentences: What does it mean? What does he mean?

Grammatically, the two sentences are the same. Yet clearly they mean different things. The first sentence can be understood as: "What is the significance of this thing?" But the second would *not* normally mean, "What is the significance of this person?" Rather, "What does he mean?" would connote "What does this person intend by his or her words or behavior?" The verb *mean* implies something fundamentally different in the two cases.[27]

Meaning is inseparable from intention.[28] The original definition of *meaning* was, in fact, "intention." A sentnece means, first of all, what the speaker intends, although the cultural context also limits the meaning.

The meaning question, then, is really the question of intention. Remove the actor or speaker, and meaning expires. We are left only with the artifact, not the artisan, which leads to the dead end of deconstructive postmodernism. Clearly meaning becomes impossible, or at least very problematic, when it focuses exclusively on an object divorced from a conscious, willing subject. So we will, and must, continue to raise the meaning question.

The Postmodern Insight

Any credible worldview of the future in a sense will be postmodernist, because we are entering a postmodern age. Emerging global society, of course, will be a mix of premodern, modern, and postmodern elements. Postmodernity, however (though not necessarily postmodern*ism*), clearly represents the direction global society is headed.

Postmodernism cannot itself give the world a sound worldview, for

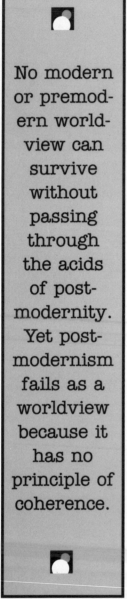

> No modern or premodern worldview can survive without passing through the acids of postmodernity. Yet postmodernism fails as a worldview because it has no principle of coherence.

the reasons already given. But any credible worldview of the future must be postmodern in the sense that it faces head-on postmodern critique and postmodern sensibilities. No modern or premodern worldview can survive without passing through the acids of postmodernity.

Postmodernism cannot serve for long as a credible worldview because it has no compelling principle of coherence. Negation itself does not cohere. The great worldviews of history have been able to move beyond deconstruction to set forth a new vision, a new paradigm, a new model of how things fit together and where history is going. By definition, postmodernism cannot do this.

Postmodernism is best seen as a pause, a wrinkle in time. It is a period of overlap between epochs and worldviews. What has been is fading; what is to be does not yet appear—thus the sense today that "All that is solid melts into air," to quote Marx. Perhaps postmodernity should be seen as the time of vying worldviews, a free market competition in models of meaning. Only a few will survive as livable and globally credible options. The rest will fade away except where small, culturally isolated, declining groups cling to them like rudderless life rafts.

Postmodernism is partly a response to globalization and the sense of living in one world of great diversity and pluralism. When Rome, London, and Washington, or Moscow and Beijing are no longer the center of the world—when the world is centerless, with diverse points of action, initiative, and influence—the inevitable result seems to be pluralism, relativism, and the collapse of totalizing ideologies and empires.

In this sense, at least, postmodernism is a response to globalization and thus an inseparable part of emerging global culture. Weak and deceptive as a worldview, it is powerful and infectious as a sensibility.

PART THREE
PERSONAL MEANING IN THE GLOBAL CITY

At
Home
in
the
Cosmos?

CHAPTER SIXTEEN

The Future and the Ecology of Meaning

> "Meaningless! Meaningless!"
> . . . Everything is meaningless.
> . . . What has been will be again,
> what has been done will be done again;
> there is nothing new under the sun.
> . . . I have seen all the things that are done under
> the sun; all of them are meaningless, a chasing
> after the wind.
>
> —QOHELETH, THE PREACHER
> (ECCLES. 1:1, 9, 14 NIV)
>
> Ecology is reordering our conception of the world
> . . . as profoundly as a great religious idea might.
> —EDITORIAL, NATURAL HISTORY, 1968

We have traced eight global trends and six major worldviews. These deep EarthCurrents are reshaping the present and future of our planet. Where do they leave us in terms of the meaning and experience of being human?

In this final section of the book we ask about patterns and connections and larger meanings. We look for signs of convergence and coherence, a place where things come together and hold together. We ask about order and beauty in a world full of surprises (pleasant and unpleasant), complexity, and seeming chaos. Our purpose is to answer the questions: What response can be given to the worldview issues that global trends bring to the fore? What kind of worldview will serve us, sustain and nourish our lives personally and collectively, in emerging global society?

In this chapter we look first at a few scenarios—possible global outcomes in light of the trends discussed earlier. Then we probe deeper. Returning to the notion of *ecology*, we ponder the ecology of meaning and the meaning of ecology. In the final chapters other matters that are necessary for a livable worldview today will demand attention: *coherence, story*, and the interplay of order, surprise, and beauty.

Alternative Futures

The trends traced in chapters 2–9 together form a global drama. Key currents are converging, perhaps approaching some major climax. What do these trends portend for the coming decades? Rather than attempt prediction, we may trace some *alternative futures*, some plausible scenarios. Over the past thirty years scenarios have become a common and helpful way to think about the future, and they will be useful here.

One possibility is annihilation—the total destruction of life, or at least of human life, due to ecological or nuclear disaster. Either calamity, or both in combination, could be the crisis of 2020 and could be fatal—end of story. (This fear is in part what motivates postmodernists to suspect that history is going nowhere.) Presumably most people would regard annihilation as an unpleasant outcome. But developments of the past decade raise also some less lethal possibilties.

The following five scenarios now appear to be the most likely. They are plausible alternative futures. One or more of these seems to be where Earth is headed—depending, in part, on human choices over the next generation.

Scenario One: Environmental Disaster

Ecological issues will not fade away. Environmental awareness is here to stay. This is the new nature of global society. The question is whether current and emerging attempts at international cooperation can avert eco-disaster. We may be cautiously optimistic. But if enough global collaboration does not come quickly, here's how the future could unfold:

- Global economic stagnation or collapse undercuts serious environmental initiatives.
- Many nations refuse to sacrifice short-term economic growth for effective action on environmental problems.

- Global warming proves more serious than anticipated, bringing critical climate changes that upset agriculture, increase cancer, and force massive resettlement of coastal populations as ocean levels rise.
- Growing ecological crises become politically destabilizing, provoking local and regional wars. These, in turn, worsen the environmental crisis in a deadly downward spiral.
- Earth gradually becomes uninhabitable through the cumulative impact of environmental calamities and inept or counterproductive attempts to deal with them. An "age of anarchy" along the lines projected by Robert Kaplan ensues.[1]

The time line for such a scenario could be anywhere from thirty to perhaps two hundred years. However, the most critical period lies in the near future, the next generation or two. If there is a major global crisis around 2020, environmental issues will surely be the cause or a major contributing factor.

Scenario Two: Friendly Fascism

A new species of political totalitarianism defines quite a different scenario. Some years ago Bertram Gross, in his book *Friendly Fascism: The New Face of Power in America,* warned of a new totalitarianism. This would be based not on force but on the increasingly cozy alliance of government, business, and the military. Pointing out the parallels between the rise of fascism in Germany, Japan, and Italy in the 1930s and developments in the United States in recent decades, Gross warns of a new kind of fascism: "super-modern and multi-ethnic . . . fascism with a smile."[2]

Most people probably consider such a scenario highly unlikely. But social chaos prompts people to want order above all else, even if it is repressive. Voices calling for more authoritarian government already clamor in Germany, Russia, and even the United States.

Such "friendly fascism" could in fact emerge in the United States or in Russia, Eastern Europe, and other parts of the former Soviet Union. This kind of seemingly benign techno-fascism could even arise globally, given the right conditions. In traditionally democratic societies, this new fascism would bring a "polite" authoritarianism in which free social institutions prosper if they go along—or be squeezed if they do not. The majority of people, increasingly self-centered, would not perceive what was happening since material and sensate needs would be lavishly met. This could be the "Singapore model" taken to a sophisticated extreme.

The scenario unfolds through a chain of developments:

- Unstable economies (nationally, regionally, or globally) with inflation spiraling out of control and/or massive unemployment bring social unrest.
- Government assumes new powers to control the economy.
- Increased crime and social confusion bring expanded anti-crime and anti-terrorist legislation and powers.
- Decreased tolerance of political dissent and free speech; restrictions on the press.
- Stepped-up surveillance of groups considered to be radical or subversive; social scapegoating.
- Urban unrest; police state mentality toward the urban poor; decreased economic assistance and greater surveillance and control.
- Voluntary social groups either cooperate with the dominant political powers or are suppressed and denied access to the media.
- The economy rebounds in a context of social control, bringing new prosperity but declining freedom.
- Parallel developments occur in many formally democratic states, producing a global undermining of democratic society but social stability and considerable prosperity, especially for elites.

This would be "soft" fascism. People's material needs and greeds would be met. Recreation and mass entertainment would abound. Most people would welcome the drift of society, preferring controlled order, high-tech pleasure, and "virtual" experiences to uncontrolled crime and economic collapse. The result would look something like China in the early 1990s (but with much higher prosperity, like Singapore), or like the "globalism" pictured by Benjamin Barber in his essay, "Jihad vs. McWorld," discussed in chapter 9.

Will this happen? This scenario appears unlikely unless triggered first by prolonged global economic crisis, because in today's world economic pragmatism and global economic prosperity require and seem to promote political freedom. But major environmental crises could bring the political and economic conditions for friendly fascism.

Scenario Three: Armageddon

Many people worldwide expect a final, cataclysmic Middle Eastern war that spells the end of history. This is a common view, especially among people influenced by fundamentalist Christianity. The final climax will be the biblical "Battle of Armageddon" (see Rev. 16:16).

Politically speaking, such a scenario is certainly imaginable. The combination of geopolitical location bridging three continents, Arab-Israeli hostility, and coveted oil make the Middle East globally strategic. The steps to Armageddon might include the following:

- Increased military build-up by Middle Eastern states, with some acquiring nuclear weapons.
- World economic crisis.
- Escalating tensions in the Middle East; several nations prepare to attack Israel.
- A military alliance between Iran and Iraq, or other states captured politically by Islamic fundamentalism, with escalating militarist rhetoric and ideology.
- The United States and its allies prepare to defend Israel and Middle Eastern oil.
- A coalition of Islamic fundamentalist states attacks Israel.
- Nuclear weapons are first used in the Middle East, followed by nuclear warfare breaking out elsewhere in the world.
- Civilization as we know it is destroyed and much of Earth made uninhabitable.

This is the grimmest of the four scenarios, but not an impossible one. The 1991 Persian Gulf War showed how quickly world events can shift and military might be mobilized. It showed other things also: the continuing importance of oil; the fact that the end of the Cold War does not necessarily mean the end of major armed conflict; and the fact that the use of nuclear weapons is still a thinkable option for some states. The Middle East peace process of the early 1990s raised hopes for long-range stability and prosperity but also fueled violent extremist movements. So this remains a plausible scenario.

Scenario Four: Nuclear Terrorism

A different scenario points to the ongoing spread of nuclear technology. Terrorists may yet acquire and use atomic weapons. The nuclear threat continues as long as tens of thousands of atomic bombs remain stockpiled. A scenario could unfold as follows:

- Terrorists in the Middle East or in former Soviet republics gain access to tactical nuclear weapons. (Some former Soviet republics already have Soviet atomic bombs.)
- Nuclear blackmail results. Terrorists (political or criminal) use nuclear threats to gain concessions, and/or expand their territory or influence.

- Large sectors of two major cities are destroyed when terrorists detonate nuclear devices; nearly a million people die.
- Nuclear panic prompts emergency measures and infringement of democratic freedoms in many nations. The global nuclear crisis overshadows other issues.
- The United States and Russia collaborate closely to contain nuclear terrorism and guard against all-out war.
- Many people turn to religion or to new messianic movements for hope and security. Society drifts toward a global version of the Middle Ages.

This scenario sees not nuclear annihilation but nuclear terror. It's a future much like the present, but with increasing fear, turmoil, and polarization rather than growing cooperation and trust. Political unrest probably would lead to repressive government action.

Scenario Five: World Spiritual Renewal

Naisbitt and Aburdene in *Megatrends 2000* predict a "Religious Revival of the Third Millennium" beginning in the late 1900s. Strauss and Howe in *Generations* show how "spiritual awakenings" or "great spiritual upheavals" may periodically renew U.S. history. Something like this might occur globally. It could take several possible shapes. One might be the rebirth of the Christian Church in a worldwide renewal of unprecedented dimensions, a global "Great Awakening." Another might be the resurgence of other historic religions or the emergence of New Age or politico-messianic movements—or these in combination. The scenario:

- Continued rapid growth of Christianity in China, with deepening impact beyond China as well. The number of Chinese Christians grows to 500 million in less than two generations (from the present 100 or so million).
- A new wave of Islamic growth arising out of ferment in Moslem regions of the former Soviet Union, Turkey, the Middle East, and among China's 18 million Muslims.
- Continued resurgence of activist Hinduism in India and elsewhere.
- A new movement of ecumenical cooperation among Protestant, Catholic, and Orthodox Christians, and possibly with or among other religious traditions as well. Influenced by globalizing trends, militant religious groups become more cooperative.

- Secularizing trends in Europe and North America are countered by major renewal in older religious bodies, once again prompting cultural renewal.
- New religious movements affirming personal integrity, family life, and working for prison reform, employment opportunities for the poor, urban revitalization, and court system reform are born.
- Emergence of effective international religious coalitions for famine relief, food supply reform, and care of the environment.

This is not an unlikely scenario. As global conditions shift rapidly (and possibly worsen, though this may not be necessary for spiritual renewal), worldview questions press more urgently. Worldviews clash and compete. Deep questions lead to deep movements. The result may well be a profound *struggle for the world's soul.* The issues traced in this book become then critical to the possibility and outcome of this scenario.

Converging Scenarios?

Some of these scenarios are rather bleak. Yet much of the evidence presented in this book might as easily suggest positive outcomes. People enamored with science and technology often see a kind of technotopia arising in the future, as forecast in the 1933 Chicago World's Fair. Such projections generally are long on technological wizardry and short on attention to broader social dynamics, however.

The more negative scenarios stand as warnings. They show what can happen if humanity sinks further into the self-centeredness and narrow self-interest that mark so much of history. Dare we hope for a millennium of unparalleled peace, cooperation, prosperity, and real meaning for all? Will the truly unique aspects of emerging global society outweigh the legacy of past mistakes? This is the key question.

These scenarios probe the future and suggest guidance in personal and political decision-making. But they don't get us very far. *Worldviews are more basic,* and ultimately more important and formative for the future. It is worldviews that fuel people's hopes and actions. History shows that worldviews shape the future.

The Deeper Quest: Worldviews and Global Ecology

Key global currents are converging. In contrast, the worldviews discussed in chapters 10 through 15 seem to clash. If trends mold worldviews, at a deeper level worldviews shape trends. They underlie attitudes and actions that coalesce into social currents. So we must examine worldviews more deeply. Each person (postmodernity notwithstanding) operates from and *must have* a worldview or a "world-sense" in order to live. Here issues of meaning, purpose, and truth are inescapable. Worldviews therefore are foundational.

But here we face a tough dilemma in the struggle for Earth's soul. None of the worldviews traced in previous chapters is adequate. We have seen strengths in each but also fatal flaws. Each worldview combines some keen insights, but the flaws remain. Something is missing. None of these views gives an adequate worldview that really serves as a Theory of Everything or a strong center of coherence.

We must probe deeper in search of a living worldview. We need one that takes seriously Earth's global trends and one that better answers the great worldview questions.

A useful place to start, it seems to me, is with the concept of ecology, exploring the meaning of ecology and the ecology of meaning. Reflection on global trends and worldviews leads us this far. We have seen that the world is beginning to think ecologically. Humanity is coming to understand that everything (literally every*thing* and every*one*) links with everything else—without exception. We are learning that this is true not only biologically but in every area. If so, this is a crucial worldview insight.

A Chain or a Web?

Looking at things ecologically is not really new. It was common 2,000 years ago, especially in Greek thought. In fact, our word *ecology* traces back to this earlier Greek understanding. *Ecology* means the study of the "household" (*oikos* in Greek, the source of our *eco-* words, as we noted in chapter 10). Ancient Greek thinkers used the words *oikonomia* and *oikumene* (the origin of our words *economy* and *ecumenical*) to speak about how everything in the city-state—indeed, everything in the cosmos—is connected. Thus "economy" is really an ecological idea, though we haven't thought of it that way in the Western world for 200 years.

In Greek thought, this connectedness was often pictured as a Great Chain of Being. As we saw in the previous chapter, the chain of being concept can be static and socially oppressive. But it *is* coherent and therefore attractive. Commenting on the ideas of "chain" and ecology, the editor of *Natural History* wrote in 1968, somewhat prophetically:

> That all things in the universe are intimately related is an ancient but still pervasive thought. . . . Not even today has it been banished as a popular notion of the moral order of the living world. . . . We are now . . . redefining and relinking the great chain. But instead of a system of rank based

on a philosophical or theological scale of values, we are developing a system that recognizes the actual workings and consequences of relationships. . . . While many of us tend to endow the word that describes the science of the new chain—and that word is ecology—with mystical properties, the fact is that the science itself is concrete, precise, and empirical. Nevertheless, it is reordering our conception of the world, of the chain, as profoundly as a great religious idea might.[3]

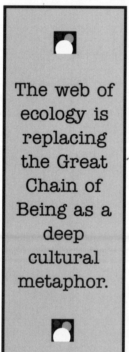

The web of ecology is replacing the Great Chain of Being as a deep cultural metaphor.

The "golden chain" or "great chain of being" metaphor traces back at least to Plato. It has been highly influential in Western thought. The idea was current in the Middle Ages and even into the eighteenth century. The jurist John Fortescue wrote in the 1400s:

In this order hot things are in harmony with cold, dry with moist, heavy with light, great with little, high with low. In this order angel is set over angel, rank upon rank in the kingdom of heaven; man is set over man, beast over beast, bird over bird, and fish over fish, on the Earth in the air and in the sea: so that there is no worm that crawls upon the ground, no bird that flies on high, no fish that swims in the depths, which the chain of this order does not bind in most harmonious concord.[4]

Thomas Aquinas, the master medieval philosopher and theologian, spoke of a chain of being beginning with God and ranging down through angels, humans, animals in the order of their intelligence, and then plants and nonliving things. Medieval cathedrals in their intricate carvings often depicted this chain of being.[5] The eighteenth-century preacher and revivalist John Wesley (founder of Methodism) pictured the created order similarly (although now disrupted by the disease of sin): "Every part was exactly suited to the others, and conducive to the good of the whole. There was 'a golden chain' (to use the expression of Plato) 'let down from the throne of God'—an exactly connected series of beings, from the highest to the lowest: from dead earth, through fossils, vegetables, animals, to man, created in the image of God, and designed to know, to love, and enjoy his Creator to all eternity."[6]

This Platonic picture is appealing, even today. It insists on the relatedness of all things; it has a principle of coherence; it provides a sense of meaning and purpose in life. It possesses a certain harmony and symmetry, even a kind of ecology.

The Great Chain image is flawed, however. It is an inadequate basis for meaning in the modern world, for several reasons. It is hierarchical rather than organic. It is nonhistorical, failing to explain the real processes of history. As a philosophical idea it lacks a scientific foundation. The "chain" that binds all things is also a chain of oppression, locking everything into a static structure. It really has no place for surprise. Its cultural implication is a social hierarchy where men dominate women, the rich rule the poor, and humans subdue and exploit all "inferior" beings.

The instinct of connectedness is sound but must be conceived more ecologically. In view of what we now know about the actual workings of nature and indeed of the cosmos, relatedness may be imagined not as a *chain* but as a *web* of being and meaning. Ecology, not hierarchy. Nature apparently has no vertical hierarchies, but it has order and system. And this complex web is historical. It shifts and changes through time, but in ways that (at least in hindsight) make sense. Here is a view based on the observable, verifiable facts of ecology, not primarily on philosophical speculation. The order is *there,* in the stuff of the cosmos, not imposed by our minds.

This still leaves open the question of larger meaning and the nature of the coherence that seems to hold things in place. Is it blind evolution, God's being and will, or something else that binds the universe together?

The emerging understanding of ecology is different from the old Greek one in two crucial ways. First, the Greek idea was heavily philosophical. It was grounded in mental speculation, not scientific investigation. Today's notion of ecology, however, comes directly from research into the links between plants and animals and their physical environment. In this sense it is inductive, not deductive. For example, learning how toxic wastes work their way up the food chain, or how chemicals dumped in rivers cut the supply of fish in the Great Lakes, shows us connections we never dreamed of. These discoveries lead in turn to others. Eventually we come to see that life is much more linked than we thought. Gradually we learn that tiny ecologies working in remote jungles or oceans tie into a much broader, grander ecology that touches all of life.

The second difference is that today's ecological understanding is profoundly global. We have information—hard facts—about our globe, about its physical make-up and its place in the planetary system, not just philosophical systems. We also know much more about the peoples of the Earth than was true 2,000 years ago.

In medieval Europe, a sort of ecological understanding tied to the Chain of Being idea persisted in Christian thought for many generations. But as centuries passed the concept was increasingly spiritualized, losing touch with the Earth. This spiritualizing tendency also traced back to Greek philosophy. Greek thinking, especially as influenced by Plato, tended to view the Earth as an imperfect, shadowy place that was only a dim reflection of the "true," ideal world of pure mind or spirit. The higher up the ladder, the less material and more perfect. For this reason, the rise of modern science spelled the death of the Great Chain metaphor. Eventually the vertical links of the Chain of Being were replaced by the horizontal links of evolution as the dominant myth.

Today, however, ecology is increasingly seen as the key concept. Ecology concerns the Earth—microbes, chemicals, insects, water, trees. So far ecology is seen as mainly a matter of the body, not of the spirit. This is really a defective view, but a change is coming. It simply will not do to allow a gap between body and spirit when we think ecologically. Increasingly, we are going to discover a broader, richer notion of ecology. This seems inevitable as science and imagination probe more deeply the interface of mind and matter, spirit and body.

Here is the real meaning of ecology: A whole ecology, not a piece-meal one. Once we learn that the lives of snails and sparrows are linked to our own in a dozen ways, the meaning of ecology gradually expands to include every other aspect of human life and well-being. And somehow the link between matter and spirit must be part of this ecology.

The Ecology of Meaning

The most crucial lesson of ecology, however, is what it teaches about meaning itself. Ecology hints that meaning is found in relationship. A big part of the significance of any one thing is found in its connection to other things. This is another key worldview insight.

At some level, we know this instinctively. We speak of "meaningful relationships," or "significant others." We feel that every individual human life may have meaning. But much of that meaning is found in the relations a person has with other people and with the world around them. People who lack healthy relationships become a menace to society.

Ecology, then, provides one key to meaning in emerging global society. How important is a newly discovered plant or insect found in the jungles of Central America? We can't answer until we really know its ecology—how it affects and is affected by its environment and other life forms. We may think the plant or insect is unimportant. But suppose we find that it produces a chemical that can cure a dreaded human disease. Suddenly something deemed unimportant becomes hugely significant! A new level of meaning emerges. (In fact, this very example has happened repeatedly in recent decades.) And if the whole Earth has value, the significance of a plant or animal is not limited to its relationship to humans. The nonuseful, nonmedicinal plant has just as much value, perhaps, in some larger dimension of meaning.

Ecological science encourages us to presume significance and meaning even where we have not yet found it. Thus ecology really leads to a deep intuition: *Everything has meaning simply because it connects with everything else.* We may not yet understand the connection or all it means. But if anything is important and everything is linked, then every part is important. Whether *equally* important or not—a key question—depends on other considerations, as we shall see.

In other words, *ecology itself provides an element of meaning.* The meaning of the universe is that everything is connected to everything else. This is certainly its *real* meaning, if not its *total* meaning. Nothing is insignificant because everything is linked. We find meaning here in two senses. First, every individual thing has meaning because it is part of a larger ecological whole. Second, the meaning of the universe is that everything is ecologically connected. Here then is a key insight: The meaning of the universe is that it shows complex patterns of interrelationship, which in themselves suggest that the universe has meaning.

Is this a circular argument? Yes. It is more an intuition than a proof. One could argue (and many have) that the complex ecology of all things is still meaningless—if one has enough faith to believe that. But something about the ecology of our own lives and minds tells us these intricate patterns of interrelationship constitute some deep meaning. We also sense, however, that this is not enough. Something still is lacking.

By definition, ecology must consider *every* dimension and influence that affects the life of a organism or ecosystem. Sometimes even ecologists forget this. A study of a city's ecology, for instance, would be faulty if it failed to consider the effect of air pollution or the economic and cultural loss from the flight of middle class professionals. And it would have to consider much more remote influences, including those from the past and economic or climatic factors half a world away.

Ecology insists, then, that every influencing factor be taken into account. When we apply this ecological thinking to society and culture, we discover that we must consider not only physical, economic, social, and political factors, but also the dimensions of mind and spirit. Ecology is not complete or whole if it ignores these more elusive elements, even though they are harder to define, analyze, or quantify. We may suspect that here, however—in dimensions of mind and spirit are to be found something that gives some transcendent meaning to ecology.

The Meaning of Meaning

What, then, is the meaning of meaning? Ecology suggests two keys: Unity (or wholeness) and diversity (or distinction). To be ecology there must be *parts*—entities that can be numbered, counted—that make up the whole. Ecology requires number (whether people, insects, elements, particles, concepts, or whatever). And meaning arises from relationships between parts.

What, then, is meaning? Meaning is correspondence and signification: one thing in relation to something else. We can say something *means* (or "signifies"—literally, "signs") something only by relating it to something else. Thus meaning requires relationship between two things. In fact, meaning involves patterns of twos and threes: One thing in relation to a second thing (and the second in terms of the first), and the meaning that arises as a third thing because of the first two—the meaning of the relationship itself. This relationship becomes, in a sense, the bond of unity between the two, and (at least metaphorically) the offspring of that relationship.

Meaning, then, is ecological—even in a sense numerical. In this understanding every part, even the tiniest, takes on meaning in itself and as part of the whole. No influence can be disregarded; no number or fact can finally be "rounded off." (Perhaps this is why mathematicians sometimes think that pure mathematics holds the key to the universe.)

This insight is neither strictly modern nor postmodern. A cogent criticism of *modern* worldviews is that they are "atomistic," seeing the world as built of separate things, related mechanistically. *Postmodern* worldviews stress relationships and patterns over things, at times going to the other extreme of denying "things" or "parts." Truth lies in affirming both. Ecology tells us this.

Relationships, patterns, and connections certainly imply that-whichis-connected, not just the connection itself, unless the connection is understood only as a Platonic idea. "Things" or "parts" can be understood in a not-exclusively-materialist sense, however. Further, one need not deny an encompassing unity and wholeness within which the parts both exist and are linked—even if that "existence" and "linkage" are both equally necessary in a synergistic, mutually supportive sense. This is what I am arguing—not atomism (or, conversely, monism).

In the Christian tradition, philosophers and theologians have dealt with this issue of meaning and relationship in part through the doctrine of the Trinity. Whatever or whoever God is, God is *not only* One. God is Threein-One. The Trinity is one way of describing the complexity and multidimensionality of God's self-awareness. The unity—perhaps the meaning— of God is found in the indivisible, ever-intercommunicating relationship of one-in-two, two-in-three, three-in-one. In the Christian view, meaning is therefore trinitarian and relational. God is Trinity—a personal unity of Father, Son, and Holy Spirit, bound together in loving intercommunion. So profound is this relatedness in the being of God that it constitutes triunitive personhood: three persons in one (not two persons united by some impersonal energy or spirit). The doctrine of the Trinity is itself, therefore, an intriguing intimation of the essential twoness and threeness of the oneness of meaning. Interestingly, it is actually an ecological conception, not a mechanical and certainly not a hierarchical one.[7]

The Meaning of Ecology

Obviously these are not the only conclusions one could reach in examining the meaning of ecology and the ecology of meaning. One might admit the intricate interrelationships and symmetries of Earth's biosphere, for instance, and yet say that this complex ecology means nothing. Believing that the patterns and linkages of the universe disclose, or at least signal, fundamental meaning is more plausible and more consistent with the nature of human mind and experience, however, even if this is not convincing to everyone.

There are four possible ways to account for ecological realities:

1. All life, and therefore my life, has meaning and significance because it is ecologically related to all other life and to everything that exists. This is the line of argument I have been following so far.

2. Everything is ecologically related, but still the universe is meaningless. Relationship or connectedness in itself is not enough to prove or provide meaning. A river and its banks are related to each other, but so what? Meaning requires something more than relationship.

3. The only meaning is the meaning of my own life. I think and I feel; therefore I am significant, at least to myself. Ecology has meaning only to the extent that it touches my own life. It does not tell me what the meaning of my life is. Rather, my life tells me what the significance of ecology is. Meaning can be found only in one's own experience. This seems to be a common assumption of many people in North Atlantic societies today. It is the postmodern temptation. This is the logical conclusion of modernity and the essence of postmodernity.

4. A fourth option would be to look to a higher level or a greater multidimensionality. One might reach beyond both one's personal existence and the ecological interconnectedness of all things. This option affirms the significance of ecology (option one). But like the second option, it says the mere fact of ecology provides insufficient meaning. In common with classical Greek philosophy and most religions, this view argues

that ultimately meaning flows from some dimension of being or existence beyond the known universe. Most fundamentally, meaning is grounded in the realm of mind or spirit, and ultimately in the being of God or the realm of the gods.

Only this fourth option is really adequate and coherent. It affirms but surpasses the first option (ecological connectedness).

The most consistent and credible view, it seems to me, is belief in a personal God who is both creative Source of the universe and also its Sustainer, Source of direction, and culmination. This is far from being an outmoded outlook. A chief strength of this view is precisely its believability today. It is credible partly because it coheres nicely with all the dimensions of human experience—including thinking, willing, acting, and storytelling.

Before we consider this further, however, some other matters must be cleared up. We will deal with these in the next chapters. At this point I simply affirm these basics:

- The world is coming to a new ecological awareness.
- We increasingly see that everything is connected to everything else.
- Much of the significance of individual things is found in their linkage to a global ecology.
- This awareness must be factored in to any contemporary worldview discussion.

In sum, if ecology means that all things are interdependently connected, the ecology of meaning shows that meaning is a complex phenomenon of many interconnected parts. Meaning is not one thing by itself; it is many things in relation to each other. It is, for example, man and woman in mutual relationship, love in relation to truth, the individual in relation to society, humanity in relation to the environment, the present in relation to past and future. It is mind in relation to matter, things in relation to the patterns of their relationships, symbol in relation to what is symbolized. The ecology of meaning is that meaning is both complex and simple, both whole and differentiated. It is complicated and yet coherent. It is like the parts of a vast computer software program. Each part is necessary to make the whole work, and conversely there is a functioning "whole" of which each element is a part. But the universe is much more than a software program. It is a reality that includes life and will, constituting the context where people (and their software!) may exist.

In the growing global market of worldviews and ideas, the most persuasive worldviews will be those that take ecology seriously.

Your worldview must be ecological.

CHAPTER SEVENTEEN

Order, Surprise, and Beauty:
The Coherence of Meaning

> Our universe is an apparently inexhaustible
> source of symmetric patterns, from the inner-
> most structure of the atom to the swirl of stars
> within a galaxy.
> —IAN STEWART AND MARTIN GOLUBITSKY,
>   FEARFUL SYMMETRY
>
> We live in the most probable of all possible worlds.
> —STEPHEN HAWKING,
>   PARAPHRASING VOLTAIRE[1]

At some point, at some dimension or level, everything is connected. Not only the four physical forces and Earth's ecosystems, but also the laws of economics, the powers of technology,
the cycles of history. The images of the hologram and the synapses of
the brain, the symmetries of science and art, all trends and worldviews—surely all things are connected, not only by the human mind,
but also more deeply, through an inbuilt or inherent order that is really
"there."

Even the grandest Theories of Everything proposed so far are not
really theories of *everything*. They are theories, at most, of how the
material world holds together. If verified, any such theory would, of
course, have implications for literally everything, including matters of
spirit, because it would affect trends and worldviews. But it would

remain something less than truly comprehensive and would prove inadequate as a worldview.

A *real* Theory of Everything, or TOE, must include not only the physical forces but all the dimensions of existence. Included should be matters of the spirit, certainly, but also matters of art, history, and culture. It would have to encompass issues of the human soul—for example, how humans have been able to survive the most harrowing circumstances, often with resilience, verve, and joy. Why is this? Certainly the human spirit is more than just a complex pattern of electrons and neutrons and neurons, more than complicated coils of DNA, more even than the "phase transitions" and "emergent structures" of complexity theory.

A real TOE is a question of *coherence* in the most comprehensive sense. How does everything hold together? The root word of *coherence* is the Latin verb *cohaerere,* "to cling together" or hold together in a connected way. It is related to the root verb *haerere,* meaning "to stick" or "to adhere." *C*oherence speaks of the connectedness of all things. Why does literally *everything* cling together?

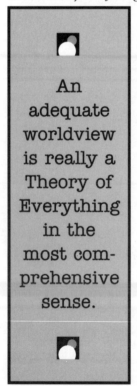

An adequate worldview is really a Theory of Everything in the most comprehensive sense.

This is a key puzzle for a *real* Theory of Everything. In fact, it is the quest we have been following since the beginning of this book. What is behind today's Earth Currents? What connects them? What makes worldviews coherent or in the end chaotic?

Is there a principle, a force, a reality that binds everything together? Is everything that exists "sticky" so it coheres? If so, why? Is there a principle or power of coherence that can guide us in the living of our lives? Some basis or source for a credible worldview?

Order, Surprise, and Beauty

The real world as we experience it, and as we long for it to be, is a place of order, surprise, and beauty. A comprehensive worldview combines these elements of order (not just randomness), surprise (not determinism) and beauty (not merely mechanistic technology). These are essential elements of genuinely human life. Order, surprise, and beauty also involve issues of symmetry and style, and they raise the question

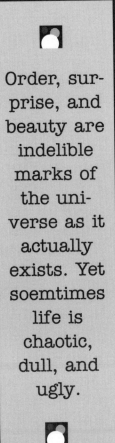

of chaos. Is chaos, for instance, merely the absence of order and meaning, or is it a clue to meaning?

Order suggests a coherent pattern in which all the parts stand in non-chaotic relationship to each other and to the whole. *Surprise*, as I use it here, means the element of freedom and unpredictability that may appear in a system and that yet turns out to be compatible with the order. *Beauty* in relation to worldviews means symmetry and balance and the ability to invoke in human beings a sense of attraction and aesthetic appreciation—a sense of wonder.

Order, surprise, and beauty seem to be aspects or marks of the universe as we experience it. All three must, therefore, be taken into account in any valid and credible worldview. Together these qualities may give us clues for discerning a sustainable worldview.

Order, surprise, and beauty are indelible marks of the universe as it actually exists. Astronomers and astrophysicists find order, surprise, and beauty in the vast universe of stars, planets, pulsars, and black holes. Gaia admirers find them in the intricacies of Earth as an organism. Postmodern science finds order, surprise, and beauty at the level of the quantum. Master artists combine order and surprise to create new expressions of beauty.

True, the universe includes pockets of chaos, ugliness, and determinism. Yet the fundamental structure appears not to be chaotic. "Chaos" itself may not be what it seems. Scientists studying chaotic systems report that even here an underlying order seems to rule. The definition of *chaos* as "complete disorder" may turn out to be obsolete.

Are order, surprise, and beauty basic marks of society and human history, as well as of the physical universe? I will argue that they are. Indeed, they constitute key elements forming the coherence of the universe in all its dimensions, including human life, consciousness, and history.

We may not always experience the world as orderly or beautiful, of course. For various reasons, one's own life may be disordered, ossified, or disfigured—whatever the case with the larger universe. And since we are all part of the uni-

> Order, surprise, and beauty are indelible marks of the universe as it actually exists. Yet soemtimes life is chaotic, dull, and ugly.

verse, we may easily doubt whether the world is a friendly place when confusion or suffering comes.

Order and Chaos

Is the universe an ordered place? Historically, two main views compete. One ancient view says the universe is deeply chaotic, but order can be maintained through religious ceremonies and rituals that in effect hold chaos at bay. The other view says that the universe is orderly. A third, less popular, claim is that the universe is totally chaotic and all order is an illusion. This has not been a very popular view because it does not square with most people's daily experience. Also, we are not able to live very long in chaos or with a worldview that affirms chaos. Living requires order.

Enlightenment science saw the universe as a great machine, as we have noted. This was the clockwork universe. Everything was in principle orderly and predictable, even if we didn't yet know fully how the machine worked. The main task of science was to discover the physical laws of the universe, to decode the machine.

Einstein's relativity theory, and more recently quantum theory, threw a wrench into the machine. It is wrecked. It no longer serves as a universe model, even though some parts of the universe do run like machines. Clearly the universe exhibits order, if not *mechanistic* order. We see this in everything from the structure of a snowflake or a crystal to human thought to the circling of planets round the Sun.

Can the universe be orderly and chaotic at the same time? No, in an absolute sense. But yes, it can be if chaos churns within a larger framework of order. It would be rationally inconsistent, an oxymoron, for the universe to be fundamentally both orderly and chaotic. Science now, however, is showing that pockets of chaos do operate within larger structures of order. In science, chaos does not mean total disorder but rather unpredictability.

It seems the universe really is an ordered place. Yet this does not rule out pockets of disorder, chaos, or instability. Any family with small children knows this.

Here *surprise* jumps in. In an orderly system (and certainly in a machine), one does not expect or welcome surprises. The worst sin of a machine is to be unpredictable. A machine is worthless if it is randomly erratic.

Surprises may be pleasant or ugly. A person may believe in an ordered world and then come to doubt this when surprised by disorder, pain, or chaos. Yet we welcome pleasant surprises. What the universe seems to be showing us is that surprise is in some way part of the order of things. An example of this follows.

Parable of the Tiled Floor

I walk into a shopping mall. In a central courtyard a beautiful floor made of different colors and sizes of tiles catches my eye. I start to wonder whether the tiles are laid out randomly or by design. I visually trace the tiles, seeking a pattern. No design seems evident within a small area, so I examine a larger section.

Gradually I think I see a pattern. A certain mix of colors and sizes seems to be repeated about every ten feet in each direction. With this hypothesis, I look further. Walking first in one direction, then at right angles, and then diagonally across the floor, I find my hypothesis confirmed. I have found a pattern in the tiles. It really exists. It's not just in my mind. I could show it to others.

Satisfied that I have solved the order of the floor, I cross to the other side to do some shopping. Absentmindedly, I continue to trace the pattern in the tiles. Then suddenly, at the far side, I note an inconsistency. A ten-by-ten section of tiles doesn't match. Here the arrangement seems to be chaotic.

Now I begin to doubt the hypothesis that I thought was confirmed. Maybe I missed the pattern. Or perhaps this section is a random exception. Maybe I have found a chaotic section within the order. Or perhaps this section follows a different pattern. Anyhow, I have to doubt the order I had assumed and figure out how to explain this oddity.

Several explanations spring to mind. Perhaps someone made a mistake; this section is, in fact, arranged chaotically, contrary to the intended design. It's also possible that this section displays a pattern that is just the reverse of the larger design I had seen. Or perhaps this section follows a totally different plan, unrelated to the larger pattern.

There is another possibility. This section of tiles may be an *intentional* exception to the larger pattern. Perhaps the designer, for whatever reason, chose to insert this oddity as part of his or her overall plan. This might be confirmed by checking out other work done by the same designer. If I discovered similar cases of disorder or chaos in other work by this person, I would conclude that this designer's pattern includes one area of seeming disorder.

In other words, disorder could be part of the design, contained within the order.

This point is reinforced when we consider the aspect of *dimensionality*. The above example is a two-dimensional analogy, a flat surface.

This is its limitation. Chaos may exist in a part of these two dimensions, as shown, if some tiles fail to follow the pattern. Yet in *other dimensions* this chaos vanishes. The whole floor is flat and stable, not chaotic; thus there is no chaos in the third dimension. The fourth dimension is also nonchaotic: the whole floor exists in the same time frame. Just so, what appears chaotic (and may really be so) within our normal dimensions of perceiving may be orderly at higher levels of dimensionality.

The Beauty of Surprising Order

This little parable speaks about the existence and design of the universe. The fundamental order is such that it allows for genuine surprises. We may think these surprises cancel the order, that the two can't exist together. Not so.

Surprise would be impossible in a clockwork or machine model of the universe. But it might be consistent with other models—for instance, an organic, ecological one. It is possible, of course, to make machines with built-in surprises—a jack-in-the-box, a Trojan horse, a virus-laden computer program. The surprise is contained within the order, within the design. But this is a predictable, mechanistic surprise, not surprise in the sense of true unpredictability and freedom. It's a clever trick.

We see then that the universe, at least as a physical place, is marked by both order and surprise. This may give some insight into human society and history as well. There can be—must be—both order and surprise in human affairs. One doesn't kill the other.

What, then, of beauty? Order and surprise are not the whole story. The universe is also beautiful. Poets and sages through the ages sing its praises. So have astronauts and cosmonauts, seeing the universe from space. So have astronomers and, occasionally, scientists peering through microscopes.

What makes something beautiful? Perhaps it is precisely (or at least partly) the joining of order and surprise.

Poetry and music give good examples. Orderly music has a certain beauty. Add the element of surprise, and the result (if done skillfully) is much greater beauty. Likewise in poetry: it is often the arresting word or image or rhythm that creates exquisite beauty. Surprise, skillfully employed, boosts the beauty of order. Incidentally, it also makes humor possible. Conversely, surprise that otherwise seems totally chaotic is made beautiful when the right touch of order is added, like just the right spices.

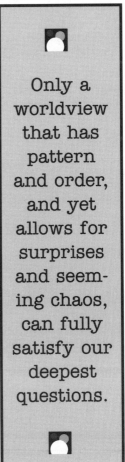
We see this in life. We are beset by surprises—unexpected and seemingly random. Seeing no meaning or pattern, we feel disorder, tension, and anxiety. We ask, why? What's happening? What is the reason? But if we later discover a pattern that makes sense of the surprises, we are reassured. We can deal with them. We may even see the surprises as enriching the beauty of our lives.

It is like reading a story that seems to make no sense. Then finally, near the end, everything falls into place. It all fits, even though it didn't seem to at first.

Another example would be a man who moves from a desert climate to one where it rains often but rather unpredictably. If the man isn't familiar with the new climate, he probably feels it is chaotic and rather unfriendly. This proves annoying. Over time, however, he discovers the pattern to the weather and learns how to live with it. He may even come to like the new climate better than the old one, appreciating the variety and perhaps even the unpredictability.

Or consider a less tangible but more personal case. Strange, seemingly random events start to upset a woman's life. She is stressed and begins searching for some way to cope. If she fails to find a meaningful pattern in the unfolding events, she may well "make up" a pattern to provide order and security. That imposed pattern may be either healthy or unhealthy; it may be actual or fictional. It may, in fact, be very destructive, as when a person concludes wrongly that bad things are happening to them because of something they or someone else has done. Sometimes people use belief in reincarnation in this way. Things are happening the way they are, these people say, because of who they were in past lives. The events of life are invested with meaning by imposing the larger pattern of reincarnation.

The point is this: The physical universe is marked by order, surprise, and beauty. Perhaps this is true as well of such intangible things as society and history. Human history, for instance, includes great ugliness. Yet, those who have lived life at its ugliest are often the very ones who are most aware of its beauty. Consider the Holocaust survivors.[2]

> Only a worldview that has pattern and order, and yet allows for surprises and seeming chaos, can fully satisfy our deepest questions.

It seems then that order, surprise, and beauty are fundamental marks of society and history, as well as of the material universe. Even things in life that appear chaotic and ugly, in some ultimate sense, may be part of a pattern of order and beauty when and if we come to see the whole picture.

All of this suggests that order, surprise, and beauty must be part of any worldview that is coherent, credible, and functional in people's lives. At this time in history, especially, humanity needs a worldview that has pattern and order, yet that allows for surprises and the seemingly chaotic, and that has a certain aesthetic appeal in the way it holds these two together. Only such a view can give really satisfying answers to the fundamental worldview questions discussed in chapter 10.

Worldviews that fail to incorporate this trinity of qualities will prove defective and perhaps deadly. Order and surprise without beauty would be a dungeon or a bare island, but not a habitable worldview. Surprise and beauty without order would be fascinating at first, like fireworks, but could be deadly and would prove unlivable. Beauty and order without surprise would become tiring and constricting, like a person trapped forever in Disney World. The monotony would finally prove fatal.

Order without surprise, or order and surprise without beauty, or surprise and beauty without order—all run counter to the very nature of the material universe and the rhythm of our lives. They prove functionally inadequate in both personal and corporate human experience. Here is one test for the rational coherence and practical livability of worldviews: Do they include order, surprise, and beauty?

Toward a Livable Worldview

Order, surprise, and beauty, then, are key elements of a worldview that is coherent, consistent with the material world as we know it, and potentially credible on a global scale. Although these elements are insufficient in themselves to provide an adequate worldview, any view that fails to incorporate them will ultimately disappoint those who hold it. Eventually it would be undermined by the force of converging global trends.

I suggested above that surprise adds beauty to a pattern when skillfully combined with order. But what does *skillfully* mean here? Clearly it implies intention, volition. Of course, one could say that the combination of order and surprise in the universe has no intentionality behind it. It is simply the way things are, or the way an evolutionary process developed. Many believe this. It is much more credible, however, to believe that the very combining of order and surprise in the world is intentional and in some way personal. The symmetry and beauty are at least presumptive evidence for the existence of a Mind—a Person—whose character includes order, surprise, and beauty. They are not proof but reasonable evidence, a "signal of transcendence," to use Peter Berger's phrase.[3]

This reminds us of the classic argument from design that has been used historically to "prove" that God exists. As we have already noted, however, worldviews are ultimately unprovable. They always demand faith. So I am not arguing proof here. I am merely arguing plausibility or reasonableness, rational and personal coherence.

Historically the argument from design was an argument from order. The argument seems to collapse, though, when disorder or chaos enters. An argument from order is not enough. If there is an underlying design (and therefore a Designer), that design must incorporate surprise and beauty as well as order. Combining them, we learn that surprise and beauty deepen rather than demolish the argument from order.

If a Designer lies behind (or above, or surrounds, or interpenetrates) the order, surprise, and beauty of the universe, what kind of Designer? Certainly order, surprise, and beauty will be consistent with the Designer's character. Further, the Designer must possess will or intention, creativity, and power. That much, at least, we may reasonably infer from the nature of the universe around us. This may serve as another useful insight in discerning a contemporary livable worldview as we enter the twenty-first century. Such a worldview could have a high degree of coherence.

Back to Coherence

We know that at the physical, matter/energy level of life on Earth, things do hold together. Coherence rules; $E = MC^2$ on Earth and in space. Electrons and planets do not randomly go spinning off into space, jumping their orbits and creating chaos. Time predictably goes forward; it does not capriciously jump back and forth between past and future like an erratic compass. Rain comes down and mists rise. If these things were not so, our lives would be impossible—true chaos.

What holds these physical facts together? Is this simply the way things are, requiring no explanation? Even if all the physical laws are eventually known, we will still be left with the deeper question of the source of coherence.

Patterns, rhythms, and cycles govern physical existence. Earth circles the sun, yet both are hurtling through space at vast speeds, racing away from all the other stars in our expanding Milky Way. The regular cycles of Earth and moon set the patterns by which we mark our days and months. The vibrations of quartz crystals keep our watches accurate. The varying wave cycles of electromagnetism set the frequencies that let us watch television, listen to the radio, talk on the telephone, and have light in our homes. The patterns of an acid called DNA make human life possible. Somehow, all these powers and patterns cooperate, and the universe works.

Why? Why doesn't everything spin apart? We know the tremendous power of atoms. Nuclear energy keeps us warm through the sun's constant explosion. Yet on Earth, atoms don't normally explode. We are kept safe from this awesome power unless it is released by human action—an atomic bomb or a nuclear generator meltdown.

Why doesn't the Earth simply explode? What is the principle of coherence? Physics can give us physical answers but not ultimate ones. We sense that there must be an answer more fundamental, more ultimate than the laws of physics. The universe is more than quantum mechanics.

We want to know not only what holds the physical universe together, but also what gives order and coherence to society and to our own lives. What holds cultures together? What makes for a healthy, stable society compared with one that is fraying or decaying? What holds families, neighborhoods, and nations together, or causes them to fail? What brings peace, health, and order—or conversely, war, disease, and chaos? Do we know? These are questions of coherence.

We all struggle to make our lives coherent. At least minimal patterns of eating and sleep are essential simply to keep going. But meaning and purpose require more than physical food. The spirit must be fed. Everyone needs some basis of coherence to give life meaning. Life needs an organizing center, a meeting point.

Worldview Coherence

That principle of coherence, whatever it may be, is in effect a person's worldview. For many people, probably, it is love for another person that gives this coherence. For some it is self-love, looking out for Number One. For many it is pleasure, or power, or getting rich. For others, it is working for world peace or seeking to glorify God. The principle of coherence may be personal and private (one's own self), interpersonal, or transcendent—or some combination of the three.

Many people lack a principle of coherence. Their lives are incoherent. Life is ruled by outside forces—job, the day's routine, or other people's priorities and schedules. Such people just go with the flow. Their only life principle is to go along and get by.

Other people find a transforming purpose or goal that gives them energy and direction. One person in his or her own experience makes a pretty small world, and a rather puny worldview. "Living in one's own world" is almost a definition of poor health. We know instinctively, and certainly upon reflection, that a credible worldview must include other people, the physical world, all of history—all that is. A tiny circle of coherence is not very satisfying to mature, healthy adults.

What about society? What about history, the connection and collection of all human lives? Is world history coherent? This is a basic worldview question and is much debated. Historians such as Arnold Toynbee and Arthur Schlesinger (both Sr. and Jr.) have written about cycles in history. Through the centuries scholars have sought patterns and meaning in historical events. We described one of these efforts as generational history in chapter 1. Some have said history is meaningless or totally chaotic. But most discern order of some sort.

Thinking of worldview coherence, and still thinking ecologically, we must remember at least one other dimension: the realm of the spirit. Throughout history most people have believed that reality is more than physical. Other dimensions beyond what we can see, feel, and touch with our senses affect our lives. We speak of mental and psychic energy. And many people (perhaps most) believe in a spiritual world at least as real as the world of our physical senses—a whole world of spiritual being or consciousness that we know perhaps dimly. What people believe about spiritual reality makes a huge difference in their worldviews.

Spiritual existence lifts the question of coherence a notch higher: What holds the life of the spirit together? How are spiritual and physical existence linked?

Personal Coherence

Probably most people feel their lives are generally coherent most of the time. We all pass through crises when we may feel that "things are falling apart." If we are stressed, we feel we are "coming unglued." But most of the time we think we are holding things together. Basically our lives are under control. If any area of life—physical, social, financial, emotional, or spiritual—is chaotic or unstable, life loses coherence and we feel stress. We do what we can to restore order. We try to make sense of things even when some part of life is out of control. We seek an explanation, try to keep our balance.

Even in the midst of chaos—especially then—we look for coherence.

Failing to find a center of coherence, a person turns violent, suicidal, or insane. It is simply not possible for life to exist without some basic pattern. If nothing holds things together, everything falls apart. This seems true physically, emotionally, spiritually, and more broadly in society and history. Humans must feel or believe that something holds everything in place. In actual fact, most of the time something apparently does hold things together, whether we are aware of it or understand it or not.

For human beings, it is worldviews, relationships, and the patterns of life built upon them that hold things together. Coherence in only one or two areas will not do. Life out of control in one area unsettles other areas. We may deal with the stress by denying or ignoring the problem. But it still haunts us. If life is out of control financially, for example, this eventually touches us in mind and spirit. Deep emotional tension stresses us in various ways and may even make us physically ill. Conversely, physical illness upsets other areas. If our physical life is incoherent in some way, this warps our relations with other people—and so on and on in the whole ecology of life.

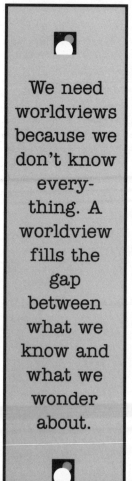

We need worldviews because we don't know every-thing. A worldview fills the gap between what we know and what we wonder about.

Coherence, in other words, is all-embracing. This doesn't mean everything always has to be peaceful or under control. But it does mean we need some underlying feeling of coherence that allows us to make sense of everything in life, including whatever disorder or dis-ease or chaos we experience. We must have some way of holding things together, even when some of the things we hold together are falling apart.

By definition, worldview coherence is all-encompassing. Coherence is the question of how everything (without exception) holds together. If ecology refers to the interrelationship of all things, coherence refers to the power that holds all things together in their interrelatedness.

Worldviews and Unanswered Questions

Here we face a problem. We do not know how literally *everything* holds together. Life has its mysteries. But worldviews help us out. This is precisely why we need a worldview. Coherence doesn't demand that we know everything about everything. It means we have a perspective, a certain viewpoint or model, that allows us to interpret all we experience—even things we don't understand.

A worldview doesn't answer every question. The conviction that there are no answers to life's questions could, in fact, be a worldview. A worldview is a framework, a pattern we use to interpret and make sense of things. It is what we feel is true, based on what we *do* know and have experienced up to this point in our lives.

It is precisely because we don't know everything that we need a worldview. A worldview fills the gaps between what we do know (or believe) and what we don't. It gives order to the chaos of the vast number of unknown things. It is plain silly to think we must know everything fully in order to believe anything surely.

So coherence doesn't mean knowing everything. It means believing in some kind of order or pattern that allows life to go on, giving it meaning, purpose, and direction.

Since we don't know everything, worldviews always require a large dose of faith. Or we might say a worldview is a matter of *intuition*. Based on what we see and experience, we intuit a larger pattern, a sort of grid in which everything fits. This, in turn, makes sense of life and enables us to see other things we would miss without the grid. Of course, we may be only "seeing things." Our intuition may be wrong or our faith faulty. Worldviews aren't infallible. The coherence we see may actually be a false coherence, one we simply impose. The trick is to find a coherence that is simply *there,* that we don't impose.

So we arrive at our worldviews by faith or intuition. This may be an example at the worldview level of what philosopher Michael Polanyi calls "tacit knowing" or "personal knowledge." Polanyi cites the way we recognize a person's face. When we see another person, we don't separately analyze the nose, eyes, and other features and then finally deduce who the person is. Rather, we take in the person's face at a glance and make a "tacit leap" of recognition. We know the person. Polanyi points out that this is neither a purely subjective nor objective transaction; it is both. It is personal knowledge.[4] (This is something like familiar perception games in which one is shown an ambiguous silhouette or pattern of dots and must decide what it is.)

Since a worldview is discerned not by answering every question but by some type of intuitive faith leap, obviously a worldview can never be fully proved or disproved—either logically or scientifically. History shows that worldviews can persist in the midst of the most contrary evidence. For example, many people still believe that their race or culture is superior to all others even though social and scientific evidence says otherwise. Perhaps some people still think Earth is flat. But as more and more contrary evidence piles up, fewer and fewer people hold that view. Another view gradually replaces it for most people. Such a change in worldview is called a "paradigm shift" and can trigger a revolution.

We should never forget, however, that a worldview—the pattern of coherence we believe in—always requires faith. This is so for the atheist as much as for the "true believer." Even agnostics must have faith to believe that they cannot know. A worldview is never just "the way things are." It is always the way we *believe* things are. However, the most coherent and livable worldviews are those in which the gap between what we believe and what really is true is relatively small—or at least not essentially inconsistent.

I have stressed that the most valid worldviews are those that accurately account for the broadest range of all the things that make up existence in all its dimensions. Any worldview that is partial is to that degree flawed. If it leaves out one part of life or "rounds off" some dimension of reality, its coherence is compromised. It is not ultimately satisfactory or satisfying and is vulnerable to the winds of change, even though it may contain much truth.

What, then, makes a worldview credible, believable? Three things, at least: How it squares with our own experience; the influence of other people who believe it, particularly people who are significant to us; and its ability to answer questions and provide meaning. A functional worldview is one that matches experienced reality, is believable to a large number of people, and suggests convincing answers to questions for which we otherwise have no clues. A worldview could be widely believable and answer our questions and still be wrong, of course. But worldviews must at least fulfill these roles.

A valid worldview could *in principle* give correct answers to all questions about everything, even though our knowledge is incomplete and many questions remain unanswered. A valid worldview would still be substantially correct even when all questions were answered. Or, to put it differently, a valid worldview would provide no essentially wrong answers, even though it might be incomplete and would need to be expanded or adjusted as new evidence piles up.

In the previous chapter we saw that a worldview must be ecological. Now we see that it must also be comprehensively coherent, even it if lacks complete knowledge.

What would a coherent and comprehensive worldview look like? How can an encompassing principle of coherence be set forth? These questions remain to be answered in the final chapters.

CHAPTER EIGHTEEN

Story, History, and Truth

> We are without a comprehensive story of the universe. The historians, even when articulating world history, deal not with the whole world but just with the human. . . . The scientists have arrived at detailed accounts of the cosmos, but have focused exclusively on the physical dimensions and have ignored the human dimensions. . . . We have fractured our educational system into its scientific and its humanistic aspects, as though these were somehow independent of each other.
>
> —**BRIAN SWIMME AND THOMAS BERRY**[1]

O rder can be oppressive. Surprises may prove fatal, and beauty may fade to ugliness. A livable worldview must include these elements, and yet something is still missing. Even a pleasant ecology of order, surprise, and beauty lacks something.

This missing element is *story*. It is story that gives meaning to history and to worldviews. It is narrative with meaning, which means story with an open future that gives purpose to the present and the past. We hope that it is a good story.

We have seen how trends shape worldviews and worldviews focus our choices and decisions. New trends and worldviews alter history (the story), sending it in new directions. We act out what we believe is true, making our own story and interacting with the world's story.

Often it is story that gives meaning and coherence to life. The stories we believe and live give us a center, a foundation for our lives and choices. Here we confront truth and metaphor; imagination and meaning; reality and consequence.

From Worldview to Story

Every worldview is rooted in metaphor. For Enlightenment modernism this root metaphor was the machine, the very embodiment (or better, product) of reason and technique. Some have suggested art as the root metaphor for constructive postmodernism,[2] but decomposition and death more accurately mark deconstructive postmodernism, the more dominant form. Each of the worldviews outlined in previous chapters has its own root metaphor: Economics, quantum uncertainty, Gaia, Cosmic Designer, Fate as force, deconstruction.

At this hinge of history, any plausible and globally credible worldview must include story as well as ecology and rational coherence. The root metaphor for a new and yet historically grounded worldview will be *story* and *parable*. Earth needs a compelling story that makes sense of life and history and thus serves as a strong worldview.

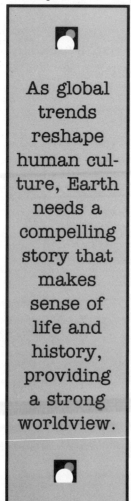

As global trends reshape human culture, Earth needs a compelling story that makes sense of life and history, providing a strong worldview.

The category of story brings many related ideas: parable, fable, myth, drama, narrative, as well as journey and history. Actually, *story* and *history* are at root the same word (as they still are in some Romance languages). The root is the Greek *istoria,* meaning knowledge or information gained by inquiry, or simply a narrative or tale.

Story, parable, drama, and similar forms share some interesting features—especially in the light of modern and postmodern sensibilities. In all stories we normally find:

- a central and unique place for personality
- choice and action—presumed to be free and often central
- no subject/object split

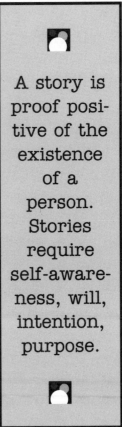

- direction; plot and climax in most cases
- ecological and historical dimensions combined
- complexity, without negating cause and effect in history
- some basis for morality (good and evil) provided by or assumed in the story
- a storyteller

Not every story includes all of these elements. In late modernism and postmodernism, stories have been written precisely to negate some of these features—for instance, to deny freedom, direction, or meaning. The same is true of much modern art. But these very negations accent the affirmations.

These story features are important for worldviews and their uses. From a worldview perspective, the two key aspects are *the need for a storyteller* and the connection between *story* and *history*. It is surprising how consistently these two keys are ignored in discussions of story and storytelling.

You simply can't have a story without a storyteller. A tale demands a teller as surely as *tale* and *tell* come from the same root.[3] No teller, no tale. Without a novelist, no novel; without a dramatist, no drama. This is obvious, yet its major meaning is often missed: A story requires a person as surely as lungs need air. The existence of a story is proof positive of the existence of a person. This means that story requires *consciousness*, that strange fact of self-awareness, including will, intention, imagination, and purpose, the constituents of personality.

Here is another key worldview insight. If the world fundamentally has the character of story, then personality is basic to and constituent of the universe. This is not just personality in the abstract, or even persons only as characters in the story; it is the person of the storyteller.

The storyteller transcends the story as its source and creator, or at least teller. Thus the story of the universe—if it is a story—implies a creating storyteller who transcends (dimensionally surpasses) the universe as we know it. Perhaps this story character is another "signal of transcendence."

> A story is proof positive of the existence of a person. Stories require self-awareness, will, intention, purpose.

Story and History

Story is essential to human existence. We tell stories because our lives *are* stories. Collectively, generationally, they form history. Many have argued, of course, that history has no meaning, no pattern except what people impose. History is "a random sequence of meaningless occurrences," says Mark Taylor.[4] It has no story, which means there is no history. But this is an extreme and ultimately unlivable view. Humanity has always been fascinated with the story of history, whether in the modern historically conscious sense or in more mythic forms. History is story because it is populated by people. Life lived is the connection between story and history.

History is the larger story—the combined, intertwined saga of society. If there is any real difference between history and story as we commonly use the terms, it is only that history refers to the story of more than a few persons over extended time. We may think of history as the story of the past, "a narrative of events" that have happened, while story may be present or ongoing. Or conversely, history may appear more open-ended than story because we're still living it. But these are fuzzy distinctions. Our story is part of history, and vice versa. At times we speak of "history in the making" or "current history." This is increasingly so in our interconnected, instant-access world.

There is no *essential* difference between history and story. Both embody meaningful narrative, a complex of meaning reaching beyond mere spacetime to the dimension of intention, plot, and resolution.

History is *ecological* in the sense that all stories interact. No story is finally complete in itself. Every story is part of the larger story we call history. This is a facet of the universe's fundamental ecology. An ecological connectedness seems to run through everything: material existence, Earth's ecosystems, and all human history. But history itself is a key dimension to the ecology of human life.

A comprehensive, serviceable worldview today will affirm that history is story, not haphazard happenstance. History has an "external" as well as an "internal" meaning. The meaning of history is not merely the accumulated stories within it. There is a wholeness to history that is more than the sum of its parts. History is ecological in this sense and also in the sense of the complex interrelatedness of all the acts and facts within it.[5]

If history is really a story, then its external meaning derives not simply from its internal meaning. It is the other way around: The external meaning of history is the source—fundamentally, if not wholly—of the meaning of each smaller story within it. Meaning is more than the tale itself, for there is a teller and thus a larger context of meaning.

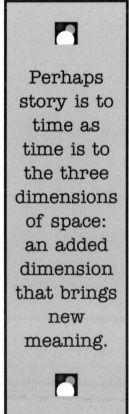

If history has this character of story and this kind of "external" meaning, what is the source of that larger meaning? It can be found only in the storyteller or the history maker. If story requires a storyteller, then history requires a history creator—requires, not in the sense of external necessity, but in the sense of the structure and logic of reality itself; just as action requires an actor and breathing a breather.

The Dimensions of Story

Life is story as much as it is a DNA string. Even after we've figured out how things cohere scientifically, we face the continuities and intricacies of historical change through time: plots and subplots, characters and conundrums, crises and climaxes. A large part of life's meaning lies in its story.

Matter, alone, lacks story. We are really speaking metaphorically (personally!) when we talk about "the story of the atom" or even "the story of the ant." What matter does give us, of course, is *time* in addition to the three dimensions of space. By itself time does not make story, but story requires time. Perhaps story is to time as time is to the three dimensions of space: a kind of added dimension bringing new levels of meaning. Story builds on the four dimensions of spacetime. Without time there can be no story, at least in the physical world.

People tell tales and inhabit stories because they are conscious creatures dwelling in space and time. Human life doesn't simply run in cycles. It stretches out into a line because people change with each experience. Unique events happen that can't be recycled. Even when the story seems to repeat itself, or when we pass through cycles and rhythms in life (days, months, years, generations), we never simply repeat ourselves or relive the story. We store up the story and make history. We build our own story and are part of larger stories. Memory changes us, so that no tomorrow can really be just like yesterday. We change as the story unfolds; rather, the changes in our lives and relationships gradually build a story. People make the story, primarily. Secondarily, the story makes

> Perhaps story is to time as time is to the three dimensions of space: an added dimension that brings new meaning.

people, as they live out the story as they understand it, fulfilling their roles.

The key to the meaning of the universe and of every life, yours and mine, is found in the *story* of the universe. The universe, that is, of conscious beings, not just of matter. Is this a coherent story, or not? That is a difficult question, because the story isn't over yet. It is often hard to figure out the meaning of a story before you reach the end.

Try living through a story. Some of the time everything goes well. We see order and beauty and hope. Then crises come. We encounter tension, perhaps even violence and the vilest evil. At these points it seems naive or cruel to say the story has some ultimate meaning. Only at the end of the story, perhaps, do we discover its coherence. Only then can we say with confidence how the good and the bad, the crisis and tension, the hope and despair fit together. The ecology of the story doesn't become clear until the end. Only then do we find the "happy ending" or the "sad ending."

Story seems to be deeply embedded in the coherence of the universe. There is a story and history to the world's coherence. Coherence is not static or frozen. Neither is it some changeless structure simply stretched out into time. It is more.

This is key for worldviews. A livable worldview in coming decades will have to manifest the character of story and be tuned in to history and its meaning. That history has meaning cannot be proved, of course, in any absolute sense. For one thing, the story of history has not yet been fully "told." But belief in historical meaning more adequately accounts for the facts and human experience of history than does any other worldview.

In sum, the worldview question is a story question. So a story or two may help.

A Simple Story of Complexity

Once upon a time a novelist wrote a book about a man named Fred. The novel had seven long chapters. The first chapter introduced Fred and told a little of his story. Fred was a novelist, a writer of mysteries. In chapter one he is depicted planning a novel about a man named Tom.

To make a long story short, here is a sketch of the other six chapters of the novel about Fred:

In chapter 2, Fred tells about Tom, the main character in his novel. Tom is a science fiction writer. He has been accused of a murder he didn't commit, and he is writing a sci-fi story about a man named Dixon.

Chapter 3 introduces Dixon: who he is, his background, the key events of his life. Dixon is both a scientist and a novelist. He is currently developing a book about a woman named Harriet.

In chapter 4, Dixon tells the story of Harriet. We learn of her family background and the things that influence her. She has grown to be a beautiful woman, and in the story she falls in love with and marries a novelist named Fred. They live happily ever after.

Chapter 5 completes Tom's story about Dixon. Dixon completes his novel, which ironically gives him new insight into a scientific problem he had pondered for years. This is a key event in his life. It sets in motion a chain of events that leads to the culmination of Tom's sci-fi novel about him.

In chapter 6 we learn that Tom was unjustly imprisoned in the murder case, but while in prison he completes his novel about Dixon. This book is a great success and focuses such attention on Tom that the investigation is reopened and eventually Tom is cleared and freed. His success as a writer gives him the freedom to write a heuristic book on science in the form of a novel that turns out to be his masterpiece.

Chapter 7 brings the novel about Fred to its conclusion. It tells how Fred's novel about Tom becomes a best seller and makes Fred famous. The book finally turns out to be a romance: Fred meets and marries a beautiful woman named Harriet and they live happily ever after.

Now, actually this is not a true story. We can imagine such a seven-chapter novel, even though it has never been written and probably never will be! But suppose it were. We might imagine that the novelist's name was J. Rutfield Crank.

We can fill in some details about Mr. Crank. His seven-chapter novel about Fred (and all the other characters) was called *Celestial Hierarchies*. It turned out to be a moderate success and added to Crank's growing reputation as a world-class writer.

Toward the end of his life, having written seven novels and three books of poetry, Crank became so famous that he was the subject of a major literary biography. His biographer, a man named Dixon, had himself gained fame through a series of brilliant biographies of prominent people. Eventually, Dixon died and an intriguing biography was, in turn, written about him. (It could have been written by J. Rutfield Crank, who survived Dixon, but it wasn't. Crank didn't like to write biographies, preferring fiction. He always said he thought fiction was stranger than truth, but he may have been wrong about this.)

The name of Dixon's biographer is unimportant, and in any case I don't remember it. I can assure you, however, that writing the biography of Dixon was no easy task. The biographer had to discuss not only

Dixon and all the major events of his life, but he also had to introduce the reader to J. Rutfield Crank and all the characters in his novel, *Celestial Hierarchies!* And of course he had to help the reader not confuse the Fred and Harriet of Crank's novel with the Fred and Harriet of the fictional Dixon's novel (who, of course, were also characters, indirectly, in Crank's novel).

As you see, all of this storytelling gets rather complex. But that's life. Personally, I find it ironic that Fred, the main character in *Celestial Hierarchies,* ends up marrying a beautiful woman named Harriet, just as the Harriet of Dixon's novel marries a novelist named Fred! It's also rather ironic that Crank's biographer was named Dixon, since Dixon was the name of a character (indirectly) in *Celestial Hierarchies.* There are a few other ironies here also, though that itself is probably not ironic. Irony, of course, is a part of good fiction because it is part of life. It signals life's mystery. On the other hand, I shouldn't make much of these ironies because they're rather intentional; I made them up. They flow from an ironic mind.

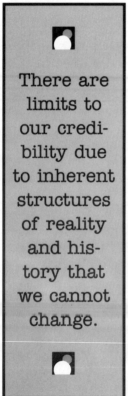

There are limits to our credibility due to inherent structures of reality and history that we cannot change.

A True Story?

Is any of the above story (or stories) true? Not really. I made it all up. However, now that I have created this scenario, it *is* true (for example) that there are two Freds and two Harriets, and also two Dixons, and that one of the Dixons is a character in Tom's book—and therefore also in Crank's book. It is true that the second Fred is a character in both Crank's and Dixon's books, but the first Fred *cannot* be a character in Dixon's novel because Dixon was created by Tom, who was created by the first Fred. So it would certainly be *untrue* to say the first Fred was a character in Dixon's book. Impossible! There's no way to beat the logic.

What seems to be true here, then, is not the story itself (which is totally imagined) but some inherent structure of reality that even I don't have the power to change. Here is a truth before which I am not omnipotent. True, I could claim that both Freds (or both Harriets) are really the same person. I could say that Crank's novel was really written by the novelist Dixon, or that in fact Harriet, the heroine of chapter four of *Celestial Hierarchies,* was really the author of *Celestial Hierarchies.* But the reader wouldn't buy it—no more than people today could be convinced that Huckleberry Finn brought Mark Twain into existence by writing a novel about him, or that Albert Einstein discovered the source of the Nile. There are limits to our credibility because there are inherent structures of reality and history that we cannot change. (True, some philosophical or literary types might argue that *in some sense* Huck Finn created Mark Twain, but that stretches our credibility. We know it is untrue in a historical sense.)

I have often thought it would be amusing—and totally mystifying—if I were to pick up a book printed, say, in the 1700s and find it contained names and facts about people in our time. So far this hasn't happened.

Consider again the novel *Celestial Hierarchies.* How is it possible that its characters exist as fictional people? Where do they come from? And what does "exist" mean here? They could not exist even as fictional characters unless Crank were to write his novel. But they *do* exist as fictional characters; yet Crank didn't create them, because Crank never lived. He is simply another fictional character. Crank didn't create the characters of *Celestial Hierarchies;* I did. They are really my characters. It is a fiction that Crank created them, except in a fictional sense. I just made up these characters. But I made them up as characters in the novel by Crank, whom I also made up. Now, it is true that within my fictional account Crank created Tom, Dixon, Harriet, and the other characters of the novel. But that is true only within my fiction. In actual fact, I made up the whole thing. The novel *Celestial Hierarchies* doesn't really exist. We're just imagining it.

There is, then, a rational explanation for the appearance in these pages of the characters of *Celestial Hierarchies.* We've pretended that Crank created them. But I have confessed that I did. The explanation for these characters' existence (even including Crank) is that they were created by a creative mind, whose identity I have slyly let slip.

But we can't stop here. We face another question: Who created me? How is it that I exist? We could pursue a long line of heredity: my parents, their parents, etc., all the way back to the point where we don't have data and so are forced to say (1) we don't know; (2) it just happened by some evolutionary process; or (3) there is a greater dimension of reality, probably a greater Mind—an Author within whose sphere of being he (or she) has chosen to create other beings and other minds.

Take your pick. For me, the third alternative is much more credible and satisfying. I brought the above cast of characters into existence within the rather limited dimensions of fiction. Within those limits they live and move and have their being, such as it is. But maybe fiction is to history what history is to spirit, for spirit is the dimension or dimensions of God's being. If God (or some dimensionally greater Mind than mine, for whom the name *God* seems most fitting) created me or my earliest ancestor, directly or indirectly, then it is no mystery that I can create a whole cast of fictional characters. And they in turn can create other fictional (or "subfictional") characters if I let them.

This is no proof that God exists, of course. That would be a little like J. Rutfield Crank trying to prove my existence, or like his characters trying to prove *his* existence. They could of course *try*—if I let them—but they could never succeed, for they have no way of transcending the limits of their existence (in this case, fiction). It can't be done because we're speaking of qualitatively different dimensions. Yet from this angle God's existence and activity are as plausible (at least!) as the claim that I created J. Rutfield Crank and all his characters. (If the truth be known, I actually invented J. Rutfield Crank over thirty years ago, but this is the first time I've gotten around to letting him out in public.)

What does this whole imagination game mean? Simply this: We had better not limit the dimensions of meaning or reality to what we can prove or explain or even imagine. We can imagine and manipulate many things. But there are dimensions and structures to existence that we simply cannot control. They are just *there,* dimensions that transcend our reality and our power.

This doesn't mean the higher dimensions of reality, whatever they may be, are totally unlike our own life and the world we taste and touch about us. More likely the opposite is true: The broader dimensions of reality are found or are hidden in our own being in some way. We do, in fact, transcend space and time in small ways in our everyday experience. Our dreams at night seem to lift us beyond spacetime. One morning I awoke early, then fell asleep again and enjoyed an elaborate dream that seemed to cover many hours. When I awoke again, only five minutes had passed. Somehow, in the world of dreams we are not limited to clock time or bedroom space.

Reality comes in multiple dimensions. Maybe the universe in all its dimensions really is a hologram. That is, maybe each part does in some diminished way contain the whole. Maybe spirit is hidden in rocks and ants, and every event of history signals universal history. Maybe every human being in some way images God.

Go to the Ant

Consider the ant, for example. Ants are fascinating critters. As a child in Michigan, I occasionally used to find anthills in the fields near our home. Some were two or three feet high, mounds of gray earth with a scattering of green blades of grass.

Sometimes I would poke a hole in the mound with a stick, or scrape away a few inches of honeycombed earth, and watch the ants scramble. Repairs began immediately. Ants, it seems, are as busy as bees.

I wonder: Do the ants have a story? Not in the human sense of story. In some sense they do have a history. They built their elaborate hierarchical home over months and years. Now I have disturbed them. There are billions of ecosystems on Earth, most of them smaller than this ant hill. Within them life goes on undisturbed, or perhaps changed or destroyed as more powerful creatures move in—like humans.

So I poke into the ant hill, walk on home, and go on with my life in my family and in the small town that was my childhood home. The ant hill is forgotten. Life goes on. I live oblivious to most of what happens in the larger world. But if a nuclear bomb hits our town or a meteor crashes to Earth, my little ecosystem will be demolished. Good-bye ant hill.

If there is a Mind, a Power, a Being who lives above and beyond (though not absent from) all our human and material systems—or, better, One who inhabits a broader range of dimensions that perhaps include and interpenetrate ours—then the circle of reality is much larger still. If this One not only observes but interferes in human affairs, then this is essential to the human story. Of course, we have no way of proving scientifically that this is the case, or not the case. But we see some possible evidence and wonder. We may see the hole poked in our anthill. And because we are more than ants, we may think and reflect and draw some conclusions.

So far as we know, ants don't think and wonder like we do—even if they *are* better organized. We can wonder, and we can imagine. We can build and destroy ecosystems and ponder their meaning.

We seem to experience history and story in a way that other creatures don't. A hole in an ant hill is swiftly fixed, and ant life goes on in its recurring cycles. But a hole poked into human society changes history. The story will ever after be different. In some way, the meaning is changed.

So we imagine another story—a cosmic one—a story bigger than a child looking at an ant hill, or a novelist pondering fictional characters. We raise our imagining a few notches on the dimensional scale. We imagine a cosmic drama. The global trends and consciousness we've examined in this book make us increasingly aware of larger, more cosmic dimensions to the universe. Is there a story behind these global streams? Conceivably we are all characters in a cosmic drama.

Cosmic Drama

Let us imagine that God is the great Playwright. God works out a dramatic plan on the stage and in the stages of history. God is sovereign as the playwright is sovereign over the drama he or she creates. Yet as every artist knows, in the creative process sovereignty does not mean lack of engagement, emotional detachment, or total independence from the persons and the action in the play. The playwright feels herself personally involved with the characters; she puts something of herself into them. In fact, each character probably embodies some aspect of her own character.

Since this is a cosmic drama, it is ecologically all-encompassing. Everything is included: all creatures, great and small; all things on Earth and in space; everything visible and invisible. But all this doesn't simply exist or evolve. A central story binds them together. We see movement, climax, resolution. During the play, of course, only the Playwright sees this clearly. The actors in the midst of the story don't fully grasp the plot. Meaning and ultimate purpose—or, for that matter, meaninglessness and chaos—are to them still questions of faith. The actors believe certain things about the character of the Playwright, the nature of the drama, and what the final outcome will be.

We can imagine the universe in this way. Some might object, claiming that drama isn't "real" or "true"; it remains a work of fiction, however much truth it embodies or reveals. Most people don't want to see themselves as the projection of someone else's fantasy, as someone's dream, even God's dream—much less as merely playing a part already written, predetermined.

But what if the Playwright is exceedingly clever? Then the cosmic drama model meets this challenge—provided we remember that this is a metaphor for a mystery that transcends our imagining. In actual fact, in real history (we may imagine) the Dramatist allows the characters to come alive, to improvise, to make real decisions—even possibly to ruin the play or steal the show. At issue is not so much the *power* of the Playwright (who can call a halt if things get out of hand) but rather the Playwright's intelligence, creativity, and insight—in short, his *creative genius*.[6]

The greatest dramatic genius who ever lived on Earth could not grant full freedom to the actors on the stage. He couldn't be sure the story would turn out as he intended, even if he knew all the actors intimately. But if the Playwright were *God*—not a God who predetermines people's actions but a God who gives people genuine freedom within the limits of his ultimate power, a super clever God—the story would be different. It would be genuinely open, genuinely free, yet definitely glorious in final outcome. It would be a breathtaking story!

Myth Become Fact

Playwright, drama, actors, world—here are elements of a worldview. But how could such a worldview or worldstory be true? True, not just as fiction or myth is true, but true even in a historical sense? True the way that it is true that humans have genes, electrons orbit nuclei, and you are now reading this page?

The British author and fantasist C. S. Lewis once pondered this. He wrote about myth becoming fact. As a student of literature, Lewis recognized that the world's great myths express truth in some sense. But he went on to make a startling suggestion. Maybe all the great myths in the world—all those that are in some sense true—point beyond themselves to *the* Myth, a myth that actually happened in history.

Lewis used this reasoning to explain his faith. In his spiritual autobiography, *Surprised by Joy* (partially captured in the film *Shadowlands*), Lewis tells not how he found God, but how God found him—surprised him into believing in Jesus Christ. That experience, that conversion, led him to write: "The heart of Christianity is a myth which is also a fact." Once in history, all the world's myths of suffering and salvation, of pain and healing, came true. The truth of the world's myths is that they dimly show an actual story of redemption, a cosmic drama whose secret and meaning are seen in spacetime history.

This historical myth is the story of Jesus Christ: his birth, life, death, and resurrection. The story of Jesus brings myth and fact together. "Perfect Myth and Perfect Fact: claiming not only our love and our obedience, but also our wonder and delight, addressed to the savage, the child, and the poet in each one of us no less than to the moralist, the scholar, and the philosopher."[7]

This is a perfectly coherent way to view things. All human dramas and myths point to a more profound truth: a story of redemption that is both poetry and history and is also consistent with science. Truth, in the final analysis, must be just so: A beautiful story in which evil is finally overcome (or self-destructs) so that in the end we see the harmony, the symmetry, the beauty. Imagining history as God's redemptive cosmic drama hints at how such a story just might be true, not only poetically or mythically but also historically—and also scientifically, no doubt, if we knew enough to see the connections.

If history *is* such a cosmic drama, it is not over yet. We are in the middle (more or less) of the story. Its culmination lies in the future. Yet the future is partly present now. Those who know the secret shape their lives to fit the story, to share the adventure and the wonder and the joy.

This could serve as a coherent worldview. It respects history. How is history unfolding? We see both crisis and development. Any good story combines gradual development and climactic moments as it moves toward final resolution. As Playwright, God is the chief agent—initially, finally, and throughout. And yet human action is real, free, and significant. People actually contribute something to the final outcome. There is room for many subplots, counterplots, even attempts to subvert the story. Actors may be tempted to think they are the playwright, or deny that there is any meaning. Yet the drama progresses and finally reveals meaning. *In the end it all makes sense.*

How do the dimensions of matter and spirit relate in this cosmic drama? A *deus ex machina* model won't do. But one can imagine that the cosmic drama happens in more than our four spacetime dimensions. It occurs in multiple "spaces," yet is unified in the being and mind of God. C. S. Lewis was a master of such multidimensionality. He made multiple yet coherent levels of reality believable, as, for example, in his *Perelandra* trilogy of novels and his children's series, *The Chronicles of Narnia.*

Great drama shows both outer behavior and inner reality. We perceive motives as well as acts. Seeing God's involvement with human history as a cosmic drama has this strength as well. Also, as it unfolds in history the drama combines both personal and environmental concerns, and the drama can be explored through various symbols and images.

The historian Herbert Butterfield hinted at the usefulness of the cosmic drama model years ago in his book *Christianity and History.* Butterfield suggested the analogy of a composer and an orchestral composition to picture God's activity in history. "It is better worldly-wisdom, even when we are only looking for a pictorial representation, to think of history as though an intelligence were moving over the story, taking its bearings afresh after everything [people] do, and making its decisions as it goes along," he wrote. "There is no symbolic representation that will do justice to history save [that of] the composer . . . who composes the music as we go along, and, when we slip into aberrations, switches his course in order to make the best of everything."[8]

Cosmic symphony is a good metaphor. Cosmic drama is even better, for as a form of story it more fully portrays human action.

Truth and Metaphor

Cosmic drama remains, of course, a metaphor. It is not the whole truth, but it may suggest the wholeness of the truth. It points to a reality beyond the metaphor.

Some people try to wring truth out of metaphors. Precisely speaking,

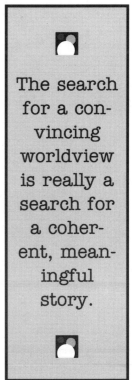

truth does not come from metaphors. It is the other way around. Metaphors hint at truth only to the degree that there is some deeper (or higher) truth that backs up the metaphor—a correspondence or resonance. Metaphors suggest that which is "metaphored." They reveal truth to us only when, by analogy, they help us see some truth we had not previously seen. A metaphor may be a mediator of or catalyst for truth.

Where, then, does truth come from? Where is it anchored? It seems to be grounded in some dimension beyond our own mind and experience. This is where the above inquiry leads us, even though the conclusion is starkly unmodern and unpopular.

I personally believe that truth is grounded in the Cosmic Mind—the Divine Person, God. For the fundamental reality of the universe must be personal, with mind, will, and emotion; therefore, in some sense with a story, or the potential for story. Human personality must be a reflection or image, a sort of incarnation, of the Divine Personality. This Person must exist in higher or fuller dimensions, not be something *less* than humanity. Of course, since these dimensions transcend time, even story is a sometimes weak metaphor. Story in our human conception requires time, as already noted. Story is what happens to personality in time. Yet God must exist in some range of personal dimensions that are at least analogous to what we, in spacetime, experience as story.

Some connection (or multiple connections) must exist between the Divine Person and the physical world, and especially with humankind. This must be more than a spiritual connection. It must penetrate the natural world. It must be dynamic, have movement, not be static. In short, the perception of a *story;* a *history* requires this relationship with a divine personality.

Worldview as Worldstory

This study of story and history means that the search for a worldview is really a search for a coherent, meaningful story. The coherence of the universe is the coherence of story. Any search for meaning in the universe that overlooks the dimension of story misses a key to its actual coherence. The meaning of the universe is found in the coherence of story, for it is the story of coherence.

> The search for a convincing worldview is really a search for a coherent, meaningful story.

What we need, then, is not so much a *worldview* as a *worldstory.* The issue is not just how we see the world but how we experience it, live in its story, find the meaning of our own story there.

What is this story? This now becomes the key question. Is there a Story behind every story? Some kind of Master Story? Is there in fact an ultimate metanarrative? Postmodernism rejects all metanarratives as manipulative, oppressive, and inherently impossible. But maybe that's only part of the story. Maybe even postmodernism will finally fit into a larger story. The term *postmodern,* looking backward rather than forward, implicitly suggests that the story isn't over yet.

The story *isn't* over yet. In the final chapters we explore the idea of worldstory and its implications for trends and worldviews.

CHAPTER NINETEEN

Worldviews and Worldstory

> There is a principle of organization connecting all things.
>
> —**Chinese proverb**
>
> History . . . is the price that God pays in order to have men [and women] who are free.
>
> —**Edgar S. Brightman**[1]

Entwined with global trends are deep worldview issues. These issues press harder and harder as converging trends become increasingly global. How shall we deal with them?

There are many particular, partial answers. More basic, comprehensive answers, however, require a coherent worldview. The issue comes down to a question of *worldstory*. Earth needs a worldstory that cogently links not only trends and ideas but also personality, ecology, and history.

The struggle for the world's soul is more than a contest for its mind, though it surely is that. It is a struggle for its whole being, for all humanity and the life of Planet Earth. It is not a dispute among intellectuals but a deep personal struggle involving every person and all of life. If this is not consciously recognized by most people, it is increasingly *felt* by everyone under the growing pressure of global trends.

People live by stories. The stories may be their own, their parents', their grandparents', or some broader story that forms an ideology or a religious quest. Whatever the story that shapes their lives, that is for them their worldstory.

Two key questions surface when we consider the need for a world-story: What are the essential criteria for a plausible, livable worldstory today, in the light of global trends? And can we find such a worldstory?

Worldstory Criteria

A worldstory that is coherent, believable, and livable today must meet seven key tests. These arise from the discussion in previous chapters. A few have already been explored somewhat, others only implied. Now we must draw the strands together. In listing these seven criteria or basic elements, I will show why each one is essential for what we might call a "good worldstory." Though some of these criteria overlap, each is distinct enough to require emphasis.

1. *A livable worldstory will first of all be a comprehensive story.* It must incorporate all that is, at least potentially and in principle. It must literally be a Theory of Everything. Anything less would be only part of the story, a sub-story, not the whole. People feel the need for a story that is truly comprehensive. Granted, most people live by partial or private stories. But eventually a private story will let you down.

A comprehensive worldstory is one that is both *transcendent* and *immanent,* as those terms are generally understood. It will answer both big and little questions without dissolving either into the other. It will make room for those dimensions of reality that stretch beyond spacetime existence, and yet will show the reality and significance of material things.

The word *transcendence* suggests going beyond, and *immanence* suggests dwelling within. A transcendent worldstory is one that goes beyond all distinctions between matter and spirit, person and thing, time and non-time, past and future, showing the interrelationship of all that exists. An immanent worldstory is one that "dwells within" all the dimensions of personal, daily material life as we experience it. These two need not—indeed, must not—be seen as contradictory, though the implications are deeper than we can grasp.

2. *A truly adequate worldstory will also be ecological.* The global trends outlined in the earlier part of this book press home this worldstory requirement. This has always been true for worldviews and worldstories: they must show how everything is linked to everything else. More deeply, they must have *an inherent ecological sensitivity,* reflecting a profound consciousness of the interwoven nature of all of life. This is the primary strength of the Gaia hypothesis and its useful contribution to contemporary worldview discussions.

An ecological worldstory is one in which all the elements are deeply intertwined. Nothing is finally superfluous or irrelevant. It makes one

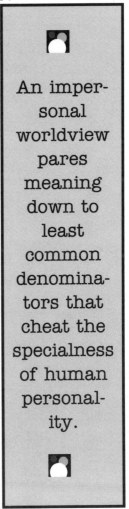

believe that small events and acts can have large consequences and that complex systems are not fundamentally chaotic, even if it cannot demonstrate this in every case.

This ecological character is especially needed today. Science in particular, and human knowledge generally, is increasingly demonstrating the deeply ecological nature of the universe. This sensitivity adds great strength and coherence to the worldstory. Any worldstory that is not truly ecological will finally prove unconvincing. It would be a split-level worldview.

3. A worldstory that wins the world's soul will also have to be personal. Personality is a profound and precious gift shared (or squandered) by all human beings. Yet many worldviews ultimately dissolve personality into impersonality and nonbeing, or reduce it to a mix of meaningless molecules. A worldstory must affirm human personality by showing that the universe is in some deep and wise sense personal as well as ecological. Often ecological thinking today, in its urge to show human dependence on the nonhuman environment, fails to do justice to the uniqueness of human personality—what writer Philip Yancey calls "the ache of cosmic specialness."

A livable worldstory must be personal to be fully rational. An ultimately impersonal worldstory or worldview is reductionist, paring meaning down to least common denominators, niches that cheat the specialness of personality. This personal aspect is necessary also pragmatically. An impersonal or nonpersonal worldview is dehumanizing. Unless it is personal it lacks the element of story. Only a worldview that is personal can be a worldstory, as we saw in the previous chapter.

4. A fourth essential of a coherent worldstory is that it be historical. This follows from the personal character of the world and is part of the dimension of story, as we have seen. The worldstory is not a mere myth floating in some nonhistorical space, however profound or "true" in a philosophical or psychological sense. A believable worldstory takes actual historical events seriously in their spacetime concreteness and in their historical flow and relatedness.

> An impersonal worldview pares meaning down to least common denominators that cheat the specialness of human personality.

Why? Because this is how life is. History exists, even apart from its interpretations. The telling of history is, of course, partly interpretation. But there is that to be interpreted, or the interpretation would be wholly fiction (as deconstructive postmodernism maintains). People live and move in history, and this history provides much of the meaning of their lives.

More than just a story *about* history, a true worldstory must actually *be history*. It must be grounded in history itself, not be an abstraction from history. The acts and events of history must be part of the story. Even though history is not yet ended, world history and worldstory must finally be one.

5. A useful worldstory will be public, not merely private. If a worldview is truly universal and historical it will be in some sense public, of course. But many worldstories really are private worldviews. They deal only or essentially with the interior life. Or they are held more or less privately by a particular community that does not take its view to the public square. Private worldviews may work fine for those who hold them, but they tend finally to be only partial or schizoid stories. They abandon much of life, society, and the environment to others and make no claim on broader culture. They thus fail the test of comprehensiveness and are implicitly dualistic. Unfortunately, this is rarely recognized.

Unless a worldstory is public, it is not the whole story. It is not really universal, ecological, or historical. A worldstory that is not a public story always remains a retreat from reality rather than an engagement with reality.

6. A credible worldstory today will be mythic—not mythological in the sense of nonhistorical or purely imagined myths, but mythic in the sense of giving larger meaning and defining right and wrong. A mythic worldstory is thus ethical, setting the basis for morality. A worldstory must be a "good story" in this sense.

This has always been a basic task of worldviews. They set people's lives in a larger narrative that answers questions of purpose and good and evil. A worldstory serves as an encircling, comprehensive story from which people can coherently deduce or instinctively infer a framework for ethical conduct. This is how people function. Whatever really forms people's acts and choices is their worldview, where admitted or not. Given today's EarthCurrents, a convincing worldstory will need to make this ethical connection clear.

7. Finally, a livable worldstory must be transforming—personally, socially, and globally—inside and out. Only a transcendent and transforming worldstory prompts hope in the face of today's EarthCurrents. Many worldviews do not. Most merely help people cope, or keep them in some kind of homeostasis with the environment. But the world today

calls for a transformative worldstory. It must provide the basis for active, catalytic roles in the story, not passive watching.

In other words, the worldstory must be *purposive*. It must transform not merely as yeast but as purpose—personal intention and action. Only this is consistent with the personal and historical character of the world and human experience. A worldstory without direction and purpose betrays the character of genuine story. The destructive tendencies of key global trends point to the need for universal healing. Humanity increasingly needs a transforming, healing worldstory.

More Than Ideas and Views

These seven tests show that a livable worldstory must be much more than just an idea. It must be concretely historical, ecological, and personal. At the same time, it must provide a moral compass and motive power for human life in all its dimensions.

It follows that such a worldstory cannot be *invented*; it can only be discovered. A worldstory of such scope would be too grand for human invention. Its roots in history would be too deep for human creation, and its ecological reality would be too complex for human creativity. A true worldstory must be something like gravity or relativity, not something invented or thought up, but something "really there," waiting to be discovered. Albert Einstein did not invent the equation $E = MC^2$—he discovered it.

Does a worldview or worldstory have to been scientific or scientifically verifiable? It's a catch-22 question. We saw in chapter 12 that the answer is yes and no. At one level the answer is obviously no, for two reasons: Science is constantly evolving, making new discoveries and outdating old theories. More importantly, science simply has no way of dealing with some of the key worldview issues.

On the other hand, a worldview should not contradict truly verified facts of science. If it does, it loses credibility with many people. It then assumes the added burden of having to explain the discrepancy with science. If a worldstory meets the above seven criteria, however, it will sufficiently coincide with science—today's science and also tomorrow's.

Can such a worldstory be discovered? Only if it already exists. If it does, it possibly could be discovered by a seeker. Or a seeker could be found by the story. But could any worldstory possibly meet these difficult tests? Is such a worldstory an impossible dream?

Surveying the six worldviews outlined earlier, we find that not one meets these tests for a fully plausible, livable worldstory. Every one fails at one or more points, profound as some of them are. In discussing the strengths and weaknesses of each worldview in chapters 10–15, we noted these fatal flaws. The seven criteria above show the depth of those flaws. We have yet to find a worldview or worldstory that can withstand the winds and acids of today's EarthCurrents.

Can we, then, find a convincing worldstory, or what James Sire calls "a likely story"? Can we be sure of the meaning of a story when it's not over yet? To answer this, we must return to an essential aspect about any credible worldview: the fact of faith. A plausible worldview, we noted earlier, doesn't answer *every* conceivable question, just as an adequate principle of coherence doesn't answer every question. So we must examine the options and activate faith.

Seeking the Good Worldstory

> A worldview functions as a person's religion or philosophy of life. At root the worldstory question is really a religious quest.

Where can we find a story with deep enough meaning to base a worldview upon? How does one discover a worldstory, a worldview that illuminates all of life? Science and economics cannot provide one; their scope is too small. Politics is too reductionist. Art and music are broadly inclusive and suggestive, but ultimately too ambiguous and inarticulate. Mythology suggests answers but slights or relativizes history. Philosophy is too abstract and speculative to provide a common worldstory. Religion is often seen as being unscientific or irrational and irrelevant to the big, practical issues of life.

Yet it is religion and philosophy that specialize in worldviews. A worldview functions as a person's religion, his or her philosophy of life. This means that the worldstory question is really a religious quest. Many people shy away from religious language and "religiosity." Yet everyone seeks a worldstory, consciously or not. The religious and irreligious alike, both philosophers and non-philosophers—all seek or believe a worldstory.

Socially and psychologically speaking, the chief function of religion is to provide a livable worldview or worldstory. This has been true historically and still is today. Emerging global society is if anything *more* religious than past ages, not less. (A notable exception to this would be vocal academic and media elites in technologically advanced societies.)

We can discuss worldviews and worldstories without resorting to traditional religious language. The need and the quest remain. The key worldview questions are at base religious and philosophical, whatever language we use.

Typically religion answers worldview questions through some kind of story (mythological[2] or historical) that gives moral meaning to life. Thus we have the stories of the Buddha, of Jesus, of Mohammed. We know of the myths of ancient Greece and of Hinduism, or of Scientology. More philosophical currents (religious and ostensibly nonreligious) give us maxims, proverbs, propositions, and theories. Examples include Confucianism, some streams of Buddhism, Marxism, and (when taken as worldview or worldstory) capitalism and science (or more accurately, scientism). Humanism, agnosticism, and atheism function in the same way.

What do we make of the various philosophies and religious options? We could study each in turn, examining them by the worldstory crtieria outlined above. We need only raise the issue of *history*, however, in order to narrow the options. Today any credible worldstory must be historical, as we have seen. Many religions and philosophies have profound insights and helpful maxims but fail the test of history. As global society progresses, these will increasingly lose their persuasive force—except among people who are looking for a nonhistorical escape from history.

Even the historical religions and philosophies, generally speaking, fail the test of history. Their stories may be historical, but they fail to show how *this particular* story is the key to all of history, all of life. Why should one particular story or history be relevant to anyone but me, or its own actors? Can any one story transform all others?

What about the cosmic drama model, suggested earlier? Does this give us a worldstory?

Even if the cosmic drama model is true (and I believe it is), it fails to give us a complete worldstory. By itself, it fails for at least three reasons: the drama is not over yet (we can't be sure how it will turn out); too much of the story even now is unknown to us; and the story is too complex to grasp. The story must be embodied in one concrete revealing story in history that gives us the decisive clue to grasp the meaning of the whole story.

Why should there be only *one* revelatory story? In theory there might be many. But not in history. A revelatory story is not simply an explanatory myth. It is part of the actual web of the contingency and complexity of history. It makes all the difference in the world whether it happened or not. If it happened, it changed history.

C. S. Lewis claimed that the history of Jesus is such a story. The Jesus story is rooted in history, yet it has great mythic and transforming power. Empires have risen and fallen because of it. People by the millions have found that it answered their deepest questions, satisfied their most disquieting quests. Here is a worldstory, Lewis argued, in which myth became historical fact. It changed his life.

This is my experience, as well. I have come to see and believe that God acted in Jesus Christ, creating history and recreating history. God has made Jesus Christ the key to history.

The story of Jesus answers the worldview questions and squares with the seven worldstory criteria. I am speaking specifically of Jesus Christ—not of the Christian religion, which in many of its versions has very little to do with the person and spirit of Jesus. The issue is the actual life and history of Jesus of Nazareth, who lived on Earth from approximately 4 B.C. to A.D. 30.

The story/history of Jesus satisfies the worldstory criteria in a profound and moving way. It appeals to mind, emotion, and will. The story is coherent and persuasive, once one grasps it or comes under its power. This was the experience of C. S. Lewis when he discovered Jesus Christ and was "surprised by joy." Change the time and place, and you find similar stories in the lives of people ranging from Augustine and Francis of Assisi to Malcolm Muggeridge, Mother Teresa, and Charles Colson.

The story of Jesus complements and completes the cosmic drama model. It gives it flesh and blood—*literally*. We may come to see that this is the decisive story—because of who Jesus was and is, because of God's action through the story, and because of Jesus' voluntary death and surprising resurrection. Here is a story that is unique, not just in its ideas or moral power, but also in its historicity. It happened. More accurately, God acted.

The Story of Coherence

A cosmic drama with Jesus as the key actor builds on and accents many of the points we have considered throughout this book. The story can be told in bare-bones fashion as follows:

The most fundamental reality in the universe, the source of the story and the one who provides meaning for everything else, is God, the Divine Person. God is not absent from the physical universe, but God's being transcends its every dimension: space, time, human consciousness, and human history. (Thus far the Divine Design worldview rings true.)

God is the great Storyteller, the Master Chronicler and History-maker. God is not held captive in the dimensions of space and time. These dimensions actually hint at higher dimensions that (to us) are hidden in the energy and being of God. God is working out a coherent story in the universe and in human affairs. Of course we don't fully grasp that coherence yet. For now, we can only believe—or disbelieve—it is there. We must wait until the end of the story, the final act, to see and experience its full coherence.

The key to the story, its central plot, is the history of Jesus Christ. In Jesus we see the nature of God and the meaning of the story. Here we see the order, surprise, and beauty of the story of the universe—and its ultimate irony. Frederick Buechner writes that with the birth of Jesus:

> the whole course of human history was changed. That is a truth as unassailable as any truth. Art, music, literature, Western culture itself with all its institutions and Western man's whole understanding of himself and his world—it is impossible to conceive how differently things would have turned out if that birth had not happened. . . . And there is a truth beyond that: for millions of people who have lived since, the birth of Jesus made possible not just a new way of understanding life but a new way of living it.[3]

It may seem impossible or absurd that the meaning of the universe could be revealed in the story of one person. But that is the big surprise. It is the shock to our sensibilities that has been a stumbling block for 2,000 years. In Jesus Christ, God shed some of the dimensions of his being to enter the dimensions of human existence. He become part of our story; he inhabited it. In this way God transformed the story, gave it new meaning, set it going in new directions that will lead to surprising ultimate coherence. And in Jesus, God continues to be active in the story. For Jesus rose from death, transforming the possibilities of history.

How did God do it? "Unimaginably, the Maker of all things shrinks down, down, down, so small as to become a single, barely visible fertilized egg. And that egg divides and redivides until a fetus takes shape, and finally a baby comes from Mary's loins to join puny human beings on their speck of a planet," writes Philip Yancey.[4] God did it through becoming human in Jesus Christ. To us, of course, it looks like a miracle. Here we sense the uniqueness and power of this person: Jesus. Yancey writes:

> The God who roared, who ordered armies and empires about like pawns on a chessboard, emerged in Palestine as a baby who could not speak, who depended on Mary and Joseph for shelter, food, and love. Here on earth, for 33 years, God experienced what it is like to be a human being. And in the stories he told, and the people whose lives he touched, he answered for all time the question, Does one person matter?[5]

Here is a marvelous story, one just incredible enough to be true, to be a likely story. The story is nowhere more beautifully sketched than in an early Christian hymn:

[Christ Jesus,] being in very nature God,
    did not consider equality with God
      something to be grasped,
but made himself nothing,
    taking the very nature of a servant,
    being made in human likeness.
And being found in appearance as a
    man,
    he humbled himself
    and became obedient to death—
      even death on a cross!
Therefore God exalted him to the
    highest place
    and gave him the name that is above
      every name,
that at the name of Jesus every knee
    should bow,
    in heaven and on earth and under
    the earth,
and every tongue confess that Jesus
    Christ is Lord,
to the glory of God the Father.

(Phil. 2:6-11 NIV)

As this hymn suggests, the key to Jesus' life is his death and resurrection, and the key to these is his identity as divine and human. Jesus came to live, but more. He came to die—the only way to defeat death and bring life. Why die? This goes to the heart of the good news, the good story of Jesus Christ. There is great power, great irony, and great anguish in Jesus' death. Great power, in that Jesus died innocently and voluntarily. Great irony, because through his death Jesus turned defeat into victory. Great anguish, because this was real flesh-and-blood suffering for ungrateful people.

Did Jesus have to die? He denied any external necessity: "I lay down my life—only to take it up again. No one takes it from me, but I lay it down of my own choice. I have power to lay it down and power to take it up again" (John 10:17-18; author's paraphrase). Jesus could have escaped capture and the cross, but his dying was needed for two reasons: To maintain the consistent coherence of his life and message, and to defeat death and evil by his resurrection. He did this historically, as God, by taking upon himself the full weight of evil and human rebellion and self-fixation. Those who respond in personal faith and utter loyalty to Jesus feel this resurrection power and purpose in their own lives— personal transformation. This seems to be what the apostle Paul meant in one of his letters: "Anyone who is in Christ is a new creation. The old has gone; the new has come" (2 Cor. 5:17; author's trans.).

This is not the whole story of Jesus, of course. But it is the key to the story, and it is history's central meaning. The history of Jesus is the perfect hologram of the cosmic story—as the source of the light, not just its refraction. The complete story involves many other things: the conundrum of sin and evil, the connection between spirit and flesh, the re-creation of community. All these are part of the story. But the center and meaning are found in Jesus Christ. When history reaches its climax, we will finally see how everything ties together, the whole cosmic ecology. In the biblical vision, this will be a time of universal reconciliation when all tears are dried, all evil is judged and destroyed, and all nature enjoys its full harmony.

To deal with these many important but secondary issues would take another book. I simply offer this focus on Jesus as both essential conclusion and unique starting point. The most satisfying and credible worldstory—considering life and existence in *literally* all its dimensions—is the story and history of Jesus Christ.

The central storyline was summed up by the apostle Paul some years after Jesus' resurrection: "God was reconciling the world to himself in Christ, not counting [people's] sins against them." So anyone who is "in Christ" is a "new creation." The biblical picture of Jesus Christ is both personal and cosmic: "The creation waits in eager expectation for the [children] of God to be revealed. For the creation . . . itself will be liberated from its bondage to decay and brought into the glorious freedom of the children of God." Jesus himself put it more poignantly and personally: "Come to me, all you who are weary and burdened, and I will give you rest" (2 Cor. 5:17-19; Rom. 8:19-21; Matt. 11:28).

One of Jesus' closest friends, John the Evangelist, penned a powerful picture of Jesus about half a century after Jesus left Earth. He called Jesus "the Word." Here is how he tells the worldstory:

> The Word was in the beginning, for the Word was with God. In fact, the Word was God. He was with God from the start. All things were made by him. Without him not one thing came into being. In him was life, and that life was a light for all people. The light keeps shining in the darkness, and the darkness cannot blot it out . . . .
>
> The Word, the true light that enlightens everyone, entered our world. He was in the world, the very world he made. Yet the world did not recognize him! He came to what was his own, but his own would not accept him. But to everyone who did receive him, who believed in him, he gave power to become God's own children—not just humanly speaking or by human effort, but by God's action.
>
> This Word became flesh and blood and lived among us. We have seen his glory—the glory of the Father's only child, overflowing with grace and truth. . . . We have all received grace and more grace from him. The law was given through Moses, but grace and truth came through Jesus Christ.

Though no one has ever seen God, his only Son, always with the Father, has made him known. (John 1:1-5, 9-14, 17-18; author's paraphrase)

This picture of Jesus jolted and jarred the best-selling worldviews of the first-century Roman Empire. Here was a new worldview: "strange new teaching," some Greek philosophers said. It was a worldstory that would shake and remake history. Today, as the world changes in new ways, this picture takes on renewed force and meaning rather than turning obsolete.

Weighing the Worldviews

A review of the seven worldstory criteria shows how fully the history of Jesus Christ meets tests for coherence and credibility. Clearly this is a *comprehensive* story, even a kind of Theory of Everything. It encompasses all the material universe but also transcends it. This worldstory includes all the dimensions of existence, from human hopes and dreams to hard physical facts.

The Jesus worldstory is *ecological* in a deeper sense than any scientific ecology. This worldstory is *inherently* ecological. It sees all things as coming from the same source, as now interrelated, and as sharing a common history and goal. A special strength of this worldstory is its profound *personal* character. We find personality in the universe because its source, God, is a person. Further, the meaning of life is inscribed not in philosophies or theories but in the life and history of Jesus Christ. In him we see what it means to be person and to be human. This worldstory is personal and personally healing. It heals the splits of today's world: subject/object, private/public, interior/exterior, particular/general, parent/child, male/female. A contemporary worldstory requires this comprehensiveness.

Another strength of the Jesus worldstory is its *historical* nature. Person, story, and history are joined in Jesus. Jesus is rooted in and yet transcends the actual, datable events of world history, even of "secular" history. In the accounts of Jesus we read about the Roman Emperor Augustus and many other historical figures. The uniqueness of Jesus' history is seen in the remarkable quality of his life and his actual resurrection within history. The New Testament seems to suggest that Jesus' life, death, and resurrection form the paradigm and pattern for all of history.

Jesus' resurrection is, of course, the signature event in his life and in the whole story. Some Christians have naively said that it makes no difference to the power or meaning of the story whether Jesus actually, historically rose from the dead. It's still a great story, they say, even if not historically true. That, however, is like saying it makes no difference whether or not the atomic bomb fell on Hiroshima and Nagasaki; it's still a powerful story. But it *does* make a difference, a crucial difference.

To deny this ignores completely the significance of history, and its pain and joy. World history has one meaning and end to the story if Jesus rose from the dead. It would have quite another if he did not, even if his followers believed and acted as though he did.

We do not know exactly how Jesus rose from the dead, and we obviously can't explain it scientifically, though from a quantum science viewpoint his resurrection looks less "unscientific" than Enlightenment science thought. The New Testament teaches that Jesus' resurrection was real, historical, and physical, but also that after the resurrection Jesus' body was in some ways different, not subject to spacetime limitations. The risen Jesus could be seen and touched and ate food, yet he could pass through closed doors and apparently move instantly from place to place.

The story about Jesus is also a *public* worldstory. These things were "not done in a corner," Paul the apostle told King Agrippa II (Acts 26:26). The events of Jesus' life, death, and resurrection were public knowledge, however they were interpreted. The meaning and implications of this worldstory are public as well. The Jesus worldview is not just a religious story for religious people. It concerns the public square as much as the private soul. It has foundational implications for global trends as well as global worldviews. If we take Jesus seriously, for example, we will care for the environment while we continue to explore science. We will seek the economic welfare of all people, and especially the poor, not just the prosperous. We will be concerned with individuals, families, and community, and with the rights and responsibilities of all, for this is what Jesus teaches and shows.

Although historical and public, the Jesus worldstory is also profoundly *mythic*. Jesus gives us the most powerful myth of all time. It has moved people to remarkable courage and heroism, from early Christian slaves to Mother Teresa of Calcutta. When distorted and twisted for political ends, it has produced horrific suffering. The medieval Crusades, the persecution of Jews, racial repression in the United States and South Africa, and terrorism in Northern Ireland and Lebanon are all terrible examples.

The Jesus worldstory, in contrast to its religious distortions, shows us how to live lovingly and justly and gives the power for such a life. Early Christians said the story about Jesus was "good news." It was, and is, a good worldstory. Taken seriously and on its own terms, it provides the foundation for social ethics, personally and globally. This is so because the Jesus worldstory is not a moral theory but a life lived and a battle over evil won. Through their experience of Jesus early Christians could say, "Death has been swallowed up in victory" (1 Cor. 15:54; see Isa. 25:8).

This power of the lived, victorious life we see in Jesus means that the Jesus worldstory is a *transforming* story, personally, socially, and globally. Already it has transformed history remarkably. Most of Earth's great humanitarian movements trace directly or indirectly to the inspiration of Jesus. Hospitals, schools, civil rights movements, and thousands of other efforts to end human suffering have sprung from the same source. Even non-Christians like Mahatma Gandhi have been inspired by him. Even Karl Marx's communist dream was a secularized, distorted version of the Christian hope.

The world's literature abounds with witnesses to the personal and social power of Jesus and the worldstory he embodies. In fact, the story of Jesus is believed today by more and more people worldwide—at the rate of several thousand a day, according to studies. These are not "primitive," superstitious people, given to believing incredible things. They are people like Tatiana Goricheva. As a young philosophy student in Leningrad, Tatiana rejected dialectical materialism and embraced existentialism, yet she found that unsatisfying. She turned to yoga, but still found no answer to her despair. She tells what happened next:

> In a yoga book a Christian prayer, the "Our Father" [the prayer Jesus taught] was suggested as an exercise. . . . I began to say it as a mantra, automatically and without expression. I said it about six times, and then suddenly I was turned inside out. I understood . . . that he exists. [God], the living, personal God, who loves me and all creatures, who has created the world, who became a human being out of love, the crucified and risen God.[6]

Thousands of such stories arise around the globe. Among the Sawi tribe of West Irian, Jesus is discovered to be the "Peace Child" who brings reconciliation to warring tribes. Among the Masai of Tanzania Jesus Christ is found to be the one who brings hope and a new sense of community, as recounted in the remarkable book *Christianity Rediscovered* by the Roman Catholic missionary, Vincent Donovan.[7] The story of Jesus Christ is still proving to be "the power of God for the salvation of everyone who believes" (Rom. 1:16).

The Jesus worldstory concerns not only Jesus as a person but also God's purpose to bring peace and reconciliation to Earth through him. Early followers of Jesus expressed this sense of overall purpose and direction in many ways. Paul the apostle gave classic expression to it, arguing that God is carrying out a plan, an "economy," through Jesus Christ "to bring all things in heaven and on earth together" in him. "God was pleased to have all his fullness dwell in" Jesus, he argued, "and through him to reconcile to himself all things, whether things on earth or things in heaven, by making peace through his blood, shed on the cross" (Eph. 1:10; Col. 1:19-20).

There is remarkable cogency, energy, and inspiration in the Jesus worldstory. Part of this strength is due to its ability to satisfy all worldstory criteria. Nothing beats a true story.

CHAPTER TWENTY

End of Story/ Beginning of Story

> If the whole universe has no meaning, we should never have found out that it has no meaning: just as, if there were no light in the universe and therefore no creatures with eyes, we should never know it was dark.
>
> —C. S. Lewis[1]

> I am the First and the Last, the beginning and the End.
>
> —Jesus Christ

E arth is experiencing an unprecedented global struggle. Powerful trends point to a possible global crisis around the year 2020. Issues of meaning and purpose are equally important and, heightened by global trends, suggest that the next two generations will be uniquely critical for human history.

This is nothing less than a struggle for the world's soul—for its sanity and integrity, its sense of wholeness and worthwhileness, its human and spiritual vitality and resilience. As we have seen, this quest is at once social and ecological, political and economic, spiritual and philosophical. It encompasses all these dimensions and the whole constellation of issues arising from them. This is why the current global marketplace of worldviews and ideas is so significant.

I have argued that these global trends and worldviews must be taken seriously. They must be carefully understood and faced. I have even committed the popularly unthinkable, arguing for a particular worldview as coherent and true: the story of Jesus Christ. Here is a worldview and a faith that seeks no oppression or domination, that respects all peoples and faiths, and that yet provides comprehensive and reliable answers to the great human questions.

This is often *not* the way the Jesus worldstory has been understood, both inside and outside of Christianity. But the global convergence of worldviews and ideas perhaps sets the stage for a rediscovery of the power of Jesus Christ and of the hope he offers for the renewal of Earth and the "restoration of all things."

All trends and worldviews begin to converge as we grasp the Jesus worldstory. The story of Jesus opens the door to a genuine Theory of Everything. Jesus gives coherence to the universe and its history—so argued the earliest Christian writers. The unknown author of the *Letter to the Hebrews* called Jesus "the radiance of God's brilliance and the exact image of his being. He upholds everything by his powerful word." Similarly, the apostle Paul said that Jesus "is the image of the invisible God, the firstborn over all creation. By him everything was created— things in heaven and on earth, things visible and invisible. Everything was made by him and for him. He is before all things, and in him every- thing coheres" (Heb. 1:3; Col. 1:15-17; author's paraphrase).

Compared with other views, this worldstory centered in Jesus Christ does in fact display a remarkable coherence. It provides plausible answers to all the worldview questions, particularly at the level of basic perspective. On the other hand, it brings its own set of difficulties.

In this chapter we will see how the key worldview questions find answers in Jesus Christ. We will also inquire whether the Jesus story conflicts with or affirms other worldviews and see how it has often been distorted or misunderstood by Christianity. Finally, we will ask what this perspective has to say about today's key global trends.

Worldview Answers

The Jesus story satisfies the key worldview questions, *purpose, design, relationships,* and *history*. It is a coherent worldview, in part because it is more than a worldview.

1. Jesus gives *purpose* to life, both personally and cosmically. The whole universe, says the story, reflects God's glory and creative energy. The universe is made to radiate and revel in God's majestic beauty. Birds and flowers, even rocks and planets exist to glorify God and to display God's creative beauty. Human beings find their purpose in praising God, mirroring his glory, enjoying the Earth, and pursuing God's purposes in the world. This is not demeaning, not bondage or slavery, because God is love, care, and creative energy. We know this when we look at Jesus.

The purpose of personal life is to know Jesus Christ as a living person. God offers this gift to us, through our repentance and faith. Jesus invites us to deepen that relationship, becoming the hands and feet of God's healing love in the world. Our purpose is to know and show God's loving brilliance in every sphere of life: art, science, commerce, human relationships, social structures, all of culture. We become part of a new humanity, a new community bonded together in Jesus and committed to Jesus-style life in the world.

Here we find the answer to the meaning question. If meaning is rooted in intention, then it is found in God's self-disclosure. If God exists, then life means what God intends.

2. The *design* of the universe is an open-ended order that permits surprise and beauty. The universe *is* a kind of organism, but in a larger, deeper sense than the Gaia theory knows. Designed and formed by God, the universe exists not just for itself, nor exclusively for humankind, but to fulfill its potential to show God's beauty and love.

The universe shows a remarkable consistency of design, from the smallest neutrino to the largest constellation. This is because of its Designer. The universe is made to be the home for man and woman, who are unique, so far as we know, among all creatures in their combining of material and conscious spiritual existence. But Earth is also home for all other material creatures God has made. Human beings have responsibility both to God and to their co-inhabitants of the cosmos to live in harmony with the created environment. This is their ecological task as they experience the various dimensions of the universe's true ecology.

The design of the universe includes the four physical forces as well as the higher dimensions to which the material world seems to point—whether seven, ten, or twenty-six. Humankind continues the age-long adventure of uncovering what this design really is. The frontiers of discovery have moved from atoms and the shape of the globe to the levels of the quantum and the cosmic. In the Jesus-based worldview, each new discovery shows further the wisdom and glory of the Divine Mind. Truth is never a threat.

In Jesus Christ we see that the universe is more than the material world. Jesus lived about thirty-three years on Earth. But as God, he created all things and continues living and acting in dimensions of life that are more than physical. We don't know what other beings or consciousnesses live at higher dimensions than our spacetime world. Human beings may be but a small part of the conscious universe. The Bible speaks of various kinds of angelic beings. Some of these are in rebellion against God's design and have perverse influence on Earth.

3. As a person in constant multidimensional communion with God (in the Trinity), Jesus provides the key to all relational questions. In a remarkable prayer recorded by his disciple John, Jesus said he wanted all who believed in him to "be one as we are one: I in them and you in me. May they be brought to complete unity to let the world know that you sent me and have loved them just as you have loved me" (John 17:22-23; author's paraphrase of NIV). As the Persons of God's being—traditionally, Father, Son, and Holy Spirit—are one, so Jesus wants all people to be joined in loving community. Jesus made it plain that only in relationship with him could people find such community. On any other basis, human self-centeredness seeps in and sours the relationships.

Every human relationship is a spacetime (at least) reflection of God's internal communion. Here is an awesome basis for human community, whether in marriage and family, neighborhood and nation, or globally. When we are in harmony with God through Jesus Christ, we are potentially in harmony with every other human and sing the song of the cosmos.

4. Jesus Christ is also the key to *history*. The story of the cosmos is the story of what God is doing in and through Jesus. History is the story of creation, alienation, and restoration through Jesus Christ. We learn from Jesus' own words that this reconciliation has begun but is far from completed. A battle rages between good and evil, light and darkness, hope and despair, justice and oppression, reconciliation and alienation. Every person is caught up in this battle, this struggle for the world's soul, whether they know it or not.

So the story is not over yet. The drama continues. We are some of the characters. Other characters also act in the drama, but with our spacetime limitations we are scarcely aware of them. We don't know in detail how the story will turn out. But we do know the central plot, and we know that the story will end in harmony and peace, order and beauty.

We know this by faith because we see what God has already done in Jesus Christ. The decisive act in history was the resurrection of Jesus Christ. He was betrayed and crucified, but two days later he rose again. This was the key triumph over death and despair, the reversal of discord and incoherence. The battle continues; there will yet be many casualties. But we are energized by the assurance that the one who won the decisive victory over evil in his resurrection at a specific point in history will bring the story to a final, glorious climax in history. The goal of history is final harmony and reconciliation, justice and moral symmetry—the ultimate triumph of truth and love. Shortly after Jesus' resurrection, the apostle Peter called it "the restoration of all things" (Acts 3:21; author's paraphrase).

Comparing Worldviews

The Jesus worldview/worldstory contrasts sharply with the views examined earlier in this book. Yet it shares several features. Like the New Economic Order, this worldstory knows the importance of economic forces and relations and of viewing these globally. Economics is critical because it deals with value and with material and social relations among people. Scholars calculate that Jesus talked more about economics than about any other subject. Jesus cast economic relationships in terms of justice, respect for individual value and initiative, and special concern for the poor.[2]

Quantum worldviews also give us fascinating insights into the nature of the universe. But these worldviews are necessarily incomplete. Quantum mystery can't tell us much about the deeper dimensions of human character and history. But placed in the larger framework of the Jesus story, the quantum view illuminates. Quantum physics, as it pushes to the frontiers of spacetime, may help us see how both spirit and matter fit in a multidimensional universe. We already know that matter and energy are in principle interchangeable. Science may eventually show us that spirit is existence (personal energy) at higher dimensions. Perhaps better, we may learn that space, time, and matter are merely the "slowing down" or jelling or patterning of four of the spiritual universe's many dimensions, forming the material world as we know it.

Quantum physics itself forms too small a circle to build a worldview. But it may help enrich and even clarify aspects of the Jesus worldstory. Since all truth is God's truth, quantum physics, as science, is no threat to the Jesus worldstory. But a worldview *limited* to physics would be misleading and possibly dehumanizing.

The Gaia worldview is not essentially incompatible with a worldstory grounded in Jesus. It is just incomplete. It doesn't include some important dimensions of reality, as noted earlier. Gaia thinking and research can even enrich a Jesus-centered worldview, provided it is set in the larger story of God's work through Jesus Christ. Its stress on organism and ecology echoes many things Jesus said. Gaia thinking must properly be seen, however, as part of the larger story of cosmic redemption through Jesus. Earth appears as an organism not because it evolved that way but because it reflects the nature of a personal Creator God.

We noted in chapter 13 that Divine Design is the underlying worldview of all the great monotheistic religions. Yet we also saw its flaws. It is just these flaws that the Jesus story fills. Jesus Christ shows us not only where the universe came from, but also how God continues to be involved with it, and where history is headed.

Jesus actually affirmed many of the key claims of the Divine Design model. But he showed more fully how God is linked with the world and how God's purposes are worked out. The Divine Design view needs the story of Jesus to be fully coherent.

The Jesus story necessarily rejects Fate as a worldview option. As we have seen, this view is fatally flawed. Jesus was not chained to fate; he was not "fated" to be born or die or rise again. Nor was God under any external necessity in creating the world. Rather than affirming fate, the Jesus worldstory celebrates the mystery of the wisdom, character, and purposes of God. It affirms God's active providence, not blind fate. Fate is the easy way out. The Jesus story refuses to yield to fate. It believes in God's good purposes even in the midst of evil and despair. Like Job, who refused the temptation to "curse God and die," followers of Jesus say: I *will* believe in God's good purposes; I *will* hold on to see the end of the story when evil dies and goodness reigns.

The other worldview discussed earlier was postmodernism. As we saw, this is really not so much a worldview as an anti-worldview. It is the stage to which history is bringing global society. Though postmodernism is inadequate as a worldview, it does raise questions for the Jesus worldstory.

Even constructive postmodernism fails at crucial points. Its fundamental error, at least in most of the forms articulated so far, is its weak conception of God and divine agency. Some forms of constructive postmodernism claim to be Christian, yet they abandon the central truth of the biblical worldview: its picture of God as Person who creates the universe and continues active in its history, but is not contained within it.

Constructive postmodernism of this kind still imprisons God within the historical process. "God" comes to mean not a personal, acting Being, the Creator of all and therefore essentially distinct from space, time, and history. "God" is just the term applied to some anonymous creative energy within, and part of, the universe itself. God seems to be imprisoned within his own story—that is, within history. Griffin says, quite rightly, "If there be no central, all-inclusive perspective, then 'the truth' is an abstraction without a home"; "the very nature of *truth* is constituted by this divine perspective." Yet he denies the possibility of "supernatural, divine inspiration or revelation." God is not all-powerful; he "cannot unilaterally determine the utterances of any voice, the writing of any book, the thought processes of any mind." Further: "To say that God knows the truth does not mean that God already (or eternally) knows those events that are still future for us."[3]

However lofty this may sound, such talk suggests essentially a pantheist, or panentheist, view. God is not fundamentally distinguishable from the universe. As a result, it is not clear what the statement "God exists" or acts really means. This view is really *atheistic* about a transcendent, personal, volitional God.

Another failing of constructive postmodernism is its uncritical acceptance of the modern (Enlightenment) criticism of classical texts, especially the Bible. Despite its critique of modernism and the negative features of postmodernism, this version of postmodernism actually marches to the same music. It begins by uncritically assuming that the Enlightenment critique of the Bible is valid—even though the dominant nineteenth- and twentieth-century biblical criticism was largely based on rationalist assumptions that postmodernism discredits.

Today much biblical criticism is so under the thrall of modernity that it shuts itself off from much of the power and pulse of the biblical record. Its presuppositions prevent it from really taking the Bible seriously, on its own terms. It has declared the biblical worldview "no longer believable," except perhaps for selected elements and "insights," such as "prophetic imagination" or the example of Jesus' servanthood. Scholars advise students to "suspend disbelief." Biblical criticism makes no convincing case for this dismissal of biblical revelation but uncritically accepts the "results" of modernism's naturalistic, rationalistic critique. Just like modernity, this postmodernity rejects the biblical worldview or "plausibility structure," preferring its own more enlightened one—a curious move.

Worldviews of this kind imprison God within the world process. God appears at the end of the cosmic timeline, not at the beginning. The universe creates God instead of the other way around. Somehow unconscious, lifeless matter or energy leads to conscious Mind, rather than the reverse. But our experience and intuition lead us to believe the opposite: Existing things must have their conscious creator.

Postmodernism generally bypasses these questions altogether, but it raises other important issues. Many intelligent people believe that postmodernity makes Jesus obsolete and the Jesus worldstory unbelievable. What do we discover if we look at Jesus postmodernly?

The Postmodern Jesus

Ironically, postmodernism actually sheds some light on the person of Jesus Christ. Rather than obsolescing him, postmodern sensibilities make Jesus look all the more remarkable. The irony is that Jesus embodies and transcends the postmodern sensibility.

Here is, perhaps, the strangest irony of all: The most postmodern person of history lived not in the twentieth century but in the first century A.D. This person whom millions throughout history have seen as the most selfless and self-giving of persons was also decidedly self-centered. Jesus often spoke of himself and even made faith in him the exclusive door to final truth. He went so far as to say, "I am the Way, the Truth, and the Life. No one can come to the Father except through me." He claimed, "I and the Father are one" (John 14:6, author's paraphrase; 10:30). Here is the great irony and the great conundrum of Jesus. His claims suggest that he was either deluded, mentally ill, or insufferably vain. Yet his life shows the opposite. He was uncommonly compassionate, self-giving, and humble, "the man for others." What sort of man is this? How does one handle the mystery of Jesus?

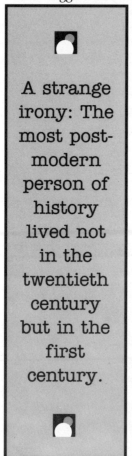

A strange irony: The most post-modern person of history lived not in the twentieth century but in the first century.

Perhaps Jesus really is the ultimate postmodern, incarnating the very concerns of postmodernism. Yet, most pointedly, he transcends the postmodern critique, standing it on its head. Jesus Christ carries the irony and self-reference of postmodernity to new dimensions of meaning. Ironically, Jesus melts irony into meaning and self-reference into self-identity and therefore self-giving.

In some respects, Jesus fits postmodern sensibilities better then he does modern or premodern ones. The premodern worldview locked Jesus in a box of static order and changelessness. Much medieval theology and Christian orthodoxy reflect this. Then the modern worldview remade Jesus in its own image, whether as poet, philosopher, philanthropist, or lawgiver. Postmodernity helpfully shatters these earlier worldviews—possibly, just possibly, making Jesus winsome and believable as never before.

Remarkably, Jesus anticipates and embodies postmodern concerns. In Jesus we find self-reference without selfishness. We find the ultimate irony of an irony that transcends irony. Ironically, Jesus lived a brief life on Earth and yet is the most abiding figure in history. No one's life appears more free, more contingent, more open-ended. Yet he said he came to fulfill God's purposes and spoke as though the very events of his life were preplanned.

Two features of postmodernism are the mixing of styles and a deep suspicion of ideology, power, and the political use of universal claims. Here again, Jesus shines as the quintessential postmodern. He fits no one's style. He fit no one's mold in the first century nor since. He was one of the most outspoken characters in history—the most merciless in exploding hypocrisy, self-interest, and the use of power or ideology for selfish or political ends. He told the religious leaders of his day, "You nullify God's word by your traditions. You teach your traditions as if they were divine law!" (see Matt. 15:6; Mark 7:8).

In the postmodern view, life and meaning are what you make of them. Yet here also, Jesus is postmodern. Fitting no one's pattern, Jesus constantly amazed and surprised people by his sense of purpose and inner direction—even his own followers. He knew what he was about and who he was. He did not fit the mold of the political zealot, the religious mystic, or the champion of religious law. Yet his life shone with coherence and purpose.

How can one explain Jesus Christ? Given the remarkable person he was, we should weigh the explanation Jesus himself gave. He claimed to be sent by God, to have a divine mission, to be faithfully doing God's will. He claimed to be the Messiah, the Christ, the promised one through whom God would keep his promises to save Israel and bring justice and peace on Earth.

Fixing on Jesus' own words, several first-century writers argued that he was unique among all people who ever lived. They spoke of Jesus as both human and divine, the "incarnation" of God in human form, "the Word made flesh."

If true, this claim solves the riddle of Jesus. The reason he is unlike every other human being is that he is God in human form. Yet this is also the reason he is *like* every other human being. Jesus was fully and in every way human, God assuming the dimensions of space, time, and matter. As Michael Card sings, "He's unlike any other man, and yet so much like me."

Truth in Paradox

This still leaves us, of course, with a great mystery. How can Jesus be both divine and human? No one has ever figured that out. The Christian faith has always struggled with this conundrum. At times groups have veered off to the right or left, seeing Jesus as fully human but not really God, or as fully God but not really human. Admittedly, those are easier answers. Yet finally the only way to make sense of the paradox is to affirm its mystery. Jesus as the God-man, the divine-human person, unties a whole knot of questions in a coherent, symmetric way. If that mystery can be accepted by faith or as a hypothesis, it provides plausible answers to every other question.

There are three great mysteries to the Jesus worldstory: the Trinity (God existing as Three, yet One), the Incarnation (God taking on human form in Jesus Christ), and the Resurrection (Jesus' return to life after his crucifixion). Interestingly, there is a sort of rational coherence, a kind of symmetry, in these paradoxes, even as they remain mysteries. And, we may plausibly believe, all these mysteries find their "explanation" (humanly speaking), or their resolution, in multidimensionality. This is not, of course, an explanation but rather the reason why we lack, at present, an explanation.

We naturally have trouble with any truth that reaches beyond spacetime experience. Human beings are "dimensionally challenged."

From these deep mysteries flow many others. Not least of these is how women, men, and children are transformed when they meet and come to fully believe in Jesus Christ. Early Christians described this mysterious transformation through a wide range of powerful images: being "born again," made a "new creation," "made alive," "adopted" into God's family, being "risen with Christ" or being made part of "the body of Christ," and many others. It is a mystery hard to put into words, though often put into song.

Perhaps the paradoxical nature of these mysteries is profound evidence for the truth of the Jesus worldstory. Any worldview so shallow as to contain no mysteries or seeming contradictions would be suspiciously superficial. Truth has its paradoxes. Yet, these testify not so much to the nature of truth as to the limits of our dimensionally bound understanding. When it comes to anything beyond our spacetime experience, human beings are "dimensionally challenged." To us, the curvature of spacetime or quantum uncertainty seem paradoxes. But this is partly because we cannot fully grasp higher dimensionalities and partly due to human self-centeredness and what the Bible calls "the deceitfulness of sin" (Heb. 3:13).

Jesus' life and acts, flowing from his essential identity, attune us to other strange but wondrous paradoxes. Love is stronger than violence. Faith is more potent than despair. Evil can be swallowed up in good. Suffering, in the end, is not evil. Bad stories can turn out good. Here is paradox, we believe, without contradiction.

Finding truth often requires assuming that paradox is not contradiction but limited comprehension—limited by lack of knowledge or experience, lack of moral wisdom, or the lack of being "dimensionally qualified" to grasp the whole picture.

The deepest paradox of the Jesus worldstory is his existence as the God-man. Yet this is the key to a coherent worldview. It means that Jesus is the source and goal of history. He is the pivot, the meaning of the story; he is the one on whom all else turns. It is true historically that Jesus came to be seen as "the hinge on which history turned and therefore [became] the basis for a new interpretation of the historical process and for a new historiography," says Jaroslav Pelikan.[4] Jesus is the primary actor and orderer of history, as God. He is history's end, not as terminal or terminator but as *telos* or goal. Jesus is the goal that opens into new life, new levels and dimensions and meanings of existence in the limitless space of the spirit.

Christian Misunderstandings of Jesus

Christianity has had a terrible time figuring out what to do with Jesus. Through twenty centuries Christianity as a religion has often remade and reduced Jesus to fit the fads and philosophies of the age. This is still true of major parts of Christianity. Perhaps today's dominant misunderstandings of Jesus are these: seeing him as a wise moral teacher but not really God incarnate (theological liberalism); seeing him as an almost exclusively spiritual savior who forgives sins but doesn't transform society (theological conservatism); or seeing him as a remote sovereign who grounds and legitimates our religious traditions (whether Catholic, Protestant, or Orthodox). Perhaps it is these as much as first-century Pharisees whom Jesus warns, "You nullify God's word by your traditions."

Yet Jesus continues to inspire and provoke. New biographies and historical studies pour forth, even in the 1990s. Malcolm Muggeridge in his later life chronicled his encounter with Jesus in *Jesus Rediscovered*. Oxford novelist and biographer A. N. Wilson in 1992 published a book entitled simply, *Jesus*. Though Wilson misunderstands Jesus as being only human, he recognizes his power: "Jesus remains too disturbing a figure ever to be left to himself." Christianity has largely ignored Jesus' teachings, Wilson argues. "Few of the Christian Churches have ever viewed the teaching of Jesus with anything but contempt."[5] Even so, Jesus' influence continues:

> Christianity gave to the human race a sense of the worth of the individual, slave or free, male or female, Gentile or Jew. Without it, there would

have been no St. Francis, kissing the beggar, and no Mother Teresa of Calcutta, living among the poorest of Calcutta's poor. In Christ's name, Wilberforce freed the slaves, and Elizabeth Fry campaigned for the prisoners, and Christian Aid attempts to feed the hungry. In Christ's name, "little unremembered acts of kindness and of love" have been performed throughout the centuries.[6]

Despite frequent betrayal of Jesus and massive confusion about him within Christianity, Jesus continues to shape history and heal lives. One of today's amazing Earth Currents is the thousands of people, literally, around the globe who each day become first-time followers of Jesus. History may show that the greatest turn-of-millennium revolution was the quiet multiplication of small, loving communities of Jesus' followers within the great majority of Earth's 20,000 people groups. All of this is happening in spite of Christianity's frequent misrepresentations of Jesus. Being who he is, Jesus necessarily transcends and perhaps ultimately transforms even those institutions and movements built upon him. He continues to show us that while religion is our search for God, Jesus is God finding us.

There is still hope, though, for deep renewal within Christianity. Perhaps the church will again discover Jesus. This has happened before, as popular renewal movements met Jesus Christ anew, shook the church and revitalized society. The noted Dutch church leader, W. A. Visser 't Hooft, once wrote of "the extraordinary capacity for renewal which characterizes the Christian Church," the way history has repeatedly witnessed "the rebirth of the Church" precisely at those times "when everything would seem to point to its approaching death."[7] One thinks of the remarkable twelfth-century renewal sparked by Francis of Assisi and others, or the revivals in central Europe, England, and North America of the seventeenth and eighteenth centuries.[8] These instance the "spiritual awakenings" phenomenon described by Strauss and Howe in their book *Generations*. As Earth's society increasingly globalizes, perhaps we will see the first truly global discovery and rediscovery of Jesus Christ.

World Trends and Worldstory

We began this book by looking at key trends shaping global society. How do these trends look in the perspective of a worldstory based on Jesus Christ?

We saw that every trend presents both dangers and opportunities and that the underlying current is globalization. The key question, therefore, is how humanity can work together to enhance the positive side of world trends and to overcome the dangers presented by their negatives.

The Jesus model helps here. It calls us to global cooperation and understanding. Jesus challenges us to live our lives for others. The story of Jesus as worldstory helps us see global trends in a larger perspective. In other words, Jesus provides both a cosmic worldview and a pattern for life at both personal and collective levels.

People often live below their ideals and possibilities. Too seldom do we live loving and cooperative lives. We need help, a power to lift us beyond ourselves and give us the energy to live for others and for the sake of the world. Jesus, the Way, the Truth, and the Life, offers precisely this. As we come to know him relationally, personally, as intimate friend and center of life, we discover new power. Jesus, no longer confined by the spacetime dimensions of physical existence, comes to live within us as Spirit—the Spirit of Jesus, the Holy Spirit. Here is the source of the personal and communal energy needed in coming decades to overcome our self-centeredness, rebuild society, and confront global trends. Here is hope for the global city and everyone in it. Here is a worldstory with meaning, hope, and power.

The Struggle for the World's Soul

Am I suggesting that the only hope for the world is for everyone to become a Christian? Not necessarily. Jesus still is Lord and History Maker, even if many deny this. And even if everyone did accept Jesus, too many Christians would fail to live the Jesus life-way. As in the past, many people and groups claiming the name of Jesus Christ would continue to betray him by their lives and actions. History isn't kind to nations that adopt the Christian religion but betray the spirit of Jesus.

Yet Jesus is the key to the future, the only door to eternal life, and the answer to the struggle for the world's soul. This is true at three levels, at least:

Personal significance. Much of the crisis of emerging global society is rooted in a loss of a sense of personal meaning. At the deepest level, government, politics, and material prosperity cannot provide that. Relationship with Jesus Christ can.

People who come to know Jesus personally find that their lives take on new and deeper meaning. Jesus is the basis for personal identity and significance. In him people find meaning for their lives that transcends, and yet transforms, them. Faith in Jesus gives inner purpose, unity, calmness; a confidence that at some deep level, everything is all right. It gives the assurance of endless life beyond the grave. Yet it also gives a sense of calling and mission and a consciousness of connection with the world. People criticize pie-in-the-sky Christians for being "so heavenly minded they're no earthly good." But throughout history those people most closely associated with Jesus, and thus most heavenly minded and inwardly grounded, have often given the most to social justice and human welfare.

Life in community. Not isolated personal significance, but the reality of cooperative, shared life at many levels—this also is a gift from Jesus. By lifting people above themselves, above their fears and prejudices, Jesus brings people together. The greatest, strongest gift of faith in Jesus Christ all down through history has been new, redemptive forms of community.

Can the global human family live in community? Jesus shows this can happen through respect and openness to every person and all peoples, through attitudes of cooperation and concern for general welfare. Jesus is the example. For those who know Jesus personally and truly form his body, the church, Jesus provides the power to model community in millions of local situations and to build community globally.

World history. Whether we like it or not, history is going someplace. Not history as some autonomous force, but history as the story of humanity and the universe. Those with faith in Jesus Christ believe that he is the key to history—past, present, and future, to speak in human, spacetime terms. Jesus is the hope of history, because in him all things hold together and all things will find their final reconciliation and restoration. Thus Jesus is a hope that extends even beyond history.

Jesus is the hope for history through his example and the selflessness he engenders, but also in a much more ultimate sense. Jesus has reserved the right to bring history to its conclusion. During his days on Earth, Jesus talked not only about the present but also the future. He spoke of appearing again at the end of history to bring all things to their culmination—to end the story, or at least the spacetime chapters. He spoke of a day when there would be "one flock and one shepherd" (John 10:16 NIV). Shortly after Jesus' resurrection and ascension the apostle Peter said that Jesus would "remain in heaven until the time comes for God to restore everything" (Acts 3:21 NIV). We look forward, he said, "to a new heaven and a new earth" (2 Pet. 3:13 NIV). The apostle Paul said that because of our faith in Christ, we know that "the creation itself will be liberated from its bondage to decay" and brought to glorious freedom (Rom. 8:21 NIV).

During dark days of persecution a couple of generations after Jesus' resurrection, suffering followers of Jesus were strengthened by these words that the Spirit spoke to the aged apostle John, Jesus' old friend:

"Then I saw a new heaven and a new earth, for the first heaven and the first earth had passed away. . . . There will be no more death or mourning or crying or pain, for the old order of things has passed away" (Rev. 21:1, 4 NIV).

History is going someplace. Because of who Jesus is, we know that place will be glorious. But Jesus also said our ability to participate in these broader dimensions of life depends on our commitment to him.

The struggle for the world's soul is really the same struggle Jesus faced during his earthly life: love or hate, justice or oppression, hope or fear and fatalism, truth or manipulation and distortion, respect or arrogance, character or moral confusion, healing and wholeness versus disease and exploitation. Jesus showed in his life, death, and resurrection the way to confront and resolve these issues, not through force and manipulation but through a life committed to truth, compassion, and understanding. Intimate friendship with him, and community grounded in him, provide the center and source for personal coherence and for cosmic healing.

The Jesus worldstory is more than a philosophy to be adopted or a moral code to be lived. It is a call to commitment and engagement. If the history of Jesus were *only* a worldview or worldstory, our attitude toward it could be primarily intellectual. But the call that comes to us is not just an intellectual challenge. It is the appeal of a person: Jesus, who calls us to follow him in faith and learn from him how to live on Earth. He calls us to a life centered in him, not to a mere set of ideas.

The Jesus worldstory is friendly to all that is positive and humanizing in the world's EarthCurrents, but it is deathly hostile to all that is destructive, dehumanizing, or pathological. It is friendly toward information access for all but hostile to any manipulative use of information, as Jesus' own words make clear. The Jesus worldstory encourages global economic well-being, but it warns of economic injustice. It affirms the full worth and freedom of women but negates any shattering of gender partnership and complementarity. It cherishes Earth as good and worth caring for but opposes reducing humankind to nothing but one more species in the ecosystem.

The Jesus story rejoices in the marvels of DNA and quantum mysteries, seeing there God's genius. It affirms the continuing human unraveling of these mysteries, but it denounces using such knowledge for oppressive or manipulative ends. The Jesus worldstory is no foe to computers, artifical intelligence, or even virtual reality. It insists only that these marvels be kept subservient to Earth's well-being and that the controlling reality and experience be found in our relationship to God, not in electronic wizardry.

This Jesus worldstory lifts no race or nation in domination over others. It values all peoples, East and West, North and South. From its perspective we learn why civilizations rise and fall. This worldstory opposes any new world order that oppresses people or demeans human dignity and freedom. Yet it promises a New World Order of global peace, health, and prosperity, an order whose power and endurance permeate but stretch beyond the span of spacetime existence.

Life in the Seventh Dimension

In this book we have encountered many dimensions of life and the universe. We have seen that life is fundamentally multidimensional, not only in the scientific sense, but also in the sense of the dimensions of story, imagination, human experience, history, and spirit. It is more than space, time, and matter.

It is possible to live multidimensionally. We can inhabit more than merely spacetime. We experience broader dimensions as we come to know God through Jesus Christ. To experience Jesus is to know the meaning of the universe. In Jesus we transcend spacetime limits. We begin experiencing new dimensions of the spirit, and of story and history, that will continue beyond the limits of this life.

We might call this Life in the Seventh Dimension. It means living beyond the confining dimensions of spacetime, of material existence only. It means transcending fate, shattering the chain of physical cause and effect. Yet this life enriches and illumines our material life as we experience a deeper, higher, larger coherence.

Jesus is, then, the end and the beginning of the story. He is the end of the worldview quest and the opening of new worldstory possibilities.

This is what Jesus' aged friend John the Evangelist, exiled by Roman authorities on the island of Patmos, saw around A.D. 100. He heard Jesus say: "I am the Alpha and the Omega, the First and the Last, the Beginning and the End" (Rev. 22:13 NIV).

It's still true today.

NOTES

Introduction

1. Alvin Toffler, *Powershift: Knowledge, Wealth and Violence at the Edge of the 21st Century* (New York: Bantam Books, 1990), 83, xviii, xix.
2. David Harvey, *The Condition of Postmodernity* (Oxford: Basil Blackwell, 1989), vi.
3. Quoted in Richard Stengel, "Bang the Drum Quickly," book review in *Time,* July 8, 1991, 58.
4. Alexander King and Bertrand Schneider, *The First Global Revolution: A Report by the Council of the Club of Rome* (New York: Pantheon Books, 1991), xx.
5. Mikhail Gorbachev, speech to the opening of the Fourth International Global Forum Conference, Kyoto, Japan, April 20, 1993.
6. Toffler, *Powershift,* 82.
7. Contemporary English writers increasingly speak of *world view, world-view* or (more and more commonly) *worldview*. The English use derives from the German *Weltanschauung*. Although *worldview* is a compound of two words, it is one concept, so I have adopted the compound form, without hyphenation.
8. Walter Ong points out that world *view* is a somewhat limiting concept in that it is restricted to the sense of sight. The world is more than something we see, he points out; it is also something we touch and feel with senses that are more intimate and interactive than sight. He suggests that "world view" be supplemented with "world sense" or, even better, "world-as-presence," implying the use of all the senses. Walter J. Ong, "World as View and World as Event," *American Anthropologist* 71 (1969): 634-47.
9. James W. Sire, *The Universe Next Door: A Basic World View Catalog* (Downers Grove, Ill.: InterVarsity Press, 1976), 16.
10. Thomas F. Banchoff, *Beyond the Third Dimension: Geometry, Computer Graphics, and Higher Dimensions* (New York: Scientific American Library, 1990), 3.

1. Looking to 2030

1. Leonard I. Sweet, *FaithQuakes* (Nashville: Abingdon Press, 1994), 8.
2. John Naisbitt and Patricia Aburdene, *Megatrends 2000: Ten New Directions for the 1990s* (New York: William Morrow, 1990), 16.
3. Gerhard Casper, "A Golden Age of Education," *University of Chicago Record* 25 (August 8, 1990): 2.
4. William Strauss and Neil Howe, *Generations: The History of America's Future, 1584 to 2069* (New York: William Morrow, 1991), 14, 382.
5. Ibid., 426.
6. In Strauss and Howe's analysis, a "generation" is all of those people born during a specific time frame, not strictly a biological generation. Tracing generations biologically soon becomes meaningless because of the widening span of birth years over several generations due to variations in the age at which adults bear children. Thus second or third cousins may belong to quite different generations, sociologically speaking.
7. Strauss and Howe, *Generations,* 74, emphasis added.
8. Ibid., 75-76.
9. Ibid., 78.
10. Michael D. Lemonick, "Architecture Goes Green," *Time,* April 5, 1993, 48-50.

11. Michael D. Lemonick, "Blinded by the Light," *Time,* December 20, 1993, 54.
12. John Naisbitt, *Megatrends* (New York: Warner, 1982), 261-62.
13. Bureau of National Affairs, *The Future of Work and Family; Shaping Programs for the 21st Century,* Special Report no. 34, October 1990.
14. Jacques Ellul, *To Will and to Do,* trans. C. Edward Hopkin (Philadelphia: Pilgrim Press, 1969), 185, 190.
15. These three paragraphs are summarized from my book, *The Problem of Wineskins* (Downers Grove, Ill.: InterVarsity Press, 1975), 118-19.

2. Online: The New Shape of Global Culture

1. Peter H. Salus, "Net Resources: What's There and How to Approach It," *Internet World* (June 1994): 76.
2. Harley Hahn and Rick Stout, *The Internet Complete Reference* (Berkeley, Calif.: Osborne McGraw-Hill, 1994), xix, xx.
3. Wilson Dizard, Jr., *The Coming Age of Information* (New York: Longman, 1985), quoted in Jerome M. Rosow, ed., *The Global Marketplace* (New York: Facts on File, 1988), 98.
4. James E. Olson, "Toward a Global Information Age," in Rosow, *The Global Marketplace,* 94.
5. Quoted in Rosow, *The Global Marketplace,* 100.
6. Bill McKibben, *The Age of Missing Information* (New York: Penguin Books, 1993), 9.
7. Ibid., 10.
8. Robert B. Reich, *The Work of Nations: Preparing Ourselves for 21st-Century Capitalism* (New York: Alfred A. Knopf, 1991), 3.
9. Ibid., 6-7.
10. Ibid., 9.
11. Parker Rossman, "The Emerging Global University," *The Futurist* 25, 6 (November/December 1991): 19-20.

3. Global Web: The Emerging World Economy

1. Tadahiro Sekimoto, "Meeting the Challenge of the 21st Century," in Jerome M. Rosow, ed., *The Global Marketplace* (New York: Facts on File, 1988), 161.
2. Kenichi Ohmae, *The Borderless World: Power and Strategy in the Interlinked Economy* (London: Fontana, 1990), ix.
3. Lester Thurow, *Head to Head: The Coming Economic Battle Among Japan, Europe, and America* (New York: Warner Books, 1993), 15-16.
4. Otto Reich, guest on "The McLaughlin Group," Public Broadcasting System, August 28, 1993.
5. John McLaughlin, host on "The McLaughlin Group," Public Broadcasting System, August 28, 1993.
6. Thurow, *Head to Head,* 216.
7. Ibid., 205-7.
8. Robert B. Reich, *The Work of Nations: Preparing Ourselves for 21st-Century Capitalism* (New York: Alfred A. Knopf, 1991), 97.
9. Ibid., 82.
10. Ibid., 84.
11. Ibid., 87.
12. "The Battle for Europe," *Business Week* (June 3, 1991): 44-52.
13. Ibid.
14. Although the economic recession of the early 1990s and other factors slowed the drive toward a common European currency, in the long run underlying trends toward greater unity will likely prove dominant.
15. *Time,* March 1, 1993, 14.

16. Bureau of National Affairs, "The Future of Work and Family; Shaping Programs for the 21st Century," Special Report no. 4 (October 1990).
17. Reich, *The Work of Nations*, 84.
18. Ibid., 88.
19. Ibid., 89.
20. Ibid., 90.
21. Ibid., 113.
22. Ibid., 174-77.
23. Ibid., 178, emphasis added.
24. Greg Stricharchuk, "Workers Take Charge: Fewer Bosses, More Quality at Plant," *Dayton Daily News,* June 30, 1991, 1F.
25. Quoted in Leonard I. Sweet, *Quantum Spirituality: A Postmodern Apologetic* (Dayton, Ohio: Whaleprints, 1991), 112.

4. Gender Power: The Feminist Revolution

1. Kathleen Newland, *The Sisterhood of Man* (New York: W. W. Norton, 1979), 4.
2. Riane Eisler, *The Chalice and the Blade: Our History, Our Future* (San Franciso: Harper & Row, 1987), xix.
3. Quoted in Frank Feather, *G-Forces: Reinventing the World* (Toronto: Summerhill Press, 1989), 73.
4. Emily MacFarquhar, "The War Against Women," *U.S. News and World Report,* March 28, 1994, 44.
5. Newland, *The Sisterhood of Man,* 3.
6. Monika Guttman, "Separating the Sisters," *U.S. News and World Report,* March 28, 1994, 49.
7. Feather, *G-Forces,* 73.
8. Donald Meyer, *Sex and Power: The Rise of Women in America, Russia, Sweden, and Italy* (Middletown, Conn.: Wesleyan University Press, 1987), xiii.
9. Newland, *The Sisterhood of Man,* 7.
10. Feather, *G-Forces,* 74-75.
11. *Time,* November 22, 1993, 38.
12. Feather, *G-Forces,* 74.
13. See Howard A. Snyder and Daniel V. Runyon, *Foresight: 10 Major Trends That Will Dramatically Affect the Future of Christians and the Church* (Nashville: Thomas Nelson, 1986), 95-110.
14. Patricia Aburdene and John Naisbitt, *Megatrends for Women* (New York: Villard Books, 1992), 313.
15. Meyer, *Sex and Power,* 69-71.
16. Feather, *G-Forces,* 76.
17. Ibid., 78.
18. See Mary Field Belenky, Blythe McVicker Clinchy, Nancy Rule Goldberger, and Jill Mattuck Tarule, *Women's Ways of Knowing* (New York: Basic Books, 1986).
19. Aburdene and Naisbitt, *Megatrends for Women,* 320.
20. Feather, *G-Forces,* 74.
21. Ibid., 81.
22. Meyer, *Sex and Power,* xiv, emphasis added.
23. Feather, *G-Forces,* 81.
24. Renée Weber, *The Tao of Physics Revisited: A Conversation with Fritjof Capra,* in *The Holographic Paradigm and Other Paradoxes: Exploring the Leading Edge of Science,* ed. Ken Wilber (Boston: New Science Library, 1985), 220.
25. Donald M. Joy, *Bonding: Relationships in the Image of God* (Waco: Word Books, 1985), 91-95. Many other factors of heredity and environment also affect mental behavior, of course.
26. Eisler, *The Chalice and the Blade,* xiv.
27. Meyer, *Sex and Power,* xiv.

28. Robin Morgan, ed., *Sisterhood Is Powerful: An Anthology of Writings from the Women's Liberation Movement* (New York: Random House, 1970), xvii. Quoted in Meyer, *Sex and Power*, xvi.

5. Fragile Greenhouse: The Environment at Risk

1. Quoted in Leonard I. Sweet, *Quantum Spirituality: A Postmodern Apologetic* (Dayton: Whaleprints, 1991), 116.
2. Al Gore, *Earth in the Balance: Ecology and the Human Spirit* (Boston: Houghton Mifflin, 1992), 238.
3. Sweet, *Quantum Spirituality*, 300.
4. Gore, *Earth in the Balance*, 2.
5. There had been, of course, an earlier conservation movement in the United States and elsewhere. On the American scene, the writings of Henry David Thoreau (1817–62) were especially influential in this regard.
6. Gore, *Earth in the Balance*, 24.
7. Alan Durning, "How Much Is 'Enough'?" *World-Watch* 3 (November/December, 1990): 15.
8. Jonathan Weiner, *The Next Hundred Years: Shaping the Fate of Our Living Earth* (New York: Bantam, 1990), 29.
9. R. Monastersky, "Global Warming: Politics Muddle Policy," *Science News* 137, 25 (June 23, 1990): 391.
10. Paul Raeburn, "New Report on Ozone Cites Peril," *Dayton Daily News*, October 23, 1991, A-1.
11. *Time*, January 21, 1991, 65.
12. Barbara W. Tuchman, *A Distant Mirror: The Calamitous 14th Century* (New York: Alfred A. Knopf, 1978), 92-125.
13. Thomas F. Homer-Dixon, Jeffrey H. Boutwell, and George W. Rathjens, "Environmental Change and Violent Conflict," *Scientific American* (February 1993): 38.
14. Ibid., 40.
15. Quoted in Sweet, *Quantum Spirituality*, 116.
16. Gore, *Earth in the Balance*, 12.

6. Vital Strings: DNA and Superstrings

1. Stephen Hawking, *Black Holes and Baby Universes and Other Essays* (New York: Bantam Books, 1993), ix.
2. Steven Weinberg, *Dreams of a Final Theory* (New York: Pantheon Books, 1992), ix.
3. *Time*, May 17, 1993, 52-53.
4. John Pekkannen, "Genetics: Medicine's Amazing Leap," *Reader's Digest*, September, 1991, 24.
5. Christine Gorman, "The Race to Map Our Genes," *Time*, February 8, 1993, 57.
6. Pekkannen, "Genetics: Medicine's Amazing Leap," 23.
7. Quoted in Leon Jaroff, "Giant Step for Gene Therapy," *Time*, September 24, 1990, 74.
8. Jaroff, "Giant Step for Gene Therapy," 76.
9. Ibid., 76.
10. Hawking, *Black Holes and Baby Universes*, 64.
11. John D. Barrow, *Theories of Everything: The Quest for Ultimate Explanation* (New York: Oxford University Press, 1991), 17-19.
12. Hans Christian von Baeyer, *The Fermi Solution* (New York: Random House, 1993), 69, italics added. Hawking explains similarly: "To see where a particle is, you have to shine a light on it. . . . This packet of light would disturb the particle and cause it to move at a speed in some direction. The more accurately you wanted to measure the position of the particle, the greater the energy of the packet [i.e., the more light] you would have to use and thus the more it would disturb the particle." Hawking adds, "This uncertainty principle of Heisenberg showed that one could not measure the state of a system exactly, so one could

not predict exactly what it would do in the future. All one could do is predict the probabilities of different outcomes" (Hawking, *Black Holes and Baby Universes*, 77).
13. Ernest C. Lucas, "The 'New Science' and the Gospel," in Martyn Eden and David F. Wells, eds., *The Gospel in the Modern World* (Downers Grove, Ill.: InterVarsity Press, 1990), 129.
14. Hans Moravec, *Mind Children: The Future of Robot and Human Intelligence* (Cambridge, Mass.: Harvard University Press, 1988), 64.
15. It must be remembered, however, that this model really can't be visualized because it includes more than the spacetime dimensions we experience. These models are verbal and visual crutches. But they do (or may), by analogy, point to the truth.
16. "Hanging the Universe on Strings," *Time,* January 13, 1986, 56-57.
17. Quoted in Richard Morris, *The Edges of Science: Crossing the Boundary from Physics to Metaphysics* (New York: Prentice Hall Press, 1990), 146.
18. Ibid., 163.
19. Ian Stewart and Martin Golubitsky, *Fearful Symmetry: Is God a Geometer?* (New York: Penguin Books, 1993), xviii, 17, 5.
20. Hans Christian von Baeyer, "Fang's Universe," *The Sciences* (May/June, 1991): 12.
21. See Morris, *The Edges of Science,* 48-52.
22. Banchoff, *Beyond the Third Dimension,* 40.
23. Hawking, *Black Holes and Baby Universes,* 72.
24. Ibid., 82.
25. On the dimensions of space and time from a philosophical perpsective, see Richard Swinburne, *Space and Time* (London: Macmillan, 1968), especially 136-41, 207-11.
26. Quoted in John Monczunski, "A Wrinkle in Time," *Notre Dame Magazine* (Autumn 1991): 46.
27. Hawking, *Black Holes and Baby Universes,* 45.

7. Electric Minds: Artificial Intelligence and Virtual Reality

1. Howard Rheingold, *Virtual Reality* (London: Mandarin Paperbacks, 1992), 15.
2. Hans Moravec, *Mind Children: The Future of Robot and Human Intelligence* (Cambridge, Mass.: Harvard University Press, 1988), 109-10.
3. Ibid., 110-11.
4. Ibid., 1.
5. Bart Kosko, *Fuzzy Thinking: The New Science of Fuzzy Logic* (New York: Hyperion, 1993).
6. Philip Elmer-Dewitt, "In Search of Artificial Life," *Time,* August 6, 1990, 64.
7. Moravec, *Mind Children,* 72.
8. Ibid., 116.
9. I don't mean such a worldview would be "scientific" in the sense of having empirically proved validity. This kind of speculation moves beyond science into imagined scenarios. My point is that such speculation is a *logical, reasonable extension* from known science into areas beyond science. The starting point (or launching pad) is science, not philosophy or religion.
10. Moravec, *Mind Children,* 116-17.
11. Gene Bylinsky, "The Marvels of 'Virtual Reality,' " *Fortune,* June 3, 1991, 142.
12. Carmen Miller, "Online Interviews Dr. Thomas A. Furness III, Virtual Reality Pioneer" *Online* (November 1992): 14-27.
13. Rheingold, *Virtual Reality,* 17, 19.
14. Ibid., 16.
15. Ibid., 347-48.
16. Miller, "Online Interviews Dr. Thomas A. Furness III."
17. Philip Elmer-Dewitt, "Orgies On-Line, *Time,* May 31, 1993, 61.
18. Amy Harmon, "Computer Offers Mousey Moments of Interactive Sex," *Dayton Daily News,* December 5, 1993, E1-2.
19. Bylinsky, "The Marvels of 'Virtual Reality,' " 150.
20. Rheingold, *Virtual Reality,* 19, 350.
21. Michael D. Lemonick, "Those Computers Are Dummies," *Time,* June 25, 1990, 74.

22. Roger Penrose, *The Emperor's New Mind: Concerning Computers, Minds, and the Laws of Physics* (New York: Oxford University Press, 1989), 448.
23. See the discussion in Heinz Pagels, *The Dreams of Reason: The Computer and the Rise of the Sciences of Complexity* (New York: Simon and Schuster, 1988), 203-40.
24. Ibid., 205, 207.
25. John Horgan, "The Death of Proof," *Scientific American* (October 1993): 103.

8. Western Decline: America's Final Hour?

1. Tad Szulc, "The Greatest Danger We Face," *Parade Magazine*, July 25, 1993, 4.
2. Robert N. Bellah et al., *The Good Society* (New York: Alfred A. Knopf, 1991), 3.
3. Os Guinness, *The American Hour: A Time of Reckoning and the Once and Future Role of Faith* (New York: The Free Press, 1993), 19-20.
4. Howard Fineman, "The Virtuecrats," *Newsweek*, June 13, 1994, 31. Public opinion and perceptions are, of course, notoriously fickle. However, several studies show a decades-long decline in confidence and optimism on the part of the public.
5. "Poll Finds Americans Moody About New Year," *Dayton Daily News*, January 1, 1994, 1A.
6. Kevin Phillips, *Boiling Point: Republicans, Democrats, and the Decline of Middle-Class Prosperity* (New York: Random House, 1993), 194.
7. Ellen Goodman, "Time has become lean, mean economy's biggest prize," *Dayton Daily News*, October 9, 1994, 158.
8. Phillips, *Boiling Point*, 253.
9. Arthur M. Schlesinger, Jr., *The Cycles of American History* (Boston: Houghton Mifflin, 1986).
10. An excellent study of this is Roy Beck, "The Ordeal of Immigration in Wausau," *The Atlantic Monthly*, April 1994, 84-97.
11. Charles Krause, "Muslims in America," *The MacNeill/Lehrer News Hour*, Public Broadcasting System, August 26, 1993.
12. Paul Gray, "Whose America?" *Time*, July 8, 1991, 13.
13. Ibid., 17.
14. Arthur M. Schlesinger, Jr., *The Disuniting of America* (New York: W. W. Norton, 1992), 16-17.
15. These statistics are only very rough approximations, but they give some sense of the extent of family fragmentation.
16. Amitai Etzioni, "How to Make Marriage Matter," *Time*, September 6, 1993, 76.
17. Amitai Etzioni, *The Spirit of Community: Rights, Responsibilities, and the Communitarian Agenda* (New York: Crown Publishers, 1993), 60.
18. Etzioni, "How to Make Marriage Matter," 76.
19. Pat Conroy, quoted in Bellah et al., *The Good Society*, 46.
20. Daniel Patrick Moynihan, interview, "Meet the Press," NBC News, September 19, 1993. Moynihan, formerly a professor at Harvard University, is referring to studies of urban family life, which he conducted in the 1960s.
21. Quoted in Etzioni, "How to Make Marriage Matter," 76.
22. Bellah et al., *The Good Society*, 46. The French jurist quoted is Alain Bénabent.
23. Etzioni, "How to Make Marriage Matter," 76.
24. Etzioni, *The Spirit of Community*, 55-56.
25. Ibid., *The Spirit of Community*, 73.
26. Some of America's most incisive and concerned critics are people like Hughes (from Australia) and Guinness (British), whose roots are non-American.
27. Schlesinger, *The Disuniting of America*, 101-18.
28. Neil Postman, *Amusing Ourselves to Death: Public Discourse in the Age of Show Business* (New York: Viking, 1985).
29. Ralph Waldo Emerson, "The American Scholar," *Essays and English Traits* (New York: Collier and Son, 1937), 6.
30. Philip Elmer-DeWitt, "Take a Trip into the Future on the Electronic Superhighway," *Time*, April 12, 1993, 52.

31. By "moral leadership" I mean leaders who articulate a broader, higher vision for the nation, calling for shared sacrifice in pursuit of goals that benefit all people and the Earth, rather than catering to individualistic or parochial self-interest. By "spiritual renewal" I mean the recovery of a sense of shared vision for the nation that unifies and uplifts, transcending merely material and economic concerns.

32. William J. Bennett, *The Book of Virtues* (New York: Simon & Schuster, 1993). Bennett's best-selling 820-page tome celebrates such virtues as self-discipline, compassion, responsibility, honesty, and faith.

9. New World Order: Global Culture or Clash of Civilizations?

1. Lance Morrow, "Welcome to the Global Village," *Time,* May 29, 1989, 96.

2. The new IMF standard of measurement gauges each nation's economy in terms of internal purchasing power rather than by international currency exchange rates. By this measure the world's six largest economies are the United States, Japan, China, Germany, France, and India. See "Zooming Up in the Charts," *Time,* May 31, 1993, 18.

3. Barry Hillenbrand, "America in the Mind of Japan," *Time,* February 10, 1992, 20.

4. Ibid., 23.

5. Benjamin Barber, "Jihad Vs. McWorld," *The Atlantic Monthly,* March 1992, 59.

6. Hernando de Soto, *The Other Path: The Invisible Revolution in the Third World* (New York: Harper & Row, 1989).

7. David Martin, *Tongues of Fire: The Explosion of Protestantism in Latin America* (Oxford: Basil Blackwell, 1990), 284.

8. David Stoll, *Is Latin America Turning Protestant? The Politics of Evangelical Growth* (Berkeley: University of California Press, 1990), 331.

9. Marvin Cetron and Owen Davies, *Crystal Globe: The Haves and Have-Nots of the New World Order* (New York: St. Martin's Press, 1991), 221, 228.

10. Ann Scott Tyson and James L. Tyson, "Deng Struggles to Set Reform Back on Track," *The Christian Science Monitor,* February 26, 1992, 9, 12.

11. Robert D. Kaplan, "The Coming Anarchy," *The Atlantic Monthly,* February 1994, 60.

12. Herman Kahn, *World Economic Development: 1979 and Beyond* (New York: Morrow, 1979), 60-65.

13. Kahn's broad analysis, which lumps nations together, also masks large pockets of poverty in the richer nations. It is simply a distortion, for example, to call the total U.S. population rich, or to average out the wealth in nations where a small elite controls the vast majority of resources. Kahn himself admitted that his relatively rosy projections could be undermined by "potentially disastrous" consequences of "bad luck and bad management," "complicated, complex, and subtle ecological and environmental issues," or other problems. Thus in the final analysis the pro-gap argument comes down to this: Things probably will get better if they don't get worse.

14. See, for example, Norman Cohn, *The Pursuit of the Millennium,* rev. ed. (New York: Oxford University Press, 1970); Frances Fox Piven and Richard A. Cloward, *Poor People's Movements: Why They Succeed, How They Fail* (New York: Vintage Books, 1979); William D. Morris, *The Christian Origins of Social Revolt* (London: George Allen & Unwin, 1949).

15. Benjamin Barber, "Jihad Vs. McWorld," *The Atlantic Monthly* (March 1992), 53.

16. Ibid., 55, 58.

17. Ibid., 59.

18. Ibid., 59-60.

19. *Time,* November 22, 1993, 16. The largest numbers of refugees (as of 1993) were Afghans, Palestinians, Mozambicans, and Ethiopians.

20. Barber, "Jihad Vs. McWorld," 62 63.

21. Kaplan, "The Coming Anarchy," 46, 48.

22. Ibid., 72-73.

23. Ibid., 46.

24. Samuel P. Huntington, "The Clash of Civilizations?" *Foreign Affairs* 72, 2 (Summer 1993): 22.
25. Ibid., 24.
26. Ibid., 25.
27. Ibid., 25.
28. Ibid., 49.
29. Mikhail Gorbachev, Speech to the Fourth International Global Forum Conference, Kyoto, Japan, April 20, 1993.
30. Margot Hornblower, "States of Mind," *Time*, February 1, 1993, 36-37.

10. Global Economics: A Pragmatic Worldview

1. Peter F. Drucker, *The New Realities* (New York: Harper & Row, 1989), 256.
2. John Maynard Keynes, quoted in Robert L. Heibroner, *The Worldly Philosophers: The Lives, Times, and Ideas of the Great Economic Thinkers*, 4th ed. (New York: Simon and Schuster, 1972), 12.
3. James W. Sire, *The Universe Next Door: A Basic World View Catalog* (Downers Grove, Ill.: InterVarsity Press, 1976), 17-18.
4. Ibid., 18-19.
5. Danah Zohar, *The Quantum Self: Human Nature and Consciousness Defined by the New Physics* (New York: William Morrow, 1990), 232-33.
6. In essence, these questions restate Sire's five questions, above.
7. E. P. Sanders, *Jewish Law from Jesus to the Mishnah: Five Studies* (Philadelphia: Trinity Press International, 1990), 323. Quoted in Leonard I. Sweet, *Quantum Spirituality: A Postmodern Apologetic* (Dayton: Whaleprints, 1991), 129.
8. Drucker, *The New Realities*, 255-56. The shift to a mechanistic model was not this simple or sudden, of course; it was underway well before 1700. But this shift truly was fundamental for world views.
9. Mikhail Gorbachev, *Perestroika: New Thinking for Our Country and the World* (New York: Harper & Row, 1987).
10. Marvin Cetron and Owen Davies, *Crystal Globe: The Haves and the Have-Nots of the New World Order* (New York: St. Martin's Press, 1991), 4, 300.
11. Kenichi Ohmae, *The Borderless World: Power and Strategy in the Interlinked Economy* (London: HarperCollins, 1991), 269-70.
12. Lester Thurow, *Head to Head: The Coming Economic Battle Among Japan, Europe, and America* (New York: Warner Books, 1993), 220.
13. See Mark Holloway, *Heavens on Earth: Utopian Communities in America 1680–1880* (New York: Dover Publications, 1966); Rosabeth Moss Kanter, *Commitment and Community: Communes and Utopias in Sociological Perspective* (Cambridge, Mass.: Harvard University Press, 1972); Howard A. Snyder, *Models of the Kingdom* (Nashville: Abingdon Press, 1991), 114-15.
14. Drucker comments on this in *The New Realities*, 256.
15. Jacques Ellul, *The Political illusion* (New York: Alfred A. Knopf, 1967).
16. Herman E. Daly and John B. Cobb, Jr., *For the Common Good: Redirecting the Economy Toward Community, the Environment, and a Sustainable Future* (Boston: Beacon Press, 1989), 202.

11. Quantum Mystery: A New Scientific Worldview?

1. Steven Weinberg, *Dreams of a Final Theory* (New York: Pantheon Books, 1992), 3.
2. Fritjof Capra, *The Tao of Physics: An Exploration of the Parallels Between Modern Physics and Eastern Mysticism*, 3rd ed. (Boston: Shambhala Publications, 1991), 325.
3. Gary Zukav, *The Dancing Wu Li Masters* (New York: William Morrow, 1979).
4. Lawrence Krauss, "The Holy Grail of Physics," *The Sciences* 33, 5 (September/October, 1993): 41.

5. Weinberg, *Dreams of a Final Theory,* 241-61.
6. Many people do, in fact, commit this divorce, especially in postmodern society. To do so, however, is inconsistent and unwise from a worldview standpoint.
7. Weinberg, *Dreams of a Final Theory,* 6-7.
8. Fritjof Capra, *The Tao of Physics,* 3rd ed., 7. The original edition was published in 1975.
9. Ibid., 12.
10. Ibid., 8.
11. Ibid., 328-35.
12. Ibid., 334-35.
13. Danah Zohar, *The Quantum Self: Human Nature and Consciousness Defined by the New Physics* (New York: William Morrow, 1990), 28.
14. Ibid., 219-20.
15. Ibid., 234-36.
16. Ibid., 237.
17. Ibid.
18. Ibid., 226-27.
19. Pierre Teilhard de Chardin, *The Phenomenon of Man* (London: Fontana Books, 1966), 243.
20. Zohar, *The Quantum Self,* 73.
21. Renée Weber, "The Enfolding-Unfolding Universe: A Conversation with David Bohm," in Ken Wilber, ed., *The Holographic Paradigm and Other Paradoxes: Exploring the Leading Edge of Science* (Boston: New Science Library, 1985), 51.
22. Michael Talbot, *The Holographic Universe* (New York: HarperCollins, 1991); Alex Comfort, *Reality and Empathy: Physics, Mind, and Science in the 21st Century* (Albany: State University of New York Press, 1984).
23. Henry P. Stapp, "Quantum Theory and the Physicist's Conception of Nature: Philosophical Implications of Bell's Theorem," in Richard F. Kitchener, ed., *The World View of Contemporary Physics* (Albany: State University of New York Press, 1988), 54.
24. Zohar, *The Quantum Self,* 73-74.
25. Ibid., 237.
26. Capra, *The Tao of Physics,* 341.

12. Life on a Living Planet: The Gaia Worldview

1. James Lovelock, *The Ages of Gaia: A Biography of Our Living Earth* (New York: Bantam Books, 1990), 12.
2. Lawrence E. Joseph, *Gaia: The Growth of an Idea* (New York: St. Martin's Press, 1990), 1.
3. Theodore Roszak, *The Voice of the Earth* (New York: Simon and Schuster, 1992), 136-59, 202-5.
4. Riane Eisler, "The Gaia Tradition and the Partnership Future: An Ecofeminist Manifesto," in Irene Diamond and Gloria Feman Orenstein, eds., *Reweaving the World: The Emergence of Ecofeminism* (San Francisco: Sierra Club Books, 1990), 26.
5. Quoted in Joseph, *Gaia,* 3. See also James Lovelock, *The Ages of Gaia.*
6. James Lovelock, "Gaia: The World as Living Organism," *New Scientist* (December 18, 1986): 25.
7. Joseph, *Gaia,* 1.
8. Lovelock, *The Ages of Gaia,* 28.
9. Ibid., xiv-xv, 11.
10. Ibid., 27.
11. Ibid.
12. Ibid., 217-18.
13. Roszak, *The Voice of the Earth,* 156.
14. Ted Peters, *The Cosmic Self: A Penetrating Look at Today's New Age Movements* (San Francisco: Harper, 1991), 45.
15. Quoted in Joseph, *Gaia,* 6.

13. Divine Design: God in the Shadows?

1. Peter Kreeft and Ronald K. Tacelli, *Handbook of Christian Apologetics* (Downers Grove, Ill.: InterVarsity Press, 1994), 81.
2. James W. Sire, *The Universe Next Door: A Basic World View Catalog* (Downers Grove, Ill.: InterVarsity Press, 1976), 23.
3. Summarized from Sire, *The Universe Next Door*, 24-55.
4. Émile Bréhier, *The History of Philosophy*, vol. 5 (Chicago: University of Chicago Press, 1967), 14, quoted in Sire, *The Universe Next Door*, 51.
5. Since God is personal, and since human nature, including the division into male and female, derives from God, logically God could be designated either "he" or "she." God transcends sexuality, but we have no personal pronouns that do not imply gender.
6. Sire, *The Universe Next Door*, 55-56.
7. This view is presented convincingly in Michael Polanyi, *Personal Knowledge: Towards a Post-Critical Philosophy* (New York: Harper Torchbooks, 1964).
8. John Monczunski, "A Wrinkle in Time," *Notre Dame Magazine* (Autumn 1991): 46.

14. The Force of Fate: Determinism Revisited

1. Quoted in Christopher Lasch, *The True and Only Heaven: Progress and Its Critics* (New York: W. W. Norton, 1991), 50.
2. Quoted in Will Durant, *Caesar and Christ*, vol. 3 of *The Story of Civilization* (New York: Simon and Schuster, 1944), 304.
3. Sydney E. Ahlstrom, *A Religious History of the American People*, 2 vols. (Garden City, N.Y.: Doubleday, 1975), 2:39.
4. Ralph Waldo Emerson, "Fate," *The Prose Works*, rev. ed., 3 vols. (Boston: Houghton Mifflin, 1883), 2:319-23.
5. Ibid., 325-26.
6. Ibid., 327.
7. Ibid., 329, 333.
8. Ahlstrom, *A Religious History of the American People*, 2:40.
9. Emerson, "History," in *The Prose Works*, 1:219-37.
10. Jeffrey Burton Russell, *Dissent and Reform in the Early Middle Ages* (Berkeley: University of California Press, 1965), 185-86.
11. Jon Butler, *Awash in a Sea of Faith: Christianizing the American People* (Cambridge, Mass.: Harvard University Press, 1990), 21.
12. Ralph Waldo Emerson, *Self-Reliance* (New York: H. M. Caldwell Co., 1900), 9.

15. Postmodernism: The Death of Worldviews?

1. Leonard I. Sweet, *FaithQuakes* (Nashville: Abingdon Press, 1994), 11-12.
2. Cited in Page Smith, *Killing the Spirit: Higher Education in America* (New York: Viking, 1990), 3.
3. Daniel Bell, *The End of Ideology*, rev, ed (New York: The Free Press, 1965); Francis Fukuyama, *The End of History and the Last Man* (New York: Basic Books, 1991); Richard O'Brien, *Financial Integration: The End of Geography* (London: Pinter, 1992).
4. Charles Jencks suggests this event as the symbolic end of modernism in architecture. Cited in David Harvey, *The Condition of Postmodernity: An Enquiry into the Origins of Cultural Change* (Oxford, England: Basil Blackwood, 1989), 39.
5. Ibid., 39, 38.
6. Cited in Smith, *Killing the Spirit*, 3.
7. Ibid., 3-4.

8. Terry Eagleton, "Awakening from Modernity," *Times Literary Supplement,* (February 20, 1987). Quoted in Harvey, *The Condition of Postmodernity,* 7-8.

9. Ibid., 9.

10. Cited in Harvey, *The Condition of Postmodernity,* 10.

11. I. Hassan, "The Culture of Postmodernism," *Theory, Culture and Society* 2, 3 (1985): 123-24. Reprinted in Harvey, *The Condition of Postmodernity,* 43 (slightly condensed).

12. Quoted in Harvey, *The Condition of Postmodernity,* 39.

13. Os Guinness, *The American Hour: A Time of Reckoning and the Once and Future Role of Faith* (New York: The Free Press, 1993), 129.

14. Ibid., 129-30.

15. Robert D. Kaplan, "The Coming Anarchy," *The Atlantic Monthly* (February 1994): 72.

16. Harvey, *The Condition of Postmodernity,* 48.

17. Quoted in ibid., 21.

18. David Ray Griffin, ed., *The Reenchantment of Science: Postmodern Proposals* (Albany: State University of New York Press, 1988), 13.

19. Fritjof Capra, *The Tao of Physics: An Exploration of the Parallels Between Modern Physics and Eastern Mysticism,* 3rd ed. (Boston: Shambhala Publications, 1991), 325.

20. Ibid., 325.

21. David Ray Griffin, "Introduction to SUNY Series in Constructive Postmodern Thought," in David Ray Griffin, William A. Beardslee, and Joe Holland, *Varieties of Postmodern Theology* (Albany: State University of New York Press, 1989), xii.

22. Alexander Pope, "An Essay on Man" *Selected Works,* ed. Louis Kronenberger. See Arthur O. Lovejoy, *The Great Chain of Being: A Study in the History of an Idea* (New York: Harper Torchbooks, 1960).

23. Griffin, "Introduction . . .," xii-xiii.

24. Ibid., xiii.

25. Ibid., xiii.

26. David Ray Griffin, "Postmodern Theology and A/Theology," Griffin et al., *Varieties of Postmodern Theology,* 51. Griffin is following A. N. Whitehead here.

27. "What does he mean?" *could* signify "What is his importance or significance," but in order to clarify that the subject's intention is not meant, we usually would say, "What does he mean *to me?*" (or to you or perhaps to the story, history, or some particular group—as in, "What does Mohammed mean to Moslems?") Otherwise, we naturally infer that *intention* is implied.

28. I am indebted to Milo Kaufmann and E. D. Hirsch for this clarification.

16. The Future and the Ecology of Meaning

1. Robert D. Kaplan, "The Coming Anarchy," *The Atlantic Monthly* (February 1994): 44-76.

2. Bernard Gross, *Friendly Fascism: The New Face of Power in America* (New York: M. Evans, 1980).

3. "Ecology: The New Great Chain of Being," *Natural History* (December 1968): 8.

4. Quoted in ibid.

5. Jeffrey Burton Russell, *Medieval Civilization* (New York: John Wiley & Sons, 1968), 82, 510, 536.

6. John Wesley, sermon no. 56, "God's Approbation of His Works," in Frank Baker, ed., *The Works of John Wesley,* Vol. 2, *Sermons II,* ed. Albert Outler (Nashville: Abingdon Press, 1985), 396-97. Wesley's view is less static than the traditional view because of his dynamically personal understanding of God and his strong stress on the image of God in men and women, making them "capable of God" (i.e., with the capacity for deep, transforming communion with God). Like most orthodox Christians, Wesley viewed this original harmony as now fundamentally distorted because of sin.

7. The social and cultural implications of the doctrine of the Trinity—never adequately developed in the Western Christian tradition—are very helpfully explored in Colin E. Gunton, *Enlightenment and Alienation: An Essay Towards a Trinitarian Theology* (Grand Rapids: Eerdmans, 1985); *The Promise of Trinitarian Theology* (Edinburgh: T & T Clark, 1981);

and *The One, the Three, and the Many: God, Creation, and the Culture of Modernity* (New York: Cambridge University Press, 1993). Gunton shows how a proper conception of Trinity provides the basis for community, personhood, and ecology.

17. Order, Surprise, and Beauty: The Coherence of Meaning

1. Stephen Hawking, *Black Holes and Baby Universes and Other Essays* (New York: Bantam Books, 1993), 63.
2. Several studies and autobiographical accounts of Holocaust survivors have shown that in many cases victims of dehumanizing imprisonment and cruelty manifest increased sensitivity to beauty, compassion, and the suffering of others.
3. Peter L. Berger, *A Rumor of Angels: Modern Society and the Rediscovery of the Supernatural* (New York: Doubleday, 1969).
4. Michael Polanyi, *The Tacit Dimension* (London: Routledge & Kegan Paul, 1967).

18. Story, History, and Truth

1. Brian Swimme and Thomas Berry, *The Universe Story* (San Francisco: Harper, 1992), 1.
2. Specifically Joe Holland and Gibson Winter. See Joe Holland, "The Postmodern Paradigm and Contemporary Catholicism" in *Varieties of Postmodern Theology,* 18-21.
3. Both *tale* and *tell* are related to the Old English term *talu,* as is the word *talk. Tell* and *tale* are respectively the verb and noun form, as in "to tell a tale."
4. Mark C. Taylor, *Erring: A Postmodern A/theology* (Chicago: University of Chicago Press, 1984), 164. Quoted in David Ray Griffin, "Postmodern Theology and A/theology: A Response to Mark C. Taylor," *Varieties of Postmodern Theology* (Albany: State University of New York Press, 1989), 34.
5. History is both what happens and what is recorded. Yet in a broader sense, what is recorded is also part of what happens—the writing of history is part of the story of history. My point here is that, even more basically, history is not so much what happens (a passive phraseology) as what persons do, stressing the priority of acting persons.
6. I recognize the limitations of the Cosmic Drama analogy. Clearly, a fictional character is fundamentally different from a living, breathing, thinking person. My point is that the category of mulitdimensionality makes the analogy seem more apt and convincing—not to press the analogy beyond its metaphorical (i.e., dimensional) limits.
7. C. S. Lewis, "Myth Became Fact," in *God in the Dock* (Grand Rapids: Eerdmans, 1970), 66-67.
8. Herbert Butterfield, *Christianity and History* (London: Fontana Books, 1964), 143. On myth, history, and cosmic drama, see also Howard A. Snyder, *Models of the Kingdom* (Nashville: Abingdon Press, 1991), 141-44.

19. Worldviews and Worldstory

1. Edgar S. Brightman, "A Personalistic Philosophy of History," *The Journal of Bible and Religion* 1 (January 1950): 10.
2. In the study of religion, "myth" often has the technical meaning of a religiously explanatory story that is not necessarily nonhistorical. But most people understand *mythological* as the opposite of *historical,* and I use the term in this popular sense.
3. Frederick Buechner, *Listening to Your Life,* quoted in *Christianity Today,* December 13, 1993, 47.
4. Philip Yancey, "Do I Matter? Does God Care?" *Christianity Today,* November 22, 1993, 21.
5. Ibid., 21-22.
6. Tatiana Goricheva, *Talking About God Is Dangerous* (New York: Crossroads, 1986), 17.
7. Don Richardson, *Peace Child* (Glendale, Calif.: Regal Press, 1974); Vincent J. Donovan, *Christianity Rediscovered,* 2nd ed. (Maryknoll, N.Y.: Orbis Books, 1981).

20. End of Story/Beginning of Story

1. C. S. Lewis, *Mere Christianity* (New York: Collier Books, 1960), 56.
2. See especially Ronald J. Sider, *Rich Christians in an Age of Hunger: A Biblical Study* (Downers Grove, Ill.: InterVarsity Press, 1977).
3. David Ray Griffin, "Postmodern Theology and A/Theology: A Response to Mark C. Taylor," *Varieties of Postmodern Theology* (Albany: State University of New York Press, 1989), xii. Griffin's understandable concern is to avoid "premodern authoritarianism" and any tendency toward "debilitating fatalism or complacent determinism." But he overreacts. Divine transcendence and omnipotence don't require authoritarianism and determinism, even though historically the two have often been linked. There can be authority without authoritarianism, ultimate control of history without canceling human freedom and historical openness.
4. Jaroslav Pelikan, *Jesus Through the Centuries: His Place in the History of Culture* (New Haven: Yale University Press, 1985), 26.
5. A. N. Wilson, *Jesus* (New York: W. W. Norton, 1992), 252, 253. Overstated, but we get the point.
6. Ibid., 255.
7. W. A. Visser 't Hooft, *The Renewal of the Church* (London: SCM, 1956) 68.
8. See especially Marie-Dominique Chenu, *Nature, Man, and Society in the Twelfth Century* (Chicago: University of Chicago Press, 1968); W. R. Ward, *The Protestant Evangelical Awakening* (Cambridge: Cambridge University Press, 1992).

INDEX

Abortion, 65, 69, 126
Aburdene, Patricia, 23, 70, 237, 307, 309
Acid rain, 76, 78
Adams, Douglas, 12
Advertising, 129
Aesthetics, 216, 227, 249
Afghanistan, 51, 313
Africa, 32, 50, 84, 142, 146, 148; Central, 32; West, 146
Agnosticism, 166, 181, 184, 283
Agriculture, 45, 78, 80, 89, 234; innovations in, 161
Ahlstrom, Sydney, 206, 316
AIDS, 32, 50, 83, 90, 112
Alchemy, 211
Alienation, 154
Alzheimer's disease, 90
Americo-Japanese Culture, 136-39
Anarchy, 234
Anderson, W. French, 91
Angels, 240, 293
Anthropology, 221
Apollo Space Program, 37
Apricot Corporation, 54
Aquaculture, 80
Arab peoples, 236
Architecture, 110, 215, 221, 224, 316
Argentina, 50, 119
Armageddon, Battle of, 235
Armenia, 150
Armstrong, Neil, 37
Arrhenius, Svante, 79
Art, the arts, 23, 38, 55, 59, 62, 137, 158, 208, 216, 220-25, 247, 263, 272, 282, 285, 293
ASEAN (Association of Southeast Asian Nations), 48
Asia, 48, 51, 133-36

Astrology, 167, 198, 202, 207, 209Astronomy, 14, 38, 92, 249, 25
Astrophysics, 81, 92, 249
AT&T, 40
Atheism, 166, 260, 283, 296
Augustine, St., 284
Augustus, Roman Emperor, 288
Australia, 39, 128, 130, 131, 141, 143, 145, 200
Authority, cultural, 126, 130, 148, 319
Automobiles, 30, 38, 39, 138; solar-powered, 31
Azerbaijan, 51

Bach, Johann Sebastian, 186
Bacon, Francis, 168
Baker, Frank, 317
Banchoff, Thomas, 18, 99, 186, 199, 307, 311
Bangladesh, 85, 127, 146
Banking, 53, 59
Barbados, 59
Barber, Benjamin, 138, 144, 235, 313
Barrow, John, 93, 310
Baseball, 137
Batwa Pygmies, 150
Baudelaire, Charles, 216
Beardslee, William A., 317
Beauty, 158, 183, 232, 247-61, 266, 273, 285, 292, 317
Beck, Roy, 312
Beijing, China, 134, 230
Belenky, Mary Field, 309
Belief, see faith
Bell Effect, in physics, 95, 315
Bell, Daniel, 316
Bell, John, 95
Bellah, Robert, 116, 125, 312
Benedictine Order, 161

Index

Bennett, William, 131, 313
Berger, Peter, 255, 318
Berlin Wall, 16, 132
Berry, Thomas, 75, 87, 261, 318
BGH (Bovine growth hormone), 89
Bible, the, 195, 297
Big Bang theory, 92, 96, 172, 175, 199
Billings, Paul, 91
Biology, 36, 61, 85, 178
Birch, David, 67
Birth control, 65
Black Death (Plague), 50, 83
Black holes, 185, 249, 310, 317
Bloom, Allan, 126
Boeing Corporation, 60
Bohm, David, 173, 315
Bohr, Niels, 71
Bombs, atomic - see nuclear weapons
Bonaparte, Napoleon, 201, 206
Books, book publishing, 39, 138
Boorstin, Daniel J., 116
Boscovich, Roger, 93
Bosnia, 144
Boutwell, Jeffrey H., 310
Brain, human, 18, 36, 102-05, 170, 173, 182,
    247; and consciousness, 170
Brazil, 15, 37, 50, 76, 119
Bretton Woods Conference, 133
Bréhier, Émile, 188, 316
Briggs, John, 143
Brightman, Edgar S., 277, 318
Budapest, Hungary, 118
Buddhism, 121, 145, 173, 283
Buechner, Frederick, 285, 318
Bulgaria, 39
Bureau of National Affairs, 34, 56, 308
Bureaucracy, 53
Bush, George, 149, global, 41, 220, 226
Butler, Jon, 211, 316
Butterfield, Herbert, 274, 318
Bylinsky, Gene, 311

CAD/CAM, 112, 129
Cahoone, Lawrence, 170
Canada, 40, 49, 54, 55, 66, 68, 128, 141
Cancer, 32; environmental causes, 32, 79, 81,
    234; genetics of, 90
Capitalism, 44, 48, 141, 145, 160, 283
Capra, Fritjof, 71, 104, 167, 173-76, 223,
    309, 314
Carbon dioxide, 78, 180
Card, Michael, 299
Carlson, Rachel, 78
Casper, Gerhard, 24, 307
Cathedrals, medieval, 240
Cause and effect, 187, 191, 199, 306

Celebrities, 213, 215
Central America, 139, 242
Central Intelligence Agency (CIA), 109
Cetron, Marvin, 140, 157, 313, 314
Chance, 202, 207, 217
Chaos, 12, 29, 78, 178, 189, 196, 198, 202,
    209, 232, 248-58, 272, 279;
    and symmetry, 96; chaotic systems, 249;
    social, 84, 122, 143, 146, 234
Character, 219, 272, 295, 305
Chemicals, 179, 242; environmental risks of,
    76, 78, 241
Chenu, Marie-Dominique, 319
Chernobyl disaster, 82
Child care, 34, 56, 65, 71, 125
Children, 112, 125; abuse of, 123, 126
Chile, 50
China, Peoples Republic of, 16, 24, 38, 40,
    46-49, 117, 130, 149, 235, 237, 313;
    democratization of, 141; trends in, 132-36,
    138; women in, 69
Chlorine monoxide, 79
Chlorofluoro-carbons (CFCs), 79
Christian Aid, 302
Christianity, 117, 121, 129, 137, 166, 172,
    182, 186-97, 203, 206, 211, 235, 237, 241,
    244, 273, 284, 289, 292, 298, 301-04, 317;
    growth of, 137, 200, 290, 302
Chromosomes, human, 90
Churches, 56, 122, 124, 237; Protestant, 68,
    140, 206, 237, 301
Cigna Corporation, 53
Civil War (U.S.), 27
Civilization, civilizations, 13, 29, 77, 147,
    236; and global trends, 148; and religion,
    148, 169; and technology, 155; and world-
    views, 148; clash of, 44, 132, 147;
history of, 35, 135, 153, 156, 210, 306
Climate, 38, 234, 243; study of, 38, 79
Clinchy, Blythe McVicker, 309
Clinton, Bill, 131
Cloward, Richard A., 313
Club of Rome, 13, 307
CNN (Cable News Network), 41, 138
Coal, 79
Cobb, John B., Jr., 162, 314
Coca-Cola, 53, 138
Coherence, 12, 29, 133, 189, 191, 196, 224-
    33, 241, 246, 247-60, 265; and world-
    views, 154, 170-75, 183, 221, 230, 239,
    255-58, 262, 273-95, 299, 305
Cohn, Norman, 313
Cold War, 82, 117, 133, 147, 149, 162, 236
Colombia, 49
Colonialism, 225
Colson, Charles, 284

Comfort, Alex, 173, 315
Commerce, global, 36, 144, 293
Common Market, see European Community
Communications, 144; electronic, 13, 15, 25, 37-45, 48; global, 36; online, 37-45; symbolic nature, 41; trends in, 29, 34, 108, 144
Communism, 24, 47, 133, 141, 171, 200, 290; collapse of, 39, 140, 162
Communities, 161, 221, 289, 293; utopian, 161; monastic, 161
Community, 13, 15, 29, 34, 128-31, 140, 161, 211, 287, 302, 304; virtual, 113
Compassion, 193, 298, 305, 313, 317
Complexity, 153, 198, 232, 248, 263, 279, 283
Computers, computerization, 25, 29, 152, 155, 305; living computers, 104; neural, 38, 106; optical, 38; trends in, 29, 37-45, 52, 81, 89, 102-15, 144
Comsat system, 40
Confucius, 48, 148, 283
Connections, linkages, 62, 167, 172, 177, 223, 232, 240-60, 264, 275, 277, 303
Conroy, Pat, 312
Conscience, 191
Consciousness, 18, 36, 62, 102, 170-76, 190, 199, 215, 219, 222, 249, 263, 265, 284, 293; cosmic, 182, 193; ecological, 32, 76, 80, 85, 147, 160, 168, 223, 257, 278; global, 25, 62, 77, 182; physics of, 171; spiritual, 36, 257
Consciousness Revolution, 15, 25, 27, 119, 161, 214, 222
Consultants, 59, 62
Consumerism, 127
Corporations, 52-55; high-value, 52, 63; new styles, 52; stateless, 53, 58, 143
Cosmology, 166
Cosmos, 16, 153; see universe
Counterculture, 15, 214
Creation, 189, 217, 226, 286, 292, 297
Crick, Francis, 89
Crime, 24, 41, 127, 142, 146, 235
Crisis of 2020, 27, 28, 32, 83, 233, 291Croatia, 145
Cronos, 178
Crusades, the, 289
Cuba, 66, 133
Culture wars, 44, 121, 145; global, 147, 219
Culture, 27, 51, 54, 62-65, 120, 130, 144-49, 171, 175, 191, 248, 256, 259, 280, 293; continuity of, 29, 85; global, 39, 42, 132-50, 218, 220; popular, 12, 25, 39, 117, 126, 136-39; postmodern, 13, 115, 170, 197, 213-30, 280, 314; Western, 13, 116-31, 187, 214, 218, 223, 240, 285

Cybernetics, 102-14
Cyberspace, 108-14
Czeck Republic, 136

Daly, Herman, 162, 314
Darwin, Charles, 72, 180
Data processing, 39
Davies, Owen, 140, 157, 313, 314
De Soto, Hernando, 140, 313
Death, 154, 208, 262, 286, 289, 294, 305
Debt, international, 51, 139; U.S., 119, 128, 135, 139
Deconstruction, 217, 223, 226, 230, 262
Dee, John, 211
Deficits, 118
Deforestation, 84, 142, 146
Deism, 187, 189, 191, 194
Democracy, 25, 50, 116, 122, 130, 134, 140, 145, 206, 214, 234, 237
Demographic changes, 146; in China, 142; in U.S., 34, 119,120, 126
Denmark, 3
Desertification, 78
Design, 154, 159, 174, 183, 194, 209, 217, 221, 224, 251, 293, 295; argument from, 255
Determinism, 161, 199, 201, 204, 217, 223, 248, 272, 318
Diamond, Irene, 315
Dimensions, dimensionality, 18, 96-101, 162, 175, 186, 190, 197, 199, 243, 247-52, 257, 260, 263, 269, 274, 281, 284-87, 291, 293, 295, 299, 306, 311
Discipline, 128, 313
Disease, 32, 207, 256, 258, 305; environmental factors, 81, 83, 90, 146; genetic, 89
Disneyland, Disney World, 137, 214, 220, 254
Divorce, 123f
Dizard, Wilson, Jr., 40, 308
DNA, 36, 88-92, 95, 181, 248, 256, 265, 305
Donovan, Vincent, 290, 318
Double helix (genetics), 87, 95
Drama, 26; cosmic, 271-76, 283, 294, 318
Dreams, 270, 272, 288
Drucker, Peter, 152, 155, 314
Drugs, illegal, 44, 128, 146
Dualism, 189, 280
Durant, Will, 316
Durning, Alan, 78, 310
Dusseldorf, Germany, 55

E-mail, 29
Eagleton, Terry, 216, 316
Earth: as Gaia, 177-85, 278; as symbol, 13, 25, 178; threats to ecosystem, 75-87;

Index

viewed from space, 16; uniting of, see globalization
East India Company, 53
Ecofeminism, 182, 315
Ecology, 24, 32, 45, 54, 73, 136, 160, 162, 175-79, 227, 232-46, 257, 261-64, 277-80, 287-95, 317; and economics, 77, 80, 83, 136, 144, 160, 162, 233, 239, 313; and meaning, 242-46, 264, 272; as model, 36, 76, 85, 149, 177-84, 252, 317; global, 116, 220, 241; trends in, 30, 49, 75-87, 144, 146, 233
Economic Cooperation Organization (ECO), 51
Economic growth, 51, 80, 119, 129, 131, 134, 139, 143, 235; ecological constraints on, 80; sustainable, 85; vs. decline, 119
Economics, 12, 38, 116, 123, 128, 133, 138, 141, 235, 247, 291, 295, 305; and ecology, 77, 80, 83, 136, 144, 160, 162, 239; and worldviews, 152-63, 191, 223, 262, 282, 295; cycles in, 57, 118; global, 14, 24, 33, 41, 46-63, 77, 87, 136, 152-63; "informal," 140; shift to market economy, 134, 140; 230; trends in, 39, 41, 46-63, 139, 146
Economy: divine, 290; global, 43, 87, 131, 136, 140; U.S., 119, 131
Ecosystems, 181, 191, 247, 27
Eden, Martyn, 311
Education, 41, 50, 65, 126, 128, 137, 290; corporate-sponsored, 56; trends in, 34, 44, 55, 110, 115, 121, 127; women and, 67
Egypt, 119, 137
Einstein, Albert, 36, 71, 92, 94, 250, 269, 281
Eisler, Riane, 64, 72, 178, 309, 315
Electricity, 31, 190
Electromagnetism, 17, 39, 92, 165, 185, 256
Electronics, trends in, 37-45
Electrons, 93, 248, 255
Elizabeth I, Queen, 211
Ellul, Jacques, 35, 162, 308, 314
Elmer-Dewitt, Philip, 311, 312
Elvisland (Japan), 137, 220
Emerson, Ralph Waldo, 127, 203-09, 212, 312, 316
Empires, 117, 132-36, 145, 230, 284; economic, 136
Employment, 34, 149; at home, 56; part-time, 35, 56; temporary, 53, 56; trends in, 35, 56, 65
Energy, 38, 80, 189, 245, 257, 290, 292, 295, 303; and matter, 80, 92-99, 255, 295; conservation of, 30, 78; renewable, 30, 78, 84; geothermal, 31; trends in, 30, 38
Engines: internal combustion, 30, 38; deisel, 32

England, 54, 59, 117, 128, 133, 135, 140, 150, 189, 211, 302
Enlightenment, the, 36, 63, 144, 168, 189, 214, 218-21, 225, 228, 250, 262, 289, 297, 317
Entertainment, 24, 39, 45, 109-14, 124, 127, 137, 220, 226, 235
Entrepreneurs, 155, 159
Entropy, 80, 181
Environment, environmentalism, 13, 25, 75, 87, 160, 171, 175-79, 238, 246, 274, 280, 289, 293, 310, 313
Environmental dangers, 25, 30, 41, 50, 75-87, 142, 146, 149, 158, 160, 182, 233f
Episcopalians,
Estée Lauder Corporation, 53
Estonia, 150
Eternity, 196, 216, 228, 303
Ethics,   43, 72, 91, 126, 153, 158, 176, 188, 190, 193, 206, 212, 220, 280, 289
Ethiopia, 313
Ethnicity, ethnic identity, 25, 60, 120, 130, 134, 137, 144, 156
Etzioni, Amitai, 123, 125, 312
Eurocentric tradition, 121
Europe, 15, 38, 40, 41, 48-51, 53-57, 63, 110, 116, 120, 130, 133, 137, 149, 200, 225, 238, 302; Eastern, 38, 48, 55, 76, 132, 141, 234; medieval, 146, 160, 210, 240
European Community (EC), European Economic Community (EEC), 48, 54, 133-36, 157, 308
Euthanasia, 126
Evangelicals, 140
Evil, 197, 205, 208, 266, 286, 289, 294, 296, 300; origin of, 197
Evolution, 172, 175, 179-84, 186, 190, 204, 228, 241, 254, 269
Existentialism, 290

Fables, 262
Fads, 12, 15, 29
Faith, 19, 158, 166, 172, 181, 183, 188, 197, 213, 215, 297, 300, 303, 313; and worldviews, 198, 205, 207, 216, 220, 243, 255, 259, 272, 282, 285, 291, 294
Family life, 13, 29, 72, 160, 208, 256, 289, 294; and government policy, 124, 131; origin of, 24, 122-26, 134, 312, future of, 126; in U.S., 122-26, 130; trends in, 33, 55, 65, 69, 113, 119, 122-27, 137, 309
Family, definition of, 33, 35, 122
Famine, 33, 76, 85, 238, 302
Fascism, friendly, 234
Fashion, 38

Fate, fatalism, 186, 189, 196, 198, 225, 305, 316, 318; as force, 202; as worldview, 201-12, 262, 296
Feather, Frank, 66, 70, 309
Feketekuty, Geza, 41
Feminism, 65, 72, 182, 227; in North America, 65
Feminist revolution, 64-74; and social change, 73
Fiber optics, 39
Films, movies, 15, 39, 111, 113, 125, 137, 215, 220
Finance, international, 38, 41, 54, 62, 119, 149
Financialization, 119
Fineman, Howard, 312
Finland, 66
Food, 138, 149, 158, 193, 241; global supply of, 33, 238
Ford Motor Company, 139
Ford, Henry, 32
Forecasting International, 56, 157
Foreign policy, 146
Fortescue, John, 240
Fossil fuels, 79
Foucault, Michel, 221
France, 67, 136, 149, 189, 313
Francis of Assisi, St., 284, 301
Free enterprise, 48, 133, 140, 159
Freedom, 154, 202, 235, 237, 249, 262, 272, 304, 319
Freud, Sigmund, 87
Friedmann, Theodore, 91
Frisians, 150
Fry, Elizabeth, 302
Fujitsu Corporation, 54
Fukuyama, Francis, 316
Fundamentalism, 171, 195, 235
Furness, Thomas, III, 109, 311 [Ed.: This is the Third, not the number 111.]
Future, 16, 26, 29, 132, 147, 153, 196, 201, 210, 225, 232-38; alternative futures, 233-38; as worldview question, 155, 160, 175, 278, 303; prediction of, 97, 250
Futurists, 130

Gaia, 249, 315; as hypothesis, 177-80, 278; as worldview, 177-85, 190, 262, 293, 295; Greek goddess, 177
Galilei, Galileo, 178
Gandhi, Mahatma, 290
GATT (General Agreement on Tariffs and Trade), 48, 52
Gender revolution, 25, 64-74
General Media Corporation, 112
General Motors Corporation, 59, 61

Generations, 141, 265; and continuity of culture, 34, 128, 148; study of, 16, 26-29, 257, 302, 307
Genetics, 14, 25, 36, 78, 97, 106, 215, 310; ethical issues, 91; trends in, 32, 81, 88-92
Geography, 44, 113, 213
Geology, 179
Georgia, nation of, 150
Germany, 39, 53, 59, 133-36, 234, 313; reunification of, 132, 135
Ginsparg, Paul, 96
Gitlin, Todd, 213, 215
Glashow, Sheldon, 96
Glasnost, 141
Global information grid, 40, 59, 145
Global information society/economy, 43, 48, 62, 145, 149, 156
Global marketplace, 54, 144, 162; of worldviews and ideas, 153, 155, 202, 230, 246, 291
Global Positioning System (GPS), 139
"Global teenager," 25, 38, 112, 137
Global warming, 76, 78, 234
Globalism, 144-50, 235; vs. tribalism, 144, 150
Globalization, 14, 24, 46-63, 82, 118, 140, 144, 200, 220, 230, 302
Globalstar system, 40
Globex Corporation, 54
Gluck, Fred, 157
God, 154, 165, 172, 181, 202, 206, 220, 225, 240, 245, 256, 269, 284-92; as creator, 186-95; as personal, 190-94, 199, 244, 288, 296, 316, 317; as Playwright, 271-75; conceptions of, 19, 186-200, 217; immanent, 172, 187, 192; proofs for, 188, 270; transcendent, 172, 187, 190-94, 255, 284, 296, 319
Goddess-worship, 178
Goldberger, Nancy Rule, 309
Golubitsky, Martin, 96, 247, 311
Gorbachev, Mikhail, 11, 13, 134, 141, 150, 156, 307, 314
Gore, Al, 75, 77, 87, 310
Goricheva, Tatiana, 290, 318
Gorman, Christine, 310
Government, 123, 142, 235, 303; as source of employment, 56; U.S., 120; world, 149
Grand Unification Theories (GUTs), see Theory of Everything
Gravity, 17, 39, 92-97, 165, 185, 190, 281
Gray, Paul, 121, 312
Great Chain of Being, 173, 178, 226, 239-42, 317
Great Lakes, 78, 241
Greco-Roman culture, 117, 136, 139, 202

Greece, 117, 136, 139, 160, 195, 202, 239, 241, 283
Green Revolution, 14, 50
Greene, Susan, 34
"Greenhouse" gases, 30, 78
Greenpeace, 41
Gridlock, political, 120
Griffin, David Ray, 223, 225-28, 296, 317, 318
Gross Domestic Product (GDP), 136
Gross, Bertram, 234, 317
Guangzhou, China, 47
Guinea, 146
Guinness, Os, 117, 126, 219, 312, 317
Guns, 127; control of, 130; see also weapons
Gunton, Colin E., 317
Guttman, Monika, 65, 309
Hahn, Harley, 37, 308
Harmon, Amy, 311
Harvey, David, 13, 214, 221, 307, 316, 317
Hassan, I., 216, 222, 316
Hawking, Stephen, 88, 92, 100, 247, 310, 317
Health, 32, 65, 70, 81, 119, 256, 288, 292, 305
Heaven, 185, 240, 286, 290, 292, 304
Heilbroner, Robert, 160, 314
Heisenberg, Werner, 63, 94, 311
Hellenization, 136
Henzler, Herbert, 157
Heredity, 75, 269, 309
Heroes, 213, 215
Hierarchical model, 36, 58, 60, 226, 241, 245
Hierarchy, hierarchies, 25, 36, 148, 217, 226, 241, 271; vs. networking, 25, 58, 60, 70
Hillenbrand, Barry, 137, 313
Hinduism, 121, 145, 148, 195, 237, 283
Hirsch, E. D., 317
Hispanics, in the U.S., 121
History, 16, 26-29, 116, 148, 154, 160, 174, 183, 188, 215-22, 228, 233, 241, 248-63, 269, 271, 318; American, 27-29, 120-23; and economics, 160; meaning of, 188, 191, 195, 202, 206-09, 224, 228, 257, 263, 271-90, 294, 301-06; medieval, 146, 160; patterns or cycles in, 26-29, 120, 224, 247, 257; women in, 65, 73
Hitler, Adolf, 133
Holism, 14, 45, 167, 171-74, 176, 182, 196, 221, 223, 244
Holland, 54, 117
Holland, Joe, 317, 318
Holloway, Mark, 314
Hollywood, 138
Holocaust, the, 253, 317
Holograms, 16, 91, 172, 247, 270, 287
Holographic model, 172, 182, 270, 309, 315

Homelessness, 120
Homeostasis, 182, 196, 281
Homer-Dixon, Thomas F., 84, 310
Homosexuality, 65, 72, 221
Honda Corporation, 55, 59, 138
Honeywell Corporation, 56
Hong Kong, 44, 46, 49, 136, 141, 215
Hood, Leroy, 90
Hope, 19, 220, 266, 288, 290, 294, 303
Horgan, John, 312
Hornblower, Margot, 314
Horoscopes, 210
Howe, Neil, 26-29, 237, 302, 307
Hudson Institute, 142
Hughes, Robert, 126, 312
Human Genome Project, 32, 89-92
Human rights, 158
Humanism, 283
Humor, 221, 252
Hungary, 136
Huntington, Samuel, 132, 147, 313
Hussein, Saddam, 41
Huxley, Julian, 172
Huyssens, A., 218
Hyperinflation, 119
Hypersphere, 98

IBM Corporation, 59, 105
ICL Corporation, 54
Idealism, 118, 171, 303
Ideology, 25, 122, 131, 140, 143, 156, 219, 222, 277, 298; shift away from, 47, 57, 141, 156, 158, 213, 230
Image of God, 172, 187, 190, 195, 240, 270, 275, 292, 317
Images, 41, 60, 109, 172, 252, 274
Imagination, 18, 208, 242, 262, 270, 306
immigration, immigrants, 44, 119, 120
Incarnation, 285, 299f
India, 41, 119, 144, 237, 313
Individuality, individualism, 131, 171, 208, 211, 215, 221, 224, 227, 246
Indonesia, 119
Industrial Revolution, 32, 36, 136
Industrialization, 23, 31, 66
Inflation, 119, 131, 235
Information, 12, 24, 40-44, 156, 308; access to, 43, 59, 305; and symbols, 11, 40, 59, 109; as business asset, 40, 43, 48; information industry, 56
Information Superhighway, 40
Intelligence, 72, 105, 187, 240; artificial, 102, 105, 305; military, 109
Intention, 187, 196, 209, 229, 251, 254, 263, 281, 293, 317
Internal combustion engines, 30

International Green Cross, 13
International Monetary Fund (IMF), 133, 136, 313
International Olympic Committee, 134
Internet, the, 37, 308
Interotica Corporation, 112
Intuition, 71, 259, 297
Investment, transnational, 43, 53
Iran, 50, 236
Iraq, 41, 236
Ireland, 53, 59
Iridium system, 40
Iron Curtain, 132
Irony, 202, 215-22, 225, 268, 285, 297
Isaiah the Prophet, 192
Islam, 117, 121, 145, 148, 166, 186, 195, 200, 236; growth in U.S., 121
Israel, 236
Italy, 39, 40, 110, 234
ITN (International Television News), 41

Jackson, Michael, 137, 215
Jamaica, 41
Japan, 40, 49-60, 66, 110, 133-39, 141, 148, 234, 313; comparative economic growth, 51; ecological issues, 78; global influence, 117; trends in, 130, 200, 220; women in, 66, 69
Jaroff, Leon, 310
Jencks, Charles, 316
Jesuits, 117
Jesus Christ, 191, 194, 273, 283-306; history of, 273, 284-89, 294
John, Apostle, 287, 293, 304
Joseph, Lawrence, 179, 315
Joy, Donald M., 30
Judaism, 69, 121, 129, 145, 166, 187, 193, 211, 289
Jung, Carl, 87
Justice, 73, 81, 158, 188, 193, 203, 289, 294, 299, 304
Kahn, Herman, 152, 313
Kanter, Rosabeth Moss, 314
Kaplan, Robert, 142, 146, 220, 234, 313, 317
Karaoke, 138
Kaufmann, U. Milo, 317
Keen, Sam, 13, 307
Keeton, Kathy, 112
Kennedy, Paul, 118
Keynes, John Maynard, 152, 314
King, Alexander, 307
Kingdom of God, 196, 240
Kitchener, Richard F., 315
Knowbots, 108
Knowledge, knowing, 42, 81, 154, 170, 260, 301; as process, 168, 223; personal, 182, 198, 259, 281
Kosko, Bart, 311
Kowsnowski, Melvin, 214
Krause, Charles, 312
Krauss, Lawrence, 165, 314
Kreeft, Peter, 186, 315
Kurds, 150
Kurylo, Michael, 80

Lake Biwi, 78
Land, destruction of, 78, 84, 142, 146
Langton, Christopher, 106
Language, 30, 122, 169, 213, 215, 219, 229
Language translation, computerized, 30
Lanier, Jaron, 113
Lasch, Christopher, 316
Lasers, 32, 172
Latin America, 38, 48, 120, 139, 143, 148
Latvia, 150
Le Corbusier, 216
Leadership, 141; moral, 130, 312
Lebanon, 145, 289
Lemonick, Michael D., 307, 311
Lenin, V. I., 16
Leptons, 93
Letterman, David, 215
Lewis, C. S., 273, 284, 291, 318
Liberia, 146
Libraries, electronic, 45
Life, as story, 265, 278; meaning of, 35, 91, 104, 107, 114, 154, 161, 169, 175, 184, 194, 197, 207, 211, 218, 223, 245, 262-65, 272-80, 297, 303; new forms of, 89, 92; quality of, 35; simulation of, 104, 114; value of, 126, 176
Lifestyle, 31, 81, 138, 216, 219
Light, speed of, 39, 42
Lilly, William, 211
Lindisfarne Association, 178
Linguistics, 30
Literacy, 70
Literature, 215, 219, 221, 223, 273, 285, 290
Lizhi, Fang, 98-101, 311
Lobbying, 120
Logic, 196, 210, 220, 268, 311; "fuzzy," 105
London, 41, 118, 230
Lord Corporation, 60
Los Alamos National Laboratory, 106
Love, 113, 188, 194, 207, 246, 256, 289-94, 300, 302, 305; and truth, 246, 294
Lovelock, James, 177-81, 315
Löwith, Karl, 202
Lucas, Ernest C., 95, 311

Lunn, E., 222
Lytton, Edward Bulwer, 201, 203

MacFarquhar, Emily, 309
Machine model, 36, 61, 93, 106, 156, 171, 175, 189, 191, 194, 209, 223, 244, 250, 252, 262, 314, and patriarchy, 168
Macintosh Computer, 144
Madonna, 215
Magazines, 39, 41, 62, 129
Magic, 202, 207, 209, 229; as "science," 210
Malaysia, 48, 117, 119
Management, 53, 60
Manufacturing, 44, 48, 53-56, 59, 119, 129, 141
Maps, 220
Margulis, Lynn, 179, 183
Marketing, 129, 162
Marriage, see family life
Mars, 179
Marshall Plan, 135
Martin, David, 140, 313
Marx, Karl, 161, 230, 290
Marxism, 161, 171, 283, 290
Masai People, the, 290
Massachusetts Institute of Technology, 105
Materialism, 162, 171, 181, 290
Mathematics, 18, 92, 115, 166, 223, 244
Matter, 14, 19, 80, 162-66, 170, 189, 242, 255, 265, 278, 293, 295, 297, 306; structure of, 89, 92-99, 101, 185
Mazda Corporation, 139
McDonalds Restaurants, 46, 53, 138, 144
McKibben, Bill, 42, 308
McLaughlin, John, 308
McLuhan, Marshall, 54
Meaning, 12, 19, 30, 35, 62-65, 86, 91, 104, 150, 170, 175, 216, 229, 238, 241, 247-65, 272-76, 317; and ecology, 85, 223, 232-46, 264, 288; and genetics, 91; and intention, 229, 293, 317; as worldview question, 154, 184, 189-96, 199, 207, 212, 218-28, 238, 263, 283, 291, 293, 299, 303; transcendent, 194, 217, 243, 246, 255, 263, 278, 303
Medicine: genetic, 89-92; preventive, 32; trends in, 30, 32, 38, 89-92, 106, 110, 176
Megatrends, 23, 237
Memory, 102, 265
Mercosur treaty, 50
Metanarratives, 216, 226, 276
Metaphor, metaphors, 13, 15, 169, 173, 177, 217, 244, 262, 265, 272-75, 318; and truth, 274; root, 168, 262
Metaphysics, 166, 175, 198, 216, 222
Methodist Revival, 140, 240

Methyl bromide, 80
Mexico, 49, 55, 119, 140
Meyer, Donald, 66, 69, 73, 309, 310
Michigan, State of, 270
Microbiology, 178
Microorganisms, 179
Middle Ages, 23, 237, 240
Middle East, 235
Migration, 26, 85, 142, 145
Military force, 41, 49, 76, 116, 118, 135, 139, 141, 162, 227, 236; control of, 149;
Milky Way, the, 255
Millenium, 23
Miller, Carmen, 311
Miller, Lawrence, 112
Mind, 18, 36, 102, 150, 170, 208, 242, 247, 255, 258, 269, 284, 293, 297; and body, 114, 171; cosmic, 182, 206, 275
Miniaturization, 30, 105
Miracles, 187
Mitchell, Edgar, 177
Mitsubishi Corporation, 54, 139
Models, 219; worldview, 35, 61, 85, 152-230, 258
Modernity, 145, 197, 202, 213-21, 225-30, 244, 262, 297, 316
Mohammed, 283
Mohawk Tribe, 150
Monasterky, R., 310
Monasticism, 161
Monczunski, John, 311, 316
Monsma, Stephen, 126
Montagu, Ashley, 72
Montreal Protocol (1987), 80
Morality, 13, 16, 25, 113, 122, 131, 170, 187-94, 204, 212, 215, 263, 280, 305; ecological, 45; technological, 35
Moravec, Hans, 104, 106, 311
Morgan, Robin, 73, 310
Morgan, Thomas, 125
Morris, Richard, 96, 99, 311
Morris, William D., 313
Morrow, Lance, 132, 313
Mortality rates, 85, 128
Moscow, Russia, 138, 230
Moslems, see Islam
Mother Earth, 178, 182, 184
Motorola Corporation, 40
Movements, 16, 119, 131, 143, 147, 164, 175, 238, 289, 302; political, 143, 237; religious, 143, 237
Moynihan, Daniel Patrick, 124, 312
Mozambique, 313
MTV, 115, 144, 220
Muggeridge, Malcolm, 284, 301
Multiculturalism, 121, 126

Multidimensionality, 18, 97-101, 162, 186, 199, 245, 251, 269, 274, 284, 291-301, 306, 318

Multiservers, 38

Murder, 127

Music, 38, 39, 47, 129, 137, 144, 252, 282, 285; country, 129; rock, 38, 39, 129, 137, 210, 215

Muslim trade zone, 50

Mysticism, 16, 167, 170, 174, 181, 193, 195, 299

Myth, mythology, 177, 202, 262, 264, 273, 279, 280, 282, 289, 318; and ethics, 280; and facts, 273, 284

NAFTA (North American Free Trade Agreement or Area), 48, 55, 136, 140

Nagas People, the, 150

Naisbitt, John, 23, 33, 70, 237, 307, 309

Nanotechnology, 30, 105

Narrative, narratives, 216, 226, 228, 261-90, 318

Nation, concept of, 43, 54, 117, 131, 144-47, 221, 256

National Aeronautics and Space Administration (NASA), 109

National Association of Working Women, 34

National Audobon Society, 31

National Center for Atmospheric Research (U.S.), 80

National Institutes of Health (U.S.), 89

Nationalism, 48, 131, 227; as ideology, 131

NATO (North Atlantic Treaty Organization), 133, 135

Natural History Magazine, 232, 239, 317

Nature, 166, 178, 204, 226, 241; and culture, 171; control of, 168

NEC Corporation, 46

Neighborhoods, 56, 123, 131, 208, 256, 294

Networks, networking, 25, 40, 46, 58, 70, 129, 147, 157, 164, 167, 175, 219; among women, 70; as metaphor, 168; computerized, 45, 62; economic, 46-63, 140, 143, 156; global, 150

Neutrinos, 97, 293

New Age, 170, 177, 182, 193, 195, 237

New Economic Order, 155, 158, 163, 295

New World Order, 44, 116, 132-50, 306

New York City, 31

New York State, 41, 59

Newland, Kathleen, 64, 67, 309

Newton, Isaac, 36, 93, 169, 170, 178

Niche marketing, "Niching," 129

Nigeria, 146

Nintendo, 115

Nitrogen, 180

North America, 40, 48, 53, 78, 137, 238, 302

North Korea, 132; reunification with South Korea, 132

Northern Ireland, 289

Norway, 66

Nuclear energy, 31, 38, 80, 82, 92, 185, 256; environmental risks of, 76, 78, 82; fusion, 31

Nuclear weapons, 39, 80, 82, 133, 162, 233, 256, 271, 288; control of, 83; proliferation of, 82, 236

O'Brien, Richard, 316

Oceanus, 178

Ogonis People, the, 150

Ohio, State of, 41, 59, 139, 215 Ohmae, Kenichi, 46, 157, 308, 314

Olson, James E., 40, 308

Ong, Walter, 307

OPEC (Organization of Petroleum Exporting Countries), 78

Optics, 30, 113

Optimism, 205

Order, 174, 183, 188, 209, 215, 220, 226, 232, 240, 247-61, 285, 293; and chaos, 250; and disorder, 189, 266; implicate, 173; moral, 239

Orenstein, Gloria Feman, 315

Organism, as model, 36, 61, 106, 176, 179-83, 195, 241, 249, 252, 293, 295, 315

Organization, corporate, 52

Organochlorines, 81

Orthodox Church, 237, 301

Ottoman Empire, 135

Outler, Albert, 317

Oxygen, 180

Ozone layer, depletion of, 76, 78

Pacific Rim, 23, 48, 133-36

Paganism, 182

Pagels, Heinz, 115, 312

Pakistan, 51

Palestinians, 313

Pantagonia, Inc., 34

Pantheism, 200, 296

Parables, 251, 262

Paradigm shifts, 14, 167, 174, 218, 230, 260, 288, 298

Paradox, 299

Paraguay, 50

Parenting, 125

Parkinson's disease, 91

Pasteur, Louis, 168

Patriarchy, 168, 227

Index

Patriotism, 128
Patterns, 62, 107, 224, 232, 244, 251-60; of relationships, 171, 173, 183
Paul, Apostle, 286, 290, 292, 304
Peace, 73, 81, 227, 238, 256, 290, 294, 299, 306
Peace of Westphalia, 146
Pekkannen, John, 90, 310
Pelikan, Jaroslav, 319
Pennsylvania, State of, 60
Penrose, Roger, 114, 311
Pentecostalism, 68, 140
People groups, 302
People's Bank of China, 69
People, as national asset, 44
Perestroika, 156, 314
Persian Gulf War (1991), 15, 41, 118, 236
Person, personality, 36, 75, 182, 187, 190, 193, 198, 228, 245, 254, 259, 262, 265, 272, 275-79, 281, 288
Personal digital assistants (PDAs), 30, 139
Peru, 140
Pesticides, 81
Peter, Apostle, 294, 304
Peters, Ted, 182, 315
Philippines, the, 119
Phillips, Kevin, 119, 312
Philosophy, 13, 17, 48, 63, 107, 114, 129, 154, 195, 206, 240, 244, 273; and world-views, 154-60, 165, 167, 198, 208, 219, 228, 240, 279, 282; political, 152, 288, 291, 301, 305
Physics, 25, 36, 61, 71, 88, 92-99, 165, 169, 173, 178, 198, 256; Newtonian, 36, 93, 169; see also quantum physics
Pishey, Ognian, 39
Piven, Frances Fox, 313
Plastics, 30, 38
Plato, 114, 201, 206, 240-44
Plausibility structures, 297
Pluralism, 219, 221, 230
Poetry, 161, 170, 252, 273
Poland, 136
Polanyi, Michael, 259, 316, 318
Politics, 12, 44, 86, 116, 162, 208, 282, 291, 303; and ecology, 80, 234; global, 14, 24, 32, 41, 78, 132-50; 220; trends in, 39, 65, 72, 81, 119, 127, 139, 214
Pollution, 78, 85, 146, 243
Pope, Alexander, 226, 317
Population growth, 24, 26, 31, 32, 49, 120, 142, 160; and environmental crisis, 84, 146
Pornography, 112
Portugal, 117
Postman, Neil, 127, 312
Postmodernity, Postmodernism, 13, 115,

170, 178, 196, 202, 207, 213-30, 233, 239, 244, 249, 262, 276, 280, 296-99, 314; con-structive, 226, 262, 296, 318; difference between, 219, 229
Poverty, 24, 33, 43, 50, 83, 119, 123, 127, 139, 142, 147, 160, 207, 235, 238, 289, 295, 313; and population growth, 85
Power, 222-25, 255, 270, 272, 284, 286, 289, 292, 298, 303
Pragmatism, economic, 47, 57, 155-62, 235
Prayer, 113, 290
Premodernity, 146, 202, 217, 228
Prison population, 128, 302
Privacy, 91, 113
Progress, 24, 214, 218, 223; technological, 36, 80
Promise Keepers movement, 131
Proofs, scientific, 169, 243, 281, 311
Prosperity, economic, 46, 51, 159, 161, 235, 238, 303, 305
Protons, 93
Providence, 203, 296
Psychology, 87, 167, 169, 205, 219, 279, 282; and ecology, 87
Pulsars, 185, 249
Purpose, 12, 30, 154, 158, 169, 174, 182, 187-91, 194-99, 207, 212, 217, 223, 229, 239, 241, 256, 259, 263, 272, 280, 286, 290-93, 298, 303; transcendent, 224, 228, 255, 263, 296, 303

Quantum mystery worldview, 164-76, 262, 295, 305
Quantum physics, 14, 16, 61, 71, 88, 92-99, 164-76, 185, 190, 249, 256, 289, 293, 295, 300, 305
Quarks, 93, 97
Quasars, 185

Racism, 289, 306
Radio, 38, 129, 256
Raeburn, Paul, 310
Railroads, 32
Rain forests, 76
Rathjens, George W., 310
Rationalism, 218
Reagan, Ronald, 119, 135
Reality, 109, 153, 170, 190, 215, 219, 224, 260, 269; and worldviews, 153, 158, 164; dimensions of, 270, 274, 285, 293; percep-tions of, 17, 111, 115, 153, 176; spiritual, 257, 301; structures of, 269; vir-tual, see virtual reality
Reason, 19, 197, 215, 255, 259, 262, 268, 311
Reason, Age of, 36; see also Enlightenment

Recession, economic, 119, 233, 308
Reconciliation, 287, 290, 294, 304
Recycling, 30, 35
Redemption, 172
Reform, 238
Reformation, the, 218
Refugees, 26, 145, 313
Regionalism, 49, 136, 145, 221
Reich, Otto, 50, 308
Reich, Robert, 43, 52, 57-60, 308
Reincarnation, 263
Relations, relationships, 36, 63, 154, 160, 167, 171-75, 183, 188, 195, 209, 220, 223, 239, 242, 244, 258, 275, 292; ecological, 241; personal, 36, 45, 67, 122, 160, 194, 208, 212, 242, 265, 293
Relativism, 13, 14, 25, 171, 196, 200, 225, 230
Relativity, theory of, 36, 71, 80, 92, 95, 100, 164, 190, 250, 281
Religion, 12, 25, 39, 51, 56, 116 , 121, 127, 148, 157, 193, 229, 232, 237, 244, 250, 291, 299, 301, 318; and history, 283, 288; and science, 107, 167, 181; and world-views, 161, 168, 178, 181, 197, 218, 220, 227, 277, 282, 289, 295; globalization of, 25, 45; new religions, 26, 237
Religious awakenings, 27, 29, 302
Renaissance, the, 63, 218
Renewal, 238, 292, 302; cultural, 122, 130, 147; spiritual, 23, 27, 50, 130, 139, 237, 312
Research, military, 109
Resurrection, 273, 284, 288, 294, 299, 304
Reuters News Service, 41
Revelation, 283, 296
Revolutions, 260; scientific, 166
Rheingold, Howard, 102, 109, 113, 311
Rich and poor, gap between, 142, 241, 295, 313
Richardson, Don, 318
Ritchie, Donald, 137
Ritual, 250
Robots, robotics, 103-07, 113
Roman Catholic Church, 69, 145, 237, 290, 301
Roman Empire, 136, 202, 288
Romanticism, 218, 220
Rome, 117, 136, 139, 230
Rose, Karol, 56
Rosow, Jerome M., 308
Rossman, Parker, 45, 308
Roszak, Theodore, 182, 315
Runyon, Daniel V., 309
Russell, Jeffrey Burton, 210, 316, 317
Russia, 40, 49, 66, 82, 132-36, 149, 234, 237

Sakhas People, the, 150
Salman al-Saud, Sultan Bin, 11
Salus, Peter, 37, 308
Samsung Corporation, 53
Sanders, E. P., 155, 314
Satellites, communication, 39, 45, 97, 109
Saturn Corporation, 61
Saudi Arabia, 41, 145
Sawi Tribe, 290
São Paulo, Brazil, 140
Scenarios, 233-38
Schlesinger, Arthur, Jr., 120, 122, 126, 257, 312
Schlesinger, Arthur, Sr., 257
Schneider, Bertrand, 307
Schneider, Stephen, 80
Schopenhauer, Arthur, 64
Science, 12, 16, 24, 35, 41, 61, 70, 116, 133, 238, 242, 247, 250, 293; and worldview models, 61, 85, 88, 91, 97, 161, 164-85, 197, 200, 215, 218, 227, 240, 261, 273, 279, 281, 289; breakthroughs in, 71, 88-97; globalization of, 25, 45, 144; postmodern, 222, 227, 249
Scientists, 59, 165
Sea level, changes in, 78, 80, 146
SEATO (Southeast Asia Treaty Organization), 133
Seattle, Washington, 215
Secularization, 200, 238
Sekimoto, Tadahiro, 46, 308
Self-consciousness, 215, 219, 222, 263, 293
Seneca, the, 203
Service industry, 59, 63, 130
Sex roles, 65, 70, 122, 131, 223, 305; see also gender revolution
Shakers, 161
Shakespeare, William, 137
Shanghai, China, 47
Sheng, Kang, 141
Shenzhen, China, 46, 141
Shopping malls, 57, 117, 251
Sider, Ronald J., 318
Sierra Leone, 146
Sin, 172, 188, 195, 240, 287, 300, 317
Singapore, 41, 49, 59, 117, 130, 133, 141, 234
Singer Corporation, 44
Sioux Tribe, 150
Sire, James, 17, 153, 187, 191, 282, 307, 314, 316
Slovakia, 136
Small groups, in business, 58, 129
Smarr, Larry, 109
Smith, Page, 316
Snyder, Howard A., 309, 314, 318

Index

Socialism, 145; market, 23, 141
Society, 195, 246, 249-58, 264, 271, 280; global, 24, 34-45, 132-58, 214, 219, 225, 229, 233-38, 283, 294, 296; structures of, 123, 217; urban, 130, 235, 238
Sociobiology, 36
sociology, 221
Socrates, 114
Software, 52, 58, 63, 104, 107, 138, 246
Sogo Corporation, 137
Solar energy, 31
Solomon, King, 197
Sony Corporation, 137
South Africa, Republic of, 50, 128, 289
South Korea, 49, 59, 133, 141; reunification with North Korea, 132
Space, dimensions of, 18, 39, 98-101, 162, 191, 199, 265, 284, 296, 299, 306
Space, exploration of, 14, 18, 25, 37, 80, 82, 97, 110, 133, 135, 179; international cooperation in, 82
Spacetime, 18, 98-101, 162, 169, 173, 191, 199, 219, 264, 270, 275, 278, 284, 289, 293-96, 299, 303, 306, 311; curvature of, 98, 300
Spain, 39, 41, 117
Species, depletion of, 76, 78
Spirit, 18, 36, 102, 113, 150, 190, 242, 245, 248, 270, 278, 287, 303, 306; and worldviews, 36, 87, 150, 154, 163, 175, 257, 295, 301
Spirituality, 15, 23, 87, 113, 140, 170, 220, 227, 291
St. Louis, Missouri, 214
Stalin, Joseph, 134
Stapp, Henry, 173, 315
Star Wars (Movies), 201
Stars, 249, 255
Steam engine, 32, 156
Stewart, Ian, 96, 247, 311
Stoll, David, 140, 313
Story, 191, 228, 233, 246, 253, 261-90, 301, 318; and worldviews, 261-90, 306; cosmic, 271-76; in relation to history, 263-66, 301; see also history
Storyteller, need for, 263
Stout, Rick, 308
Strauss, William, 26-29, 237, 302, 307
Stricharchuk, Greg, 60, 309
String theory, see superstrings
Strong nuclear force, 17, 39, 92, 165
Style, styles, 15, 39, 42, 137, 214, 219-22, 225, 248, 298
Subject/object split, 168, 170, 174, 182, 191, 198, 262, 288
Suburbs, suburbanization, 122

Suicide, 126, 257
Sun, 185, 250, 255
Supermarkets, 137
Superstrings, 88, 95
Supersymmetry, 96
Support groups, 129
Surprise, 232, 241, 247-61, 285, 293
Surrealism, 218
Sweden, 39, 53; women in, 69
Sweet, Leonard, 23, 76, 213, 229, 307, 309, 310, 314, 316 Swimme, Brian, 261, 318
Switzerland, 53, 145
Symbiosis, 180
Symbols, 41, 48, 59, 62, 105, 178, 214, 217, 246, 274; and information, 41
Symmetry, 96, 164, 241, 247, 254, 273, 294, 299, 311; and chaos, 96; breaking of, 96
Synergy, 244

Szulc, Tad, 312
Tacelli, Ronald, 186, 315
Taiwan, 49, 59, 133, 136, 141
Talbot, Michael, 173, 315
Tanzania, 290
Tarule, Jill Mattuck, 309
Taxes, 119
Taylor, Mark, 264, 318
Teams, teamwork, in business, 58-61, 208
Technology, 12-15, 23, 33, 116, 133, 145, 149, 161, 238, 248; and ecology, 75-78; and morality, 35, 113; and worldviews, 35, 113, 155, 161, 168, 210, 216, 223, 262; breakthroughs in, 27; information, 60, 144; medical, 126; trends in, 29-32, 37-45, 52, 55, 102-14, 122, 129, 144
Teilhard de Chardin, Pierre, 172, 315
Telecommunications, see communication, electronic
Television, 15, 29, 37-42, 45, 124, 139, 220, 256; cable, 42; trends, 108, 129
Temperature, rise of atmospheric, 79
Teresa, Mother, 284, 289, 301
Terrorism, 82, 83, 235, 289; nuclear, 236
Theism 166, 186-200
Theology, 187, 240, 244, 317; medieval, 298
Theory of Everything (TOE), 13, 17, 39, 88, 92-97, 212, 247; and worldviews, 97, 165, 176, 239, 278, 288, 292
"Third World," 24, 147
Thomas Aquinas, 240
Thoreau, Henry David, 310
Thurow, Lester, 48, 50, 160, 308, 314
Tiananmen Square massacre, 16, 49, 141
Time, 164, 169, 191, 199, 265, 278, 284, 296, 306; and eternity, 196; curvature of, 100; dimensions of, 18, 39, 98-101, 162, 275, 299

Time Warner Corporation, 56
Toffler, Alvin, 13, 307
Tolba, Mostafa, 80
Topology, of universe, 97
Torus shape, 98
Totalitarianism, 128, 132, 145, 234
Tourism, 138
Toynbee, Arnold, 257
Toyota Corporation, 55
Trade zones, regional, 48, 140, 146, 157
Trade, international, 25, 36, 44, 48-51, 117, 139, 143, 155, 162
Transformation, 289; personal, 286, 300; social, 176, 280, 301
Transportation, 31, 44
Trends, global, 11, 16, 19, 23-29, 130, 148, 215, 232-38, 248, 254, 291, 302; and worldviews, 153, 186, 238, 261, 271, 277; as Earth Currents, 15, 88, 93, 116, 148, 153, 225, 232, 248, 280, 302, 305; continuity of, 130
Tribes, tribalism, 144, 150, 156, 208, 221
Trinity, the, 244, 293, 299, 317
Truth, 18, 113, 166, 176, 218, 200, 222, 239, 246, 262, 273, 293-305, 311; as correspondence, 168, 225, 275; as story, 273; vs. approximate description, 168, 223
Tuchman, Barbara, 310
Turkey, 50, 82, 135, 237
Turkmenistan, 51
Twain, Mark, 269
Tyson, Ann Scott, 142, 313
Tyson, James L., 142, 313

Ukraine, 82
Uncertainty principle, 93, 165, 300, 310
Unemployment, 131, 235
United Nations, 33, 65, 79, 80, 84, 128, 145, 149; reform of, 149
United States, 15, 34, 38, 43, 48-51, 82, 109, 133-39, 149, 157, 200, 219, 234, 237, 289; decline of, 116-31; economy of, 54-57, 59, 119, 313; women in, 67, 128, 131
Universe, 75, 92-99, 154, 172, 181, 186-90, 197, 228; and meaning, 12, 86, 164, 170, 184, 196, 207, 241-76, 279, 285, 291; as hologram, 173, 182, 270; as machine, 194, 252, 262, 314; dimensions of, 18, 162, 199, 247-57, 293, 306; origin of, 199; story of, 261-66, 285, 304; structure of, 92-99, 154, 159, 167, 173, 183, 241, 251-56, 293
Universities, 44, 55, 138, 215; electronic, 45
Unrepresented Nations and Peoples Organization (UNPO), 150
Urbanization, global, 26, 34, 122, 134, 140
Uruguay, 50

USSR, 16, 24, 50, 82, 128, 132-36, 141, 144, 149, 234, 236; disintegration of, 135
Uzbekistan, 51

Values, 15, 27, 128, 150, 167, 176, 219; conflict in, 134; cultural, 15, 86, 126, 139; moral, 25, 35, 43, 122, 130
Venezuela, 48, 49
Venus, 180
Victoria, Queen, 117
Video games, 108-14, 220
Viet Nam, 133
Violence, 13, 83, 111, 120, 124, 126, 128, 159, 195, 208, 236, 257, 266, 300
Virtual reality (VR), 102, 108-15, 235, 305, 311; and virtual sex, 108, 111-14
Virtue, 131, 219
Viruses, computer, 105, 252
Visser 't Hooft, W. A., 302, 319
Voltaire, François, 247
Volvo Corporation, 54
Von Baeyer, Hans Christian, 94, 99, 101, 310
VPL Research Corporation, 113

War, 15, 26, 36, 49, 73, 132-36, 155; and economics, 155; as way of life, 146; nuclear, 236; threat of, 82, 143, 146, 234f
Ward, W. R., 319
Washington, DC, 59, 120, 214, 230
Water, shortage of, 76, 78, 84, 146
Watson, James, 89
Wave/particle duality, 93, 169
Weak nuclear force, 17, 39, 92, 165
Wealth, 47, 51, 58; differences in, 24, 43, 51, 83, 119, 140, 142, 159, 226, 241, 313
Weapons, 44, 141; see also nuclear weapons
Weather, study of, 25, 76; disruption of, 80
Web, global economic, 46-63, 136, 140, 143
Weber, Renée, 309, 315
Weinberg, Steven, 88, 164, 166, 310, 314
Weiner, Jonathan, 310
Wells, David F., 311
Wells, H. G., 45
Wesley, John, 240, 317
West Irian, 290
West, Cornel, 13
Western society, 14, 116-31, 137, 214, 223, 240
"Wetware," 105
Whitehead, Alfred North, 317
Wilber, Ken, 173, 309, 315
Wilberforce, William, 302
Wilkinson, Barry, 55
Wilson, A. N., 301, 319
Wind, as energy source, 31
Winter, Gibson, 318

Index

Wisdom, 42, 81, 167, 296, 301

Witten, Edward, 95

Women: as pastors, 68; education of, 67; in business, 67, 72; in science, 71; roles of, 14, 25, 305; trends regarding, 34, 56, 60, 64-74, 81, 128, 131; vs. men, 71, 241, 246

Worden, Alfred, 16

Work, 60, 156; definition of, 34

World Bank, 134

World Health Organization (WHO), 84

World Soul, 178

World War II, 27, 52, 64, 69, 117, 120, 133-36, 138, 157

Worldstory, 273-90; criteria for, 278-81

Worldviews, 11, 14-18, 35, 42, 48, 63-67, 85, 91, 131, 137, 148, 150, 152-230, 232, 238-305; and philosophy, 17, 63, 152, 169, 198, 219, 282, 301; and technology, 35, 113, 161; as Theory of Everything, 17, 97, 165, 239, 247, 278; definition of, 153, 259, 307; scientific, 169, 198, 281, 283, 311; shifts in, 65, 88, 97, 217, 298; women and, 70, 72, 241

Worldwatch Institute 65, 67, 78

Writing, invention of, 113

Xavier, Francis, 117

Xiaoping, Deng, 47, 141

Yancey, Philip, 279, 285, 318

Yaohan supermarkets, 137

Year 2000, 23, 26

Yoga, 290

Youth, 136, 219; culture of, 219

Yuan, Chen, 48

Zedong, Mao, 134, 141

Zohar, Danah, 154, 170-75, 314, 315

Zukav, Gary, 165, 314